The Race to Fashoda

Colonialism and African Resistance

DAVID LEVERING LEWIS

An Owl Book

Henry Holt and Company
New York

Henry Holt and Company, Inc.
Publishers since 1866
115 West 18th Street
New York, New York 10011

Henry Holt® is a registered trademark
of Henry Holt and Company, Inc.

Published in Canada by Fitzhenry & Whiteside Ltd.,
195 Allstate Parkway, Markham, Ontario L3R 4T8.

Library of Congress Cataloging-in-Publication Data
Lewis, David L.
The race to Fashoda: Colonialism and
African resistance / David Levering Lewis.
p.   cm.
"An Owl book."
Originally published : New York :
Weidenfeld & Nicolson, 1987. With new introd.
Includes bibliographical references and index.
1. Fashoda Crisis, 1898. 2. Europe—Colonies—Africa.
I. Title.
DT156.6.L49   1995   94-36013
962.4'03—dc20   CIP

ISBN 0-8050-3556-7 (An Owl Book: pbk.)

Henry Holt books are available for special promotions
and premiums. For details contact: Director, Special Markets.

First published in hardcover in 1988 by
Weidenfeld & Nicolson.

First Owl Book Edition published in 1995 by
arrangement with the author.

Designed by Irving Perkins Associates

Maps by Arnold Bombay

Printed in the United States of America
All first editions are printed on acid-free paper.∞

1   3   5   7   9   10   8   6   4   2

To T. S. Currier, synoptic historian

Contents

Illustrations follow page 146.

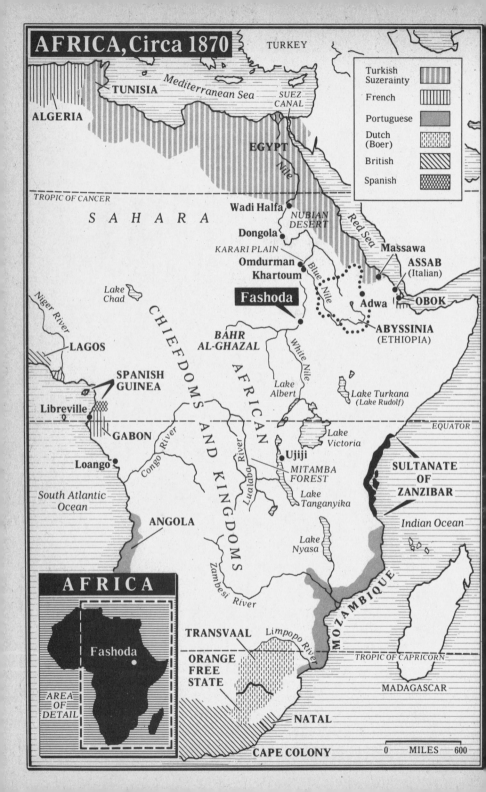

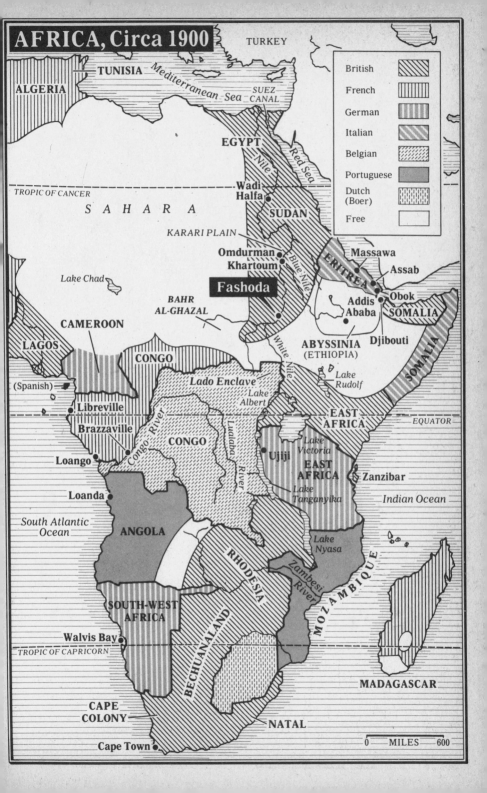

"If it should be friendship that you want, then I am ready, today as always. But I will not be your subject. . . . If it should be war that you desire, then I am also ready."
—SULTAN MASEMBA of Tanganyika
to a German commandant in 1890

"Always in a very real sense Africa is giving us something new or some metempsychosis of a world-old thing."
—W. E. B. Du Bois in 1915

Preface

This book is a venture. It was written to satisfy a personal desire to know much more about Africa's near past, specifically that period when the quickening commercial and political evolution of African societies was abruptly and decisively altered by Europe. This era, which stretches from the late 1870s to the end of the century, is commonly known as the Scramble for Africa. The desire to learn more antedated by a number of years my novitiate in Ghana, nearly a quarter century ago, as a university lecturer in European history. But, curiously, it became far more compelling while I was writing a book about a crisis in the French Third Republic, almost a decade after leaving Africa.

While I was pursuing Captain Alfred Dreyfus in the French National Archives and the Section Outre-Mer, an intuition matured into reasonable certainty that the Fashoda incident of 1898 might provide a superb paradigm of African and European interaction. Through this, I sought to retrieve a significant part of the African response to the Scramble for Africa. Although the focal incident of this book—what I call the "race to Fashoda"—has generally been considered little more than an historical footnote, it is in fact one of the great galvanic moments of the last century, a cynosure of the imperial energies of several European states and (ignored by both African and European students) an equally energizing moment in the defensive strategies of several African states. When Captain Jean-Baptiste Marchand and his one hundred fifty-odd Senegalese soldiers began their walk across Africa from the Congo in 1896, they set in motion a vast international and interracial drama which, until now, has been presented only quite partially.

How much of this drama, I wondered, could be recaptured through documents? It was clear to me even then, as I finished the Dreyfus book, that European archives—especially those in France and Belgium—contained documentary caches at which previous scholars in this field had only wisely guessed. With the appearance of the first careful French treatment of Fashoda, Marc Michel's *La Mission Marchand* (1972), most of the missing sources finally became available. Until then, however, the relevant archives had been restricted. The author of the most recent American study of Fashoda (1969), Roger Glenn Brown, was compelled to thank the director of the Quai d'Orsay library for telling him about sources that he could neither see nor cite. Indeed, with one valuable exception, all of the principal works in English were published before Michel's *La Mission Marchand*. I have been able to reconstruct fully Fashoda as Europeans saw it because I was fortunate in the timing of my research. The reappearance of the Fashoda dossier, said to have been destroyed by the minister of the interior as the Germans bore down on Paris in June of 1940, has made that possible, as did access to the handwritten journal of a forgotten French NCO, who subsequently reconstructed a daily, sergeant's-eye view of his walk across most of the middle of Africa with Marchand—to name only two of the new and newly construed European sources. And so, aside from being intriguingly complex, teeming with fabulous characters, and immensely seductive to narrative-minded historians and readers alike, the story has revealed itself to be a piñata of previously unexplored facts, motives, and ramifications.

From intuition I progressed to hypothesis—without evidence and, for an honest historian, remarkably without shame. African peoples, I decided, must have resisted the late-nineteenth-century coming of the Europeans aggressively and chronically, notwithstanding the apparent paucity of corroborating documents. I had yet to read, then, the collection of pathbreaking papers from the 1965 International Congress of African Historians, sponsored by University College, Dar es Salaam; my ignorance exceeded even my temerity. But if my hypothesis was a reinvented wheel, the wheel has even now only just begun to turn. And the claim of the Dar es Salaam congress, that "the main evidence for [the colonial experience] is contained in the Archives of African states rather than the Archives of colonial powers themselves," does not yet seem to be common currency in most of the developed world. Moreover, although in many parts of Africa it may well prove to be a claim devoid of reality, such sources remain a very promising avenue of research.

By the time I returned to Africa, I was certain that what I had begun to call the race to Fashoda could be reconstructed—documented—in a context that stressed the African role as much as the European. Starting from the Republic of Djibouti in the summer of 1982, sojourning in troubled Ethiopia and then in the deceptively placid Sudan, moving on to Cairo to go up the Nile to the Second Cataract at Wadi Halfa, I was richly rewarded by the reality of the Dar es Salaam prediction. In Addis Ababa not only was the formal treaty between Ethiopia and the Sudan made available, but the staff of the Institute of Ethiopian Studies (IES) devoted two days to translating from Tigriniya, the old language of the province of Tigre, crucial political correspondence of the young Negus Menilek, future emperor of Ethiopia. The Central Record Office (CRO) of the Republic of the Sudan made available the invaluable "Critical Edition of the Memoirs of Yusuf Mikha'il," the khalifa's minister of foreign affairs, originally translated into English by Reginald Wingate's Oxford "Blues."

Because of the Scramble for Africa, no part of the continent would be left to the natural course of its cultural and political evolution. The pace of European advance, depth of penetration, and degree of dominion, however, were never to be within the exclusive power of the intruders to determine. Which European nation finally stole the best and largest amount of real estate depended not only upon its own aggressive appetite and the effectiveness with which it was contested by its sister states, but also upon the counterforces and unpredictabilities of Africa itself. Much of what African rulers did was necessarily uncoordinated, and much of it was injurious to other Africans. But because of African resistance, the evolution of European politics in Europe was affected almost as deeply as the African continent was affected by the politics of colonial exploitation. Whether it was the "barbarous anarchy" of Congolese, the "religious fanaticism" of Sudanese, the long-lived warfare of Tukulors and Mandinkas, or the tactical resourcefulness of Ethiopians, the argument here is that African resistance was broader, deeper, and more concerted and more effective than the intruders themselves usually recognized, or than most of the later accounts reveal.

D.L.L.
Jersey City, N.J., and
Washington, D.C., 1986

The Race to Fashoda

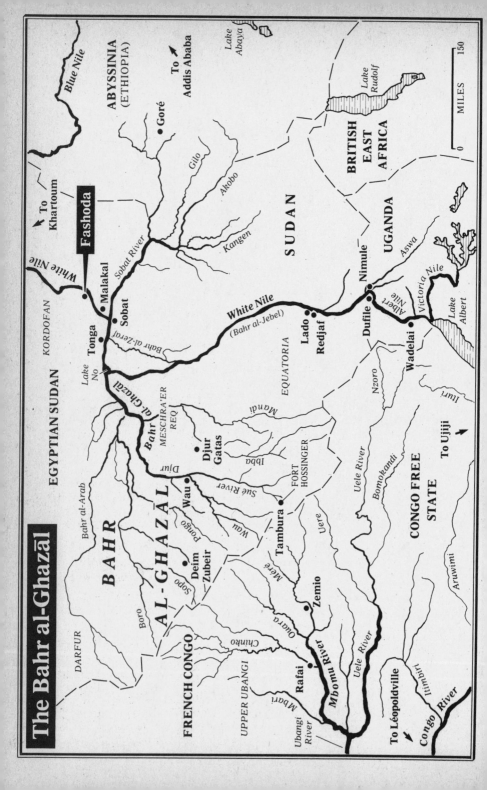

The Bahr al-Ghazāl

Introduction

Among the people of Zaire at the turn of the century there was a saying: "The white men's country must be a very bad one, since they prefer coming to live with us, although our climate kills them." But while the African climate and people killed Europeans, the Europeans killed in return, and on a grand scale. The Europeans killed according to the multiplying demands of conquest, order, conversion, labor, and profit. The Africans killed because they had to. They were fighting for their freedom and for the integrity of their cultures. This is a book about European impact upon Africa and African impact upon Europe in the late nineteenth century, about colonial encroachments and African responses, small and large, random and collective, to the invading and technologically awesome outsiders. Through the high grass of European grand designs, it cuts a way into clearings where African opposition to occupation, usually led by traditional rulers or power-holders, stands in bold relief. It takes the fortress at Fashoda, in one of Africa's remotest places, as its focal point.

Before it disappeared from the map of colonial Africa, the place called Fashoda lay 469 desolate miles due south from Khartoum in an Oklahoma-sized province of the Sudan called the Bahr al-Ghazāl—"river of the gazelles." Named by the Arabs after a vicious, crooked, brown waterway, the province—with its blazing heat, solvent humidity, elephant grass, enveloping mud, and (when the rains began in May) horizon-to-horizon mosquitoes—undermined the health and willpower of the staunchest intruders. Fashoda had begun, in 1855, as an Egyptian antislavery patrol station established by Muhammad Sa'id, viceroy of Egypt and African statesman adroit at impressing the powers of Europe (especially the British) by his enlightened policies. It was on the left, or west, bank of the White Nile, in the heart of densely populated Shilluk country, seventy-three miles south of Lake Kaka and sixty-one miles north of the Sobat River. Between Lake Kaka and reed-clotted Lake No,

3

Fashoda was about the only spot where boats could be unloaded over a total distance of slightly more than one hundred miles. A strong fortress was built there in the mid-1860s, some twenty miles upstream from the Shilluk ruler's village capital, the original Fashoda.

Fashoda grew in the sweltering noonday sun of Egyptian imperialism, its garrison sometimes numbering as many as five hundred men. Most likely, the first two Europeans to enter the Lower Sudan, the Russian-born physician Wilhelm Junker and the German naturalist Georg Schweinfurth, reached the enclosure several years apart—the German first, in January 1869. There, at "the limit of the Egyptian empire," was the nearly new fort which Schweinfurth's enormously influential *The Heart of Africa* described as presenting "a formidable appearance," its long walls looking "at a distance as though they were mounted with so many cannon" because of hundreds of waterspouts. For almost a hundred miles in either direction from Fashoda, and for a depth of ten, there were thousands of high, conical Shilluk huts anchored to mud outcroppings in the great river and along its sides—so many that Schweinfurth greatly overestimated the population as more than a million. "No known part of Africa," he was certain, "scarcely even the narrow valley of the Nile in Egypt, has a density of population so great." By the time Junker arrived in 1876, Fashoda had become "a considerable trading place," the "last outpost of civilization, where travellers plunging into or returning from the wilds of equatorial Africa could procure a few indispensable European wares from the local Greek traders."

Egyptian rule in the Sudan was one of ubiquitous corruption, extortion, and brutality, of laws arbitrarily and venally applied, of taxes repeatedly collected and repeatedly stolen, and of collusion in the enslavement and export of Shilluk, Nuer, and Dinka families to the Arabian peninsula, Zanzibar, Egypt, and Mozambique (despite the official policy of anti-enslavement). Slave corpses littered the ivory trails to Bagamoyo and Mombasa on the coast. The Sudan became a cauldron. The animist black Shilluks, Nuers, and Dinkas of the south fought among themselves, even as they rebelled against Muslim Egypt. The Arab populations of the northern towns simmered under the extortionate weight of an alien bureaucracy. The boil-over came with the Sudanese holy war in the winter of 1881. Soon thereafter, the religious union of the Sudan under Muhammad Ahmad, the Mahdi, yielded to the transforming despotism of his anointed successor, Abdullahi, the khalifa. By 1895, except for the British-defended coastal enclave at Suakin, and an almost-forgotten garrison far up the Nile in the province of Equatoria, virtually all trace of Egyptian presence in the Sudan had been swept away.

Undermined by ten seasons of blitzing rains, the walls of Fashoda fort crumbled, many of its large bricks carted off by local people to make simple ovens. The potential significance of this dilapidated outpost to European rivalry in Africa escaped all but a small group of Frenchmen at the beginning of 1895. In Great Britain, perhaps no more than a half-dozen persons had ever heard of Fashoda until March of that year. Except for King Léopold II of the Belgians and confidants of the Italian prime minister, Francesco Crispi, Belgian and Italian ignorance of this part of the world was matched only by indifference or mistrust; nor did their king see fit to disclose to the Belgian people his improbably outsized imperial designs. And even at the highest levels of government and society, Germany and Russia had minimal interest in this part of Africa, although both knew better than to ignore it completely.

But fateful decisions were being made at that moment, whose consequences would all but result in war between Britain and France. Egypt, "discovered" and "awakened" by Bonaparte's legions and made part of the modern world by the French-built canal at Suez some twenty years before, had, as the French saw it, been stolen by the unprincipled British. As the British saw it, however, Egypt had been saved from anarchy by Her Majesty's redcoats and its waterway to India magnanimously secured for the benefit of international commerce, only to be menaced by the imperial plottings of the insatiable French.

On February 28, 1895, the leading colonialist of France, François Deloncle, rose in the Chamber of Deputies to announce baldly that the British must be compelled to settle the paramount Egyptian question. If Great Britain would not keep the 1882 promise to evacuate Egypt once internal order was restored, then France would "take Britain in the rear" by marching across Africa from the Atlantic into the Upper Nile, forcing its rival to the conference table. One month later to the day, Sir Edward Grey, British undersecretary for foreign affairs, surprised most of the House of Commons with an even more provocative declaration: that from its mouth in the Egyptian delta to its source in the Uganda-Tanganyika lakes, the entire Nile waterway was British. Any advance by a

French expedition into the Nile watershed—into the Bahr al-Ghaz-āl—"would be an unfriendly act, and would be so viewed by England." France accepted the dare before the end of the year—if somewhat nervously and irresolutely. Placed off-limits by Great Britain, Fashoda became the centerpiece of a great imperial gamble by France.

Three charged years—from 1896 through 1898—were to determine the final course of colonial Africa. These were the years of the European race to the abandoned fort of Fashoda, the dogged contest by steamer, train, dugout, and footpath to be the first to arrive at a footnote in history. To get there, France would send, in the summer of 1896, eleven marine officers and more than one hundred fifty African troops commanded by Captain Jean-Baptiste Marchand marching, west to east, across the middle of the continent. To beat them, the British would invade the Sudan from Egypt in March of that same year. Until the beginning of the year, seeking full membership in the club of empire, Italy had recklessly invested the most men and treasure in the Horn of Africa; but it was now reeling from misfortunes in Ethiopia. On the first day of March, a crack Italian army had been destroyed by the forces of the emperor of Ethiopia at a place called Adwa. Meanwhile, a Belgian expedition —the largest European-commanded force ever to cross Central Africa—had left its base in the northern Congo to strike for the Upper Nile before either Britain or France sent troops there.

On July 10, 1898, commanded by marine infantry Captain Marchand, ten officers and NCOs and their Senegalese *tirailleurs* (sharpshooters) arrived at Fashoda, near the junction of the White Nile and the Sobat River in southern Sudan. Having alternately marched and steam-paddled nearly four thousand miles in two years across the upper middle of Africa—from Loango on the west coast—Captain Marchand hoisted the tricolor and claimed for France the vast belt above the equator stretching from the Atlantic to the Red Sea. The consequences of his act were immediate and just short of cataclysmic for European peace. The point of the Congo-Nile expedition (the Marchand Mission, as it came to be known popularly) was to force a resolution of the nagging Egyptian question. Just as Algeria's French destiny had been resolved during the July Monarchy of 1830–48, so Egypt's annexation by France during the Second Empire of 1852–70 had seemed certain. But the 1870 Franco-Prussian War had retarded French designs. Then had come the loss of the controlling shares in the Suez Canal to the

British in 1876, wounding French pride and greatly diminishing French influence in Cairo. The debacle had come six years later, on July 11, when a collapsing ministry and too much concern about international reactions caused a French naval squadron to be withdrawn from Alexandria, leaving the British to invade Egypt alone and shortly to suppress at Tel al-Kēbir the Egyptian nationalist movement led by the dashing Colonel Urabi Pasha.

French anguish was soothed somewhat by formal British promises of withdrawal as soon as the situation in Egypt was stabilized. In the Commons, Prime Minister William Gladstone gave a solemn, seemingly ironclad pledge that Britain would never take Egypt as a possession: "Undoubtedly of all things in the world, that is the thing which we are not going to do. It would be absolutely at variance with all the principles and views of Her Majesty's Government and the pledges they have given to Europe." But no sooner had Colonel Urabi's army, with its war cry of "Egypt for the Egyptians," been defeated and the feckless Egyptian ruler, the Khedive Tewfik, been shored up the better to serve the interests of the European banking community, than the Egyptian Sudan exploded in religious revolt. Telegrams received from an unknown Arab from Dongola Province, one Muhammad Ahmad—the Mahdi, or "Messenger of Allah"—summoned the khedive of Egypt, the queen of England, the kaiser of Germany, and the president of France to submit to the rule of Islamic righteousness. In a series of astonishing victories, the Mahdi rolled back British-officered Egyptian armies, so that by 1885 the Sudan (or the Mahdiyya, as it proclaimed itself) was independent of alien rule from the Second Nile Cataract at Wadi Halfa in the north to the distant frontiers of Uganda and Ethiopia in the south and southwest. Britain cut her losses, compelling Egypt to renounce formally its rule in the Sudan. Despite repeated promises, the British settled down to permanent Egyptian occupation. The French settled into a mood of permanent rage.

The specific objective of Marchand's 1896 Congo-Nile expedition, then, was to panic Britain into negotiating over Egypt, either by sharing it with France or, more likely, by sanctioning and supporting France's annexation of Morocco, a land surely destined by geography and commerce to fall to France from the tree of empire, were it not for recent German interference there. The threat perceived by the British was the truly unnerving prospect of a string of French posts from west to east through the Nile basin to Djibouti on the Red Sea—a deadly achievement that would bisect the grand design of Cecil Rhodes and other British Empire architects of an uninterrupted rail and telegraph connection running from the Cape of South Africa north to Cairo in Egypt. The Fashoda scheme was an overly ambitious, brilliant ploy to determine, as the century ran out, the final European boundaries in Africa. The soldier-diplomat Sir Rennell Rodd, a major player in this contest, put the matter straightforwardly in his memoirs: "At the end of the last century the issue which stood out above all others in the African problem was whether a line of cleavage in the great continent should run from south to north, or from west to east."

The French went to great and innovative lengths to insure success for the Congo-Nile stratagem, calling upon the ruler of Ethiopia to help them. The Ethiopian story is a complicated one, poignantly instructive for its ethnocentrism and individual folly, but what needs be said at this point is that the French government (or at least some of those trying to govern France) mistakenly and doggedly believed that it had persuaded Emperor Menilek II (by arms shipments and technical assistance) to support with troops a French-led thrust from the Ethiopian highlands into the swamps of the Bahr al-Ghazāl—a thrust timed to reinforce Marchand and his Senegalese and to set up a supply line stretching back from Fashoda through Addis Ababa to Djibouti on the sea. Securely installed, Marchand was to negotiate with the Sudanese Mahdi's successor, the Khalifa Abdullahi, offering arms and loans to strengthen the Mahdiyya against the inevitable Anglo-Egyptian invasion of the Sudan. Once that was done, the pragmatic British would realize that they faced a formidable coalition, as potentially lethal to their imperial ambitions as French-backed Ethiopia had just been to the Italians at the humiliating Battle of Adwa.

Unfortunately for France, almost nothing went right. A three-month delay at the outset in 1896 on the west coast, caused by the closing of the interior trails by religiously agitated Bakongo, and the delayed cresting of the Sué River on the last leg of the expedition, cost Marchand nine crucial months. The Ethiopian "allies" took the arms and gifts of the French and Russians, but their army retreated to the highlands after the briefest wait for Marchand on June 25, 1898, two weeks before the Congo-Nile expedition reached Fashoda. Menilek secretly agreed to aid France, then quietly signed a treaty with the British committing himself to neutrality, while clandestinely negotiating an alliance with the khalifa of the Sudan.

Meanwhile, the Anglo-Egyptian army of thirty thousand men led by Herbert Kitchener, starting out three months before Marchand in 1896, had Maxim-gunned the Sudanese from Wadi Halfa up the Nile to Kosti; defied received engineering wisdom by constructing a railroad arrow-straight across the desert from Wadi Halfa to Abu Hamed; and then marched on beyond the Sixth Cataract to Omdurman, where it met the khalifa's sixty-thousand-man army on Karari Plain on September 1, 1898. On September 19, Marchand and Kitchener exchanged champagne toasts aboard a British gunboat anchored off Fashoda before politely threatening to destroy each other. An important segment of the public clamored for war, but France was precluded from serious military preparations because of the state of its navy, the neutral posture of Russia, and the political disarray caused in large part by the Dreyfus Affair. On November 4, Paris ordered recently promoted Major Marchand to abandon his fortress.

During the many months that Marchand's band and Kitchener's regiments were heading for a collision, servants of Belgian King Léopold II were carrying out orders that would have given much of the "abandoned" Sudan to their sovereign. It has, perhaps, long since been forgotten that Léopold II, already private owner of a million square miles of the Congo, once schemed to double his African real estate by capitalizing on Anglo-French rivalry. Léopold wanted as much of the Sudan and the Red Sea littoral as possible. Through well-financed policies, often of Byzantine complexity, he made himself increasingly important to the antagonistic British and French, each of whom tried to use Léopold in the Congo to block the expansion of the other. By the Congo-French convention of August 1894, the Belgian sovereign (under duress from Paris) had finally agreed to collaborate with France in her march across Africa. The truth was that Léopold remained as determined as ever to play both powers against each other and out of Central and East Africa. But two years later, the Belgian Congo was convulsed by rebellion. The king of the Belgians was finally eliminated from the Scramble for Africa by Africans themselves.

How this happened is the subject of much of what follows. The Swahili War of 1892, and its recurring eruptions late into the decade, shows African resistance to and competition with the European intruders in a manner at once heroic and ignoble. The Swahili War in the Congo has almost vanished from the record of history, whether European or African. Circumstantial evidence indicates that it may have been planned from Zanzibar by the island ruler

Sultan Barghash and the almost-mythic African ivory-rubber-slave magnate Hamed bin Muhammad bin Juna al-Marjebi, known to history as "Tippu Tip." Estimates of the gross value of ivory, rubber, rare wood tonnage, and approximately ten thousand slaves trans-shipped from the Interior by Swahili merchants are largely conjecture (healthy females fetched upward of fifty dollars on the coast in the late 1880s), but profits were obviously enormous. Just as obviously, Léopold's move into the eastern Congo and control of the Congo River traffic would increasingly divert that ivory, rubber, and wood to the Atlantic and interfere with slaving.

The battle for the Congo began on October 22, 1892, commanded by Tippu Tip's son, who was called Sefu. The Swahili grand strategy called for a sweep by river and land across the Congo to the Atlantic. A breakthrough to the ocean was likely, they believed, to spark uprisings throughout the west coast. After all, the French had been locked for years in struggle with various Islamic sultans in Mali and Guinée. Samori Turé, larger-than-life leader of the Mandinka people in what was called the French Sudan, had proven such a military handful in the mid-1880s that Paris had come close to abandoning most of the territory, much as the British had jettisoned the Egyptian Sudan. Swahili leadership planned to attack from the east and endanger European supply lines on the Atlantic, hoping that Belgian public opinion might turn against Léopold's now-costly enterprise. The Belgians were saved by the defection of ten thousand Batetelas commanded by one of Tippu Tip's former slaves and principal lieutenants, Ngongo Leteta. Even so, much of the Swahili plan initially succeeded, with most of the eastern Congo falling to them, and even after the Swahilis were beaten, hard and bloody battles against African guerrilla fighters, many of them politicized by the war, continued until the turn of the century.

Generalizing from long experience as de facto overlord of Egypt, the extremely knowledgeable Earl of Cromer (the former Sir Evelyn Baring) lectured the British public in a widely read essay, "We need not always inquire too closely what these people, who are all, nationally speaking, more or less in *statu pupillari,* themselves think is best for their own interests." Whether participant or spectator, virtually every European embraced the dogma that the scramble for territory beginning in the last quarter of the nineteenth century was as beneficial for Africans as it was beyond the power of Africans to resist. That was the unquestioned article of faith, the perception and premise of conduct and policy in Africa, as well as elsewhere in the nonwhite world. And it was true enough that Africa could not have been conquered without African peoples loyal to European masters. The race to Fashoda was run, literally, on African legs. But in the larger sense, the Earl of Cromer was mistaken. Africans were not universally passive subjects of the Scramble. A great number resisted foreign intruders, even while many collaborated with them. The scale of resistance to Europe ranged from village to nation-state. It was omnipresent.

The race to Fashoda, more than any other chain of events unleashed by the Scramble, reveals just how significantly—almost decisively—European history was rewritten by Africans as, simultaneously, African history was being forever altered by Europeans. If one understands the race to Fashoda as a saga spanning West Africa, Central Africa, North Africa, and East Africa, involving different stages of technological and political development; if one recognizes its climax as greatly determined by the diplomatic and military behavior of the peoples of the Congo and of two highly developed North African societies (those of the Mahdist Sudan and the Ethiopian empire), Fashoda becomes that rare device for retrieving the past—a panoptic lens through which the many parts become vivid, intelligible, and whole. Turned upon Africans, the lens shows that, if there was never a master plan of resistance, by the early 1890s at least the conceivable prospects and outlines of parallel and complementary resistance had emerged. Moreover, the grand politics of the Powers unwittingly encouraged the Africans' struggle. In their determination to force the British from Egypt, or wring from them territorial compensations elsewhere, the French drew West and East African peoples into their fantastic, but not unworkable, design to forge a French belt across the middle of the continent, with its buckle at Fashoda. Reacting to this threat to their Cape-to-Cairo master plan, the British mobilized their own African forces.

What neither the French nor the British—nor, for that matter, the Italians or Belgians—noticed was that Egyptians, Sudanese, Ethiopians, Ugandans, Nilotes, Congolese, Malians, and Guineans, among others, were taking increasing advantage of opportunities to exploit rivalries between the Powers. The respective rulers of Egypt, Ethiopia, and the Sudan—the Khedive Abbas II, the Negus Negusti Menilek II, and the Khalifa Abdullahi—understood quite clearly that the outcome of this European contest around Fashoda would determine their countries' futures. Menilek II knew that if

Ethiopia were to escape being fatally drawn into the imperialist maelstrom, then it must contrive to appear indispensable to the conflicting schemes of both the British and the French, while secretly doing its utmost to cultivate the unfriendly Sudanese neighbor. Abbas II, for his part, knew that if Egypt were ever to end the debasing protectorate status, then his country must use French ambitions in the Sudan to lever the British out of Cairo. The Khalifa Abdullahi understood much less about the world beyond his borders, but he knew that the Sudan must fight all foreigners. Egyptians and Ethiopians preferred diplomacy to war; the Sudanese preferred war. Central Africans, in impeding the passage of the French and the Belgians, used both. Across the continent, African peoples steadfastly opposed the enveloping imperial strategies.

If Fashoda can be a powerful lens, it is nevertheless the case that its African images tend to be badly distorted. What flesh-and-blood Africans specifically did when confronted by hostile Europeans (as opposed to what may reasonably be inferred from vague episodes) is not easy to know. Much is, simply, everlastingly unknowable. Most of what is known is found in the records of the intruders. And the intruders almost always saw only what they wanted to and remembered almost always only what pleased their prejudices. After the European contest for real estate slammed forward in high gear, everything that was done in Africa had powerful religious, racial, commercial, or political justification. Well before the ideology of imperialism distilled itself into slogans and images familiar to every European worker and schoolchild, however, the veil of misunderstanding was already firmly in place. A process of antipathetic conditioning, at least in embryo, had been present in Europe for centuries. But in the decades immediately before the Scramble began in earnest, the process began rapidly to transform itself: fascination with Africa evolved into distorted familiarity, which then hardened into rationales for exploitation.

Africans drew from the behavior inspired by this process usually correct but no less simplistic conclusions about the outsiders. Fashoda unfolded against this elaborate backdrop of ignorance and suspicion.

Much of the African response in the Interior to white colonialism had been conditioned by the outstanding causal event in the Scramble—Henry Morton Stanley's voyage down the Congo River. Its significance was this: the Anglo-American explorer's advent on the Lualaba, at the end of 1876, revealed the dismay of the peoples of the Interior at whiteness. By and large, Africans equated whiteness with death and the unnatural. They described the spirits of their dead as white, strange of movement, and emitting odors of sickly staleness. If, in the eyes of most Europeans, Africans were primitive automata, peoples devoid of complexity (though not of mystery) and, when not firmly disciplined, perversely at variance with their own interests, in African eyes, the coming of the whites signified more than the menace of Remington repeaters. It presaged death itself.

Stanley's best-selling *Through the Dark Continent* told of a significant colloquy near Lake Albert with the Buhaya people: "Do you know that we believe you to be *Wanyavingi*?" "What, are they white people like us?" Stanley asked. "They have no clothes like you, nor do they wear anything on their feet like you," the African explained, "but they are tall, big men, with long noses and pale color." Stanley pressed for more details. What were these *Wanyavingi*? *"Abaluga kuzima,"* he was told—"those from the dead." A few years after Stanley's first Congo voyage, the Reverend George Grenfell, crossing a part of the Congo's Manyema Province unexplored by whites, wrote of hearing cries of *"Bedimo! Bedimo!"*— "Ghosts! Ghosts!"

At the root of these perceptions was the visceral sense of unpleasant strangeness, and what was imbedded in African psychology was shortly reinforced by experience. The people along the Upper Nile had been among the first to speak of a fall from grace, of a pervasive sense of ancient relationships irreparably damaged in a few seasons —of what the Dinka people deep in the Sudan called "the time when the world was spoilt." Despite the undeniable mercies of European medicines and the triumph of its technology, black African culture was affronted by forces so alien that the invaders' material superiority only confirmed the intuition that these forces were, in the sweep of history, diabolical and unfeeling, anti-human. "The European is devoted to dead metals," goes a late-nineteenth-century Herero saying. "We are more intelligent, we get our joy out of living creatures." Clearly Europeans were cursed, for how else were Africans to explain the appearance out of nowhere of men and even women who condemned polygamy and were ashamed of the naked body, of others who settled vast tracts of land they claimed had no previous owners, and of still others who stumbled about savannahs and rain forests renaming lakes and rivers that had been there since the beginning of time?

Not all Europeans in late-nineteenth-century Africa were calculating, cruel, or uncomprehending. Junker and Schweinfurth, for
example, were perceptive, in the manner of thorough collectors of
the unusual. David Livingstone's ingenuous proselytizing on Lake
Tanganyika was widely admired. The constant diplomacy of
France's Savorgnan de Brazza near Stanley (Malebo) Pool had its
imitators, as did Joseph Thomson's deference near Lake Nyasa
(camping under trees until village headmen granted passage
rights). Their interest, patience, and gentleness were, nevertheless,
special cases that, as the century closed, became increasingly rare.
The famous globe-trotter Richard Burton, to press the argument,
would never have been so sickened by Arabs massacring Africans
in the town of Nyangwe as to turn away from discovering the source
of the Congo River, which a deeply grieving Livingstone did in July
1871. And if it is true that, as a contemporary student of these
whites in Africa wrote, to get across the continent "they negotiated
more than they coerced, and only in rare instances were they the
swashbucklers that they portrayed themselves to be"—they
nonetheless demonstrated the need, at least autobiographically, to
posture. Most of the centurions of the Industrial Revolution and the
White Man's Burden were too arrogant or self-absorbed to take
seriously the Africans who got in their way. "The blacks give an
immense amount of trouble," was Henry Morton Stanley's typical
reaction.

Missionaries, explorers, soldiers, and exploiters came to Africa to
test their moral and physical stamina, capacity to dominate, right-
ness of geographical and water-source hypotheses, money-making
acumen, and luck. Many, as well, sought escape from the social,
religious, or political unease they felt in middle-class Europe.
Which is not to say that they were any better attuned to the realities
of Africa than their compatriots. "I am not an empire builder. I am
not a missionary. I am not truly a scientist," Joseph Thomson confessed. "I merely want to return to Africa to continue my wanderings." Africa was the romance of mystery, a chance for renown, for
captaincies well before thirty, for the social cachet of national geographical society gold medals, or, more nobly, for countless be-
nighted souls harvested for the Lord. And Africa was escape from
the straitjacketing morality of the homeland into alcohol, sex, and,
too often, sadism.

For the most part, the literate public learned almost nothing of
the world their marines, merchants, and missionaries spoiled, a

world whose most widely read interpreters were the likes of Henry Stanley and his equally presumptuous fellow explorers. The continent, for these readers, meant constant expansion and strange nomenclature that had the sound of drums—Bagamoyo, Gondokoro, Fouta Jalon, Abeokuta, Timbuktu. For all that, without knowing—or wanting to know—what it all meant, the European written record preserved enough of the African response to an alien presence to reveal a great deal of "the time when the world was spoilt."

CHAPTER ONE

The Spoilt World

1

Both the Scramble for Africa and African resistance to European invasion and settlement began virtually at the same moment: with the attempted crossing of Zaire's Lualaba River by Henry Morton Stanley, his three British companions, and some three hundred Zanzibari porters, in December 1876—an event that was to lead inexorably to the rending and partitioning of the sub-Sahara. It was the electric moment when all the predisposing factors of technology, ideology, and commerce fused. Stanley's advent announced the end of amateur expeditions, of aleatory strolls, with local permission, across Africa, like Livingstone's and Silva Porto's in 1853, Gerhard Rolfs's in 1862, or Verney Lovett Cameron's almost a decade later. Backed by James Gordon Bennett's *New York Herald* and the London *Daily Telegraph,* Africa's most methodical, indomitable, and unfeeling explorer departed Zanzibar in November 1874. With every tent peg, quinine bottle, and Remington cartridge calculated for the trek, the business of Stanley's expedition was business. The world-famous deliverer of Livingstone intended to scoop his predecessors for the greater glory of the *Herald,* the *Daily Telegraph,* and himself. Richard Burton still insisted that Lake Tanganyika was the source of the Nile. John Hanning Speke had gone to his grave arguing for Lake Victoria. Livingstone had died with a prayer on his lips that it be the Lualaba. Sir Samuel Baker was sure that Lake Albert spilled into the Nile. Stanley announced the solution: with a budget far larger than the sum of all expeditionary allowances previously expended, he would chart and measure the three great lakes—Victoria, Albert, and Tanganyika—determining whether or not they connected and if any appeared

16

to be the primary source of the Nile. Then he would march to the Lualaba and sail into the Interior until he reached either the Nile or the Congo.

The diminutive, illegitimate Welshman had a reputation for being a master at manipulating people and publicity. The many months spent in the company of David Livingstone, perhaps the single man he ever truly respected, had softened Stanley some-what; still, when he wrote of that extraordinary experience, he concluded that the missionary's kindly ways and disorganization were fatal to the grand enterprise of civilizing the "dark conti-nent." Thousands of miles blazed through the continent revealed almost nothing to Stanley of the human face of Africa. "I had no time to give, either to myself or to [the Africans]," he regretted later. He was the fourth white man after Speke, James Augustus Grant, and the American Charles Chaillé-Long to reach Uganda, the temperate country Stanley called the "pearl of Africa."

Uganda in 1875 was a collection of warring city-states (the largest and most imposing being Buganda), each boasting a divine-right ruler quakingly supported by counsellors, governors, administra-tors, pages, and standing armies. Astounded by what he saw in Buganda, but incapable of true admiration, Stanley praised the better to highlight the flaws. Mangassa, the zealous twenty-year-old emissary sent with scores of white-robed officials and warriors to welcome Stanley, aroused in him the "painful suspicion that the vast country which recognized his power was greatly abused, and grieving that the poor people had to endure such rough treatment for my sake, I did my best to prevent Mangassa from extorting to excess." Capable of raising an army of 150,000 warriors and a war fleet on Victoria Nyanza* of 325 sleek, intricately decorated canoes (some of them seventy-two feet long), the Kabaka Mutesa I of Buganda impressed Stanley. Mutesa was "sedate and composed in manner, intelligent in his questions and remarks beyond anything I had expected to meet in Africa." But this was, after all, Africa, and after much palaver in Swahili, Stanley reassured himself about Mutesa: "I saw that he was highly clever and possessed of the abili-ties to govern, but his cleverness and ability lacked the mannerisms of a European's." Bountifully provisioned and ceremoniously es-corted to the Buganda border by Mutesa's legions, the American-ized newspaperman lamented, "Oh for the hour when a band of

*Lake Victoria

philanthropic capitalists shall vow to rescue these beautiful lands, and supply the means to enable the Gospel messengers to come and quench the murderous hate with which man beholds man in the beautiful lands around Lake Victoria!"

Uganda and Lake Victoria behind him (warfare prevented a visit to Lake Albert), and after nearly a year circumnavigating and exploring eel-shaped Lake Tanganyika (which he eliminated as a source of the Nile), Stanley arrived on foot at Kasongo on the Lualaba. It was the capital of Tippu Tip—Hamed bin Muhammad bin Juna al-Marjebi—son of a Zanzibar Arab father and an unmixed African slave, master of East Africa from the Tanganyika coast to where the swift Lualaba halfway runs its course to the Congo River. Over four centuries of Negro admixture, Arab culture, and indigenous languages mixing with Arabic had produced a new African people—the Swahili—of whom al-Marjebi was an outstanding example. "Tippu Tip" was the name the Africans had given him, possibly from the "tip-u-tip-u-tip" sound of the muskets made by his slave-hunting caravans, but more probably because of a nervous tic of batting his eyelashes. Lean Tippu Tip was as cold-blooded as the short, strutting Stanley. Stanley offered him five thousand American dollars (Tippu Tip claimed it was seven) if he and his men would come with him for sixty camps down the Lualaba, as unknown and forbidding to the Arab Africans as it was to the Europeans.

Almost four years earlier, another white man had come to Kasongo hoping to obtain help exploring the Lualaba and the Congo rivers. The Englishman Verney Lovett Cameron was as singular and as mysteriously fortunate in his peregrinations as Livingstone, whom he had been on his way to find just as Stanley was arriving at Ujiji on Lake Tanganyika to bring the missionary his memorable salutation in 1871. Cameron walked through Africa alone, often without cloth or beads to buy food and porters, trusting his God and his radiant humanity to see him through. He thought he got on well with Tippu Tip, "a good looking man and the greatest dandy I had seen among the traders." One of the benign negrophobes, Cameron found the lord of Kasongo, black as he was, "a thorough Arab, for, curiously enough, the admixture of negro blood had not rendered him less of an Arab in his ideas and manners." Very likely, Tippu Tip had been amused by this quixotic guest who certainly presented much less of a threat to the region's Arab monopoly than would Stanley with three white lieutenants and a battalion of veteran fighters. But although harmless in himself, Cameron's successful voyage into the unknown Congo would have inspired emulation and, ultimately, European competition. Tippu Tip convinced the Englishman that his ambition was impossible, directing him, instead of due north, in a westerly direction to Luanda in the Portuguese colony of Angola on the Atlantic. As such, Cameron became the second European after Livingstone to walk across Africa from coast to coast.

Tippu Tip immediately realized that Stanley was too determined and resourceful to be eliminated in the manner of Cameron. Poison or a fatal accident may have been a tempting solution, but the merchant prince's fine house and investments on Zanzibar would never have survived the outrage of the explorer's suspicious demise. Tippu Tip knew, too, that the world was changing; the situation required tact. And besides, he wanted the five thousand dollars. The bargain was struck. Explorer and trader set out together for Nyangwe, the last Swahili outpost on the Lualaba River. Later, Nyangwe would become a double settlement of nearly thirty thousand people: a malarial, malodorous sprawl of African huts on the mud banks of the river, and a colorful "Arab" town on the high, healthful promontory on the right bank. But even when Stanley saw it in 1876, sixteen years before the peak of its prosperity, the slave capital of East Africa, although smaller and less developed, was already a rich town, raw, teeming and steamy, and always potentially deadly—like the Old South's Natchez, also situated at the extremity of one of the world's mighty rivers.

On November 5, a Sunday, the caravan of more than a thousand gun bearers, porters, women, and children streamed out of Nyangwe into the Mitamba forest. Stanley's plan was to march due north, parallel with the Lualaba until the forest was behind them and then, before Tippu Tip and his men turned back, to continue by river. Moving the two-mile-long caravan through the primeval Mitamba proved almost too great an ordeal for the experienced explorer. The forest was crowded with enormous trees whose interlaced foliage more than a hundred feet above squeezed out the sunlight. On the forest floor, life moved in slow motion through the vaporous heat and chemical riot of decaying vegetation. Strangest of all in this ochre chiaroscuro was the silence, an oppressive absence of sound that began to magnify an awful sense of heroic pointlessness. Porters, men as well as women, who normally balanced seventy-pound loads on their heads for twenty miles a day,

stumbled and plodded on at an ever-slower pace, sometimes failing
to advance more than eight miles.

Throughout the Congo, as in most of Africa, endless trails were
ribbons of life from point to point. Always they followed a path of
least resistance, sharply veering from sudden irregularities in the
landscape, concentrations of dangerous animals, the broadest
stretch of a stream, or even large fallen trees, sometimes zigzagging
for miles before returning to a point not far beyond the casually
ignored obstacle. With calendars on their minds and compasses in
hand, European travellers found these trails almost a cultural
offense, although only the most experienced or foolhardy strayed
from them unless absolutely necessary. But the silent Mitamba soon
became trailless.

Day after day, Stanley's caravan hacked its dimly lit, exhausted
way through a rubbery growth. The expedition was pure European
folly, Tippu Tip protested. "Ah yes," he had declared on November
16, refusing to continue, "if you *Wasungii* [white men] wish to
throw away your lives, it is no reason we Arabs should. We travel
little by little to get ivory and slaves, and we are years about it
. . . but you white men only look for rivers and lakes and mountains,
and you spend your lives for no reason, and to no purpose." Stanley
managed to keep him going a few camps longer, paring the
Swahili's recompense to twenty-six hundred dollars. Three days
later, they reached the Lualaba, which Stanley immediately rechristened the Livingstone. This was the farthest edge of the zone
penetrated by the Arabs.

A Wagenia leader watching Stanley's caravan making ready to
cross to the river's west shore no doubt recognized the enormous
threat posed to the heartland. "Where from?" he demanded. Approaching the expedition by boat from the opposite bank, and hearing "Nyangwe," the Wagenia leader intoned Africa's first warning
to this newest generation of intruders. "Not for ten thousand shells,
brother," he told Stanley's translator upon the latter's offer of shells
for boats. "We do not want you to cross the river. Go back! *Wasambye* [uncircumcised]; you are bad! *Wasambye* are bad, bad, bad!
The river is deep, *Wasambye!* Go back, *Wasambye!* Go back,
Wasambye are bad, bad, bad! The river is deep, *Wasambye!* You
have not wings, *Wasambye!* Go back, *Wasambye!*" Stanley pretended to make light of his translator's warning—"That is a war cry,
Master"—but his mind was far from easy. As the Wagenia paddled
back across the river, they sang the "wildest, weirdest note" Stanley

had ever heard, sending it "pealing across the river.... In response, we heard hundreds of voices sing out a similar note!" Tippu Tip had already understood that the peoples of the forest and river would sacrifice themselves in droves. Again, Stanley narrowly managed to keep their bargain intact a bit longer. Splitting forces near the Lualaba, they struggled on along different trails until November 26, when they reunited.

Suddenly the forest came alive, and the expedition was pounded day after day by thousands of what were probably Bakuma along the river's eastern shore. "Sometimes the muzzle of our guns almost touched their breasts," Stanley recalled with a twinge of uncharacteristic horror. "The shrieks, cries, shouts of encouragement, the rattling volleys of musketry, the booming war horns, the yells and defiance of the combatants, the groans and screams of the women and children in the hospital camp, made together such a medley of hideous noises as can never be effaced from my memory." Tippu Tip had had enough. On December 27, at the village of Vinya Nyaza, the Swahili slaver and his men quietly but firmly took their leave. Stanley floated his aluminum boat, the *Lady Alice*, having managed to find and hollow out trees for enough canoes to transport most of his men on the river. Meanwhile, the cry to stop the white explorers was passed from the Wagenia to Batetela, and from Batetela to, among many others along the Lualaba and Congo rivers, Bakusu, Basoka, and Bateke. Through Bobangi, the lingua franca, the numerically dominant Bantu-speaking people, as well as the Mangbetu of the smaller Sudanic groups, responded to a summons of survival transcending their ancient gulfs of language, religion, and territorial jealousy.

There were no grand conferences among the peoples; no coordinated military strategy. Each prepared to meet the river-borne threat alone. In twenty-seven gory combats from the Lualaba to the northern arc of the Congo River, people and clans hurled themselves at Stanley. But arrows, spears, and darts, and even the odd Arab musket, fizzled against Remingtons and Sniders. The Mbuti pygmies inflicted only slight casualties as the expedition swept past, rifle barrels red-hot from volleys. The blood of "Niam-Niam" warriors (possibly Mituku) turned the river red as they died in heaps along the banks. Then, the proud Mangbetus rushed down the Aruwimi River to intercept the Europeans in a battle so sanguinary that reports of it sickened and embarrassed many of Europe's Africa-watchers.

At Wagenia Falls the Lualaba became the Congo River proper (Stanley persisted in calling it the Livingstone), and Stanley had begun to expect to arrive at the Atlantic Ocean rather than in the Valley of the Nile. Two hundred miles above Wagenia Falls—the waterfall that spills its tonnage at the equator and was once named for Henry Morton Stanley—the Aruwimi River joins the Congo as it makes a sweeping left turn toward the Atlantic. It was here, in early February 1877, that the Mangbetu threw their full naval might into the balance. In fifty-four monster war canoes propelled by ten-foot-long, carved paddles capped with large ivory balls and tipped with iron, the Mangbetu fleet careened into the Congo River across Stanley's path. It carried two thousand warriors brandishing copper spears. Long, carved, finely worked knives hung at their sides. Others waved heavy, double-headed sword-spears, axes, war hatchets, and hammers. Such deadly sufficiency of arms proved to a momentarily distressed Stanley that "the people on the banks of this river are clever, intelligent, and more advanced in the arts than any hitherto observed since we commenced our descent of the Livingstone." What could be described as the Mangbetu admiralty staff—ten young officers in crimson and gray headdresses of parrot feathers, much of their bodies caparisoned with copper and ivory amulets—danced on a platform in the bow of a dugout canoe whose dimensions struck their adversaries with fear and amazement. An enormous drum throbbed and ivory war horns blared as this lead ship, its forty oarsmen straining, skimmed toward the Europeans' tight formation. But Remingtons and Sniders, firing only at the last moment, did their work to perfection. Charge after charge was turned back, the heavy Snider projectiles ripping out bark at the waterline and raising a fine spray of tissue, marrow, and blood. By the time Stanley's men outran them, the naval power of the Mangbetus had been devastated.

Bangala followed Mangbetu to the slaughter, evoking in their death agonies the sporting admiration of their enemies. "A very superior tribe" were the Bangala.* The Great Explorer regretted "the singular antipathy they entertain toward strangers, which no

---

*As it happens, they were not "Bangala" at all, because the Bangala were created by Stanley. Never doubting for a moment Stanley's appellation and characterization of these river people, Belgian administrators decided that they wanted only "Bangala" for soldiers and workers. Hence, a "tribe" and a language, "Bangala," soon created themselves to satisfy European beliefs. Seventy-five years after Stanley labeled and slaughtered them, a leading Belgian ethnographer conceded, "We know today with certainty that, in all the Belgian Congo, there exists no ethnic group bearing this name."

doubt they will continue to show until, like the Ashanti [Asante of Ghana], they have been taught by two or three sharp fights to lessen their pretensions to make targets of aborigines and strangers." In this case, they were taught a sharp lesson indeed.

Stanley arrived, reluctantly on foot (standing in the prow of a boat had more panache), at Boma on August 9, 1877, "the 999th day from the date of our departure from Zanzibar." Forty-odd miles from the Atlantic and at the tail of an inlet, Boma was then the easternmost European settlement in the Congo. The instantly telegraphed news of Stanley's emergence at the mouth of the Congo (his three white companions and half his Zanzibaris dead) electrified Europe. The mysterious Lualaba and Congo were proven to be potential highways for commerce and Christianity, navigable for a thousand miles through the heart of Africa. No unscalable "Mountains of the Moon" blocked the penetration of Africa's heartland, as the ancients had believed. If the natives were hostile, they could in time be persuaded to accept the superior offerings of Western civilization. If the rain forests were lethal to whites, medical advances would soon attenuate the problem. The Bible, the Maxim gun, and quinine, preferably but not necessarily in that order, were sufficient tools with which to begin the mighty work of progress. "Not only, sir, have you opened up a new continent to our view," Premier Léon Gambetta, an avid expansionist, toasted the Great Explorer upon the latter's arrival in Paris, "but you have given an impetus to scientific and philanthropic enterprise which will have a material effect on the progress of the world. . . . What you have done has influenced governments—proverbially so difficult to move—and the impetus you have imparted to them will, I am convinced, go on growing year after year." East and Central Africa were open for business.

2

If East and Central Africa were open for business to Europeans, they were equally open now to Arabs. East Africa had already been exploited by Arabs for several centuries, and by a combination of stealth, seduction, and strong-arm tactics, they had been slowly advancing westward toward Africa's Interior for more than a quarter century. Stanley and Tippu Tip perfectly personified the European and Arab competition for Africa, and before the forces represented by Stanley could win, those of which Tippu Tip was the incarnation had to be destroyed. Arab penetration of East and Central Africa was powered from three markedly different sources. There were the Arabs of Oman and Zanzibar, who began their advance to the great lakes of Uganda and Tanganyika in the early 1840s under the brilliant leadership of Sultan Ahmad bin Sa'id—or Seyyid Sa'id, as he chose to title himself. There were the Egyptians under the Albanian empire builder, Muhammad Ali, who pushed deep into the southern Sudan about the same time. Then, after the early 1880s, came the Arabs of the Sudan, inflamed by their leaders the Mahdi and the khalifa, who broke into Chad and the northeastern Congo.

Appearing in East Africa as the naval allies of the centuries-old, highly mixed coastal populations, the Omani Arabs had quickly displaced the dominant, hated Portuguese after 1700. By 1840, the year Seyyid Sa'id moved his official residence from Muscat to Zanzibar, the great Omani families like the Mazrui were well on their way to becoming more African than Arab. It was the Omani Arabs who turned slave trading into an industry of remarkable prosperity by the 1860s, some twenty to twenty-five thousand Africans from the Interior being sold each year in the markets of Zanzibar alone; two decades later, about half that number reached the coast. As the Omanis grew richer, they also grew darker and culturally hybrid. It was often the case that the more African they became, the more they protested the purity of their Arab blood and Muslim culture, but the reality was that forty-odd years later the Omanis would constitute the latest infusion into the more-African-than-Arab culture of the Swahili: the urban, coastal culture of Africans, Persians, and Arabs who embraced Islam, used the Arab alphabet, and spoke and wrote the composite language of KiSwahili.

By naked force or through trade, the Swahili displaced or coopted local rulers. The sale of outmoded rifles, often accompanied by arrangements enriching the chief and his family, usually resulted in a relationship between clan ruler and Swahili trader, making the trader or his agent first welcome guest, then resident counsellor, and finally de facto ruler or even "sultan" of the region. Wholesale, if perfunctory, conversion to Islam of those dependent upon his goodwill usually followed. The Arab scramble was a complicated phenomenon, then, involving Swahili, Sudanic, and Egyptian invasions of the Interior, as well as competition with Europe, stiffening of African resistance, and transformation of this resistance into a struggle against European hegemony and, frequently, Arab rule.

From the early 1820s onward, Turco-Arab armies and administrators of Egypt, followed by traders from as far away as Yemen,
pushed up the Nile into lands unknown to them. The naval expedition sent out in 1839 by Muhammad Ali, the aggrandizing founder
of modern Egypt, quickened the pace of penetration in a way
comparable to Stanley's later feat on the Congo River. Once it was
discovered that beyond the river's dreaded *sudd* (many miles of
tangled, floating vegetation) lay solid ground again—on the edge of
a vast belt rich in ivory, wood, and enslavable people—armies,
administrators, and caravans inserted themselves into the remote
Bahr al-Ghazāl and its even more southerly neighbor, Equatoria
Province.

Then Muhammad Ali's grandson, Ismail, borrowing prodigiously
from European bankers, tried to leapfrog his country into the nineteenth century. While the British had not yet begun to fasten their
power over Nigeria and had only just mangled the proud Asante of
Ghana, and while the French had but recently resumed their desul-
tory push into the Senegal hinterland and were still unready to take
on the imperious Tukulor along the Niger, by the late 1870s the
Arabs were already well advanced as methodical and comprehensive empire builders in the east.

Turkey's former dependency, the racially heterogeneous African
province of Egypt, seemed destined to be the dominant "civilizing"
power from Suez to the equator. Its Circassian-officered armies
were stiffened by American Civil War veterans, its Ottoman-
formed bureaucracy harried into unaccustomed activity by
strangely driven Europeans such as Baker, Gordon, Romolo Gessi,
Frank Lupton, Rudolf Slatin, and Eduard Schnitzer (Emin Pasha).
Its expanding possessions were garrisoned as far east as Kassala
Province, as far south as Equatoria, and riveted along the Upper
Nile at Khartoum, Sennar, Fashoda, and Lado. In but a few years,
however—by 1883—Egypt would be occupied by a British army;
its new ruler, Tewfik, obedient to a British proconsul; and its forty
thousand troops ignominiously withdrawn from Bahr al-Ghazāl,
Darfur, Kordofan, Kassala, Berber, and most of the rest of the
Sudan.

Developments in Egypt would drastically alter the balance of
power in Africa. With Stanley's arrival at Boma-Matadi, they were
the most decisive developments in the competition for African real
estate; for once French and British interests in Egypt were no
longer able to coexist, the leisurely pace of European exploitation

necessarily sped up to become a free-for-all. But what became inevitable might well have remained only contingent had it not been for the grandiose schemes of the visionary Ismail. His first extravagance had been the payment of a huge sum Egypt could scarcely afford to the Ottoman sultan to make the title of khedive (viceroy) hereditary. More beneficial but no less prodigal outlays for schools, hospitals, and roads followed over the decade. Ports and palaces added to the red ink on the accounts ledger. A standing army, expensively equipped and rapidly growing, required new campaigns for new garrisons. Above all, there was the great sum of almost fifty million dollars for Ferdinand de Lesseps's canal at Suez —the sea-level parting of the sands that, in 1869, at long last commingled the Mediterranean and the Red Sea through what was henceforth the globe's most strategic ditch. With the frenzied boldness of borrowers whose debts are too large to be denied endless credit, Ismail and his wizard Armenian advisor, the unflappable Nubar Pasha, had, by 1875, run up the stupendous national debt of nearly five hundred million dollars to various Rothschilds, the Crédit Foncier, and the Crédit Lyonnais, among other sources. (Subsequent estimates, after deductions for interest, handling charges, and creative bookkeeping, placed the actual amount reaching the Egyptian treasury at about half that sum.) The first repayment installment was due that December. The collateral was Egypt.

Ismail had no choice but to sell his controlling interest in the Suez Canal: 177,652 shares valued at twenty million dollars. Because their vaults were already brimming with Egyptian debt, and because the Duc de Décazes's aristocratic cabinet was so grateful for British solidarity during a recent German war threat that it refused government financial backing, the French bankers allowed their Suez shares option to expire. With Rothschild money, the British prime minister immediately met the price. Explaining the transaction's haste and slight irregularity to Queen Victoria, Disraeli wrote, "The Canal should belong to England, and I was so decided and absolute with Lord Derby on this head that he ultimately adopted my views and brought the matter before the Cabinet yesterday. . . . We telegraphed accordingly." To the satisfaction of all European states—except the furious French and the suspicious Russians—the canal became the property of the British government, and Egypt became the property of the European bankers.

Economic crisis encouraged military adventurism. Ismail sent his

well-equipped armies south into Ethiopia. But two battlefield catastrophes in less than one year—including the loss of four thousand
men, eighteen thousand new Remingtons, and thirty artillery
pieces to the Ethiopians—wrecked the army's morale and halted
the Egyptian Arabs' advance southward for more than a decade. In
May 1876, the desperate khedive was forced to create the infamous
Caisse de la Dette, whose European commissioners mandated the
orderly rearrangement of the country's finances and resources to
fund the repayment. The few thousand Europeans in Egypt at the
beginning of Ismail's reign had by then grown to more than one
hundred thousand. In a final throw of the dice, Ismail turned to the
liberal elements in Egyptian politics, refusing to pay the full interest on the gargantuan debts and boldly firing a widely detested
European financial advisor. He then announced plans for conven-
ing an Assembly of Notables in an attempt to overhaul the realm.
On orders from the apoplectic British and French creditors, the
sultan's *firmin* (edict) arrived from Istanbul in a matter of days to
depose the khedive, and install Tewfik, his pouty, harem-raised son,
in his place.

An important sign of a world in transformation above the Second
Cataract of the Nile appeared in November 1881. A thirty-seven-
year-old Dunqulawi ascetic named Muhammad Ahmad, who lived
with his disciples in a cave on a small island in the White Nile,
announced that he was the Mahdi, the Expected Guide sent by the
Prophet to return the *ansār* (faithful) to the pristine tenets of Allah.
The Sudan having been atremble with messianic expectations for
most of the nineteenth century, occasionally some exceptional person was identified as the long-awaited Mahdi: Muhammad Ahmad's
incarnation as messenger of the Prophet was thus not wholly unexpected.

But Muhammad Ahmad's swift acceptance by the people of the
Sudan had as much to do with Egyptian policy as with a holy man's
baraka, or supernatural power. Khedival policy on the Sudan's
most lucrative industry—the sale of human beings—had often been
ambiguous. Endorsing the heavy-handed punishments meted out
to slavers by the bullish Sir Samuel Baker in the early 1870s, the
khedive had nonetheless appointed Zubayr Rahman Mansur, a man
whose businesslike rapacity rivalled Tippu Tip's, as governor of the
Bahr al-Ghazāl. Zubayr's armed caravans rampaged through Kordofan and into Darfur Province, slaughtering troops and even the
sultan of Darfur. Throughout the southern Sudan, the *zaribas,* or

fortified markets, did a brisk commerce in slaves, reaching an annual outflow of about twelve thousand

When the ramrod-principled Charles Gordon came to the Sudan
as governor of Equatoria in 1873, he set about dismantling this way
of life and profit. Gordon, like the Mahdi who would destroy him
and his work, was a charismatic molder of men, an Englishman who
sheathed his sword in the Bible and drew it to smite evil with a
dogmatic vengeance. Ismail, near the close of his reign, had found
it helpful to public relations and revenue-raising in Europe to abol-
ish slavery; in January 1877, he made Gordon governor general of
the entire Sudan. In the name of the khedive, Gordon immediately
outlawed the sale of men and women. Flying columns zigzagged
the desert in search of slave caravans. Troops were sent to oversee
the evacuation of the *jallaba* (merchants) from the zone south of
El Obeid, the provincial capital of Darfur, and harsh punishments
were meted out to malefactors. Zubayr's son Suleiman was arrested
by Romolo Gessi, Gordon's Italian lieutenant, and shot. "Thus does
God make gaps in [the ranks of] His enemies," Gordon noted
sternly in his diary. At the same time, ivory was declared a government monopoly.

The *jallaba* poured discontentedly into Khartoum, El Obeid,
Sennar, Kosti, and other centers, while the inspired Gordon and his
multinational cadre of administrators strove mightily to transform
the Sudan into a model of justice and order. God and Gordon's own
star, the general was certain, would see the great enterprise safely
through. But the khedive's star was beginning to flicker, and was
finally extinguished by the sultan's 1879 deposition *firmin*. Crushing taxes and brutal pashas returned to devour the southern provinces. A new governor general was appointed. Enriched and un-
troubled, he permitted extortion and corruption to blanket his
domain like sands from a desert storm. Ismail's dethronement by
the sultan also accelerated the social discrimination in the officer
corps which had worsened during the khedive's last years.

Lieutenant Colonel Ahmad Bey Urabi, unlike the overwhelming
majority of senior officers, was not a blue-eyed Circassian from the
highlands of Anatolia, but a dark-skinned *fellah*—an Egyptian
peasant. Ahmad Bey Urabi had entered the army at fourteen, been
promoted to his rank when only twenty, and, at thirty-five, seen
action on the disastrous Ethiopian front—although not as a combat
officer but in the stigmatized transport corps. The handsome, vigorous, and plain-spoken Urabi became the magnet for *fellahin* offi-

cers whose personal and professional lives had been marred by caste prejudice, as well as for a small but growing number of privileged Egyptians whose distress about their country's humiliation and corrupt institutions made them ready for drastic action. On the morning of September 9, 1881, Colonel Urabi's regiment mustered with two others in Cairo's Abdin Square to demand the dismissal of the cabinet, convocation of a constitutent assembly, and a six-thousand-man increase in the size of the army. For a few months, under the colonel's electric slogan, "Egypt for the Egyptians" (crafted by the maverick English Catholic Wilfrid Blunt), khedive and rebels made common cause.

Unhappy but uncertain about what course to follow, Italy, Austria, Germany, and Russia informed Egypt's nominal overlord, the sultan of Turkey, that after six months of watching, they favored the tense alliance of khedive and the colonel as the best formula for keeping Egypt from social revolution and total insolvency. France and Britain, though far more agitated because of their enormous stakes, joined with the others in signing, on June 25, 1882, the Self-Denying Protocol of the conference of the Powers meeting in Istanbul. By its terms, each solemnly pledged not to seek territorial gain or exclusive position in Egypt, whatever the ensuing developments.

The Self-Denying Protocol quickly fell apart, however, destroying what remained of Egyptian autonomy. Fourteen days before the bemedalled plenipotentiaries affixed signatures to the highsounding document, rioting broke out in Alexandria. Thirty-eight Europeans (most of them Greeks) were slaughtered and the British consul badly mauled. There was a double irony in this tragedy: the French were so determined to display force that Léon Gambetta's government had formally invited the competing British to sail with them; the combined naval force had anchored within shelling range of Alexandria, fuelling the explosion in the city.

In theory, the Anglo-French naval force served the will of the Self-Denying Powers and of the Ottoman sultan. But the bluff commander of the British fleet interpreted his orders loosely; and while his French counterpart fretted, awaiting new instructions, and the new government dissolved in Palais Bourbon debate, Admiral Sir Beauchamp Seymour hurled an unacceptable ultimatum on July 10 for the instant surrender of the forts ringing Alexandria. British marines landed the next day, and the French fleet returned to home port. By the end of the month, the flexible khedive had welcomed General Garnet Wolseley's troops as liberators and formally requested them to secure the canal. On September 13, 1882, the British defeated Urabi's army at Tel al-Kēbir. Three days later, Wolseley's Highlanders and fusiliers marched into Cairo to begin two generations of occupation—even though Prime Minister Gladstone, little more than a month before, had piously informed the House of Commons, "Undoubtedly of all things in the world, that is the thing which we are not going to do." Elimination of Egypt from the Scramble for Africa merely shifted the centers of Arab nationalism farther south—and sharply intensified them.

It was now only a year since Muhammad Ahmad dreamt three times that the Prophet had come to Aba Island to announce that he, Ahmad, was the Mahdi. His proclamation promised to lift the heavy, unjust burdens laid upon the Ja'aliyyin and Ta'isha people by the khedive's governors. "If the crop is good," wrote the *Times* correspondent at Khartoum, "[peasants] pay double taxes (one for the private purse of the Pasha and one for the government at Cairo). If they don't grow the corn, they can't pay the taxes at all, and are kourbashed (good hippopotamus hide) and put into prison."

"Verily, these Turks"—as the people of the Sudan knew both Egyptians and Europeans—"thought theirs was the kingdom and the command was in their hands," Ahmad preached:

> They transgressed the command of [God's] apostles and of His prophets and of him who commanded them to imitate them. They judged by other than God's revelation and altered the Shari-ā of Our Lord Muhammad, the Apostle of God, and insulted the Faith of God and placed poll-tax on your necks together with the rest of the Muslims.

Although Muhammad Ahmad himself made no explicit appeal to those whose lucrative slave raiding had been both suppressed and monopolized by the "Turks," it was obvious that his triumph would mean the return of such profits. The sacred book did not discourage ownership of slaves, and the Mahdi's own clansmen, the Danaqla, had been most grievously deprived by khedival policies. Summoning the khedive, the sultan, the emperor of Ethiopia, and Queen Victoria to submit to the true faith, Muhammad Ahmad swept the Sudan clear of infidels in a series of crushing victories by lightly armed, spear-wielding "Dervishes," beginning with the fall of El Obeid in January 1883. An indifferently trained but well-armed

Egyptian army of ten thousand men was annihilated almost to the last soldier that November, with General William Hicks and his British officers gamely resisting until they were skewered. Darfur collapsed the following month, and the entire Bahr al-Ghazāl succumbed in April 1884. The summons went out once more to Gordon, just about to sail for the Congo, who returned immediately as governor general. Having twice entreated Gordon to save himself and submit to "the Successor of the Apostle of God," the Mahdi commanded a last furious assault upon Khartoum before the advance column of the British relief army arrived. The city fell on January 26, 1885.

With the fall of Khartoum, only the Austrian Emin Pasha's Equatoria Province and parts of Kassala contained Egyptian forces. By then, under pressure from his British advisors, Egypt's ruler, the hapless Tewfik, had formally abandoned the Sudan. The Mahdists occupied Redjaf at the upper end of the White Nile and pushed across the vague frontiers of what had recently become the Congo Free State. In place of the comparatively restrained rule of Egypt, there was now in East Africa a perpetual *jihād* in the form of a centrally ruled theocracy: the Mahdiyya, formidably armed with the discarded and captured arsenals of the khedive's armies.

In the years immediately before the rise of the Mahdiyya, Swahili competition with Europe had sprung into a new phase after the rulers and merchant princes in the Arabian peninsula and on the islands of Pemba and Zanzibar learned that Henry Morton Stanley had survived the Congo River obstacle course. The spell protecting the Manyema, the vast stretch from the Lualaba's right bank to Lake Tanganyika, was broken. Over the next years, an Arab pincer movement from Sudan and Chad in the north and from Tanganyika in the south cut deeper into the once-mysterious Interior. Slave and ivory raids accelerated tremendously, a great many of them conducted by Tippu Tip and his lieutenants. From his Zanzibar headquarters the grasping old flesh-and-ivory merchant had waited for news of Stanley's fate, carefully filing every piece of information for the day when his own caravans might follow the Great Explorer's trail beyond Vinya Nyaza. While geographical societies awarded Stanley their gold medals and his brash, brutal *Through the Dark Continent* went through several international editions, Tippu Tip slashed into the Interior, killing, enslaving, and extracting ivory and rubber.

Now more chairman-of-the-board than a swashbuckler, Tippu Tip tended increasingly to leave the gory fieldwork to his son Sefu and Sefu's subalterns, Lupungu and Ngongo Leteta. The latter was a tall, well-built, dark brown man whose spidery fingers restlessly curled and extended as he spoke, his face inscrutable and impassive. Born among Bakusa, he had been enslaved by Tippu Tip and freed when his fighting and organizing abilities were recognized. Sidney Langford Hinde, the Englishman serving King Léopold of the Belgians in the Congo Free State, wrote admiringly of Ngongo Leteta's leading "his warriors through the country at a run for hours together."

When Stanley returned to the Congo in the summer of 1879 to shape the gargantuan expanse for King Léopold, he was aghast at what the Swahili had done to the Interior. From the deck of his steamer, Stanley chugged past shores where, on his first voyage, aroused Africans had charged his expedition from heavily populated villages enveloped in tropical growth. Now, even the "superior" Bangala were cowed, and "not a drum nor a horn was sounded to raise the alarm of war." The splendid war canoes had been gashed before being rammed upright into the river bank, macabre cenotaphs of progress. Cannibalism had always been a predilection among some of these peoples: enemies captured in war were often eaten, and the flesh of slaves was sometimes consumed to give strength to ailing persons. But until the Swahili infestation, it had been held in check by traditions of warfare and ritual. By the time of Stanley's return, however, territorial dispossession, institutional chaos, collective panic, and disease and famine had ignited a wave of flesh-eating that spread from inveterate cannibals like Bakusa to Batetela, the Mangbetu, and much of Zande. Before the end of the decade, the felon interplay of raids, migrations, and animal and crop wastage would open the Interior to tsetse fly. Trypanosomiasis, sleeping sickness, would soon devastate whole peoples from the mouth of the Congo to Lake Victoria. Much of Africa was becoming as anarchic, pestilential, and brutal as the arriving missionaries, physicians, soldiers, and commissioners never tired of reminding the outside world that it had always been. The black African world of self-sufficient villages merging with slowly expanding regional economies (as coast and interior became slowly interlinked by river and overland commerce in rare woods, ivory, cotton fiber, precious metals, nuts, gums, and oils) was being strangled. After the collapse and chaos spawned by the intruders would come forced labor and total economic subordination—would come an Africa that could be looked upon by Europeans as being in as desperate need of European uplift as the gospel of the White Man's Burden proclaimed.

CHAPTER TWO

The Spoilers

1

The Belgian Léopold II had a voracious appetite for territory, even by imperial standards, as he sought control of the last African acreage still unclaimed by Britain and France. As heir to the throne, the young Léopold had tirelessly addressed commercial groups, learned societies, and military assemblages with his exhortations for Belgians to look beyond the Meuse. "There is no time to lose," he would warn, "unless we wish to see all the best positions, already scarce, occupied successively by nations more enterprising than ourselves." As king, he would scheme to acquire North Borneo, the Philippines, part of China, Uganda, and Eritrea, but his preference was always centered on the Nile.

Egypt fascinated this otherwise phlegmatic prince. It stimulated a romantic, almost mystical yearning in what was one of the most calculating royal personalities of Europe. "I dare not call him treacherous," a cabinet minister later wrote of Léopold. "He hides his thoughts, and advocates what he does not believe in order to protect his inner reflections from attack." Egypt was different; his emotions about it broke through the controlled Saxe-Coburg demeanor, giving rise to what French politicians called with aspersion Léopold's *"folie de grandeur."*

His first trip to the Land of the Pharaohs was as an impressionable eighteen-year-old, a "stick of asparagus" on a nuptial voyage with his lovely, unloved Habsburg bride, Archduchess Marie Henriette. He returned in 1862, this time following the Nile to its Second Cataract at Wadi Halfa, Egypt's ancient Nubian frontier. Two years later, Léopold again came to Heliopolis and Luxor on his way to India. Long before tales of Central African exploits lured his imagi-

34

nation and avarice to the Congo, he dreamed of a Nilotic empire. Knowing that Egypt was bound to fall to either Britain or France, he looked far beyond the last projection of pharaonic might on the Nile—Ramses II's stupendous statuary at Abu Simbel—to the southern Sudan and farther still. The king gave rein to his imagination and bided his time until the moment when he could take a slice of "this magnificent African cake."

That moment appeared to have come with news of Verney Lovett Cameron's astonishing stroll into Luanda on November 22, 1875. The Lualaba was part of the Congo, Cameron asserted confidently. Five months later, supposedly incognito but by then a familiar figure to Londoners, the king of the Belgians received Cameron in his rooms at Claridges. What the alcoholic explorer had to say about the kindliness of the peoples, wealth of the region, and probable navigability of the Congo was enough to convince Léopold that his first slice of Africa lay in the heart of the continent. The Nile would have to wait.

Slow of speech and evasive (Léopold I had thought his son retarded), Léopold II efficiently manipulated the quick-witted, the vigorous, and the altruistic. The high-minded men of action and science invited to the Brussels International Geographical Conference in September 1876 assembled with the inspiring expectation of royal patronage for good works. Léopold's invitational letter, stressing the "completely charitable, completely scientific and philanthropic nature of the aim to be achieved," was carefully composed to excite them. Looking down his elongated nose at the multinational audience of thirty-five savants—Sir Bartle Frere, Sir Henry Rawlinson, and William Mackinnon of Great Britain; Admiral de la Roncière le Noury and Ferdinand de Lesseps of France; Baron von Richtofen of Germany; Count Zichy of Austria; others from Italy, Russia, and the United States; and the explorers Cameron, Nachtigal, Schweinfurth, and Rolfs—Léopold opened the conference with a noble charge:

> The subject which brings us together today is one that deserves in the highest degree to engage the attention of the friends of humanity. To open to civilization the only part of the globe where it has not yet penetrated, to pierce the darkness enshrouding entire populations, that is, if I may venture to say so, a crusade worthy of this century of progress; and I am happy to discover how much public sentiment is in favor of its accomplishment. The current is with us.

Forswearing national rivalry, territorial gain, and commercial warfare, the delegates returned home to form national committees dedicated to the uplifting principles of the Declaration of the International Association for the Exploration and Civilization of Central Africa. While men of affairs raised funds and geographers and physicians planned expeditions, the honorary president of the Association Internationale Africaine (AIA), Léopold, schemed behind his supposedly disinterested title to steal the Congo.

Returning to England in January 1878, after his Congo saga, Stanley was approached by Léopold's agents with a generous offer of employment. Demurring until *Through the Dark Continent* was at the publisher's, and then until it became clear that British interest in Central Africa was practically nil, the Great Explorer eventually accepted the king's invitation to the fanatically clean Laeken Palace (Léopold was a hypochondriac) in the summer of 1879. Léopold cunningly placed Stanley in the service of something called the Association Internationale du Congo (AIC), confusingly similar to the AIA but in fact a wholly Belgian operation under Léopold's exclusive control. "Care must be taken not to make it evident that the Association du Congo and the Association Africaine are two different things," he warned a confidant. Stanley arrived at Boma-Matadi again in August 1879 and began the colossal work of road building and station construction which would keep him in the Congo until June 1884. Planting the association's flag—blue with a gold star—at intervals as they went, Stanley's force of one hundred whites and six hundred Africans, equipped with four machine guns, twelve Krupp cannons, and a thousand rapid-action rifles, chopped and blasted its way up the Congo River bank until it reached N'Tambo, shortly renamed Léopoldville. On December 1, 1883, Bula Matari—"smasher of rocks," Stanley's new African name—hoisted what had now become the flag of the as-yet-unrecognized Congo Free State over Stanley Falls on the equator in the eastern Congo.

Stanley's achievement had been prodigious. Paradoxically, it also seemed to mellow Bula Matari somewhat. Brutal and obsessive as he was, he confessed sorrow at having earlier shot his way across the continent. He preferred Zanzibaris to the starched Belgian officers who, indifferent to the terrain and ignorant of the languages, barked and marched across the colony's stupendous surface. But Stanley's era was already closing. Now was the time of the professional soldier, the civil servant, and, above all, of the cartel agent.

Bula Matari was withdrawn in 1885. The French government had made his recall a precondition to Congo frontier negotiations, and Léopold had become increasingly uneasy with this outspoken world figure who bent instructions to fit situations. Stanley himself had grown moody with a royal employer who refused to be "so frank as to tell me outright what we are to strive for."

A flotilla of steamboats now connected the country from west to east. Stanley had assembled the nucleus of a militia, the Force Publique, which would be formally established in 1888. More than five million of Léopold's own dollars went into the Congo Free State from 1879 to 1890.

Formal recognition of the Belgian hybrid by Europe and the United States came at the Berlin Conference of 1884–85. As sole proprietor of the million-square-mile Congo, Léopold began to scheme in earnest at the close of the decade for an even greater empire, one stretching to the Upper Nile and, if possible, to the Red Sea. When Auguste Beernaert, the Catholic party's cautious leader, counselled restraint, his genuinely surprised sovereign exclaimed, "You think that it's nothing, my dear minister, to be a Pharaoh!" Léopold also believed that playing pharaoh could have long-term, salutary domestic consequences. Economic, religious, and regional tensions were building up dangerously in Belgium. The old Liberal party (the party of the urban, industrial, mainly French-speaking haute bourgeoisie), with its property franchise, secular public-education reforms, and free-trade policies, faltered and then succumbed in 1884 to forces of Catholic reaction. This reaction was a complex mix of agricultural protection, labor legislation, Flemish provincialism, and a broader franchise in order to undo the work of the previous governing elite. It was far from clear, though, whether or not franchise sops (such as full manhood suffrage in 1893) and factory inspection laws could control the new industrial working class in one of Europe's most rapidly expanding economies —an economy in which Liège coalminers, Hainault steelworkers, and Antwerp stevedores annually became poorer because of rising prices. The Belgian Workers' party, forerunner of an aggressive socialist party, appeared in 1885, and the following year there were violent and widespread labor troubles.

Abreast of the latest theories and with a Kiplingesque imagination, Léopold was certain that eventually his African fiefdom would prove a powerfully uniting symbol of little Belgium's grandeur. In

France, elaborate rationalizations of imperialism were being spun by professors like Pierre Paul Leroy-Beaulieu and politicians like Jules Ferry, according to whom colonies were "escape valves" for capitalist overproduction and rampant protectionism. In England, writers like George Henty, Rider Haggard, and Rudyard Kipling were already investing insalubrious sub-Saharan outposts with mystery and romantic danger, which appealed strongly to the fin-de-siècle male imagination—especially those males with modest inheritances.

Two years before mounting the throne, Léopold had outlined a book which he never found the time or candor to write. His ideas there somewhat anticipated those of Leroy-Beaulieu and Ferry, noting that in colonies

> We see a means of augmenting our power in the world, of opening up new careers to our fellow citizens, of providing ourselves with a new financial structure which might, as in Java, yield a surplus and give an opportunity for investing capital in places where our own laws hold sway in a manner far more advantageous than in metals or even in railroads.

Finally, Léopold intended to reverse the historical dependency of monarchy upon the middle class by enriching Belgian businesses and banks in his Congo venture.

But what this restless prince, who constantly turned up in London and Paris with unsolicited advice and bizarre proposals, wanted most was to play the game of power politics in the manner of a grand statesman—to be the Bismarck of Africa. The African schemes of Léopold, who reigned over a small population with no navy and a tiny army, would have verged on the fantastic if not for the fact that Belgium, this little geographical wedge in the heart of western Europe, was a potential buffer between the rival African schemes of France, Great Britain, and Germany. Léopold's marginal status much enhanced his crafty politics: king of a neutral Belgium ever ready to be of service in Europe; intimate Saxe-Coburg cousin to Hanoverian Queen Victoria; tied to France by language, mutual fear of Germany, and investments; European sovereign of an African state theoretically unentangled with Europe; amateur geographer and humanist presiding over African philanthropies; royal freebooter inviting investments through scores of cartels in Africa's ivory, rubber, minerals, lumber, and railroads.

Ultimately, as was to be expected, Léopold's various personae, his dissembling and hypocrisy, reduced his credibility to the point where the rulers of Europe believed him capable of the blackest infamies. Toward the end of his life, the documented horrors of the Congo Free State, exaggerated tales of the white-bearded king's lust for young girls, and public spats with his working-class mistress, the mother of illegitimate Saxe-Coburgs, were such an embarrassment to royal peers that he was sometimes cut in public. Even the concupiscent Prince of Wales found Léopold's presence insufferable. For all that, the monarch's real fault was that he had behaved with the morals of a tycoon rather than with the constitutionally fettered propriety of a king.

The French were the first to take measure of Léopold's duplicity. While Bula Matari charted the king's vast lands and ruthlessly drove his men to set up posts and stations, the elegant, Italian-born Marquis Pietro Savorgnan de Brazza unfurled the flag of France on the north bank of the Congo River. Year by year, each added to the volume of his respective Congo, Stanley conducting himself like a mining engineer short of time, de Brazza like an amateur anthropologist on a leisurely walk. De Brazza sniffed that he was never in the "habit of travelling on African soil in martial array like Mr. Stanley, always accompanied by a legion of armed men," adding that he "never needed to resort to barter, because travelling as a friend, and not as a conqueror, everywhere I found hospitable people." It was the languid marquis who reached the pool above the Congo cataracts first, staking a claim for France, charmingly welcoming a flustered and uncharacteristically tardy Stanley. De Brazza left a Senegalese sergeant and a small detachment to protect French interests and block the Belgians. Léopold was furious. In June 1882, de Brazza returned to France bringing treaties "x'd" by the Teke chief Makoko, placing his realm under the protection of France. Despite Radical Deputy Georges Clemenceau's sneers about their validity and value, and the grave misgivings of a large number of deputies, the so-called Makoko Treaties were ratified by a belatedly enthusiastic Chamber of Deputies after much adroit lobbying by champions of empire and a furious press campaign partly orchestrated by de Brazza and his friends.

Friction between the two Congos steadily increased. An April 1887 protocol between France and the Congo Free State defined Léopold's domain as stretching north and west to the Ubangi River, and, where the Ubangi's northern course remained uncharted by

Europeans, no farther north than four degrees of latitude. The French clearly meant to keep the Belgians on the river's left shore. But the Ubangi was shortly discovered to divide into two rivers—the Uele and, farther north, the Mbomu—and by 1891 troops, traders, and administrators of the Congo Free State, claiming there was no Ubangi in that part of the Congo and ignoring the latitude limitation, swarmed into territory the French had meant to give themselves. Back in West Africa as governor general of the French Congo, de Brazza and his few officers were scarcely able to oppose the stealthy, well-financed encroachments of Léopold's forces.

Most Frenchmen were either uninterested in or hostile to acquiring colonies. Overseas profits came from places where overseas investments were made—Russia, the Balkans, and Latin America. Léopold and his Force Publique, de Brazza and his Makoko domains were minor concerns. Formal, almost perfunctory protests by France's ambassador to Brussels were routinely lodged about border infractions in Central Africa. The costs of this casual approach went unappreciated until it was almost too late. For in less than three years after the 1887 protocol, a Belgian flanking movement north of the Mbomu River threatened to end all eastward expansion of the French Congo, blocking penetration of the Upper Ubangi and of the Bahr al-Ghazāl beyond. Instead of a new cone-shaped colony providing a passageway to the Nile watershed, the French realized that they were being pressed into a hinterland disappointingly close to the Atlantic. Audaciously, the monarch of three million polyglot, gourmandizing, industrious burghers of a neutral nation had all but eliminated one of the world's great powers from much of Central Africa.

While Savorgnan de Brazza's administrators were stymied in the west, Léopold plotted a further exclusion of France from the east. His newfound instrument was Sir William Mackinnon, a quixotic Scots steamship magnate who had made one of Britain's great fortunes in India. Inspired by a blend of Presbyterian mission and Highlander greed, Sir William now wished to bring the blessings of limited liability enterprise to East Africa. The Mackinnon clan planned to set up the Imperial British East Africa Company (the mighty IBEA), whose chartered mandate "to open up Africa for commerce and Christianity" was unmistakably indebted to the sainted David Livingstone's motto of "Christianity, civilization, and commerce." Mackinnon used publicity as ably as a twentieth-century public relations expert. Léopold avoided it. But each saw reflected in the other his own image of master manipulator. Long, secret discussions with Mackinnon and Stanley, again in active Congo service, resulted in a feverishly advertised bogus relief expedition to the Nile headwaters, ostensibly either to resupply or to "escort to civilization" the fabulously resourceful Emin Pasha, still commanding an Egyptian-Sudanese army near the Uganda border.

On the first day of December 1886, the boat bringing Wilhelm Junker from the Interior with news of Emin Pasha docked at Zanzibar port. Except to a few members of the Royal Geographical Society and the Edinburgh Geographical Society, the name Emin Pasha was wholly unknown in the United Kingdom. Almost instantly, the press made the commander of the last surviving Egyptian forces in the Sudan a household hero. His doughty message sent to the world through Junker—"We shall hold out until we obtain help, or until we perish"—electrified the nation as no African cause since Gordon at Khartoum. Yet Emin Pasha was neither a British subject nor a Christian, but a German Jewish convert to Islam.

Among all the complex, colorful Western personalities drawn to khedival service, Eduard Karl Oskar Theodor Schnitzer from Prussian Silesia may have been the most unfathomable. He is the paradigm of the rootless European in Africa. Reared by Lutheran parents, a brilliant medical student at Breslau and Berlin universities, and an enthusiastic member of his duelling fraternity, Schnitzer learned at the age of twenty-three what it could mean in Germany to have a Jewish father he had never known. Hurdles were suddenly thrown up to bar professional certification by the state. He sailed for Turkish Serbia almost immediately, in December 1864, returning only once, ten years later, with a retinue of Circassian slave women, which he promptly left in the care of his family and the horrified citizens of Neisse.

Emin corresponded with his sister until his death, from Antivari, Trebizond, Epirus, Anatolia, Albania, Persia, Syria, Cairo, Khartoum, Gondokoro—wherever the flag of a declining Turkish empire had been unfurled. He changed his name to Doctor Hairouallah Effendi, and Eduard Schnitzer disappeared forever beneath the fez of a Muslim official, Turkish quarantine officer of the Serbian port of Antivari, who spoke perfect Turkish, Arabic, Persian, Greek, Swahili, and several Slavonic languages, as well as English, French, and Italian. "I am now completely naturalized," he wrote his sister in 1872, "and have even adopted the disguise of a Turkish name." Whether or not his Muslim personality was really a disguise was impossible to know, because Emin Effendi, or Emin Pasha, as he chose to be known in the Sudan, left too many contradictory clues. What was certain was that this delicately slender polymath with the deeply intense, myopic eyes and dark, handsome face so attractive to women became an incomparably endowed physician, zoologist, anthropologist, botanist, ornithologist, and linguist. He was also a superb diplomat and administrator, talents which brought him to the attention of Gordon, then governor of Equatoria.

This was the great decade of Egyptian expansion. Cairo was launching dynamic European governors, unenthusiastic Egyptian officers, and stolid, seldom-paid Sudanese infantry on waves of conquest south. Steaming upriver aboard the hundred-ton *Khedive* and forty-ton *Nyanza* with a thousand well-equipped officers and men, Sir Samuel and Lady Baker had claimed ivory-rich Equatoria for Egypt in 1871. For good measure, the Bakers annexed the unvisited kingdom of Bunyoro—part of neighboring Uganda—the following year. When Gordon took over from the Bakers as governor in 1873, aggression against Uganda and Kenya (then owned by the sultan of Zanzibar) had climaxed. Two large Egyptian armies invaded Ethiopia in 1876. Gordon made Emin his emissary to the Kabaka Mutesa, who was holding captive troops sent into Buganda to extend the khedival sphere. In July 1878, after Gordon had become governor general at Khartoum, Emin was appointed governor of Equatoria. Emin devoted the next few years to suppressing the slave traffic, founding a chain of Nile stations from Lado to Lake Albert, mapping the region, studying the flora and fauna, stuffing rare birds, and raising an African daughter. Although Egyptian and Sudanese subordinates were much puzzled by his practice of deciding policy only after conferring with them, Cairo was thoroughly gratified by Emin's governorship. Equatoria's budget showed a forty-thousand-dollar surplus from ivory exports in 1882; a sixty-thousand-dollar surplus was anticipated for 1883.

The Mahdi's *jihād* shattered the pasha's idyll. El Obeid, capital of Kordofan, fell in January 1883. Rudolf Slatin, an Austrian of Jewish descent who, like Emin, had converted to Islam, surrendered the garrison at El Fasher that December, and with it Darfur *mudiriyya*, or province. A month later, Gordon hurried to the Sudan to organize Khartoum's defenses, while the former merchant seaman Frank Lupton desperately held on in the Bahr al-Ghazāl. These were distant rumblings of uncertain meaning in Equatoria until the arrival of Lupton's letter in late April 1884. "It's all up with me here," he warned Emin. "Look out, you; some 8,000 to 10,000 men are coming to you well armed." When a large Mahdist army approached at the end of the year, the pasha squandered weeks seeking a consensus among his officers before finally deciding to abandon his Lado headquarters for a post near the Uganda frontier. Depending on the *Khedive* and *Nyanza* (the Bakers' thirteen-year-old steamers) for messages and supplies between Wadelai, his new headquarters in the south, and Dufile, now the last defensible northern post, Emin positioned his several thousand troops for escape through Bunyoro and Buganda. He also moved a huge quantity of ivory with an estimated market value of three hundred thousand dollars to the new headquarters, and settled again into his routine of botanical and zoological discovery. Emin's friend Junker made his way to the Tanganyika coast with the news and letters that were to arouse the United Kingdom at the close of 1886.

Neither Her Majesty's government nor the newspaper-reading public immediately volunteered to pay for a rescue operation, however, and it was then that Mackinnon and, prompted by his British advisors, the Egyptian khedive stepped forward. The khedival government subscribed fifty thousand dollars for an evacuation expedition. Most of the balance, some fifty thousand dollars, came from Mackinnon, his Manchester business friends, and, covertly, Léopold. Junker and Schweinfurth, Emin's disinterested friends and the Egyptians' first choices, were rapidly sidelined from leadership. In late January 1887, Stanley hurried for Zanzibar as head of the Emin Pasha Relief Expedition. Egypt and Emin's friends understood that Emin was to be brought out. Mackinnon intended for him to become a servant of IBEA, Léopold schemed to employ him for the Congo Free State, and Bula Matari wanted him for a trophy. But it was Léopold who held the upper hand in these negotiations, because Stanley was still in his munificent employ, and, although Mackinnon wanted Emin for himself, the shipping magnate could also count on his East African designs being realized through substantial business entanglements with the Belgian king.

And so with elaborate public statements explaining why Emin Pasha was not to be rescued by a 980-mile dash from the Tanganyika coast—German territorial touchiness, Ganda ferocity, missionaries placed at risk, uncharted lands—Bula Matari announced that the relief expedition would sail from Zanzibar around the South African Cape to the mouth of the Congo, up the Congo and the Aruwimi rivers, then march through the near-impassable Ituri forest into Equatoria. Bula Matari and his business backers in the geographical societies praised Léopold's high-mindedness in allowing the expedition to take this circuitous, but supposedly secure, route through his lands. Secretly, in addition to the hundred thousand cartridges which Emin hardly needed, the expedition carried two business proposals: Léopold's that Emin accept the title of governor and rank of general, an annual stipend of seventy-five hundred dollars, and a budget of fifty to sixty thousand dollars in return for transferring ownership of Equatoria from Egypt to the Congo Free State; Mackinnon's that the pasha, in exchange for supplies and construction of a secure fort on Lake Albert, enter the service of the projected IBEA.

Léopold's and Mackinnon's plans were complicated, but their goals—ivory and territory—were clear. Moreover, Léopold's mischief was, if impenetrable in certain particulars, painfully obvious to the French in its broad consequences. Stanley's expedition, from Zanzibar to the mouth of the Congo, was geographically inexplicable but politically logical. For Tippu Tip, in residence at his Zanzibar mansion, was now master of the eastern Congo. Twenty-six months earlier, in November 1884, the Swahili merchant prince had angrily annulled a treaty signed by his deputy with the Congo Free State intended to bar Swahili power from moving north beyond Stanley Falls. Seven hundred Swahili troops were sent raiding, pillaging, and murdering as far north as the Aruwimi River, just to make certain the Belgians had no doubts about Tippu Tip's claims. Two years later, the interference in slave raiding and the Congo Free State's export tax on ivory and rubber caused an explosion. Swahili soldiers attacked Stanley Falls, scattering the Hausa and "Bangala" militia and driving the Europeans into the bush. Belgian power virtually disappeared from the eastern Congo. Stanley's orders were to buy time for Léopold by neutralizing Tippu Tip; race up the Congo River reaffirming Belgian authority; then buy Emin Pasha. The French were not amused, nor were the Germans.

Whether Emin Pasha accepted a salary, general's star, and annual subsidy to place Equatoria Province and its Sudanese troops in the service of the Congo Free State; or whether, as Mackinnon and even Stanley hoped, Emin chose IBEA, East Africa would be closed to France and in large part to Germany. The scheme was too clever, however. Emin's army would obey only those commands it expected to be given. The pasha was no freer to order a switch of allegiance from the khedive to the king of the Belgians than he was to sound the evacuation of the White Nile stations for duty in Uganda with IBEA. Emin found Bula Matari frighteningly insensitive and impatient. In the end, no one got anything—not even the seventy-five tons of ivory that had caused Léopold and Mackinnon to wet their lips—except the kaiser, who won Emin Pasha after Stanley dragged him to the coast at Bagamoyo in December 1889. At a cost of one hundred thousand dollars, it was a large, expensive setback for the calculating parties.

Less than a year later, the king and Mackinnon sought to accomplish through paper what Stanley had failed to bring about in the rain forest. The so-called Mackinnon Treaty of May 1890 proposed to put the Congo Free State firmly on the left bank of the White Nile from Lake Albert north to Fashoda. This region of the Bahr al-Ghazāl was of crucial importance to the French. In return for "recognizing" the Belgian Congo's extended sphere over territory belonging to neither England nor Belgium, Mackinnon's IBEA, piously busy absorbing Uganda, was "given" a slice of East Africa five miles wide, running through German claims, from Lake Tanganyika north to Lake Albert. IBEA's five-mile swath was to be an easement for Cecil Rhodes's rail and telegraph linkage of British East Africa from the Cape to Cairo. Lord Salisbury, the British prime minister, privately congratulated Sir William and instructed the Foreign Office to tell Léopold that the treaty had the unofficial blessings of Her Majesty's government.

In all, it was a jolly fine turn of affairs for Britain. Without a pound from the Treasury and without official involvement in the machinations, the nettlesome French had been checkmated. The French disdainfully announced that an agreement between a businessman and a quasi-fictional state utterly lacked international legitimacy. The best minds at the Quai d'Orsay, however, had few helpful, concrete proposals. Certainly nothing materially helpful came to Savorgnan de Brazza from France. His reports of mounting Belgian activity above Léopoldville were received, filed, and infrequently and evasively answered.

In February 1891 Léopold dispatched Major Guillaume Van Kerckhoven and nineteen officers to the Congo. Van Kerckhoven was already an experienced "African" (a term applied to Europeans having served in Africa), having been part of a Force Publique expedition to the Aruwimi River in the late 1880s. The five-hundred-strong Van Kerckhoven Expedition, ordered to bring the

northeastern Congo under Belgian rule quickly and then speed to
the Nile, was a straightforward military operation for exclusively
political ends; it was Léopold's contribution to the European dismemberment of sub-Saharan Africa. No one was to be rescued from
savage clutches, there were no unknown rivers to be mapped, nor
was there the slightest scientific or anthropological pretext. Van
Kerckhoven and his men were there to conquer Africa for king and
—its citizens' indifference notwithstanding—country. The second
phase of the expedition was finally launched on December 12,
1891. Leaving the Bomokandi River region in the northeast and
marching parallel with the equator toward Lake Albert, Van Kerckhoven's orders called for a swerve north toward the Bahr al-Ghazāl. By the fall of the following year, 1892, Van Kerckhoven and his
satellite forces had skirmished within reach of the Nile, while barely
a few dozen of de Brazza's administrators or soldiers had reached
the Upper Ubangi. Whatever the Quai d'Orsay said about the non-
validity of the Mackinnon Treaty, it could not ignore the force at
the conference table of the old expression *"titre vaut possession"*—
possession is nine-tenths of the law.

"Van Kerckhoven must already be on the Nile," de Brazza's chief
assistant, Albert Dolisie, wrote despairingly early that November.
In fact, Guillaume Van Kerckhoven's arrival on the Nile was never
to happen. The commander had kept a strong, hard pace for many
months. "The expedition passed from the valley of the Congo to
that of the Uele like a pestilence," a contemporary Belgian geographer noted. But on the twenty-ninth day of September 1892, a river
crossing about three hundred miles west of Lake Albert was Van
Kerckhoven's undoing. The Nzoro was seventy yards wide at that
point. On the far bank Africans with poisoned arrows barred the
way. Shouting for his Winchester, the commander unnerved his
boy; somehow the rifle discharged, killing Van Kerckhoven instantly. Command fell to Jules Milz, a lieutenant with a knack for
winning Arab "sultans." The second week in October he reached
the settlement of Wadelai in the southern tip of what was once
Emin Pasha's Equatoria. The nearly blind Emin, after shaking free
of Stanley and taking service with the kaiser, had tried to return to
his old headquarters at Wadelai, only to drift with Swahili caravans
into the Manyema and, that same month, to die, his throat slit by
a Swahili knife.

Lieutenant Milz was the first European the Equatoria garrison of
some four hundred men had seen in three years. These were stal-

warts. The bulk of Emin's force had moved farther south into Uganda. Like isolated Japanese forces in the mid-twentieth century, maintaining esprit de corps and fighting long after their empire's surrender, the stubborn Wadelai garrison clung to the fantasy of defending the rights of the khedive. But they were more flexible now than when Stanley had tried to budge them. The Mahdists were sure to attack before too long, and fierce Lubaris, "who feared neither white men nor repeating rifles," had begun to settle not far away in numbers too great for safety. Swearing allegiance to Léopold, the garrison accepted Milz's decision to send a contingent of 240 men to Dufile farther down the White Nile, while the remainder followed the Belgians to an abandoned Egyptian post at Ganda. What Milz had done was of great potential importance. Even if Emin's aging soldiers strained to pull tunics over ample middles, their knowledge of the people and region was invaluable. Brought back to fighting edge by the Free State's Force Publique officers, they would have been useful auxiliaries, well-forged links in the Belgian Congo's lengthening chain of posts. But the right formula for discipline and sagacity proved to be beyond the Belgians, and after about six months the Egyptians and Sudanese at Ganda would revolt against their new masters and join the Mahdists. Before that came about, however, the Van Kerckhoven Expedition had already carried the Belgians into position on the White Nile—not as far downriver as Redjaf or even Bor, but well placed for their final run.

2

Success bred arrogance in Brussels and desperation in Libreville, Savorgnan de Brazza's headquarters. It also forced a measure of resolve in Paris. French governments under the Third Republic had the durability of soufflé, their survival usually determined by how adroitly they deferred consideration of urgent matters. A coherent policy for Central Africa, adequately financed and aggressively pursued across a field of self-destructing cabinets, volatile parliaments, and increasingly polarized public opinion, demanded uncommon clarity, vigor, and deviousness. Sadi Carnot, ex-physicist and president of the Republic, possessed the first quality; Théophile Delcassé, journalist turned colonial undersecretary, abundantly the second and third. A classmate of Sadi Carnot's from the prestigious École Polytechnique had presented the president in early January

1893 with what seemed a startlingly plausible project. Victor Prompt's report convinced Carnot that French engineers, having dug the Suez Canal and begun to pierce the ill-conceived Panama Canal, could dam the headwaters of the Nile, turning the great waterway on and off like a bathtub spigot. Helped by the small but well-organized imperialists in the National Assembly, Delcassé was able to insert preliminary credits in appropriations voted in June 1893 for an expedition through the French Congo to the Nile watershed in the Bahr al-Ghazāl.

This, the French believed, would surely get the conciliatory attention of the British in Egypt. Merely sending out the expedition, or at most some detailed surveys and preliminary digging, were likely to bring the British to the conference table. Five years before, Lord Salisbury had proposed a take-it-or-leave-it solution to the Egyptian question which the French and their soon-to-be allies the Russians had considered an insult: Britain would evacuate Egypt after three years, if the country was secure and if the sultan agreed to a perpetual right of British reentry. Carnot and Delcassé imagined that Victor Prompt's scheme would reopen the Egyptian question and eventually lead either to British evacuation or sharing of Egypt, or to concessions to France in Morocco.

Experienced "African" officers may have doubted that the flow of the Nile could be managed with the ease described in Prompt's report—for one thing, the region contained no rock or suitable wood—but they were excited by prospects of leading expeditions that would run a belt of French influence from West Africa to the Red Sea. None of them had the politicians' misgivings that such a threat to South African Cecil Rhodes's rail and telegraph lines to Egypt might lead to a French disaster. As for the Belgians, it was assumed that once France began to move in force across Central Africa, their obstructionism would quickly fade away. The most desirable outcome, cheapest and least dangerous, would simply be for all parties to behave accommodatingly now that France had demonstrated a willingness to act aggressively. The Bahr al-Ghazāl enterprise, in that case, would become a chess match that need not be played to the finish, since astute statesmen in Paris, London, and Brussels could readily foresee the endgame.

Meanwhile, Savorgnan de Brazza had decided it was time to challenge the Congo Free State with his own feeble resources. News of the projected Nile mission reached him during the spring of 1893, but de Brazza knew painfully well how much stock could be placed in initiatives from Paris. On the other hand, there would be all the more need for Colonial Undersecretary Delcassé's strategy if a small force of French Congo administrators were already forging into the Upper Ubangi region and holding on to new territory with the slimmest of means. In any case, the marquis saw that his hand was being forced by the Belgians. News reached him in Libreville that the Force Publique was buying African cooperation with blanket handouts of rifles. Van Kerckhoven or his successor was said to be at Wadelai, Redjaf, or perhaps even at Fashoda. From the fork of the Ubangi, the Belgians and their African allies were multiplying and reinforcing posts. The French shut-out was almost a fait accompli. Even if they "restore these territories to us, we will have an impossible task with our present capabilities and we will need a very significant number of men to hold the posts," warned Victor Liotard, commissioner of the Upper Ubangi and one of France's outstanding proconsuls.

At thirty-five, Victor Liotard was a dark, intense ex-navy pharmacist whose abilities as a colonial administrator had been quickly appreciated by de Brazza. He was both adventurous and tactful, imposing order and permanence upon the remotest rain forest encampments and repeatedly winning the trust of Congolese rulers. With no troops of his own and only a few European assistants, he had succeeded in studding the north bank of the Ubangi River with posts at Zinga, Bangui, Kouango, and Mobaye. At the close of 1892, he had begun to probe the Belgian settlements just beyond the Ubangi's fork, on the north bank of the Mbomu. On March 16, 1893, on the southern road leading into Bangassou near the Mbomu River, Liotard, his adjutant, and about forty borrowed Algerian troops sounded bugles, unfurled the tricolor, and broke into a rapid marching stride as they reached Bangassou's outskirts. The senior Force Publique officer, warned of Liotard's advance, hurriedly spilled his troops into the road; as more Belgian Yakoma auxiliaries rushed forward, he ordered the Frenchman to halt and stack arms. A standard duet of European bravura ensued: *"Alors,* no more jokes, eh, M'sieur Mathieu," Liotard bluffed, still approaching. Outnumbered, confronted by officers ready to fight, and later told in no uncertain words by the obedient Yakoma chief that Frenchmen were unwelcome in Bangassou, Liotard settled for the compromise of camping near the town and awaiting the return of the Belgian commander's superior before planting the tricolor in "French soil." Both the French and the Belgians knew that the superior officer never *would* return, and that the final resolution of their charade would take place in Paris and Brussels. Liotard decamped after a brief, contentious sojourn.

A standoff on the banks of a river in the heart of Africa was not headline news in Paris. In the Chamber of Deputies, Liotard's strategic withdrawal from Bangassou was barely registered among the roiling events of the moment. The Panama scandal, filling the press with details of staggering wrongdoing and mismanagement and the criminal courts with politicians and financiers, was reaching its dreaded term; national elections and adjournment of the legislature were ahead; on December 9, an anarchist's bomb showered the Chamber with iron filings; and a young Jewish army captain, Alfred Dreyfus, found himself facing court martial. Military espionage and political scandal far upstaged frontier tensions in the Congo—except for Delcassé and his imperialist supporters. Léopold's behavior rankled deeply, and Delcassé pushed ahead all the more determinedly with plans for the Congo-Nile scheme. The polished, assertive Captain Parfait-Louis Monteil had already been chosen to lead the expedition to the Sudan. An imaginative officer with the gift of command and a first-rate technical education, Monteil had been the natural choice for the mission. *"Monsieur le Président,"* Monteil had said, saluting Sadi Carnot with appropriate Elysée solemnity, "you are the head of the Army, and of the Navy. Order, and I will obey."

The order had been given there and then, in May 1893, without anyone's bothering to put Monsieur Develle, the minister of foreign affairs, in the picture. With the connivance of President Carnot, Colonial Undersecretary Delcassé was playing a high-stakes game with cards that could be concealed only for a short time. For public and foreign consumption, he had told the Chamber of Deputies on February 4, 1893, that France's "colonial domain acquired during the past years will be sufficient to hold all our attention for quite some time." His powerful colonialist allies heard just the opposite from him: all that could be done to place French soldiers in the Nile watershed must be done.

Technical supplies for Monteil's mission were shipped to the French Congo during the second week of September 1893. Supplies, leadership, momentum—nothing was lacking to give France the unbeatable lead in the race to the Bahr al-Ghazāl, except collective will. The problems began in December. The new premier, timid Jean Casimir-Périer, who also served as his own foreign affairs minister, removed Delcassé and gave the Monteil mission luke-warm support. When enthusiastic President Carnot was assas-sinated by an Italian anarchist in June of the next year, Casimir-Périer was elected by the National Assembly to succeed him. Lead time was evaporating.

Monteil himself had become mired in delays and diversions. So strong was Léopold's reputation for bottomless intrigue that sophis-ticated observers, then and much later, believed that the king's men and money had kept Monteil away from the Congo until late 1894. This was partially true. Léopold had preempted one of France's most effective propagandists for empire, Harry Alis (Hip-polyte Percher). Money from Laeken Palace was reaching the jour-nalist's deep pockets, encouraging him to call for French conces-sions to the Congo Free State, extending its borders, before France sent off an expedition to the Nile. Far from feeling guilty about taking Léopold's money, the Frenchman believed in what he did, defensively boasting that he was "the most important and at the same time independent man in the world. . . . I don't know a man with greater moral force than mine." Alis followed his Brussels instructions faithfully, influencing newspapermen and lobbying politicians.

But while there were almost certainly deputies in the Chamber who pocketed money from Laeken Palace passed along by Alis, it is unlikely that Monteil was knowingly manipulated. He was one of the leaders of a band of highly political and fervently imperialist army officers for whom the march across the Congo was becoming almost a sacred undertaking. He began to think of himself not only as an accomplished explorer and soldier but as something of a diplo-mat and policy-maker. His was an ego made for exploitation by Léopold, and it may have been the case that certain politicians and members of the Comité de l'Afrique Française encouraged Mon-teil's increasing finickiness about leaving for Loango, the coastal town at the head of the French Congo caravan trail. In June the Chamber voted five hundred thousand francs for 1893, but by early the next year Monteil said he needed four hundred thousand francs more (*"Vous êtes insatiable,"* a senior foreign affairs officer wrote him). Then he wanted a telegraph line run from Loango to Stanley Pool. After that it was more men and more artillery. Yet it was clearly not a desire to serve Belgian interests that motivated Mon-teil, but his belief that, to serve France responsibly, either his expe-dition had to be powerful enough to sweep the Force Publique aside or the Quai d'Orsay had to negotiate a path for his expedition. Even Delcassé had been jolted into agreeing to delay by the news of Liotard's humiliation at Bangassou. Increased appropriations were going to be necessary, Delcassé decided; but this would not happen until the following June.

Then, suddenly, Delcassé was gone from office—temporarily. The new ministry, headed by the timid Casimir-Périer, much preferred diplomatic solutions. It fretted about making more enemies than France could handle, preferring to threaten an expedition rather than send one. In the final account, it was not so much Léopold's machinations as French indecision and British distemper that delayed Monteil. From December through early March 1894, Monteil and a senior official of the Quai d'Orsay found themselves shuttling to Berlin to negotiate a successful settlement of border problems between France and Germany in the Cameroons.

Meanwhile, negotiations with the Belgians had reached an impasse. Léopold wanted to trade the Mbomu claims for rights to the very Nile-watershed property that was indispensable to France's Congo-Nile stratagem against Britain. By now, the British had begun to take the mission seriously. Frederick Lugard, conqueror of Uganda for Britain, dashed to Paris in February 1894 to confer with "fellow explorer" Monteil. If the French followed through with their plans, Lugard reported, they would be capable of settling a large expedition down along the Nile.

French Foreign Affairs Minister Gabriel Hanotaux was still far from enthusiastic about Monteil's mission, but he had come to the Quai d'Orsay at the same time Delcassé returned to manage colonial affairs. Now a full minister himself, Delcassé took advantage of widespread French consternation over Léopold's unexpected May 12, 1894, compact with the British to keep the Monteil mission alive. What Britain and the Congo Free State had agreed to was an exchange of African properties expanding the huge concessions of the half-disavowed Mackinnon Treaty of 1890. Seeing that the French, despite Harry Alis's smooth efforts, were likely to send Monteil off without meeting the demands for an extension of the Congo Free State's borders, the Belgian king had offered himself to the British as a barrier across Monteil's path. This was effrontery that not even Hanotaux could refrain from sharply denouncing— effrontery shortly compounded by a rumor in Europe (and reinforcements on the Mbomu seemed to confirm it) that Léopold's secret instructions to his governor general were to "arrange things so that, without attacking him, [Monteil] will be made as ill at ease as possible, and so that the natives make his march difficult, cutting his communications with the rest of the world."

The language of the Anglo-Congo treaty was dense and unfathomable without careful examination and a detailed map, but its meaning for the French and Germans was, once again, enragingly clear. It gave Léopold a lifetime lease on the west bank of the Nile from Lake Albert north to Fashoda and west to the thirtieth longitude. In other words, Belgium, or rather Léopold, had been given the southern Sudan almost to the Ethiopian border—a gigantic rectangle of swamp and savannah spreading above the eastern Congo. In return for their leasing spree the British were pleased to accept from the Congo Free State the return of a sixteen-mile-wide strip running south from Lake Albert to the northern tip of Lake Tanganyika—the old Cape-to-Cairo easement. To the diplomats of the German foreign ministry it was more than curious to find again a train and telegraph route carved through regions within the ambit of German East Africa. In France, Hanotaux magisterially denounced the treaty as "zero with zero ramifications." If once there had been good reasons for delaying the Monteil mission, few French politicians now believed that the nation would be served by more palaver and temporizing.

It might have been worse for the French. Bad as the Anglo-Congo treaty was, had Léopold held a claim to Uganda his resourceful maleficence would have been greatly multiplied. In 1878, Stanley's account of Buganda had sent a battalion of British and French missionaries (the Church Missionary Society and the Pères Blancs) into the country, and by the early 1880s Mutesa had found his spiritual and political authority reduced by competition for the souls of his nobility. His refusal to circumcise himself had displeased his Muslims, and Mutesa did not understand why his statesmanlike offer to be baptized a Catholic and attend Protestant services had been icily declined. Mwanga, his young, pederastic, bhang-smoking heir, had not been able to prevent the kingdom from exploding after 1886 into a draining civil war between *Ba Ingleza, Ba Franza,* and Swahili.

By 1889, the Zanzibaris and their Muslim converts had triumphed, deposing Mwanga and two of his successors, sending Catholic and Protestant missionaries fleeing into Tanganyika. Not until 1890 did Ganda exhaustion and British maneuvering of Mwanga back to the throne bring a fragile truce. In the early 1890s,

Uganda nearly bankrupted the steamship magnate William Mackinnon's IBEA, and during much of 1891 there was a fair prospect
that the work in Uganda (including the railroad) might be forfeited.
But IBEA's buccaneering man-on-the-scene, Captain Frederick
Lugard, ignoring and exceeding instructions, rushed across Uganda
to round up several thousand of Emin Pasha's soldiers at Kavalli in
order to intimidate the already badly divided Bugandans. Lugard
won primacy for the Protestants with his rifles and forced an 1892
treaty down Mwanga's throat. The kabaka signed "with bad grace,
just dashing the pen at the paper," but the captain expedited the
smudged surrender to the Foreign Office.

After three years of rotating religious persecution, the kingdom
of Buganda was limp and faltering. In his germ-free rooms at
Laeken, Léopold contemplated the Ugandan chaos from which he
might soon greatly profit. His flair for confusion sent him to London
during the uncertain spring of 1893 with an offer to administer the
country for Britain—a proposal Queen Victoria rather liked but
which Gladstone put aside as troublingly odd. The Belgian king's
bad luck was that the East African country was fast becoming the
measure of the rising imperial tide in Britain. Queen Victoria's
"violent, mischievous and dangerous" Gladstone, aged and badly
shaken from a second rejection of Irish Home Rule, had lost his grip
over the Liberal party. Annexationists in the party were making
common cause with Salisbury's Tories while the jingo press began
to stir up public opinion. Alarming news came from abroad that the
conniving Pères Blancs had invited the explorer Karl Peters to
Buganda to sign a treaty recognizing the Germans as overlords of
the kingdom. Primed by masterful East Africa hands like Lugard
and John Russell Kirk of Zanzibar, the archimperialist Joseph
Chamberlain and others shattered Liberal resistance in the Commons in April 1893. Buganda, Bunyoro, Kitara, and Ankole were
consolidated into the British protectorate of Uganda in June of the
following year. What might have been Léopold's equivalent of the
Louisiana Purchase was removed from the imperial raffle table.

Gabriel Hanotaux believed that confrontation and crisis came
with failure of diplomacy. An honor graduate of the demanding
École des Chartes, France's elite school for historians, the elegant
foreign affairs minister understood foreign policy in the grand manner of Talleyrand. He regarded expeditions up the Ubangi as provocations of African problems, rather than—as his rival Delcassé ar-

gued—creative solutions. But there had been an abundance of provocation and a prodigal waste of time over the African problem. Widespread rumors claimed that France had warned Léopold to drop the Anglo-Congo treaty or risk losing his throne. Léopold's own ministers protested his recklessness, while Belgian newspapers like *La Réforme* reminded His Majesty that "Belgium attaches a larger price to the friendship of France than to the exploitation by its king of ivory and rubber from the banks of the Ubangi or from the Bahr al-Ghazāl." The French, everyone sensed, were finally deadly serious. Hanotaux had no intention of allowing the Belgian sovereign to block his stepladder negotiations toward a comprehensive arrangement with Britain.

Another factor in French policy had been the behavior in late June of the impetuous British ambassador Lord Dufferin. Having seen newspaper reports of a mission designed "to confront us with a 'fait accompli' by the occupation by the French of a commanding position in the neighbourhood of or within the territory" of the White Nile, Dufferin appeared at the Quai d'Orsay and haughtily insisted on knowing what Monteil was up to. Evasively, Hanotaux replied that Monteil had not yet sailed, that it would take months for him to reach the Congo basin, that there would be ample time for their two governments to resolve differences. Dufferin interrupted "that it was better I should at once inform him that . . . it would simply mean war between the two countries; and that it would be a terrible thing if we were to revive in Africa the miserable combats which had deluged India with French and British blood in the middle of the last century." Dufferin's remarks upset Prime Minister Lord Rosebery almost as much as they did Hanotaux, but the French did not know this at the time. Hanotaux and Delcassé agreed to scale down Monteil's instructions, but there could be no question now of not sending him to Central Africa. Monteil's new orders, dated July 13, confined the expedition to the Upper Ubangi. Not a single man was to be placed on the White Nile —or so the orders read.

Monteil's second-in-command, Captain Decazes, had already departed in early June; Monteil himself finally left on July 16, 1894. Then, on August 14, the Congo Free State (succumbing to French pressure) veered about completely and signed a treaty with France contradicting its agreement with Britain. The new lines were drawn between the fork of the Ubangi-Mbomu and Greenwich longitudes, and when the final terms were read Léopold had surrendered his outposts at Tambura, Zemio, Rafai, and Bangassou (where Liotard had been humiliated the year before), and been pushed firmly back across the Mbomu. But he gained more than he lost, because the French had originally wanted to roll the Free State's borders back to the Uele. And Léopold just managed to hang on to the crucial outpost on the Upper Nile. He was left with a lifetime occupation of the so-called "Lado Enclave," an area bordered on the east by the White Nile and cut off sharply to the north by the fourth parallel. The one card that Hanotaux declined to play that could have insured continued Belgian good behavior was, for reasons of prudence in triumph, withheld. Arriving at Loango on August 22, 1894, Monteil learned of orders to reembark immediately for the Kong region of the Ivory Coast. The telegram, sent on the day the Congo Free State agreement was signed, instructed Monteil to leave a small detachment behind and to sail for Grand Bassam to pursue Samori Turé, the Mandinka empire builder: "The government determines that your mission has lost much of its significance." The lieutenant colonel sailed for his new assignment on September 3.

Although Hanotaux privately suggested that he would have kept the mission alive for a while—at least until the British made up their minds about negotiating—he could not have been much displeased that Delcassé had been convinced to cancel Monteil's orders. With the Congo Free State seemingly on a leash, the French foreign minister considered a comprehensive settlement with Britain almost within his grasp. Firmness with Léopold had worked superbly and put London on notice of the new French resolve. Even though the way was paved for France's dash to the Nile, Hanotaux still feared that a provocative march across Central Africa to the Nile watershed could jeopardize his subtle diplomacy. Finally, Monteil's well-equipped force appeared to offer a final solution to the large menace to French designs in the region of Samori Turé. That its redeployment was a decision fated to cost France irrecoverable lead time in the Nile race would become obvious only four years later.

From late 1894 until late the following year, the French were alternately tantalized and dismayed by British declarations about the Upper Nile. The tentative Liberal cabinet which in March had succeeded that of the repudiated Gladstone announced that, whereas Britain had once claimed every mile from Alexandria to the Ethiopian frontier, Victoria's Egyptian empire now stopped at

Khartoum (still occupied by the Mahdists), and that the region below Khartoum to Fashoda held no interest. But what appeared to be accommodating diplomacy was in reality confusion and hesitation. For a few months, the British considered it simplest to give France the Bahr al-Ghazāl, in return for Egypt and the right to withdraw funds from the Egyptian Caisse de la Dette to build a dam at Aswan. Hanotaux believed his patience was about to be rewarded, the cancellation of the Monteil mission recompensed. But then in March 1895 Sir Edward Grey, imperialist undersecretary for foreign affairs, suddenly informed Parliament that the old claim still stood: all of East Africa from Cairo to the Cape, minus (for the moment) Ethiopia. Any advance into the territory in question, he added darkly, would be considered "an unfriendly act." Just as unexpectedly, however, Lord Rosebery's Liberals were out of office in July 1895, and Lord Salisbury's Conservatives masters of Parliament. For the moment, Salisbury appeared receptive to discussing a settlement in Egypt.

These stop-and-go Anglo-French relations delighted Léopold. The French-Congo Free State treaty he had been forced to sign had dealt his plans a major blow, but this was likely to be only temporary. Even as he had yielded to gloved French threats, Victoria's cousin was consoled by the thought that African treaties tended to rewrite themselves around the realities of actual territorial occupation. The British, after all, juggled allies in Africa like so many coconuts. France, the king shrewdly concluded, needed him much more than Britain did. Just seven days before Léopold's now-aborted 1894 agreement with them, the British had signed a treaty with the Italians. The exact terms of the "Secret Declaration" in the Anglo-Italian treaty were not all that secret. Léopold had heard enough to guess that the British were holding the Italians in reserve, either to replace or compete with the Belgians. The Italians were already being urged deeper into Ethiopia to counter growing French influence in Addis Ababa. While the French were forcing him out of his territory-grabbing arrangement with the British, Léopold realized in alarm that the British might be on the verge of a top-to-bottom African sweepstakes on the right side of the continent.

Having outraged the French, the king knew how to turn that outrage to good advantage. Secretly reversing himself at the end of 1894, he pushed his front men to fire up a French invasion of the Upper Nile. The king's confidants unofficially let the French know

that a large force stood ready to assist them in the Congo. Harry
Alis, meanwhile, mobilized the Prince d'Arenberg and other distinguished members of the Comité de l'Afrique Française. But Alis
went about his commission just a bit too pushily, and was killed in
March 1895 defending his honor against a charge of Belgian bribery
—although not before pumping up the pressure on politicians and
journalists to send off a new Congo-Nile expedition. The loss of
Harry Alis and compromising publicity must have annoyed Léopold, but the monarch had already cultivated a far more powerful
replacement: Félix Faure, a native Parisian who had fought his way
to the head of a shipping cartel at Le Havre, and who had become
a Léopold intimate. Faure, a leading politician, had his eye on the
presidency.

"Le beau Félix" or *"le Président soleil,"* as Faure soon became
popularly known, was vain, handsome, and polished—"so *grand
seigneur* and not at all *parvenu,"* Queen Victoria declared after a
chance encounter on the Riviera. But Faure had not deceived Léopold. Opportunist and priapic (Faure was to die of cardiac arrest in
the Elysée Palace in the arms of his hysterical mistress), the future
president was ideal for exploitation during lustful bachelor week-
ends at the king's rambling chalet at Ostende. Shortly after Faure's
January 1896 inauguration, rumors abounded about Belgian assistance to a French expedition upriver from Léopoldville. There was
more: Léopold urged the French to plan a pincer movement from
Ethiopia into the Bahr al-Ghazāl, synchronized to connect with the
expeditions coming from the west coast. The Franco-American ex-
plorer-adventurer Charles Chaillé-Long had earlier argued that the
quickest, surest route to the Nile was from Ethiopia. Menilek II, the
Ethiopian emperor, badly needed French help to fend off the Italians. While Hanotaux hesitated, Léopold urged a triple alliance
among France, Belgium, and Ethiopia.

French planning for a new Congo-Nile mission was already almost completed by November 1895. The elaborate screen thrown
up in Paris to camouflage what was soon known as the Marchand
Mission—all the claims as to its scientific and nonmilitary character
—fooled nobody in London. The French, if they could arrive in
time and in sufficient strength, clearly intended to throw themselves across the Cape-to-Cairo axis. The moment was right for
Léopold's next card. Arriving in London that December in what
appeared to Lord Salisbury and others to be almost a state of neuro-
sis, he warned of a fateful confrontation between England and

France that could be avoided only if England set a date for leaving Egypt and if Egypt surrendered the lands below Khartoum "to some person who was abreast of African affairs." Lord Salisbury quite failed to grasp the unique opportunity being proposed.

In mid-January 1896, Léopold again hurried from Brussels across the Channel. In return for a settlement of the Egyptian question, the king theatrically announced to Salisbury that he would take over the Sudan, destroy the power of the Mahdists, and, as a selfless extra measure, send them to fight for the British in Armenia. "It really seems as if he had taken leave of his senses," a startled Victoria confided. But Léopold believed he was the sanest player in the African stakes. England refused to evacuate Egypt; France refused to accept its loss. "We internationalized the Suez Canal. . . . Why do we not seek for Egypt—a land of so many international characteristics . . .—a formula that, without destroying every British accomplishment, modifies its excessively exclusive and menacing character?" Léopold asked in an anonymous article in *La Belgique Coloniale*. Why not, in a word, permit neutral Belgium to serve as a buffer between the two powers whose mutual enmity the Belgian sovereign was doing his utmost to aggravate?

CHAPTER THREE

The Beginnings of Resistance

Léopold wanted not only the wealth of the Congo's million square miles; more than anything he wanted to fulfill the old urge to plant Belgian troops on the Nile. At the beginning of 1896, despite the controversy over the treaties, his plans were well under way. If the British believed they had used him, and the French thought they had punished him, Léopold knew better: he knew that he had been the manipulator rather than the manipulated. But it was not so much the Europeans' competitors who now blocked his conquest of the Congo and penetration of the Nile watershed, but the Africans—especially the Swahili of the northeast, businessmen every whit as brutal and greedy as Léopold and fully determined to repulse Belgian interference with the flow of slaves and treasure eastward out of the Congo.

Eleven years after the Berlin Conference had set ground rules for plunder and outlined European spheres of influence, the king of the Belgians had still not taken full possession of the real estate assigned to him. He was now determined to end this embarrassment as quickly as possible. But if colonial domination was to become nowhere more intense, better financed, and more sustained than in the Congo Free State prior to the early 1890s, African resistance was to prove correspondingly fierce and chronic. It continually surprised and even humiliated the Belgians. The Congo was not generally known for the unity of its peoples. The realm's vast size and rain forests impeded contact and cooperation among the technologically backward, a circumstance enormously advantageous to intruders. But Belgian brutality and economic policy often nullified this advantage by forging unity where little had existed before. Moreover, all was not friction and fragmentation among the Congolese; the Zande sultanates of the northeast and the Swahili centers of the southeast, for example, were organized and formidable. When Léopold decided to entrench his power and race on to the Nile in early 1896, Zande and Swahili rulers held the keys to Belgian success.

The Zande, like the Mangbetu, belonged not to the Bantu majority of the Congo, but to the Sudanic people of the north. Their martial power was awe-inspiring; Zande warriors attacked in the massed, ordered, fifty- to sixty-man formations of *abakumba* (married men) and *aparanga* (married youths) armed with elaborately wrought shields, heavy iron-tipped spears, and the gashing *kpinga*, or throwing knife. They disdained the bow and arrow as Mbuti weapons—fighting tools fit only for pygmies. The Franco-American ex-Confederate officer Charles Chaillé-Long marvelled that he had never seen "a more perfect ideal of the warrior." By the late 1880s, of course, the spears and shields had been supplemented, where not replaced entirely, by repeating rifles.

The Zande were really more a political federation than an ethnic whole, composed of some fifty peoples—Abarambo, Basiri, Mundu, Pambia, and so on—many of whom retained their original languages and cultures. The cannibalistic, teeth-filing Niam-Niam (so called because of their *"niam-niam"* battle cry, meaning, "flesh, flesh!") were commonly taken by Arabs and Europeans during the nineteenth century for typical Zande—which they probably were not. Zande, which sprawled tens of thousands of square miles from the Mbomu River in the northeast Congo southward into the lower Sudan, was cemented by the Avungara—the Zande hereditary ruling elite—and the Zande language. Marauding down from the north in the early eighteenth century, the warlike Ambomu people subjugated others, disciplined them, and led them onward, Roman-style, to the next combat, fastening all of them in the grip of Avungara rule.

Fractious and rebellious, the major and minor Zande power centers resisted the centralizing ambitions of whatever great chief periodically appeared. A heightened degree of unity or, rather, enforced federation came only after the ascendancy of the capable, merciless Gbudwe, who ruled from 1867 to 1905. Short, stocky, ceaselessly organizing from Yambio, his capital near the Congo frontier, Gbudwe was already legendary by the mid-1870s. "His eyes sparkled like stars," an awestruck Zande nobleman recalled many years later. "When he looked at a man in anger they were terrible." From Gbudwe's imposing inner court—the *barondo,* or "court of whispers"—the Zande autocrat and his Avungara extended dominion over an amalgam of people in much the same way as the Germans managed the Austro-Hungarian Empire. Like the Habsburg empire as well, Gbudwe's Zande had begun, by about 1870, to feel the first tremors of dislocation from Arab incursions into the Sudan and the eastern Congo. Thus far, troubles in the southern regions had been more premonitory than calamitous— occasional slave raids, murderous sweeps for ivory, and the killing and replacement of a few Avungara governors with Swahili henchmen. Zande and Swahili maintained coexistence. But the eruption of the Sudanese Mahdists into their world frightened the Zande even more than did the Egyptians, who had defeated and temporarily imprisoned King Gbudwe in the early 1880s. So it was that the coming of the first Belgians at about this time evoked mixed reactions: they could be used against the Mahdists, but they were also a threat to Zande independence.

Léopold had begun sending probing expeditions into the northern Congo in the mid-1880s, intended to woo as many chiefs and sultans into Congo Free State service as possible. A large Belgian-officered force under Lieutenant Alphonse Vangèle had assembled in early 1886. More expeditions were mounted over the next half decade, and Belgian authority slowly, tenuously spread east and north from the mouth of the Congo to embrace the Mbomu and Ubangi river basin. Belgian officers repeatedly expressed the same astonishment that had overcome Stanley in Buganda and on the great river. The melding of Arabia and Africa, its relative efficiency and complexity, continually confounded European stereotypes. Charles de la Kethulle de Ryhove, a conquering lieutenant in Léopold's Force Publique, came close to abandoning regulation reserve when Sultan Rafai's Zande troops greeted him near the Sudanese frontier:

> The small army of the sultan presented arms. These fine black soldiers really looked snappy. Their uniforms were of a startling whiteness and the barrels of their rifles glistened under the shafts of great and clear sunlight. The soldiers fired salvos while the drums were beaten and the martial fanfare of the trumpets resounded through the air. After having encountered so many naked people with heads dressed with plumes, bodies covered with tattoos and rigged out with bizarre or grotesque accoutrements, I was able to see people clothed, armed, disciplined, and maneuvering with military correctness in the sunshine—and in the very heart of Africa.

The Belgians came to realize that, to retain the loyalty of the Zande sultans of Rafai, Bangassou, Djabbir, Zemio, Tambura, and others centered in the northeastern Congo, they would need to exercise an unexpected circumspection and delicacy.

While Force Publique expeditions courted the sultans of the north along the Mbomu, Léopold had been striving for more than six years to extend his rule over the Swahili Africans along the reaches of the eastern Congo—thus far with little success. His secret decree of 1885, claiming all "vacant lands" in the Congo, had been answered by a Swahili attack on the Stanley Falls fort the following year. Free State authority had been rolled back hundreds of miles. It was only then that the Belgians became aware that a powerful Swahili trading corporation, the HM Company (for Hamed bin Muhammad bin Juna al-Marjebi, alias Tippu Tip) had been organized two years earlier, with the backing of the sultan of Zanzibar. In addition to having as a full partner the chieftain of one of the region's most powerful Islamic brotherhoods, among the HM Company's other directors was the immensely resourceful Muhammad bin-Halfan—"Rumaliza"—who controlled the trade routes around northern Lake Tanganyika. There were no further Force Publique expeditions southeast of Stanley Falls into HM Company territory until the early 1890s.

When Léopold was finally ready to strike south again, he aimed first at Tippu Tip's expanding neighbors, the Yeke people of the Katanga—Tippu Tip's cultural cousins and commercial allies. Léopold's answer to the HM Company was the creation in early 1891 of the Syndicat Commercial du Katanga, the engine of much of the king's stupendous future wealth. In April, Syndicat administrator Paul Le Marinel, two Force Publique officers, and three hundred Tetela soldiers had marched into bustling Bunkeya, capital of the Katanga empire and an entrepôt for African commerce. They demanded that the ruler, Msiri, swear allegiance to Léopold and hoist the Free State flag from his palace. "I am master here," Msiri ("the mosquito") replied with dignity, before unceremoniously dismissing the Belgians, "and so long as I live the kingdom of Garenganze shall have no other." Rich in ivory, copper, salt, iron, and slaves, Msiri's realm covered an area larger than Great Britain, from the Zambia border north to the Luvua River and from Lake Mweru west to the Lualaba. In September, another secret decree of Léopold's ordered the collection of all ivory and rubber in the Aruwimi region. The Syndicat's director and three European agents were killed almost immediately by HM Company men when they began buying ivory south of Stanley Falls.

Léopold and his Antwerp banking partners wanted Garenganze quickly, before the British or Germans woke up to its potential. Force Publique officers struck again. A large delegation tramped into Bunkeya in late 1891. One of them, an English officer named Bodson, surprised Msiri in his tent and shot him dead before the ruler's bodyguard could react. Katanga was added to Léopold's private African domain.

Tippu Tip had carefully weighed the devastating power of Europe against the men and muskets of Africa and begun to doubt the future of the Swahili merchant empire. He was not alone. Sultan Barghash of Zanzibar, the overweight, lethargic grandson of Seyyid Sa'id of Oman, also seemed ready to concede the inevitable. Barghash had deputized Tippu Tip in 1882 to handle the trade from the Tanzanian coast into the Manyema (the land between the Lualaba and Lake Tanganyika), becoming a silent partner in the HM Company the following year. But the British "protectors" of Zanzibar had decided to give most of the sultan's mainland properties to the Germans. "I no longer have any hope of keeping the Interior," Barghash wrote Tippu Tip four years later. "The Europeans . . . are after my possessions. . . . Happy are those who died before now, and know nothing of this." Tippu Tip returned to the Manyema, staying on until 1890; then he left the Interior permanently for Zanzibar. His son Sefu, as sharp and as venal, took his place.

Despite his well-informed misgivings about Zanzibar, Tippu Tip must have decided that the stakes in the African lottery were high enough to justify a final, supreme effort. What was happening on the other side of Africa, deep in Mali and Guinée in the western Sudan, cannot have gone unnoticed. There, Samori Turé, Muslim leader of many of the people in the French sphere, had so badly mauled the armies sent after him in the early 1880s that Paris had very nearly followed in the western Sudan the British policy of withdrawal in the eastern Sudan. The Europeans were still weak in Central Africa, their supply lines fragile, and the peoples they ruled perhaps restive enough to fight even alongside slavers to halt them.

What was clear to Tippu Tip was that if the Belgians succeeded in planting themselves along the northernmost arc of the Congo River, in banning the slave trade, and in enforcing their confiscatory export tax, then every year would see more ivory, palm oil, rubber, and wood leave the Interior down the river to the Atlantic coast. When construction of the railroad from Boma-Matadi to Stanley Pool got under way (in 1890), the Swahili knew that it could be only a short time before they were commercially finished. But they were not finished yet, and Léopold had to some extent played into their hands with his ruse of Henry Stanley's 1887 Emin Pasha Relief Expedition. Eleven years after their 1876 encounter near Vinya Nyaza, slaver and explorer met again on Zanzibar. Tippu Tip now lived in an impressive stone mansion, and owned island properties and plantations and vast domains in the Manyema. Stanley had come to strike a deal for Léopold and William Mackinnon in order to reach Emin Pasha through Tippu Tip's realm. In Léopold's name, therefore, Stanley offered the Swahili tycoon the title of Governor of Stanley Falls (of which he was already in possession) and a modest annuity of thirty pounds a month. The transaction must have amused Tippu Tip, for the balance of Congo power was still such that Léopold, sovereign of a European nation and cousin to Queen Victoria, was compelled to beg an African trader to accept a title and retainer. Tippu Tip accepted. Then he plotted.

First had come the destruction on the Aruwimi River of Stanley's rear guard, nearly 160 officers and men who died of disease, starvation, and assaults waiting vainly for Tippu Tip's provisions and porters. When the old Zanzibari belatedly put in an appearance near Yambua, the overwrought British commander, Major Edmund Barttelot, was treated to his best amnesiac performance—he remembered almost none of the terms supposedly agreed to with Stanley. Africans along Barttelot's route vanished or refused to sell food. The promised Swahili soldiers and porters showed up in greatly diminished numbers, wholly undisciplined, and demanding almost the caravan's last pound sterling. Barttelot was murdered by a porter on July 19, 1887, and much of what was left of the rear guard wiped out in the ensuing pandemonium. Léopold's scheme to link up with Emin Pasha and maintain a line of communication from Boma-Matadi in the west to Lake Albert in the east had been effectively sabotaged. The Swahili concluded that they had little to lose by taking on their adversaries before the imbalance of forces became too great. Their grand strategy was to capture Stanley Falls station—anchor of Belgian power in the eastern Congo—by surprise, and then to skim down the Congo River, levelling every post to the Atlantic. Simultaneously, Swahili armies were to push north-west across Katanga Province in massive force to capture Léopold-ville, capital of Léopold's Congo Free State. Bakongo and Basundi people in the French territories were even then beginning to harass white traders. A Swahili breakthrough to the Atlantic was likely to spark uprisings that would ignite much of the west coast. Should that happen, the European Scramble for Africa could be-come a costly, bloody, long-term war of attrition on both sides—so prolonged and costly, perhaps, that industrialists, left-wing par-liamentarians, metropolitan military establishments, and public opinion would finally decide that dominion over jungles and sand in a barbarous continent was a nuisance rather than a mission. After all, an important body of opinion around perennial Prime Minister William Gladstone still sought an honorable British exit from Egypt. The French, for their part, seemed especially prone to imperial hand-wringing. Men and money for far-flung military sideshows were never popular, the desire to win back Alsace-Lorraine from the Germans currently being the only unifying dogma of a divided nation. When the black-pajamaed Chinese routed a well-equipped French army above Lang-Son in early 1885, cries for withdrawal from Indochina and the unceremonious overthrow of one of the Third Republic's most effective cabinets ensued. As for Belgium, except for a handful of Antwerp bankers and a few responsible politicians, almost no one cared about Léopold's Congo fiefdom.

Just how much the domestic politics of Europe weighed, if at all, in Swahili calculations is unknown. The British consul on Zanzibar, John Russell Kirk, was certain of a well-planned conspiracy stretch-ing all the way to Oman. In Sefu's imposing capital at Kasongo, ten thousand warriors were readied for the attack in late 1892. Man for man, the Swahili high command was probably superior to most of the Force Publique senior officers. Rashid, Tippu Tip's nephew; Mohara at Nyangwe, who had pushed for an early all-out war; and Muhammad bin Sa'id, at Kabambare, terrifyingly known as "Bwana Nzige" ("Master Locust"), were highly capable organizers. Then there was Rumaliza at Ujiji, by now almost as much a legend for his political and commercial wisdom as his old partner Tippu Tip. The great numbers under their command made them cautiously confi-dent, for, even with machine guns and artillery pieces, 120 white officers and 3,500 black troops (the total strength of the Force Publique) were not considered adequate to withstand a coor-dinated surprise attack by tens of thousands.

Had Sefu managed to keep the loyalty of Ngongo Leteta, his father's charismatic deputy, the Force Publique would almost certainly have been rapidly rolled back. The Belgians, who were notorious for not recognizing African qualities, appreciated Ngongo Leteta, and Major François Dhanis, commanding the Force Publique, sent the slaver a string of messages urging him to switch allegiance. Tippu Tip's former slave had lost two stinging skirmishes with the Belgians in March and April. Meditating upon his fortunes, cagily weighing the growing power of the whites, and much dispirited by Sefu's repeated failure to pay him for consignments of ivory, Ngongo Leteta accepted the Belgians' invitation to collaborate, bringing with him nearly ten thousand Tetela riflemen. Sefu demanded that the Belgians surrender Leteta, which of course they refused.

The battle began on about October 22, 1892, at a place called Riba Ribba down the Lualaba. Major Dhanis was able to mount an in-depth defense at Stanley Falls with the help of Ngongo Leteta's men. The two sides bombarded each other much of the length of the Lualaba, each furiously trying to break through the other's defense. The Swahili succeeded in crossing in force in late November, reaching the Lomami River west of Stanley Falls and Stanleyville (today's Kisangani). "It was here," laments a Belgian historian, "that the cannibal tendencies of our allies showed themselves to our eyes for the first time." The English officer Sidney Langford Hinde saw one of Dhanis's Africans shoot an enemy who turned out to be the African's relative. The soldier complained that he could not eat his own kin, and the commander ordered him to bury the corpse. Later it was discovered that the African "had given it to his friends to eat." Another of Dhanis's officers, Michaux, offered an explanation for Belgian noninterference in these practices: "Trying to punish or prevent them from feasting on the remains of their enemies would have been madness—they would have turned on us." The stench of gunpowder and, for the Europeans, a sickening smell of cooked human flesh rose over the eastern Congo.

Events turned in favor of the Force Publique the following summer. Reinforcements arrived from Belgium, including the crucial Krupp 75-mm artillery pieces. Still, Swahili forces at Nyangwe entrenched themselves along the Lualaba and fought tenaciously. To outflank the city, Dhanis needed the Wagenia's fleet of dugouts, but the Wagenia refused him, as they had Stanley seventeen years earlier, changing their minds only after seeing the Belgian arsenal.

They handed over a hundred canoes. Nyangwe was besieged in late August and reduced from a town of thirty thousand to a "fortified camp." Kasongo, Sefu's capital, fell to a two-pronged surprise attack, almost the entire population plunging into the safety of the forest. Lieutenant Hinde was delighted with his temporary accommodations—"even the common soldiers slept on a silk and satin mattress, in carved beds with silk mosquito curtains."

From occupied Kasongo, the Force Publique charged on to Kabambare. Sefu's eroded forces there had been stiffened by fresh troops brought across Lake Tanganyika from Ujiji. Hurriedly reassembling the Krupp 75 on the morning of October 13, Major Dhanis and his four Belgian officers threw their seven hundred heavily armed Hausa regulars and auxiliaries against Sefu's much larger force positioned on a rise above the Luama River. Dhanis's men were severely punished when the enemy counterattacked; Lieutenant Pierre Ponthier, one of the Force Publique's ablest officers, was killed. Victory would have gone to Tippu Tip's son had he not been fatally wounded. In January, Dhanis took Kabambare, and Rumaliza fled to Tanganyika.

But the great advantage of Sefu's death had already been counterbalanced by Ngongo Leteta's execution. Belgians in Africa demonstrated an astonishing capacity for creating enemies, a penchant for the lash and the corvée where benevolence would have worked political wonders. Ngongo Leteta had helped them turn back the Swahili onslaught, his Tetela had reconnoitered, fought, transported, and found food supplies along the scavenged battle route. As they were preparing to leave Nyangwe for the assault on Kasongo, Dhanis and his staff received a stupefying dispatch from a certain Captain Duchesne, the overbearing commander of the Lomami region. Accused of treason, Ngongo Leteta had been arrested, tried, convicted, and sentenced to death by firing squad. Hinde was ordered to take a dozen men and leave at once for Gundu to stop Duchesne. They arrived, after six days of forced marching, on September 17—two days too late. Ngongo Leteta had hanged himself with a rope plaited from his own clothing, but Captain Duchesne's vigilance saved the African from asphyxiation so that he could be duly shot at sunrise. "More than half our transport department was under [Leteta's] charge," said Hinde, "and with everything entrusted to his care he was so successful that we never lost a single load." Duchesne's idiocy was costly. Not only had the Force Publique lost an invaluable African ally, but the king of the Belgians, although he would never fully grasp the connection, had also lost the opportunity to conquer the Nile basin.

An hour after the firing squad disbanded, Kitumba Maya, one of Ngongo Leteta's most important subordinates, went over to the Swahili with six hundred new rifles. "His example," lamented Hinde, "was naturally followed by many others." The "many others" amounted to literally thousands of the Tetela, who had been the pick of the Belgian auxiliaries, and who now fell upon the Force Publique rear just as the Swahili in Manyema were being broken. Dhanis struck back savagely. Machine guns and Krupp cannons momentarily cowed the Tetela, and hundreds were dispersed throughout the Congo. By the end of 1894, little more than a year after Sefu's death, Dhanis could report prematurely to Léopold that the Swahili War was over, the Congo Free State pacified, and the path to the Upper Nile open. The commander returned to Belgium. Léopold made him a baron.

The people of the Interior had known for almost two decades that the price of what passed for civilization was outrageously high, that the commerce and religion of the Arabs, as well as the practical science of the Europeans, led fatally to subjugation. "Foreigners have always deceived us," a Mangbetu chief protested:

> We have been the prey in succession to the Zandes, the Turks, and the Arabs. Are the whites worth more? No, beyond doubt. But whatever they be, our territory is today freed from the presence of any foreigners, and to introduce another would be an act of cowardice. I do not wish to be a slave to anyone, and I will fight the whites.

Gbudwe of the Zande, having warred against Egyptians and Mahdists, detested all *abalemu* (foreigners) equally, cautiously reviling them in private as *"wasiwasi wili auro, kpekpe li aboro"* ("dirty little cropped-heads and barbarians"). Resistance flared up almost everywhere in the late 1890s. Tactics varied from people to people, some seeking the means to resist in shifting and cynical alliances, others in valiant, solitary warfare. Mirambo, the legendary overlord of Unyamwezi, had reached for the drill manuals and rifles, then sealed his country off from Arab and European political influence. Between the Victoria Nyanza and Lake Tanganyika, Mirambo carved out a domain of great commercial leverage (it straddled the routes leading from the coast to the Interior) and considerable military strength. With his musket-bearing *ruga-ruga* (hired uniformed infantry), Mirambo's kingdom of Unyamwezi rivalled Tippu Tip's domain. His Nguni people had been pushed northward across the Limpopo early in the nineteenth century by the deadly Zulu sweep into South Africa. They now brought with them their Bantu language, ancient gods, and the warfare skills learned from the once-invincible Zulus. Islam made steady inroads among them, and they became increasingly commingled with the Swahili, but for a time after Mirambo's death in 1884, Arabs and Europeans had found it wise to treat the people of Unyamwezi as equals. Sound in theory, Mirambo's plan nevertheless came too late to give Unyamwezi a permanent place in the African sun. It was no match for the kaiser's regiments and the merciless cannonading of Krupps after 1890.

In the Interior, the indigenous peoples, without a plan but with considerable solidarity, exploded as a result of the Swahili War. Sefu was gone and the Tetela mutineers largely removed, but the Belgians found that "their" Congo remained saturated with foes. Unrest and war were everywhere, being most intense in the northern spear-shaped region between the Mbomu and the Uele, where Zande, Mangbetu, and various other peoples took up the struggle from the Swahili of the east. Oscar Michaux's usually flat Force Publique combat diary quickens to life at this point, portraying the early 1894 troubles as a delayed reaction to the murder of Ngongo Leteta, whose "great intelligence no one, not even his enemies, ever denied. . . . A cry of terror, of rage, of malediction, and of horror rose over this bloody land."

Migenda, ruler of a people along the Bili River and neighbor of the Zande, was one of the first rulers to strike out independently. Consulting his oracle in April 1894, he was told to attack a Force Publique detachment led by a captain and a lieutenant. He wiped the detachment out in an ambush, inaugurating two years of fierce Bili resistance. Wily King Gbudwe, more concerned about the imperialism of the nearby Mahdists, insisted that he was neutral, but other Zande nearer the Interior saw the Belgians as deadly intruders. While Migenda was flushing the whites and their allies from his region, Ndoruma, ruler of Zande just beyond the head of the Uele, destroyed a sixty-man force.

There was no end to the warfare. Month after bloody month, the Congolese ambushed or threw themselves upon Léopold's Force Publique. Rienzi, son of Zemio, turned against the Belgians in early

1894. Sultan Zemio had been one of the Mahdiyya's most resolute enemies. He had fought to protect the populations of East and Central Africa from the advancing *ansār*, and had even made a game attempt in 1883 to rescue Gordon's lieutenant, Frank Lupton, besieged in the Bahr al-Ghazāl. He had welcomed the Force Publique as a trustworthy foil against his enemies. Rienzi continued his father's policies until Belgian support of a rival sultan and Léopold's imperial ambitions became alarmingly obvious. Declaring himself independent of both the Congo Free State and the Mahdiyya, the young sultan warred with Dhanis's able deputy, Lieutenant Jules Milz, until April 1896, when Rienzi and his people were finally overwhelmed.

Bafuka's people were not as advanced materially as the prosperous, Muslim-oriented subjects of the Mbomu sultans. Bafuka's Zande controlled the area around Dungu, a remote settlement along the approach to Lake Albert—another direction the Belgians were taking to reach the Nile. Like Gbudwe, Bafuka mistrusted all intruders and probably communicated with the paramount Zande potentate before falling on Lieutenant Lucien Francqui's troops. Retreating from a disastrous encounter with Zande and Mahdist warriors in the extreme northeast of the Congo in 1895, Francqui pitched camp on the Dungu River near the settlement of Drambu. According to oral tradition:

> The Belgians came and resided in Bafuka's country for many days. Bafuka said that he had not the slightest intention of receiving them. He admonished his subjects about them that they should keep watch on the trail going in the direction of where the Belgians were; if they saw them approaching they should come and tell him, and he would assail them on their route.

Bafuka ambushed the Belgian lieutenant, killing and scattering his soldiers after a desperate firefight. "The subjects of Bafuka were killed like grass in number, and the Belgians were killed like grass also. They continued to fight till at dusk Bafuka's men put the Belgians to flight. The subjects of Bafuka took in booty a great number of Belgian breech-loaders." Bafuka's massacre of the whites "passed from North to South till all had heard of it."

The Swahili War in Central Africa was more than a Belgian nightmare. It also signalled to the British, French, Germans, and Italians that their own dreams of empire could be dashed by the volatile reactions of the continent. In 1896, the Italians suffered the greatest of all nineteenth-century European humiliations in Ethiopia. That same year and for much of the next, the Shona and Ndebele people of the Rhodesias erupted against British rule.

The apparent victory of the Force Publique was far from edifying. There had been eviscerations, dismemberings, feasts of human flesh, and massacres of innocents. Reports of cannibalism had even reached Europe, where pious British philanthropic societies were more shocked than Léopold's ministers believed was diplomatically proper. Belgian officials denied knowledge of most of these horrors and protested stern punishment of those that had been discovered. The Congo war was seen as a credit to the grim, thankless, and necessary work of plowing under the primitive lands of the globe in order to seed them with Christianity, culture, and commerce. "The triumph of the Arabs on the Upper Congo," rejoiced a chronicler of Léopold's reign, "would have meant the obliteration of civilization and the massacre of every white man from Stanley Falls to the cataracts [of the western Congo]." "It is impossible to even surmise what would have been the effect on the future of Africa had another great Mohammedan empire been established in the Congo Basin," a Force Publique officer shuddered.

The unpleasant prospect now facing Léopold was loss of the Nile. Sefus, Bafukas, and Rienzis had delayed the march of the Force Publique far too long, giving the French time to begin assembling another mission under the command of an experienced and tireless young marine captain named Jean-Baptiste Marchand. Unlike Monteil's earlier mission, this one was not likely to be turned from its goal at the last minute. Léopold himself had pulled strings to get the French off into Central Africa again. He counted on their trek toward the Nile to rouse the complacent British into listening to his own schemes for a Belgian role in the Sudan. But first, his officers had to get there.

CHAPTER FOUR

Soldiers and Statesmen

1

When Jean-Baptiste Marchand was a scholarship student at the Collège de Thoissey, he was something of a loner. On the playground he daydreamed about great adventurers and explorers, about Faidherbe and Burton, Chaillé-Long, Stanley, and de Brazza. Jean was a tightly wound, ambitious boy with piercing blue eyes set in a condorlike face. He was a competent, if not brilliant student. But Thoissey, the town where he had been born twelve years earlier, was a long way from any place that mattered in France. A diploma from its lycée would not have won an above-average bearer the privilege of university or professional school placement. Moreover, the Marchands were hardworking poor. Even with a scholarship, family finances forced Jean to find work after the first year of high school. At age thirteen, he apprenticed himself to Maître Blondel, the local notary. But he took his playground dreams with him.

Conscientious but increasingly bored with the notarial routine, Jean (like thousands of other French boys headed for undersalaried monotony in provincial dead ends) was drawn to the military escape hatch—especially to that fighting forge of colonial empire, the Marine Infantry. While his mother lived, though, soldiering was out of the question. Madame Marchand made her son swear he would stick to the safe, stable career of notary apprentice, which he did until her death sometime in early 1883. On October 1, he reported for duty at Toulon, entering the Fourth Regiment of Marine Infantry as a private. He was seven weeks and three days shy of twenty. Within seven years Marchand would win the Legion of Honor. Five years later, he would deal with cabinet ministers in matters of state.

His military career was of a rapidity and brilliance that few officers of the era matched. Some who did served under the precocious high school dropout from Thoissey.

European officers who made their careers in colonial service tended to be socially less established than their metropolitan counterparts. Many—whatever their class background—were either flaming misfits or stunning incompetents. French colonial forces, far more so than the British, were an especially scabrous, self-reliant lot. The inner-directed Gordons, Lugards, and T. E. Lawrences were British exceptions, whereas the French colonial officer corps encouraged the recruitment of personalities characterized by stubborn independence and overheated imaginations. As a rule French officers were more excited than their British peers about what they found in Africa or Asia, more prone to conceptualizing the meaning of their experiences, and more determined to improve what was there. The East African legionary Sir Gerald Portal unintentionally caricatured both officer types in his Old Etonian's description of his Zanzibar farewell from a British general:

> The graceful facility with which any son of the Latin race would be able to clothe his sentiments in fitting and picturesque words is denied to all but the favored few of our tongue-tied and awkward nation, and our parting was what such partings always are between two English friends in any part of the world and under any imaginable circumstances—a hearty grasp of the hand, perhaps rather more sustained than usual, and with an almost involuntary extra pressure at the end, and a simple, "Goodbye old fellow."

In some respects, Jean Marchand was not one of Portal's effusive Latins; he spoke with a slow, low-registered gravity. But he possessed the fertile imagination and a florid prose style. He had remarkable self-discipline, too, and, like Stanley, reserves of energy that seemed inexhaustible. From the day he reported for duty at Toulon, his superiors became aware of Marchand's promise. He was promoted to corporal on April 1, 1884; before the year ended he became a sergeant and secretary to the regimental colonel. The colonel endorsed his sergeant's application to Saint Maixent, the officer academy for the Marine Infantry, which he entered by examination in February 1886. He returned to his regiment as a second lieutenant in mid-March 1887. The following year, the playground dream came true. Second Lieutenant Marchand arrived on

January 20 in Senegal for duty at Fort Ndiago, north of the capital of Saint-Louis.

Marchand's greatest wish was "to serve only the Fatherland," which he saw as a sun-blasted, bugle-echoing, adrenaline-filled antithesis to unheroic Thoissey. He looked upon himself as the blond warrior, the fierce Gaul, doing the lonely, dangerous work of making the nonwhite world safe for French civilization. But Marchand was not an antirepublican. He was antisloth, anticorruption, and witheringly opposed to the reigning politics of disorder in Paris that caused the Third Republic to be derided by its own citizens as *la gueuse* ("the whore") and *la République des camarades* ("the buddy-system Republic").

But energy and the uncomplicated desire to build an empire, though indispensable, were not enough by themselves. A corps of like-minded centurions was needed, and a calculating leader who was both a masterful politician and an exemplary soldier. Lieutenant Colonel Louis Archinard, the thirty-eight-year-old *commandant supérieur* of the French Sudan (today's Mali), was such a leader. Perhaps more than any other Frenchman, the mysterious Archinard was chief organizer of France's empire below the Sahara. When the expansionist cabinet of Jules Ferry was rejected in spring 1885, the navy minister then in charge of sub-Saharan Africa asked Colonels Monteil and Archinard for an opinion before deciding whether or not to order a withdrawal. Withdrawal from the Sudan would lead to the loss of Senegal, Archinard reported in the strongest terms.

The record is unclear as to precisely when Marchand attracted Archinard's notice, but six months after being posted to Fort Ndiago the second lieutenant was serving under the then major in the French Sudan. It was the beginning of Archinard's African duty, and he was assembling the first of his special breed of officers. His confidence in the lieutenant from Thoissey was quickly and fully justified. Marchand's baptism of fire came with the attack in early 1889 on the heavily armed Tukulor stronghold at Koundian, in Mali. He threw himself into the fray with histrionic fervor, receiving a flesh wound to the head for his lack of caution. A fellow officer toppled, severely wounded; his African troops crouched beneath the withering fire from the town's earthen walls. Unless a "white charged forward," Marchand recalled, the battle was lost. Lighting a cigarette, shouting for his men to follow, he dodged bullets and spears until he reached a breach in the wall, whereupon, "following all the principles of gymnastics," Marchand leaped into the fort:

> I relit my cigarette and a corporal poured his gourd over my head to stop the blood running down my forehead. I no longer felt anything. But after an hour and a half, when things were settled, when the continuous barrage of rifle fire no longer sounded, and after I'd toured the fort and come back to the hole in the wall where I'd entered, I lost consciousness. I dropped my sabre. There was a brilliant bang and I dropped in a heap against the wall. Silly, but inevitable.

Archinard owed his victory at Koundian largely to his new lieutenant, whose theatrical account detailed the contest, which was the first of what would be many single-handed tours de force.

The leader of the Islamicized Tukulor, the literate and militarily accomplished Sultan Ahmadu, believed he had adroitly conciliated France with commercial and territorial agreements generous enough to buy time for his people. But when the impetuous Archinard replaced the more deliberate Colonel Jules Gallieni in 1888, the rapid demise of the vast Tukulor empire became the order of the day. Two years later, Archinard planned his biggest offensive, an attack upon the second of Tukulor Sultan Ahmadu's two major centers: Segu, ruled by Ahmadu's son, Madani. He had already dispatched Marchand down the Niger aboard a gunboat to reconnoiter the riverside town. Anchoring the *Mage* beyond rifle range, Marchand saw a large city enclosed by high, white walls of exceptional thickness, behind which were several equally well-protected stone forts. The lieutenant submitted a self-important but well-researched report to Archinard, stressing that Segu's capture would need heavy, prolonged artillery fire and predicting heavy losses because the Tukulors would use the debris from the bombardment as cover. "You know how much all of us—myself personally—would be delighted to be sent into battle when there is much danger in doing so," Marchand added, lest his assessment be suspected of erring on the side of excess caution. "I was sent on a mission. I have observed, and I say what I think." Segu fell in April 1890. Archinard was promoted to lieutenant colonel and governor of the French Sudan. Marchand became a first lieutenant and member of the Legion of Honor. When he and Archinard returned to France on leave that year, the new first lieutenant spent most of it helping to plan the attack on Nioro, Ahmadu's capital.

At about this time, a second gifted, aggressive junior officer became part of the Archinard circle. Second Lieutenant Charles-Emmanuel-Marie Mangin was assigned to duty in Senegal in early 1890. Two and a half years younger than Marchand, Mangin was socially superior to his future commander. Charles Mangin's grandfather had been a magistrate under the restored Bourbons. Marchand's brothers had struggled through high school and into undistinguished military service, with most of Marchand's salary going to pay their way; Mangin's three brothers were graduates of the right schools and distinguished officers, each dying a notable, decorated death in a faraway place. Marchand was Saint Maixent; Mangin was Saint Cyr, the most prestigious of the military academies. For all that—at least until the experience of Fashoda—the officers were amiably united by mutual respect.

Archinard's campaigns against the Tukulors of West Africa thundered by during 1890–91. The governor had tried to deceive Sultan Ahmadu in 1888 by offering a treaty respecting the territorial integrity of the Tukulor empire, a policy favored by some of the politicians and officials in Paris who concerned themselves with black Africa. Ahmadu had been interested, but Archinard was merely buying time while he intrigued with the sultan's allies. The commandant had also been extremely anxious about the military strength of the Tukulors' enemies, the Mandinka people, led by the brutal, brilliant Samori Turé. Archinard had done what Ahmadu, understandably, was too suspicious to do quickly enough when Samori Turé again approached him in late 1889. As Tukulor and Mandinka embassies began discussions about a military alliance against the French, Archinard had temporarily neutralized Samori Turé with a friendship treaty guaranteeing the territorial integrity of his empire. Oussébougou, Kaarta, Nioro, and Jenné were quickly reduced and taken, forcing Ahmadu to fall back to his great redoubt, Massina (KeMacina), in the early weeks of 1891. There was no place in the Frenchman's imperious conception of overseas rule (as there sometimes was among British proconsuls) for powerful, semiautonomous native kingdoms—whatever the confused wishes of the Quai d'Orsay.

Several years earlier, powerful financial and military interests in France had converged upon a herculean trans-Sahara railroad project: a four-thousand-kilometer line of track, running nearly arrow-straight across the desert from Algiers to Saint-Louis, Senegal. Two hundred thousand francs for posts and surveys had been voted by the Chamber of Deputies in 1879. Unfortunately for Sultan Ahmadu, the trans-Sahara railroad (never completed) would have run across part of his empire, a geographic nuisance that Governor Archinard's political and military associates found unacceptable. The ruler of the French Sudan intended to destroy the obtrusive Tukulor empire and transform that part of Africa into a reservation where paternalistic officers took the place of sultans and chiefs.

On February 24, 1891, Archinard launched a furious assault on Jenné, Ahmadu's newest capital on the Bani River. Until the last hour the result was uncertain. Archinard's horse was shot out from under him. The regimental captain took two arrows. Marchand was shot in the elbow, and Mangin boasted to his father after three wounds, "Your blood has watered these distant lands once again, *mon cher papa.*" Lieutenant Colonel Archinard's report cited their extraordinary bravery, as well as that of Mangin's idolizing Senegalese corporal, who raved deliriously as he was carried wounded to the rear about Mangin's fine example. Sultan Ahmadu was on the run; for the moment, Archinard let him go. The French yanked out of obscurity Agibu, the feckless son of Al-Hajj Umar (the great military strategist and founder of the Tukulor empire), and promoted him as a substitute. Before his death in an explosion in 1864, Al-Hajj Umar had commanded Louis Faidherbe, governor of Senegal, to halt before the Tukulor *jihād*; signed, as equal to equal, an 1860 peace treaty with France; then swept across Mali conquering every people in the bend of the Niger River from Timbuktu to Guinée. Agibu, pliant and slow, in no way resembled his father. For about three years, until he was discarded for one of their own, the French used the puppet sultan to prevent the Tukulor and Mandinka peoples from joining forces.

It was now Archinard's intention to measure himself against the true nemesis of French power in West Africa, the Mandinka military genius Samori Turé, who had originally claimed, like the Mahdi on the other side of Africa, to be Allah's chosen one. Samori Turé's creation, beginning in the early 1870s, of a highly centralized state in southeastern Guinée was extraordinary but not miraculous. In thriving towns such as Kankan and Bissandugu, the commerce in goods and guns and the accumulation of gold from rich mines of the Buré region had long been the monopoly of African Muslims known as the Dyula—"those who frequent markets." In 1835, about five years after Samori Turé was born, the rich, city-born Dyula, intensely proud of their Islamic traditions, began revolting against the politically dominant Bambara and Mandinka, traditional animists whose roots were in the countryside. With a Dyula father and a Mandinka mother, this tall, stern African was able to turn his growing battlefield fame to special political advantage. Proclaiming himself Almamy (leader of the faith), kneading the peoples of Guinée into a disciplined whole, trading gum and gold with British merchants in Sierra Leone for modern rifles, Samori repelled the encroaching French back across the Niger with such violence in 1882 that Paris ordered further provocations discontinued.

An 1886 truce with France, an eye-opening official visit to Paris, and the brutal snuffing out, in 1888, of Bambara rebellions against Islamic excess led to a new phase of modernization. Samori now proclaimed his state to be secular, tolerant of all religious beliefs; army and bureaucracy were functionally stratified and geared to merit. African NCOs, both recruits and deserters from British and French forces in Sierra Leone and the Ivory Coast, taught his regiments European tactics. Diplomatic correspondence with European capitals presented the image of an orderly state open to trade and, two-thirds the size of France, fully contented with its borders. Turning his troops from the Tukulors, Archinard faced France's most powerful obstacle below the Sahara—as formidable, truly, and as great a hindrance to the lines of eastward communication and occupation as Léopold's Force Publique. In August 1889, however, France and Britain had come to an understanding about relations in the region, plugging the Sierra Leone arms pipeline. Archinard conducted his April 1891 campaign with lightning precision, taking Kankan in a surprise attack. Overconfident, he sent a large force against Samori himself at Bissandugu, the imperial capital, but the French were so badly mauled that Paris recalled the governor. Although his replacement managed to occupy Bissandugu at the cost of heavy casualties in early 1892, the Mandinka war machine was only slightly bruised.

Archinard returned. He was now master of most of the French Sudan, a colony of considerable potential wealth. Segu and Jenné produced high-quality cotton, and the wool products of Timbuktu, Gao, and Kano were renowned. The governor kept civilian authority in the colony to a bare minimum. Administrative policy there was military policy. In Paris, Joseph-Jacques Joffre, an Archinard loyalist, sat on the Conseil Supérieur de la Guerre (the equivalent of the Joint Chiefs of Staff), lobbying effectively for more money and a free hand for the governor. The Sudan's 634,000-franc budget nearly matched that of de Brazza's much larger French Congo by 1892. In military circles the word was out that rank and combat were to be had with Archinard, and Marchand's promotion to captain in December 1892 confirmed it. Dull duty in damp French garrison towns, where fifty-year-old captains were not uncommon, had scant appeal to ambitious lieutenants like Joseph Germain, Emmanuel Largeau, and Albert Ernest Baratier, another graduate of Saint Cyr. Handsome, quick-minded, and a good judge of men, Baratier was described by one of his colonels as "the French cavalry type in all its knightly fineness." Lieutenant Baratier brought more than combat initiative and equestrian skills to the Sudan. Like Archinard, he had begun to develop a demanding conception of France's role in Africa, a sense of mission going far beyond military pacification, medicine, and roads. Black Africa was actually to be transformed. "We are not looking to make Africa better, but to transform radically what exists. . . . We want a revolution, and a revolution is never peaceful."

Since the conquest of Algeria in the 1830s, the prevailing ideology had been that of *assimilation,* the gradual supplanting of indigenous customs and institutions by the culture and laws of France. Algerians, Senegalese, and Martiniquans were supposed eventually to become as French as the Corsicans had. But a debate over imperial policy had begun to rage in France's ruling circles during the 1880s. A countertheory, *association,* was promoted by admirers of the British policy of indirect rule, of leaving the natives to run themselves so long as they respected the ultimate authority of the district commissioner. The influential professor Paul Leroy-Beaulieu and former Premier Jules Ferry were among those who pointed to the successful Tunisian "protectorate" (France's first) as proof of the wisdom of association. By the Bardo treaty and La Marsa convention of 1882, Tunisia remained (in law if not always in reality) internally autonomous—although its tariffs, external trade, and foreign affairs were regulated from Paris. Turning alien people into Frenchmen was a philosophic excess bequeathed by the Revolution of 1789, said associationists, a preposterously demanding commitment that would, in time, lead subordinate peoples into festering disillusionment. Besides, leaving the chiefs and priests and pristine worlds intact was much cheaper. Algeria was the past; Tunisia was the model for the future.

The role of the military in this debate was complex. There were officers who swore by Colonel Joseph Simon Gallieni's policies of association, developed partly from his experience as Archinard's immediate predecessor in the French Sudan and refined after 1896 when Gallieni was master of Madagascar. Gallieni and Archinard (the latter a proponent of assimilation) fully agreed on one point: civilian rule and French settlers were bad for a colony's health. The disinterested, disciplined army was a far superior tutor of alien people, and Gallieni had seen firsthand how civilians were ruining Indochina. Warlike Tukulors or Madagascan Hovas had, it was added, much more in common with Saint Cyr and Saint Maixent graduates than with grubby traders or pasty government clerks, who would only waste away in the miserable climate. Gallieni's "oil stain" approach respected cultural diversity and integrity of native institutions and called for the slow, simple, inexpensive spread of French rule: a detachment of troops posted at a crossroads to attract a native market; digging of a well; visits by circuit-riding medical officers; maybe a school; and then a repeat of the activity at another crossroads. Archinard's followers, on the other hand, hewed to assimilation. Baratier's African "revolution" was meant to wipe out much of the past, just as, years later, Mangin's famous reply to Theodore Roosevelt about the falling French birthrate—that France had "one hundred million inhabitants" (counting Africans) —was partly forensic but largely expressive of Mangin's belief that the revolution was well under way.

These sharp distinctions in imperial development theory tended to be indistinguishable in the lives of subject peoples, of course. "Assimilated natives" and "associated natives" were equally despised and equally powerless; and Gallieni himself had ruthlessly destroyed the Madagascan monarchy. At bottom, the debate was really about speed and power. Politicians and bureaucrats were prone to worry about soldiers—whether Gallieni's or Archinard's— running an empire without more than a perfunctory salute in the politicians' direction. At the Pavillon de Flore, seat of the new Ministry of Colonies, Théophile Delcassé was determined to make it clear that, although soldiers conquered, civilians ruled. Tropical Africa was no longer administered by the navy. Then, too, Delcassé had listened to Gallieni about the Sudan, and Gallieni had argued that peace should be made with Ahmadu and that France should run the colony through the Tukulor potentates. Delcassé recommended a less aggressive policy to Archinard. What he got instead were Archinard's bloody campaigns of spring 1893.

For during the months of April and May, Marchand, Mangin, and Baratier seldom sheathed their sabers. Archinard was pulverizing what was left of Tukulor resistance. Massina, the last of Ahmadu's strongholds on the Niger, crumbled. The old sultan escaped farther east, hoping to build another empire in his four remaining years of harried life. When news reached the colonial minister of Archinard's near disaster at the second battle of Jenné on April 11 and 12, only the pleas of Lieutenant Colonel Monteil dissuaded him from ordering the governor's immediate recall. Fifteen men and two officers had been killed. Although reprieved only temporarily, Archinard's tenure was fatally compromised. He had allowed his forces to be badly mauled by Ahmadu, and finally made it possible for the new colonial service bureaucrats to plan the takeover of the French Sudan. When he ignored Delcassé's orders and began attacking Samori's large, formidably equipped forces that summer, Archinard was ordered home again and his soldiers began sharing "their" colony with civilian administrators. As it turned out, however, Archinard's influence upon imperial policy became even stronger from a Paris base.

In Africa, Marchand's star gleamed. Lieutenant Colonel Monteil was shortly on the scene, his Nile expedition having been abruptly cancelled, and was now in hot pursuit of Samori Turé in the Kong region of the Ivory Coast, where the endlessly resilient leader had recently moved his people to reconstruct an even more efficient empire. With five companies of Senegalese and two of Hausa *tirailleurs,* seventy-odd Algerian cavalry, and four batteries of artillery, Monteil's Kong column was the largest yet mounted by the French in West Africa. It included, in addition to Marchand, two new "African" officers who would be part of the Fashoda mission: Captain Joseph Germain, a Polytechnique graduate who had received his promotion in March; and Lieutenant Emmanuel Largeau, who, like Marchand, had worked his way up through the ranks and graduated from Saint Maixent. All of them—Marchand, Mangin, Baratier, Germain, and Largeau—were wounded, along with ten other officers and more than seventy of Monteil's troops, at Bonua in November 1894.

The battle of Bonua, in which Monteil was badly outgeneralled, was the high point of Samori's reputation as "the invincible one" and "the terror of the Sudan." Baratier's incredulity at meeting an enemy bugling the same calls and barking the same commands "in French!" remained with him for years afterward. Even more incredible was Mangin's account of Samori's weapons production— forges turning out or modifying "the 1874-model Gras rifle or even the 1866 Chassepôt transformed by Samori's smiths to fire a metal cartridge." Bonua was also an apotheosis for Marchand. For his incredible valor, the African soldiers called him from that day on "Paké-Bô"—"the piercer of forests." Darting and weaving with ferretlike motions, ignoring his wound as he had at Koundian, Marchand rallied his men repeatedly at Bonua to make regimental history.

2

When Marchand returned to France for reassignment on June 14, 1895, he had served nearly eight years in West Africa. Bronzed, wiry, as much at home in the desert or bush as a Tuareg or a Bambara, competent in local languages, even wearing the *jibba* and turban because of his admiration for Islam, he was known in colonial army circles as "the African." Gabriel Hanotaux recalled his first meeting with Marchand, three and a half years before the young soldier's return, on the occasion of a soirée hosted by Doctor Joseph Menard, Mangin's brother-in-law and one of the capital's empire boosters. Home on leave, Mangin had brought along Marchand, whose elbow wound from Jenné was still mending. "Both of them already had the faces of heroes," was Hanotaux's impression; "an atmosphere of initiative and courage enveloped them." Now back in Paris, the marine captain would soon present Foreign Affairs Minister Hanotaux with a more focused opportunity to gauge his initiative. Marchand, along with the recalled Colonel Archinard, was becoming deeply involved with the powerful Comité de l'Afrique Française, reading its bulletin, corresponding with Auguste Terrier, its future secretary general, and spending furloughs in the company of its co-founder, Prince Auguste d'Arenberg.

Archinard's involvement with the Comité was much deeper. From being a mere sympathizer, by 1895 he had become an active participant in its meetings and its principal recruit among senior officers on active duty. Prince d'Arenberg, Félix Faure (soon to be president of France), Eugène Étienne, leader of the Chamber's colonial party, and other political sympathizers of the Comité had smoothed the colonel's return passage with Delcassé, probably helping arrange his promotion to full colonel and appointment as head of the strategic Defense Office in the Ministry of Colonies in early 1894. The Marchand who appeared punctually at Hanotaux's office on the Quai d'Orsay on July 18, 1895, was being cued and instructed by his former commanders Archinard and Monteil, and, through the former, by the politically wise imperialists of the Comité. He came with a proposal.

Saying no to Marchand in person was not easy, not even for a suave veteran diplomat like Hanotaux. Furthermore, the foreign minister was uncertain whether or not it was wise to deny the captain's proposal. Two and a half years had elapsed since an excited President Carnot had charged Monteil to race to the Nile. Four governments had fallen since. Negotiations with Great Britain waxed and waned. One of the sturdiest colonial voices in the Chamber, François Deloncle, had recently demanded that France oppose Britain formally and aggressively: "We shall counter the English dream summed up in the formula 'From Cape to Cairo'; we shall counter with the French dream, 'From the Atlantic to the Red Sea.'" Then had come Sir Edward Grey's declaration in the Commons that French intrusion into the Sudan would be an "unfriendly" act, appearing to foreclose with arrogant finality any possibility of satisfactory solution of the Egyptian question.

Hanotaux had hoped for a diplomatic solution. And once again, just as the aloof, calculating Salisbury took office in the month before Marchand's visit to the Quai d'Orsay, the French believed they had concocted a mutually acceptable agreement. But it finally became obvious that the British were in Egypt to stay, that they planned to reextend their influence to the Sudan, and that they were stalling for time until the vastly expensive railroad from Mombasa to Victoria Nyanza was completed. Meanwhile, from his lonely outpost at Zemio in the Upper Ubangi, an exhausted Commissioner Victor Liotard signalled Paris that with just 250,000 francs and "one little European cadre" his countrymen could have the Nile watershed. Which is precisely what Marchand had come to tell Hanotaux.

Once more, the foreign minister was deeply impressed by Marchand's piercing eyes and total composure. He arranged for him to meet the sarcastic, antimilitary Minister of Colonies Émile Chautemps. On September 11, Marchand submitted his Congo-Nile report to the Ministry of Colonies. After a lesson in Central African geography, the captain presented the heart of the argument, "the Nile question from a political standpoint." It was brilliant, compelling, and characteristically a touch fantastic. The triumph of Salisbury's Tories in the recent elections was the certain prelude to a "more audacious" British colonial policy, Chautemps was told. Was France going to allow itself to be intimidated? Would it permit its "eternal rival to isolate our African colonies" and to inflict a defeat "in comparison to which the loss of our colonies in Canada and India in the last century would be no more than a forgotten date in our history?" To ask the question was to determine the answer.

What the British were up to was not merely the juncture of the Cape with Alexandria, but also of Mombasa, Kenya, with Lagos, Nigeria: what Marchand inventively called "the African Cross," as the two lines bisected the continent like ribs in a kite. To counter this "mad, arrogant dream" of the British, the captain proposed "the more modern French theory" of extending the French Congo to the Red Sea port of Obock "by way of the Bahr al-Ghazāl and Ethiopia." Ethiopia, of course, would have to "accept our offer or that of our allies [meaning Russia] of protectorate status." The Mahdiyya was also expected to welcome the French advance. Once at Fashoda, the contest would follow the laws of diplomacy, with England "compelled to accept, if not to convene herself, a European conference in which the fate of the Egyptian Sudan, i.e., the Nile Valley, is discussed and resolved."

The third paragraph began crisply with a detailed budget. "I ask for 580,000 francs in order to accomplish this mission, which will last at least thirty months," Marchand wrote: 350,000 for the first year; 40,000 for the second; the same amount for the third; and a final 150,000 for 1898. In addition to Marchand, there were to be five officers, a medical officer, an interpreter, four NCOs, one carpenter, one mason, six African sergeants, and 142 Senegalese *tirailleurs*. De Brazza, as colonial governor, commanded a salary only slightly higher than Marchand's 15,000 francs, so the captain and his men were to be relatively well rewarded for risking their necks. The wages of the loyal Africans, men and sergeants, totalled a mere 7,200 francs, while the whites required 128,180 francs.

Most of the equipment for the mission was purchasable in France. Seventy thousand meters of cloth would come from Manchester and Liverpool, and the outmoded pistols and rifles to be given Africans along the route were available in Belgium. Among the other provisions were optic telegraphs, cameras, meteorologi-cal and topographical instruments, a complete pharmacy, cooking equipment, and an aluminum canoe with navigational devices. There were also to be five hundred cases of gifts and trade goods, including cloth, sweets, beads, coral, and firearms. Two 80-mm mountain guns, 155 1890-model carbines, and 15 1895-model re-volvers were ordered. Marchand insisted on the peaceful, non-military nature of his expedition, but he intended to be formidably armed. All this material, exactly 3,049 cases weighing sixty-two pounds each, was to be prepared and packed by the Parisian firm of Monsieur Antoine Conga.

There was quite a bit here for Colonial Minister Chautemps to ponder, but while he was deliberating the cabinet unravelled. Pre-mier Dupuy gave way to Monsieur Ribot, who then stepped aside for Léon Bourgeois on November 1. The new minister of colonies, Paul Guieysse, was as ignorant of his office as the new minister of foreign affairs, Marcellin Berthelot, who replaced the able Hano-taux. Hanotaux had resigned, using fatigue to cover his aversion to serving in a "left wing" cabinet. Both asked Marchand for addi-tional information and were given, on November 10, the captain's "Supplemental Analytical Note." Evidently there were people at the Pavillon de Flore and the Quai d'Orsay who found it difficult to believe that a dozen of their countrymen and a battalion of Senegalese could march across Africa through Nilotes and Mahdists and hold the Nile basin as a bargaining chip against the British. What would happen if the Congo-Nile expedition ran into an Italian or, more likely, a British one—the Colville expedition, say, that Marchand's own report alleged to be racing for the Upper Nile by way of Uganda?

Again, Marchand reiterated the mission's peaceful character. He and his men were going to march to the Bahr al-Ghazāl "with the permission of the people there and"—as if the proposal were not totally unrealistic—"try to reach the Nile after an understanding with the Dervishes." All it amounted to, he continued blandly, was "an anonymous visit by a group of European travellers without flags or orders to the inhabitants of the territories adjacent to the Bahr al-Ghazāl, with whom they want to establish commercial and neighborly relations." Hostilities with another European force were impossible: "With the utmost urbanity and correct-ness," the commanders of the two European missions would inform their respective governments and "await their decision."

The new foreign minister thought this sounded reasonable enough. On November 30, Berthelot gave his official approval—emphatically stipulating, however, that the Congo-Nile expedition had "no military character." As far as possible, "peaceful relations with the Dervishes" were to be developed. Berthelot, like so many of his countrymen, was indulging in a great deal of optimism by alluding to such "peaceful relations." His instructions to Marchand concluded on a note of abnegation. No territories were to be occupied and no political treaties signed. The aim of the mission was uniquely to place France in a position "to settle the Egyptian Sudan question and to have the effect of hastening this settlement."

Marchand had almost won, but he still needed the full force of the colonial lobby for the final element: his marching orders from the Ministry of Colonies. As the two principal ministers involved in the Congo-Nile expedition were transient amateurs, hostile and dubious bureaucrats were able to delay the final step for several months more. Even powerful personalities like Delcassé and Clemenceau sometimes stumbled over the ministries' notorious *immobilisme,* and Berthelot was hardly in their league. Marcellin Berthelot was an illustrious chemist and well-intentioned public servant, but his incompetence at the Quai d'Orsay soon forced Premier Bourgeois to fire him. For Marchand, Berthelot's disgrace was a calamity. Exhausted, he wrote Mangin of having "to begin a new campaign for which I almost lacked the courage. I'll spare you a narration of all the ins and outs—that'd be too monotonous and disheartening." Meanwhile, Marchand had a strong and capable adversary in Ernest Roume, director of the African office in the Ministry of Foreign Affairs.

Roume had doubts about the soundness of the Congo-Nile scheme, believing (as foreign affairs officers often do) that careful planning and the strict concordance of resources and ambitions were the better part of national policy. How, Roume wondered, could Marchand and his men effectively occupy a crumbling fort at the end of a three-thousand-mile communication line when France had only 430 soldiers in the entire Upper Ubangi? Moreover, Roume was impressed by dispatches from Victor Liotard, who had reached Tambura by the end of 1895. Without an extra franc appropriated, Liotard was cultivating the people threatened by the Mahdists, consolidating an alliance with the sultan of Zemio, and preparing to go to the Bahr al-Ghazāl north through Deim Zubeir and the Bahr al-Homar. Roume saw Liotard's *"politique raisonnée"* as slower but more effective than Marchand's scheme. Above all, Liotard was a civilian and Roume believed that civilian primacy in the colonies was to be upheld at all costs. "The inescapable conclusion," he argued, "is that we must adhere to the policy recommended by M. Liotard."

On January 26, Marchand sent Roume a thirteen-page letter such as only junior officers who are heroes and have political backing can risk. There had simply been too much time wasted, Marchand lectured the Quai d'Orsay's senior Africanist. Of course he had directly approached Berthelot; Roume was reminded that he himself had granted permission:

> Any delay, during a period in which the solution to the so-called Egyptian Sudan question could fall inevitably one way or the other, is prejudicial to French interests because it benefits our rivals who are already, if I am not mistaken, well under way in the Lado region. We have to worry about being confronted by a fait accompli at any second.

Liotard's work was admirable, and there was no competition between them, Marchand continued. "But men change with the situation," and it was obvious that "a soldier is no more trained to be an administrator in the majority of cases than any administrator can be a soldier in this case." Moreover, his and Liotard's efforts would be complementary: while Liotard cultivated the Zandes and Nilotes, an alliance with the Mahdists would virtually guarantee a French victory.

Marchand's remarkable conviction that France and the Mahdiyya were destined to be allies had its source in experiences with the Muslims of the French Sudan. He believed that he understood the Muslim warrior and shared a similar view of life, and that a tenuous historical and cultural interplay between France and Islam, dating from the days of François I and Napoleon, not only existed but somehow registered in the brains of illiterate desert populations. The cultural presumptuousness of the French military was long-standing. Disembarking at Alexandria in July 1798, Napoleon had sought to win the population by proclaiming, "We are the true Muslims." Beturbaned and in flowing *jibba,* Marchand no doubt saw himself winning his first *ansār* (faithful) with the same announcement. Besides, he said, such an alliance was logical. "We must not lose sight of the fact that Muslims ought to be, whatever the price, our friends in the Nile region, our allies . . . perhaps without wishing it, but true allies finally, because it is thanks to them alone that England and the Belgian Congo are not already at Lado and Redjaf."

But politics, not argument, finally sent the Congo-Nile mission on its way. Marchand's old commanding officer, Archinard, was fighting the civilians from his perch in the Defense Office. He carefully rebutted Roume's position papers, guided Marchand to deputies who could help the campaign, and politicked to destroy the influence of civilian opponents. He prepared instructions to be sent to Liotard stating that a reduced colonial budget would "not permit him to occupy all the posts ceded to us by the Belgians." Liotard would have to stay where he was, and await the arrival of "some missions" organized to occupy the Nile basin, and to which Liotard was to lend his full cooperation. Archinard even proposed recalling Liotard. Roume strongly disapproved and Archinard's instructions were countermanded. But shortly after Marchand's impatient January letter, Roume resigned his position. His replacement was one Gustave Binger, the former governor of the new Ivory Coast colony, an active member of the Comité de l'Afrique Française, and a former army officer who had served under Archinard.

The influence of the Élysée began to register as well. Casimir-Périer, who as president remained lukewarm to the Congo-Nile idea, had huffily resigned at the end of 1894. Since January of the following year Félix Faure had reigned as president. Faure's imperialist sympathies were no secret. The minister of colonies, the gray Monsieur Guieysse, now decided that it was politic to approve Marchand's scheme for the second time. On February 24, 1896, he signed the captain's preliminary marching orders, but expressly subordinated the mission to Liotard's authority.

Marchand was finally able to relieve the anxieties of his carefully selected officers and NCOs. In a letter to Mangin in Senegal, his soaring, plunging, almost hysterical mood betrayed the strain occasioned by months of waiting:

They expect the impossible from us, and I've committed us all to giving it. . . . My heart and throat are torn by the thought of the sacrifices that are going to be necessary and the lives that I'm going to have to sacrifice. The idea that we could return home without having *completely* succeeded, without dishonor, is so utterly unac-

ceptable that, in spite of myself, I'm depressed and barely master of
my will.

The prose was more agitated than the man, however; and the
same letter abruptly gears down to instructions for selecting
Senegalese escorts, the importance of cipher communications, and
the examination of dossiers on Baratier, Germain, Largeau, "and
others that I've not yet been able to study."

Judging by some of their letters to Marchand during the long
waiting period, these men saw the chance to serve with him in
Africa as the most important moment of their careers. Emmanuel
Largeau, Marchand's twenty-nine-year-old Saint Maixent double
awaiting the word in Toulon, probably overdid his gratitude, knowing intimately his leader's exalted sense of destiny. In West Africa,
Largeau was often to exasperate Marchand by his irreverent sense
of humor. But in December 1895, he wrote, "There are those who
love movement, independence, effort, and responsibility; others
who prefer beaten paths and work close to home; there are pio-
neers as there are bureaucrats." For himself, Largeau chose those
qualities that would make "us become again what we were in the
sixteenth, seventeenth, and eighteenth centuries. If France remains shut up within her present limits, she's condemned to
depopulation and dismemberment."

For the mischievously eccentric Charles Castellani, a commercial
artist following the mission for the fashionable magazine *L'Illustration,* Marchand was the Saint Maixent reincarnation of the Maid of
Orléans. Castellani was convinced that, "from the moment he came
into the world," Marchand was destined to save France. "Absolute
decadence is always replaced by something of a renaissance." Old
companions Mangin, Baratier, and Germain, and newcomers
Pierre Simon, Sergeant de Prat, Jules Emily, and Alfred Dyé, were
a special breed, hard and sharp.

Meanwhile, events were overtaking France, just as Marchand
had predicted. On March 1, the most unexpected African disaster
of the century had taken place in the Ethiopian highlands: the
annihilation of a well-equipped Italian army by the warriors of the
Negus Negusti,* Menilek II. On March 12, Lord Salisbury had informed Europe that Britain and Egypt (whose leaders were belatedly consulted) were reoccupying part of the Sudan. Prime Minister Léon Bourgeois finally decided to appear convinced that the

*King of Kings

colonial risk was, if not small, at least calculable. On April 7, acting as his own foreign minister since the dismissal of the bewildered Berthelot, he approved Guieysse's instructions. The first ship, the *Thibet,* was loaded. "I think it's over at last," Marchand was able to inform Mangin. Then suddenly, on April 23, 1896, the Bourgeois government lost a vote of confidence. "A government collapsing while the Chamber is in recess. Who could have anticipated that?" an exasperated Marchand wrote Mangin. It was Jules Méline's turn as premier, with Hanotaux back in the Quai d'Orsay. Marchand pulled himself together for another round of high-level interviews.

Remarkably, the caretaker Bourgeois government, in a last gasp of assertiveness, stood by its permission for the mission's officers and supplies to leave France—if only unofficially. On April 24, the very day after the government's collapse, the *Thibet* carried Largeau and the first officers and supplies to the port of Loango in the French Congo, while Marchand stayed behind to await new marching orders. On May 10, Baratier left Bordeaux on the *Ville de Maranhão* for Loango with two thousand cases of supplies. Fifteen days later, Germain sailed aboard the *Stamboul* from Marseilles for Dakar and Loango. Finally, on Thursday, June 25, Marchand and Moïse Landeroin, the mission's interpreter, sailed from Marseilles aboard the *Taygète* for Libreville, capital of Gabon and the French Congo. When Marchand took his leave of Gabriel Hanotaux, the foreign minister shook his hand and, after France had taken three years to choose the weapon, dramatically exhorted: "Go to Fashoda. France is going to fire her pistol."

3

Léopold intended for the first shot fired on the White Nile to be Belgian. In truth, the unexpected and far-from-resolved troubles caused by the Swahili War and its aftermath had enormously complicated the sovereign's already intricate plans. Trying to outmaneuver the two major European powers, having to distort his dealings or conceal them from his own ministers, staking out vast claims at virtually every point of the African compass—and all this while a railroad from the coast was being forced through the forest to Léopoldville and a militia of nearly fourteen thousand was being armed and paid—might have finally overwhelmed even the most tenacious of entrepreneurs. The half-finished railroad had so far cost five million francs, most of which had come out of Léopold's pocket. Profits from ivory and rubber were at three million and one and a half million Belgian francs, respectively, by 1895, and the value of the wood and minerals from Katanga and Kasai provinces, once they had been fully policed, was incalculable.

His administrators and officers were doing all they could to increase the Congo's revenues. Month after month, two thousand Kru, Senegalese, and Bakongo were driven with hippo-hide whips up the trails from Boma-Matadi to Stanley Pool carrying everything from dismantled steamers to stationery on their heads. The Kru and the Senegalese were paid, if miserably, but the Congolese worked to discharge the Belgian-imposed "labor tax." The Congo was not quite yet the cornucopia of rubber, ivory, copper, and wood Léopold had anticipated, but an efficient system for extraction of its great wealth was already well in motion. In 1885, the king had issued an imaginatively criminal decree making twenty million Africans, by the stroke of a pen, tenants in their own country. All "vacant lands" became property of the Congo Free State, with a stiff village tax imposed for their use. Compelled to tend rubber trees and carry ivory for faceless syndicates to whom Léopold profitably leased much of the Congo, Africans were systematically maimed and murdered both as warning and punishment for "trespassing" on the crown's domain; for failing to work off taxes with exemplary industry; and, above all, for the felony of diverting to their own use the least bit of rubber and ivory chugging down the Congo for shipment to Europe. Léopold knew the anticipated wealth would come—was coming. The human cost (the Congolese population dropped by eight million in fifty years) would also be enormous; but that mattered not at all—or mattered only when meddlers such as George Washington Williams, the black American historian, or Roger Casement, the Irish diplomat, publicized Free State barbarity.

With a more deliberate pace of development, the Free State's resources would have been enough to sustain Léopold's ambitions. But the pace was furious, and the king's ambitions were not confined to his own colony. He was going to need a large and unrestricted sum of money if his scheme to place an army on the White Nile were to succeed. He had already set in motion a masterful bit of legerdemain that would result in the financing of his race to Fashoda by the citizens of Belgium. To the astonishment of Prime Minister Burlet and Foreign Minister de Mérode, Léopold revealed that he had violated the statutes under which he ruled the Congo by secretly mortgaging forty-two million acres of the Upper Ubangi to an Antwerp banking house for a five-million-franc loan, which would come due on July 1, 1895. And there was more to tell: documents had been signed in late 1894 between himself and a Colonel North of the Anglo-Belgian India Rubber Company (ABIR) advancing the Congo Free State a much-needed loan in exchange for the cession of most of the Manyema. Cession of lands required the approval of his government; would Burlet and de Mérode approve? Calculating that these low capers in high finance would shock his unnimble, principled cabinet into bailing out its sovereign, Léopold pretended to accept his cabinet's recommendation in December 1894 that the Belgian State immediately exercise its right to annex the Congo Free State. The parliament appropriated monies to retire the king's debts. At the last moment, Léopold informed his ministers that he wanted to keep the Congo as his personal property. Angry opposition to annexation from the socialists made Léopold's gambit even more feasible. Comte de Mérode resigned, but Léopold got his money plus a ten-year subsidy, and kept his colony. Many years later, his subjects discovered that the ABIR concession was a fabrication and that the Antwerp bank loan was the king's own money routed through dummy financial organizations.

He was now able to send Dhanis back to the Congo to lead the largest, best-equipped military expedition ever to cross the Interior. A terrible mutiny of Tetela near Luluabourg during the summer of 1895 was a grave obstacle to the success of the Dhanis mission. These Tetela, Force Publique irregulars who had served under Ngongo Leteta, had been transferred from the Mbomu region. Without warning they attacked Luluabourg, killed the commander of the Force Publique, and besieged Europeans at a Catholic mission before retreating into the forest with a supply of captured arms. Most of the troops Dhanis planned to use were Tetela; they were the most experienced. Whatever risks were involved in using them while many of their people were fighting a bloody guerrilla war against the Belgians was discounted because of the urgency and importance of the White Nile thrust. Sending Dhanis through the Aruwimi to the Bahr al-Ghazāl, along with a second force under Captain Louis-Napoléon Chaltin to the Mahdist stronghold at Redjaf, was Léopold's trump card in a rigged hand. Protesting neutrality to the British (who, while undeceived, were inclined to underestimate Léopold as a bothersome crank) and relying upon secret accords with the French (who, though deceived neither as to his loyalty nor as to the menace he posed, accepted the possible advantages of the Belgian risk), the king embarked on one of the greatest land grabs in history.

Dhanis's monster caravan was supposed to arrive on the Upper Nile months in advance of the French, pulverizing the pockets of Mahdist resistance and finally linking up with the French expeditions coming from the French Congo and Ethiopia. But Dhanis carried secret orders, to be opened at Fashoda. We can only guess what those orders commanded, but Léopold would have been untrue to his nature if they had not instructed Dhanis to throw aside the pretense of collaboration then and there. To block the French, the British might well have recognized Belgian possession of the Bahr al-Ghazāl—if the French, as Léopold anticipated, refused to share the territory. Had it not been for a single act of brutality, Léopold might have been able to outmaneuver the French and British and to realize the pharaonic ambitions of his youth.

Officers serving in the Belgian Force Publique were notorious for their iron discipline. Stanley had imbued what was virtually his creation with a rock-hard creed of ruthless efficiency tempered by calculating mercy. But on the Dhanis expedition, part of which had left Stanleyville in September 1896, the rule of mercy was set aside. Accelerated promotions beckoned; a sizable portion of King Léopold's private fortune was invested; high stakes in the Scramble for Africa were at risk. Never before had an African enterprise of such scale been attempted by Europeans. Five thousand well-armed Congolese troops transporting thirty-seven artillery pieces and vast stores of ammunition and supplies were driven, in three separately commanded groups and with only the briefest rest stops, for nearly five months from Stanleyville almost to Lake Albert on the Uganda frontier. From there the expedition turned north for Lado, the White Nile settlement in the swampy Bahr al-Ghazāl, some five hundred miles beyond.

The physically imposing Baron Dhanis had returned to the Congo Free State with more combat experience than any other officer. He inspired confidence and demanded flawless performance. Dividing his forces, Dhanis sent Chaltin's flying column heading for Redjaf and placed a vanguard under Captain Gustave Leroi. Ordered to hurry, Leroi force-marched his twenty-five hundred men for 150 days through the dread Ituri Forest, a steaming place of hostile pygmies and such primeval adversity as to have unnerved even Stanley. Half-starved, Leroi's troops finally stumbled out of the Ituri to Kavalli, a point on the map a few days' march from Lake Albert. Still there was no rest; for now, heading north along the White Nile, the expedition ran a gauntlet of people who vanished when approached by day and mounted deadly attacks by night. It was during this final lurch into the vast, swampy plain of the Bahr al-Ghazāl that a Belgian lieutenant snapped and "committed suicide en route out of sorrow at not making faster progress." Meanwhile, behind Leroi and straining over the same trails, Baron Dhanis had reached the Aruwimi. By then it was mid-February 1897. Despite the casualties and delays, the general timetable had been followed. Dhanis expected to reach Fashoda by April at the latest, after reuniting his huge force at Lado—by international agreement the farthest northern limits of the Congo Free State.

But the baron reached neither Fashoda nor Lado. On February 14 or 15, the troops under Captain Leroi revolted at the village of Dirfi near the Yei River. Orders had been given to apply 100 lashes to the back of an African private. That night the mutiny began. Porters fled into the high grass or cowered in the village while the Congolese soldiers made swift, awful work of their officers. Even if they had begun to read the signals of disaffection, Leroi and his subalterns were completely unprepared for the firestorm that engulfed them. By early morning, the Belgians had been shot, bayonetted, and many of them eaten. The limbs and entrails of others were smoked or dried in the sun for later nourishment. Chaos ended with the liquidation of the whites; under the Africans' natural leaders, discipline held and a new campaign plan ruled. The majority of the troops were Tetelas, who comprised the pick of the Force Publique soldiery, most of them having fought with Dhanis in the Swahili War. He owed his baronetcy and appointment as vice governor general of the Congo Free State to them. But these were also the same Tetelas who had revolted in 1893 after the Belgians had shot the idolized Ngongo Leteta. The revolt against Leroi was their long-awaited moment of revenge.

On March 18, Baron Dhanis and two thousand troops reached a clearing on the Aruwimi. They faced what had been Leroi's vanguard, now commanded by Congolese officers. Belgian sources identified the Tetela leader as a corporal with the oddly Italianate name of Arnodala. (In fact, he was not called Arnodala, but instead bore the name—portentously similar to that of twentieth-century nationalist leader Patrice Lumumba, also a Tetela—of Malumba.) Stunned and chagrined, the Belgians were too preoccupied with surviving the insurrection and, like all but the rarest nineteenth-century Europeans, too tightly wrapped in their own skins to understand an African personality that defied the stereotype. The rebel leader's motives were a mystery to them. And if not for the survival of a single written fragment we would not have a glimpse of this corporal and his men. An unsuspecting French priest, Father Achte, wandering into their perimeter, "found the camp on a plain covered with European tents and crowded with men, women, and children." He was taken to the principal tent, "in front of which were fifty Negroes dressed in European officers' clothes and seated on cane chairs." When his captors were satisfied that Achte was not a hated Belgian and was also a man of God, the priest was invited to refresh himself, take food, and then, after a few days, allowed to go in peace.

Achte found as much order in the camp as there would have been —and without the manic, martinet regime—under Captain Leroi. After a rapid return from the Bahr al-Ghazāl, the Tetelas were still a corporate body, still had their fighting edge, and their new "officers" were evidently a great improvement. What Malumba told Father Achte about the cause of the mutiny could have been placed in the mouth of his Congolese nationalist descendants. For three years, he said through the Frenchman's prose, "I had stored up in my heart hatred for the Belgians. When I saw Dhanis, face to face with my mutinous countrymen, I trembled with joy; the moment had come for liberty and revenge."

March 18 was unlucky for Dhanis. Malumba's spies had infiltrated his camp and won over not only many Tetelas but also a number of Zandes. When the firing began early that morning, the bulk of the Belgians' soldiers turned upon them. Troops who stood with Dhanis were rapidly swept aside. Officers—among them Louis Dhanis, the baron's brother—fell with saber and pistol in hand trying to stem what soon became a rout. "When the sun rose," Malumba recounted, "we saw several hundred corpses of black soldiers and seven dead Belgians. All the other Belgians fled, only escaping with their lives." Writing of these events ten years later, the editor of Belgium's *Mouvement Géographique* confessed, "the disaster was total." In Brussels, the telegraph brought Léopold the incredible news that the Belgian Congo was on the verge of being lost.

Dhanis, with a dozen or so of his surviving officers, drove hard to Stanleyville to ready its defense. His best African troops were dead or hiding in the jungle. The few white officers and sergeants in Stanleyville were clerks and garrison-duty types. The town's merchants and civil servants were generally a mangy lot who expected crack white officers and docile Congolese sharpshooters to make life safe. As bags of sand were heaped for cover on Stanleyville's east road, Dhanis worried about artillery; Malumba's people had most of it. More alarming was news brought by scouts that in addition to the huge core of Tetelas, the rebellion was attracting other Congolese people—all of them on a direct course for Stanleyville. With the loss of the town, much of the rest of the Congo would close down for Europeans. Mahdists from the north and Swahili from the southeast would fill the vacuum. Should this happen, Léopold and his servants realized, there would be neither Belgian willpower nor money enough for reconquest. In that event, either Britain or France, or both, would surely convene one of those elaborate conferences in which European statesmen, invoking burdens, Bibles, and commerce, periodically reassigned the real estate of the darker peoples.

Just as they approached the town, the Tetelas veered off, heading south past Stanley Falls to the old Swahili capital of Nyangwe. In the history of the Scramble for Africa, the bypassing of Stanleyville is an engrossing might-have-been. By July 1897, reinforcements from Europe gave the Belgians renewed momentum. On July 17, a certain Lieutenant Henri defeated Malumba's troops after a bitterly fought three-hour battle, leaving four hundred Tetelas dead. Eleven months later, on June 11, another lieutenant claimed to have broken the rebellion after a long, sanguinary match. Slowly, skirmish after skirmish, the Belgian noose tightened. Victory proclamations rained down predicting complete restoration of order before 1900. However incompetent their leadership or motivated their adversaries, quinine and rapid-firing weaponry gave Europeans an irreducible advantage. Malumba, one of Africa's first resistance fighters, disappeared from history, either killed in battle or, perhaps, succumbing to the internal politics of the Manyema. Victory seemed only a matter of time.

But time was precisely what the king could not spare; it ran as fatefully against the large ambitions of the Belgians as it did against the physical survival of the Tetelas and their allies. "In spite of the victories so pompously announced from time to time," a German officer in the Force Publique admitted in 1898, "the State troops have not, up to the present day, succeeded in bringing in a single deserter. . . . The Congo State is absolutely incapable of putting an end to the scandal." In fact, the single success of the stupendous Dhanis expedition had been that of Lieutenant Chaltin's flying column in the winter of 1897. Even then, when Leroi had been destroyed and Dhanis with his men was marching toward the humiliating battle with Malumba, Jean Marchand had sailed—after a six-month delay on his part—from Léopoldville for the Upper Ubangi. Two days after the battle at Dirfi, France and Ethiopia had signed a friendship treaty. Though Belgium fought on, the African mutiny at Dirfi had destroyed the Dhanis expedition, and with it Léopold's prodigally financed and ambitiously conceived scheme to carve an empire from the Atlantic to the Red Sea. After twenty-one years, the king of the Belgians was finally out of the race.

CHAPTER FIVE

Pawns of Pawns: Ethiopia and the Mahdiyya

1

Mysterious, isolated, diminished but unconquered, the mountain kingdom of Ethiopia saw its troubles with Europe begin in 1885, when the Italians suddenly garrisoned the Red Sea port of Massawa. Earlier, Massawa and the surrounding territory, once part of the Ethiopian footlands, had been occupied by the Turks and, more recently, by Egyptian khedives—who were themselves answerable to Great Britain. So it was understandable that the Ethiopians welcomed Great Britain's urgent maneuver to have them salvage what remained of Egyptian-occupied Sudan. Rear Admiral Sir William Hewett's mission had climbed to the imperial encampment near Adwa in March 1884, bearing decorous greetings from Queen Victoria and proposals to cede long-coveted lands in the Bogos region (Ethiopia's version of Alsace-Lorraine) in exchange for evacuation of Khedive Tewfik's troops through to the port of Massawa.

Sir William was one of many European emissaries to scale the Abyssinian highlands only to find his diplomatic skills sorely tried by Ethiopian guile. The Negus Negusti of Hewett's time was the strong but unlucky Yohannes IV of the northern province of Tigre. In addition to the Bogos country north of Tigre, Emperor Yohannes insisted on the right to occupy the towns of Kassala, al-Metamma, and Keren and to inherit the ammunition stores in these places. But what Yohannes and Ethiopian rulers before and after him wanted above all else was access to a major port. To the southeast were sand and hostile Muslim Somalis. In the east, beyond the hellish Danakil Desert and its homicidal nomads, there was French Somalia with a splendidly indented coastline, but as yet undeveloped harbors at Tadjura and Djibouti. In the northeast, successive Islamic waves since the twelfth century had rolled Ethiopia back from the Red Sea coast. When the British mission descended from Adwa in early June 1884, Article I of what became known as the Hewett Treaty guaranteed to "His Majesty the Negoosa Negust" free transit of goods through the port of Massawa.

Since the suicide of the deranged Emperor Tewodros in his mountain castle at Gondar sixteen years before, the Emperor Yohannes, through war and diplomacy, had united Ethiopia's five core provinces of Tigre, Begemder, Gojam, Shoa, and Wollo. The centrifugal "Age of Judges" (*Zamana Masafent*), during which, for more than a century, powerful feudal lords placed puppet emperors upon the throne at Gondar, had given way to centralizing imperial authority. With the signing of the Hewett Treaty Yohannes had supposed that Europe's most formidable nation would legitimize Ethiopia's surge north and west into the Egyptian vacuum. The emperor's most aggressive general, Ras* Alula Wādi Qubi, an ennobled farmer-soldier from Tigre, rapidly led some six garrisons to safety and returned to Egypt. Meanwhile, his sovereign impatiently awaited the British signal to relieve Kassala from the Mahdists. The Hewett Treaty had not offered Massawa to the Ethiopians, but once they had Kassala, Massawa too was very likely to be theirs for the taking.

Now, less than a year later, in February 1885, the Italians were at Massawa. "The Italian Government, in accordance with the English and Egyptian, and without doubt also the Abyssinian, has ordered me to take possession of the Fort of Massawa this day," the commanding admiral proclaimed. Playing for time to save the Egyptians, Britain had cynically encouraged Emperor Yohannes until its Italian surrogates were able to occupy what was left of the Egyptian Sudan and then press the Ethiopians back onto their mountains. "But why did England not warn me?" the outmaneuvered Yohannes moaned. He understood immediately that this was the greatest calamity to befall the descendants of Solomon and Sheba since the last Muslim invasion of the sixteenth century. "If we two remain united always," he wrote his ever-scheming vassal, Menilek of Shoa, "the Italians will not tire us, and with the help of God, we shall be victorious." But Menilek could be more inscrutable than the Deity.

During the four years of noble fratricide following the death of

*Duke

Emperor Tewodros in 1868, Menilek of Shoa had been Yohannes of Tigre's most powerful rival for the imperial throne at Gondar. Even after the angry magma of negusti, mardazmatches,* and rases had gradually cooled into fealty with the coronation of Yohannes at the seventeen-hundred-year-old royal city of Aksum, Menilek refused to submit. With the Egyptian Khedive Ismail's armies encircling the empire in late 1875, he had proposed an alliance with the khedive and held his armies aloof, letting Yohannes and Ras Alula grapple with the well-equipped Egyptians and their European and American officers. For his treachery, Menilek had received five hundred Remington repeaters and a promise of more if he attacked the emperor. "We will be very happy to establish relations with you, because in our eyes you are more worthy and able than others to take possession of this kingdom," Ismail's warm December letter concluded.

After the catastrophes at Gundet in November and at Gura, where, in March 1876, Yohannes's seventy thousand white-clad warriors destroyed fifteen thousand Egyptians and captured more than twelve thousand Remingtons and sixteen artillery pieces, Menilek gradually concluded it was time to make an appearance at Yohannes's camp. The parade of twenty-five thousand Shoans before the seventy-thousand-man imperial army, Menilek's ritual walk to Yohannes's raised throne with eyes downcast and a stone against his neck, and the twelve roars of the imperial cannon to signal the end of Shoan independence finally occurred in late March 1878. In return, Yohannes IV formally crowned Menilek II negus of Shoa. More than that, the emperor had decreed that Menilek was second in line to the imperial succession after his eldest son.

"If we two remain united always," the worried emperor had written Menilek in February 1886. But instinct told him that the Shoan's loyalty was determined by the preponderance of imperial power, and the Hewett Treaty, so painstakingly negotiated by Yohannes's ministers, suddenly promised nothing but trouble. Yohannes had known about his rival's flirtations with the Italians as far back as 1878, when the first emissaries from Rome had reached Shoa. By the autumn of 1887, the king of Italy and the king of Shoa had struck the first of their increasingly tricky agreements—this one implicitly recognizing Harar and Arusi in the south as part of Shoa and promising that the Italians would not annex Shoan terri-

*Princes

tory. Just as he had conspired with the khedive to undermine Yohannes, Menilek now looked to King Umberto of Italy for money and rifles to strike down his emperor when the moment was right. The moment must have seemed at hand during 1887, as General Baldissera's officers and their Somali and Eritrean *ascari* (levies) deployed from Massawa through the villages of Saati and Dogali on their march to the northern border of Tigre. Far to the south, Shoa thought it had little to fear from the cautious Italian ascent to the Tigrean plateau.

For the Negus Negusti it was a time of painful decision. He lacked Menilek's uncanny appreciation for technology, nor did he quite develop the Shoan king's knowledge of Europe. Yet he saw, more clearly than Menilek would, just how menacing the English-backed Italian presence really was. Twenty years earlier, when the nation-building energy of Emperor Tewodros had degenerated into sweeping brutality and senseless provocation to British honor, Yohannes and many of his peers had helped General Robert Napier's five thousand redcoats on their dash through Tigre. The quantity of arms and matériel pouring across the land had been so enormous, and the money distributed among local allies so prodigal, as to alter the economy and politics of Ethiopia.

Yohannes had seen the once-great Tewodros cornered and destroyed in his granite lair above the Gondar clouds; and his own ascendancy to the imperial throne had been largely due to the generous gift of guns and goods from the departing General Napier. Yohannes stood in awe of Britain, and Italy was Britain's ally. If the Mareb River was not crossed, he was ready to try to live with the Italians. "For my part," he wrote his fellow sovereign Queen Victoria, "if the Italian government does not come to take possession of my country and allows the free passage of goods at Massawa, I am disposed to make peace and come to an agreement." But by the time he dictated this letter, the faithful, impetuous Ras Alula had torn into the Italians above Asmara.

Alula Wādi Qubi was unusual though not unique in Ethiopia's hierarchical society, where court, church, and army were always willing to make use of outstanding talent from the bottom. He was born into a poor farming family in 1847. His rough playground had been a mountaintop rock high above the village of Mannawe in Tigre Province. By 1875, the time when Khedive Ismail's armies were marching to destruction, the dark-skinned, sharp-featured Alula had been raised by Yohannes to the rank of shalaqa, roughly equivalent to captain. Ten years later, the new ras was famed throughout the empire for audacity, brilliant generalship, loyalty to Yohannes, and a Tigrean chauvinism that not even his emperor matched.

Being a patriot's patriot made his relations with Yohannes often stormy, for while the emperor felt compelled to seek accommodation with the Italians and reassure Queen Victoria of his reasonableness, Alula told him that the invaders must be destroyed before they secured an impregnable beachhead at Massawa. Ignoring Yohannes's orders, Alula warned and provoked the Italians. "You Italians came to Massawa, according to your declarations, in order to facilitate commerce with Ethiopia, with amicable intentions towards our country and not in the spirit of conquest," he lectured one of their emissaries. "You, our friends, have taken not only Massawa but also other places, and now, for the sake of your friendship I demand that you withdraw the troops." Instead, Rome ordered its armies forward. The government of theatrically bellicose Prime Minister Francesco Crispi regarded African colonies as the indispensable signature of a great European nation. Ethiopians, said Crispi, were barbarians whose material progress and spiritual salvation cried out for the high ministry of Roman civilization. Moreover, the prime minister believed that the legendary Ethiopian ferocity in combat could be largely neutralized by Italian technology.

Reports of the Ethiopian attack on the garrison at Sabarguma in March 1885 reinforced Crispi's contemptuous confidence. The Italians had released manned balloons when Alula's men attacked during the day. Petrified by the apparition, "the Ethiopian soldiers . . . without listening to their commanders, turned back." Then, when the Tigreans mounted a night attack, the Italians beamed powerful electric spotlights at them. Alula's men "being illuminated like in daytime stood terrified and frightened, not knowing what to do. The Italians did not even shoot at them but remained laughing, watching the Tigreans' flight." But the next laugh was on Francesco Crispi's legionnaires. At Dogali, north of Asmara, some six thousand soldiers intercepted an Italian column racing from Massawa in January 1887 to relieve the besieged fort at Saati. Trapped in a narrow valley, 430 Italians were killed and 82 wounded out of a 550-man force. "An infernal whirl" was all that Captain Carlo Michelini remembered, aptly describing the traditional enveloping tactics of Ethiopian armies.

"As regards the Italians," Queen Victoria wrote Yohannes with characteristic ingenuousness, "we are sorry that you should have disputes with them. They are a powerful nation, with friendly and good intentions." He had not wanted war, Yohannes assured her (he may have been as angry with his ras as he said he was), but what could he do? "Ras Alula went down to inquire 'What business you have to do with other peoples' country?' The Italian chief gave an order to prepare to meet him, and fought with him." Alula made no apologies. When the alarmed Foreign Office hurried its best West Africa trouble-shooter, the very British Gerald Portal, to confer with Yohannes, he was unceremoniously delayed by Alula at Asmara. "Most insulting and aggressive," Portal harrumphed. "Italians should come to Saati only if he [Alula] could go as governor of Rome," the proud ras told the Englishman. Yohannes may have been somewhat pained by the gruff treatment and artless language served up to Victoria's emissary, but Alula had won a crucial battle in the history of modern Ethiopia. He had bought time for the empire. Because of their humiliation at Dogali the Italians fell back upon Massawa for two years, before advancing across the Mareb again. Yohannes told Portal that he would leave them alone, so long as they kept to the coast.

But the emperor's troubles from the Hewett Treaty were just beginning. Muhammad Ahmad, the Sudanese Mahdi, had been furious when, in January 1885, Yohannes's troops cut their way through his *ansār* to pluck the Egyptians at al-Metamma to safety. What Muhammad Ahmad learned from spies about the clauses of the Hewett Treaty made Ethiopia appear an aggressive ally of the hated Egyptians and British. Nor could it have been foreseen by the Mahdi that the disembarking Italians were going to make far more trouble for Ethiopia than for the Sudan. Whatever chance there might have been to avoid full-fledged war between Ethiopia and the Sudan vanished in June 1885 with the typhus-stricken Mahdi. His insecure, xenophobic disciple and successor, the Khalifa Abdullahi, had visions of an endlessly advancing *jihād*. Six months after the Italian tricolor was raised over Massawa, a sizzling challenge from one of the khalifa's vassals arrived at the imperial encampment near Adwa:

From the slave of God and faithful Mustapha Hadal to the King of Infidels, to Ras Alula his devil. . . . I know you said you would bring English troops to fight against the servants of the Prophet. But all

your sayings are delusions. They have not come, and now you say you
will fight me with an Ethiopian army; but in this you cannot succeed.
The *amir* of *amirs,* 'Uthman Bak Diqna, has now decided to conquer
every province . . . and now we have come down the hills in your
neighborhood. Therefore, come out and meet us.

The Mahdist invasion, led by the thirty-five-year-old General
'Uthman Diqna, was the darkest of portents. 'Uthman Diqna's
Kurdish ancestors had long since been absorbed into the fiercest of
the Sudanese peoples, the Hadendoa. His once-prosperous Suakin
merchant family was one of those ruined by the Anglo-Egyptian
attempt to end the slave trade. To his people's hatred of the British
and the Egyptians, he brought great shrewdness, literacy, inspiration, and his own large desire for revenge. It was 'Uthman Diqna's
howling, heedless "Fuzzy-Wuzzies" whom Kipling celebrated for
breaking a British infantry square at Abu Klea. Loved like a brother
by the Mahdi, who raised him from proud destitution to the august
rank of amir, 'Uthman Diqna also managed to keep the trust of the
darkly suspicious khalifa. His assignment from the khalifa was to
sweep Kassala Province clean of the enemy and to capture the port
of Suakin. Once Suakin fell, the Mahdiyya would have an outlet to
the Arab world for trade and arms. Most of Kassala Province fell
quickly, but the cities of Kassala and Suakin, reinforced by units
stripped from Egypt, held fast against repeated assaults.

In late summer of 1885, furious about news of Yohannes's pact
with Britain, 'Uthman Diqna veered south for Ethiopia, clearly
intending to annex large portions of the country for the Mahdiyya.
Then, as suddenly as he appeared on the Ethiopian border, the amir
departed. "We heard the news of your advance to Ethiopia," the
much displeased khalifa had written, "but my beloved, things
should be arranged according to their importance. . . . Do not attach
great importance to the Ethiopia affair. . . . Leave the Ethiopians
and do not enter their country now. . . . Return to Suakin, that is
what we want." It was also what the Ethiopians needed because it
gave them almost two years in which to concentrate on the Italian
menace without the added strain of a second front. After Ras Alula's
victory at Dogali, there was still one year to run before war between the Sudan and Ethiopia erupted.

The end of Emperor Yohannes's reign now came quickly. Early
in 1887 Ethiopian troops occupied the Sudanese frontier town of
al-Qallabāt. There had been a number of serious incidents leading

up to al-Qallabāt's seizure. But with the arrival of troops commanded by the khalifa's genial relative, Amir Unis al-Dickaim, both sides had preferred to live under a loose armistice that was good for the flourishing border trade in honey, wool, salt, cloth, wax, and dates. Then, behaving with more political perversity than was expected even of a theocratic sovereign, the Khalifa Abdullahi suddenly ordered Amir Unis to pounce upon a thousand Ethiopian traders and send them to Omdurman, where he offered to release them if the Negus Negusti embraced Islam. One of Emperor Yohannes's best generals, Negus Tekla-Haymanot, was ordered to chastise the Sudanese.

Even as the Ethiopian general mobilized, more than eighty thousand Mahdists were advancing beyond al-Qallabāt under the command of the khalifa's best general, Abu Anja, the one who had conquered Gordon and Khartoum. The well-tried Ethiopian strategy of inveigling the enemy into the country and surrounding him at the foot of a mountain failed disastrously. The Mahdists decimated Negus Tekla-Haymanot's army near Lake Tana, source of the Blue Nile, and raged through Gondar with its stone palaces, wooden churches, and monasteries, burning much of it to the ground before withdrawal to al-Qallabāt. Forty-five churches were destroyed, the fires feeding in the thin air upon hundreds of ancient illustrated manuscripts in the liturgical script of Ethiopia. "O Lord," the Coptic clergy of Gondar bewailed, "the pagans have invaded Thy preserve, Thy sacred shrine they have profaned."

Yohannes summoned his vassals from all the provinces. It was a time of much suffering throughout the Kingdom of the Second Jerusalem, not only because of the destruction of the army near Lake Tana and the sacking of Gondar, but also—as if to leave no doubt of withdrawal of divine favor—because of one of the worst plagues in memory. A blanket of locusts and caterpillars descended upon the grain, while from the northeast came cattle-rinderpest, brought to East Africa by Indian horses and mules imported by the Italians. Planting came to a halt in many places as oxen dropped. Salt became scarce due to lack of transport animals. The price of sheep began rise until, by the mid-1890s, it took six Maria Theresa dollars to buy what in 1889 had been purchased with one. So virulent was the plague that even wild animal populations were nearly wiped out. But, warriors above all, the Ethiopians rallied to the green, gold, and red banner of the empire—all except the warriors of Shoa who, on orders from a disaffected Menilek, mobilized slowly and headed lethargically for the front. For, although the emperor's son, Arya Selassie, had just died in battle, Menilek had learned that an imperial bastard was being groomed for the throne. Eight thousand Remingtons and more than a million rounds of ammunition from the Italians also encouraged his lackluster response.

Beset by famine, wary of the lurking Italians, and suspicious of Menilek, Yohannes dispatched a last-minute appeal for peace to the khalifa. He had "no wish to cross my frontier into your country," Omdurman was informed. "Let us both unite against our common enemies, the Europeans. If these conquer me, they will not spare you." Proposals from infidels were unworthy of his attention, the khalifa replied curtly. Abu Anja, the khalifa's greatest warrior, sent to replace Amir Unis al-Dickaim, had just died from swallowing a poisonous herb to treat indigestion. The equally ferocious al-Zaki Tamal, Mahdist governor of Berber, took his place. He commanded an army of more than a hundred thousand *ansār*.

On Saturday morning, March 9, 1889, the hundred-thousand-man Ethiopian army, divided into three wings, charged the Mahdist fort at al-Qallabāt. The left wing under Ras Hailu Maryam advanced slowly against fierce opposition; the right, under Yohannes's illegitimate son, Ras Mangasha, moved forward rapidly. His elaborate, cone-shaped crown gleaming amid the sea of lions' manes and dyed-handkerchief headdresses, Yohannes directed a rolling infantry and artillery attack at the head of the center wing. The first bullet passed through his right hand, but Yohannes continued running forward until a second bullet punctured his chest. Carried to the rear as the Mahdists were being driven back against the walls of al-Qallabāt, he summoned the nobles to the great silk-draped tent and, as his blood seeped away, commanded them to recognize Ras Mangasha, his bastard son, as Negus Negusti. Menilek, the absent scheming heir, was disavowed.

The leader's death in battle was the ultimate calamity. Alula, Mangasha, Hailu Maryam, and the other great nobles sounded the retreat the next morning and placed the emperor on his throne as though still alive. Stench from the rapidly decaying imperial corpse alerted a spy, and the nearly beaten Sudanese thundered out of their *zariba* to scatter the downcast Ethiopians like starlings. When the Amir al-Zaki Tamal sent Yohannes's crown and severed head to Omdurman, the khalifa ordered the head spiked and displayed before the faithful. Less than two months later, an Italian delegation headed by Count Pietro Antonelli arrived at Wichale to negotiate a treaty of friendship with Menilek II. The reason for this had perhaps best been expressed two years earlier by Italian opposition leader Fernando Martini: "Leave civilization alone, and speak of things without hypocrisy; say that all the states of Europe practice colonialism and that we must practice it too." The scramble for Ethiopia was under way.

2

"Emperor Yohannes was like a child compared to him," Augustus Wylde, the shrewd, opinionated British visitor to Ethiopia said of Menilek. Wylde could have added that Menilek's tubby little wife, Taitu, light of color and delicate of feature, matched her husband in worldliness and political sagacity. Unlike so many Ethiopian women, she had never been remarkably beautiful. Like many, however, she possessed the independence of mind that circumspectly influenced critical decisions in this status-conscious warrior society of haughty males. Ironically, it was the son of the biblical Solomon and Sheba, Menilek I, the first of the emperors, who had decreed that women should never rule the empire.

Although Empress Taitu chose and named the site of the new capital at Addis Ababa (New Flower), and actually commanded troops in the field, she truly respected the old traditions of formal subordination; direct rule of the empire was not for a woman. Besides, the attention the childless empress lavished on official business as she sat beside her husband gave her the reality of power that belied the restrictions of form. The new Negus Negusti and his wife were a formidable combination. From many years' experience as Her Majesty's vice-consul for the Red Sea, Augustus Wylde strongly suspected that "Menelikism may give a great deal of trouble in the future."

Wylde first saw Menilek in 1896, a confident yet tired, fifty-one-year-old warrior-statesman whose alert brown pupils were offset by yellowed eye-whites set in an unusually dark Ethiopian face. The deliberate, "oily" voice masked then, as earlier, nimble thoughts and explosive energy. Menilek had been forced by circumstances partly of his own making to become a past master of Machiavellian survival—and Count Pietro Antonelli, Italy's plenipotentiary to Menilek, had been a consummate teacher.

At face value, the 1889 Treaty of Perpetual Peace and Friendship at Wichale had been a political panacea for the Negus Negusti. Menilek's claim to the throne was clouded by Yohannes's illegitimate heir, Ras Mangasha, whom the great nobles had not recognized as Yohannes lay dying. Making their way back to Tigre, Mangasha and Alula had raised a revolt and were taking the part played a few months before by Menilek. Speaking for King Umberto, Antonelli offered a generous line of credit, an end to the arms embargo at Massawa and Zeila ports, formal recognition of the negus of Shoa as King of Kings—all this in exchange simply for friendly relations with Italy and acceptance of its good offices in various diplomatic matters. The formal submission of all but the Tigrean nobility in August was certainly helped by Menilek's compact with the Italians.

Yet that same month the governor of Massawa, General Baldissera, occupied Ras Alula's capital at Asmara and, on the first day of the new year, his successor would proclaim Eritrea to be Italy's new African colony. Meanwhile, on November 3, church bells pealed the elevation of Menilek and Taitu to the throne of Solomon as supreme rulers of the Amharas, Gallas, and Tigreans. Ras Mangasha, seeing that fate and Remingtons favored the new Negus Negusti, swallowed his pride in February 1890 and, holding the symbolic rock against his neck, shuffled before the throne at Addis Ababa in ritual submission. Ras Alula had begged him not to and gone his rebellious way, more royalist than the king. He had his own master, "the son of King Yohannes—why should I look for another in Shoa?"

What was going on in Italy worried the new emperor. First there had been the twenty million lire voted by the Italian parliament during the summer of 1887 for a special five-thousand-man army corps. Also, the new governor of what was now Eritrea (formerly part of Ethiopia) was an efficient, imaginative administrator and soldier with field experience fighting Ethiopians. He had been one of Garibaldi's legendary "Thousand," a member of parliament, and almost minister of foreign affairs. General Oreste Baratieri was strengthening forts, stockpiling arms, seasoning his troops, and organizing units of African soldiers—the *ascari*. But worry turned to stupefaction when Menilek learned that the Italian prime minister had notified the Powers of Europe on October 11, 1889, that Ethiopia was an Italian protectorate. Menilek's alert, worldly cousin, Ras Makonnen of Harar, had been told nothing of these designs, although he had spent two months in Rome hammering out terms of the "Additional Convention of October 1, 1889," a supplement to the May 2 Wichale friendship treaty. The convention only airily referred to future frontier rectifications based on "actual possession de facto," and the ras had gone home with a four-million-lire loan at five percent—the customs revenues of Harar Province serving as collateral.

"In the long run," wrote Sir Evelyn Baring, virtual dictator of the khedive's Egypt, to Lord Salisbury, "the Italian policy will probably collapse—more especially if they are too ambitious." In late 1891, after Prime Minister Crispi's refusal to negotiate East African questions, he added, "All I have seen and heard here impresses me greatly with the weakness of Italy as a Power." But what the stern British diplomat failed to realize was that, for Crispi and many Italian leaders, colonial possessions were the result not of their nation's modern greatness, but of the magnified status Italy would later attain from an empire carved out of Africa. Count Antonelli's booby-trapped Treaty of Wichale was designed to achieve by language what an Italian army had been unable to at Dogali. A conscientious clerk had tried to warn Menilek that Article XVII of the treaty "may not weigh one-quarter of a dollar now, but in a year's time it can be heavier than a thousand tons of lead." Summoned to the *gebi,* or royal enclosure, by the puzzled emperor, Antonelli feigned total astonishment over any ulterior meaning in Article XVII. "We are only your postman," the suave count insisted. "How could we do evil to you?" Temporarily persuaded, Menilek rewarded his clerk's sharpness by dismissal and forfeiture of property.

But then came word to all Europe that Ethiopia was now a colonial protectorate of the kingdom of Italy. For the treaty had two translations, Amharic and Italian. In Amharic, Article XVII read, "His Majesty, the King of Kings of Ethiopia, may, if he so desires, avail himself of the Italian Government for any negotiations he may enter into with other Powers or Governments." Menilek knew that access to European embassies—if only through Italian diplomatic channels—was a tremendous advantage for isolated Ethiopia. But the Italian version of Article XVII was decidedly more constraining: "His Majesty, the King of Kings of Ethiopia, consents to avail himself of the Italian Government for any negotiations he may enter into with the other Powers and Governments."

It was a mismatched encounter of High Renaissance political science and late medieval craftiness. Two millennia of written language had made the Ethiopians unique among the peoples of the sub-Sahara, imparting to their preening Amhara elites a vast cultural superiority. But the possession of Ge'ez had not made Ethiopians literate. Ge'ez, the language of black-robed Coptic priests, was to the spoken tongues of Amharic and Tigrinya what Latin was to French and Italian: a language of scholars. The great nobles had always been too busy extorting peasants and fighting among themselves to learn their alphabet. It was spoken Amharic that ruled the dealings of Ethiopian lords: elaborate, nuanced communications meticulously memorized and repeated by their emissaries. The written message only certified and identified; it almost never spelled out the essential. Ethiopians assumed that only what was *said* about the writing mattered.

When Menilek had written Crispi that he desired Italy to speak for Ethiopia, he had Antonelli's "postman" explanation in mind. But by February 1891, he finally understood where the Wichale treaty was leading his country. Fighting to stave off the collapse of his cabinet, Crispi had frantically instructed Antonelli to get Menilek's unequivocal acceptance of Article XVII. "Italy cannot notify the other Powers that she was mistaken in Article XVII because she must maintain her dignity," the count arrogantly announced during his strained audience with Menilek and Taitu. "As you, we also must respect our dignity," the empress volleyed in Amharic. "You wish Ethiopia to be represented before other Powers as your protectorate, but this shall never be."

Nor was this the last surprise of Antonelli's day. Leaving the *gebi* with what he thought was an exact Amharic copy of a new agreement letting the Amharic and Italian versions of Article XVII stand without comment, Italy's indignant plenipotentiary discovered that he had in fact signed an Amharic annulment of the article. Recalling that he had questioned Antonelli "with great seriousness" about the treaty in 1889, Menilek wrote to King Umberto a few days later that the treaty had never contained any "obligatory agreement. I am not the man to accept it, nor could you advise me to do so." He spoke with blunt defiance in his circular of April 10: "Ethiopia having been for fourteen centuries an island in a sea of pagans, I do not intend to listen quietly when governments from distant lands say they will divide up Africa." Menilek must now have known that war with Italy was inevitable. Fortunately for him, the Italians were both unwilling and unready for the contest. The far more pragmatic Marchese Antonio di Rudini had taken Crispi's place as prime minister in early February. Rudini cared very little about the Red Sea and East Africa. Kassala, Somalia, Ethiopia were worthless distractions from expansion in North Africa; and besides, they annoyed the British. The Anglo-Italian Convention of April 15, 1891, granted Italy the right to occupy Kassala (but not to keep it) and recognized Eritrea, but as far as Rudini was concerned Italian expansion south of the Sahara was adjourned.

Rudini's policies gave Menilek almost three years of respite before the bellicose Crispi returned to power in December 1893. It was barely enough time. Even without Crispi, General Baratieri was deadly. Having formally denounced the Italian treaty in a letter to King Umberto of February 12, 1893 ("I declare my will is not to renew the treaty concluded at Wichale"), Menilek began to feel the noose tightening. Arms shipments through the British Somaliland port of Zeila ceased. The kaiser and the Austrian emperor forbade their subjects to sell or transport weapons to Ethiopia; ironically, the last large shipment to the negus, two million cartridges, was brought by the Italians to Addis Ababa only days before the final, rupturing letter was sent to Umberto. The treachery in which Menilek excelled as negus was now emulated by others. Meeting General Baratieri and his staff at the Mareb River in early December 1891, Ras Mangasha declared "My enemies shall be thy enemies and my friends thy friends," and signed a convention of alliance. Ras Alula, standing by, heartily approved.

The return of Mangasha and Alula to the fold in June 1894 was small comfort. A further gift of two million bullets and arrogant Italian behavior persuaded the two Tigreans to make peace with the Negus Negusti. Leading twelve thousand of his warriors to pay long-overdue obeisance in Addis Ababa, the old campaigner Alula told Augustus Wylde that he "turned to Menilek as the only man who could restore order." Baratieri's legionnaires were crossing the Mareb River into Tigre. Fighting started at Coatit in January 1895, with the first round going to Baratieri against Mangasha. Every Ethiopian able to wield a spear or aim a rifle would be needed to face the ten thousand additional troops for whom Crispi's parliament voted thirteen million lire in August. In September, the negus officially decreed all Italians expelled from Ethiopia. Valleys ran with blood and gelignite plumes rose over mountains as battles raged throughout the year and into the next at places such as Debra Hailu, Amba Alagi, Beta Maryam, Adigrat, Makale.

At Amba Alagi confused orders sent Major Toselli's twenty Italian officers and thirteen hundred *ascari* into annihilation in Mangasha's meat grinder. At Makale, Baratieri's troops surrendered after Ras Makonnen's siege, with a promise that Italy's Muslim and Ethiopian soldiers would never again fight against Menilek's empire; they were allowed to march off with flags and arms to safety. (Later, Italian violation of the Makale pledge was to drive the Ethiopians into a vengeful frenzy.) Despite the setbacks, Baratieri's armies advanced. Tigre was proclaimed an Italian colony, and ragged peasant conscripts from Sardinia along with elite Bersaglieri from Tuscany streamed through Massawa toward the highlands. Between Christmas and early March 1896, 1,537 officers and 38,063 soldiers disembarked.

The semi-official newspaper *La Stampa* revealed that Baratieri was to continue advancing while a delegation offered the Ethiopian emperor surrender terms and demanded the imprisonment of Mangasha and his vassals. There was much deliberation and prayer in Addis Ababa and Entoto, and even a hint of appeasement in Menilek's letter to King Umberto after the long siege of Makale ended on January 20:

> From the Conqueror of the Lion of Judah, Menilek II, named by God King of Kings of Ethiopia. . . . You desire peace and friendship, and General Baratieri has informed me of this, and I am much pleased. In order to give proof of our Christian faith, as was our desire, we have sent out, with all their belongings, escorted by Ras Makonnen and in good health, those who were in the fort . . . though they were worn out by thirst, hard-pressed, surrounded, and almost trampled under our feet.

Umberto's reply was more than fifty thousand Italian troops in Ethiopia before the end of the year.

Menilek's pleas to the Khalifa Abdullahi were beginning to yield equivocal results. "In the name of Allah the All Merciful, the Compassionate," the khalifa reminded the Negus Negusti that he had begged "the doomed Negus Yohannes the Great" to embrace Islam, but Yohannes "was haughty and scorned [us] and turned off the path of righteousness." Nor had Menilek complied with the khalifa's summons to humble himself:

> Now we write to you again, inviting you to enter the creed of Islam and become enlisted in the line of the Mahdi's followers. . . . [If] you become one of the followers of the Mahdi who supervises his correct

orders, be sure that we will accept you and will appoint you as amir
on our own behalf over all your domain. . . . But you must stay within
the limits of your borders and not cross the borders of Islam.

Behind its smugness, the reply from Omdurman, the khalifa's
capital, signalled willingness to collaborate. The oral messages
brought from Omdurman were even more encouraging. They
strongly suggested that Menilek's embrace of Islam could be fudged,
that Khalifa Abdullahi's fanaticism was ultimately susceptible
to political common sense. But much time would need to be spent
in deferential and intricate negotiating before that came about.

As with all traditional peoples, religion was politics-by-other-
means to the Ethiopians. The God of Abraham and Solomon was
expected to find battalions for His people in their hour of deepest
trial. On January 11, 1895, Czar Nicholas II of Russia came to the
rescue of his brother-in-Christ and the Orthodox Church. News
blazed from Djibouti across the Danakil Desert to cool, green Addis
Ababa that a Russian caravan of three hundred men and four hundred animals was making its way to the highlands.

Twenty years before, Yohannes had sought an alliance with Alexander II against the invading Egyptians, sending the czar ("You
who are as great as Constantine and as powerful as Alexander of
Macedon") an ornate gold cross and a proposal that "now, according to our ancient prophecies, the Czar and the Negus should meet
one another in Jerusalem." Ten years had elapsed before the Ethiopian gift was publicly acknowledged by the czar's successor, Alexander III. Then, in October 1891, a personal representative from
the czar had reached Addis Ababa with a gift of ten thousand francs
and several boxes of rifles, a strong signal that Russia opposed the
April Anglo-Italian Convention. In the letter presented to the
Negus Negusti, the czar encouragingly concluded with the expression of a "desire and readiness in case of need always to extend to
the Negus the hand of brotherly assistance."

With the arrival of the official Russian diplomatic mission in January 1895 the czar lavishly advertised to Europe his interest in Ethiopia. For its part, Russia's new French ally found it highly advantageous to applaud quietly the czar's diplomacy and to allow an
increasing flow of weapons to reach Ethiopia through Djibouti. For
his part, Menilek had hesitantly approved the railway concession
from Addis Ababa to Djibouti in March 1894, a scheme in which
French capital intended to invest heavily.

When the Russian delegation finally arrived at Entoto to be received by Menilek, it had passed through the land to almost delirious cheers from the usually reserved, politely xenophobic Ethiopians. It was kept at Harar for almost a month, where grateful Amharas, despite the abating plague, slaughtered herds of sheep, served mountains of *enjerra* (the laceworklike national bread), and uncorked rivers of an amber, fermented honey called *t'ej*. The presence among the Russians of the Archimandrite Ephrem, the first representative above the rank of priest from the Russian Orthodox Church, moved the deeply religious Ethiopians. But the rich and distinguished Captain A. F. S. Eliseiev's mission, although it also contained a photographer, taxidermist, and entomologist, and was partly underwritten by the Imperial Geographical Society, was unmistakably political. Moreover, Captain Nikolai Stephanovitch Leontiev, the nobleman who replaced Eliseiev after the latter left Harar, was an aggressive adventurer who had large plans for Russia in Ethiopia. Leontiev was courageous, attractive, smarter than he was wise, and very ambitious—a superb confidence man and a good artillery officer. Menilek liked his take-charge manner instantly, so much so that Leontiev immediately gained his complete confidence and was invited to attend the war council. However, Leontiev's claim that he showed Menilek how to defeat the Italians by describing Marshal Kutuzov's famous retreat before Napoleon's Grande Armée is an exaggeration at best: the maneuver could hardly have been news to Ethiopians who had been falling back and swallowing up enemies for centuries.

What Menilek probably liked most about Leontiev was his ego, which, if harnessed to the Ethiopian cause, might excite considerable material support from Russia. The emperor was delighted to have a large delegation accompany the Russians home in April 1895, with Leontiev underwriting travel expenses. The Ethiopians were as lionized in Russia as the Russians had been in Ethiopia. A half-million rubles were spent by the government to entertain them. In Moscow, Grand Duke Sergei gave a magnificent reception, followed by forty days and forty nights of festivities. And in early July, they were received by Nicholas and Alexandra at Tsarkoe Tselo Palace. The Italian ambassador pouted and the German ambassador formally protested the affront to the Triple Alliance.

There was good reason for Italian pouting. When the Ethiopians returned home accompanied by Leontiev, they brought four hundred thousand rubles, 135 cases of rifles, a vast supply of ammunition, and several machine guns. By late September 1895, those weapons were being distributed among Menilek's troops. Shortly thereafter, a number of breech-loading, quick-firing Hotchkiss mountain guns were rushed up from Djibouti. They were the latest models, superior to anything in the Italian arsenal. Leontiev, his cossack subalterns, and a French captain named Clochette began instructing the Ethiopians in artillery and machine gun practice.

Had the Italian army not fought the Ethiopians at Adwa, it would have won the war. But Prime Minister Crispi's government wanted its colony immediately. Crispi was beside himself because of the almost even battlefield score: Ethiopian armies were defeating the best Italy could send against them. On January 18, Rome informed General Baratieri that Menilek was to surrender unconditionally. All civil and criminal authority was to be vested in an Italian governor residing at Addis Ababa, with customs, loans, defense, and political appointments subject to Italian approval. Meanwhile, General Baldissera headed for Massawa on February 22 with secret orders to replace his rival Baratieri. Three days later, wholly out of control, Crispi goaded his generals into action by telegram:

> This is a military phthisis, not a war; small skirmishes in which we are always facing the enemy with inferior numbers; a waste of heroism without any corresponding success. We are ready for any sacrifice in order to save the honor of the army and the prestige of the monarchy.

While Baratieri and his four brigadiers, Generals Arimondi, Albertone, Ellena, and Dabormida, considered the professional implications of their prime minister's vote of no confidence, Emperor Menilek's hundred-thousand-man army was on the verge of falling apart. Even the shortest campaigns imposed enormous strains on the Ethiopian war machine, with each soldier responsible for his own provisions and every village in its path obliged to yield up grain and livestock. The army had now been in the field for three months, and by the end of February had eaten the neighborhood bare. Starvation raged in the camp. The hundreds of daily desertions would shortly run into the thousands. Baratieri's 17,700 troops were only slightly better fixed for food supplies, the commander having ordered half-rations in mid-February; but Menilek was unaware of this. And short of food or not, the Italian position, with its sixty-odd

cannons, was virtually impregnable; thousands of fresh reinforcements were just arriving at Massawa.

Every instinct had prompted General Baratieri not to advance.
His communication lines with Asmara were dangerously extended,
provisions were running low, and intelligence about the enemy,
though reassuring, was less than reliable. Surprisingly, Crispi's telegram caused Baratieri to be even more cautious, and he ordered a
retreat three days later, on February 29. Friction between the
commander and General Arimondi had plagued much of the campaign. The evening of the retreat, as Baratieri held a war council,
Arimondi, joined by Generals Dabormida, Albertone, and Ellena,
heatedly argued for an attack. "Italy would prefer the loss of two
or three thousand men to a dishonorable retreat," Dabormida
stated grandly. Shaken, Baratieri promised his decision in the
morning, enigmatically mentioning some eleventh-hour intelligence he was expecting "from the enemy's camp." Ethiopian tradition holds that an Amharic double agent arrived much later that
night with news of the disintegration of Menilek's army. One messenger alone would not have decided Baratieri, who was a superb
strategist, to reel about for the attack. But there was the promise
of humiliation if the prime minister's orders were not obeyed, the
contrary opinions of his brigade commanders, news of the major
defeat of enemy forces by the crack Bersaglieri two days earlier,
and Baratieri's conviction (brilliantly encouraged by Menilek) that
the enemy army numbered well under forty thousand. The attack
was on, Baratieri told his generals the following morning—to com-
mence at 9:00 A.M. the next day.

The battle plan called for three columns to march in parallel
formation to the crests of three mountains—Dabormida commanding on the right, Albertone on the left, and Arimondi in the center
—with a reserve brigade under Ellena following behind Arimondi.
The supporting crossfire each column could give the others made
the 10,596 Italian and 7,104 Eritrean soldiers as deadly as razored
shears. Albertone's brigade was to set the pace for the others. He
was to position himself on the summit known as Kidane Meret,
which would give the Italians the high ground from which to meet
the Ethiopians. This plan was typical of Baratieri: sensible in conception and carefully drawn up in detail. Its two fatal flaws were
numbers and terrain. In another month, the Italians could have put
more than twenty-five thousand troops in the field, and by then the
Ethiopian army probably would have disintegrated. But Crispi's

telegram and Baratieri's war council settled the timing of the attack, and Baratieri's precipitate decision cost him an opportunity to send out scouting parties to double-check key features of the terrain. He might have discovered, for example, that his sketchy maps mistook another mountain for Kidane Meret. Without cavalry, however, reconnoitering the area near Adwa would have been extremely difficult even with more time. Six thousand five hundred feet above sea level, the plain near Adwa seemed designed to mock the plans of foreigners. All "rugged slopes, precipitous and broken, abounding in ravines, gorges, and crevasses; narrow and tortuous clefts in the hard rock, passes half closed and steep" was how an Italian officer described the scene—"a stormy sea moved by the anger of God."

It was Ras Alula's men who spotted the Italians on the move. Marching his forces throughout the moonlit night, Baratieri would still have had time to correct mistakes in deployment had he been able to keep the element of surprise. A peace offer sent just before advancing was intended to deceive Menilek. But things began to go seriously wrong for the Italians hours before the first firefight. Albertone's *ascari* brigade failed to keep to its narrow trail, spilling over into that assigned to Arimondi's troops at about 2:30 A.M. The tangle snarled the center's advance for almost two hours. Communicating by heliograph was not possible for another five hours, and an increasingly anxious Albertone, checking his maps and watch, had no way of knowing that Arimondi was frenziedly engaged in a traffic control problem behind him. When an Ethiopian guide informed the general that he was not at Kidane Meret, that the crucial summit lay four and a half miles ahead, Albertone jumped to the conclusion that Arimondi was waiting for him there. He gave the order to advance to the next mountain and into the exposed unknown. Shortly before 6:00 A.M., Albertone had second thoughts, ordering a halt two and a half miles from Kidane Meret —a message that failed to reach his advance guard, which continued marching toward the Ethiopian perimeter. At six o'clock, Albertone began fighting for his life. "Reinforcements would be well received," was his last message to Baratieri. It arrived at about 8:30.

Until Ras Alula's news of the Italian advance, Menilek had seen no other course than to tell his generals to break camp on Monday morning, the second of March. Early that morning, kneeling in fervent prayer for God's delivering guidance, the Negus Negusti permitted messengers to enter his silk-and-gold-cloth-draped tent. They brought incredible news: the Italians had left their fortified positions and were less than four miles away. The Ethiopian troops were given holy communion and blessed by the priests. Mounted gold and copper crucifixes soared above the green, orange, and red standards that the officers tilted before them. Taking his place at the head of the army, with Taitu beside him, Menilek ordered the long, emotional war proclamation read, a catalogue of Ethiopian forbearance and Italian unreasonableness:

> The enemy refuses to listen. He continues to advance; he undermines our territories and our peoples like a mole. With the help of God I will defend the inheritance of my forefathers and drive back the invader by force of arms. Let every man who has sufficient strength accompany me. And he who has not, let him pray for us.

A stupendous roar followed: "For the Motherland! For the Emperor! For the Faith!" The quick-firing mountain guns were set up on the real Kidane Meret, giving Menilek's artillery a clear field of fire for several miles. Eighty-two thousand Ethiopian infantry started forward on the run, accompanied by twenty thousand spearmen. Eight thousand crack cavalry advanced on their flanks. Negus Tekla-Haymanot commanded the army's right wing, which made the first contact with Albertone's vanguard. Ras Alula's men were on the far left. Ras Mangasha and Ras Makonnen commanded the center. Menilek, with an army of twenty-five thousand infantry and the pick of the cavalry, held the ground to the rear. Taitu, with three thousand infantry and six hundred cavalry, was nearby.

Forty-five minutes after the first shots Baratieri had ordered his right column to move left to reinforce Arimondi's center. Somehow Dabormida headed right, opening up a more than two-mile gap into which Ras Makonnen's men poured. The sheer weight of Ethiopian numbers threatened to crack Arimondi's brigade, but by 8:15 the sun had finally burnt off the thick morning mists and Baratieri saw the danger his army was in. What remained of Albertone's *ascari* brigade was streaming back upon Arimondi's center. Withholding artillery fire until the *ascari* were within their lines, Arimondi's gunners suddenly realized that Makonnen's soldiers were mixed in with their own Eritreans. General Albertone and his officers were already dead, slain by the splendid Gojam cavalry of Tekla-Haymanot. Baratieri galloped to the front at 9:15. Half an hour later, believing that Dabormida had moved left well in advance of Arimondi and made contact with Albertone, the commander ordered Dabormida to cover the retreat of the left column. But by then Dabormida's column, more than three miles from Arimondi's desperately engaged troops, had marched into a valley some two miles long and less than eight hundred yards wide. Within minutes they were at the center of the fatal swirling motion of the Ethiopian war machine, with Ras Mikail's Oromo cavalry whirring around them shouting their ultimate cry—*"Ebalgume! Ebalgume!"* ("Reap! Reap!"). General Dabormida's remains were never found. Months later, an old Ethiopian woman told General Arimondi's captured brother that she had given water to a mortally wounded Italian, "a chief, a great man with spectacles, and a watch, and golden stars."

Somehow Arimondi's center continued to hold. It fought with superb tenacity, repelling waves of Makonnen's Harar and Alula's Tigre regulars. At 10:30, the time of maximum engagement, Colonel Galliano's men broke just as two companies of elite Bersaglieri arrived. The Bersaglieri were annihilated. By noon, Baratieri's army was in headlong flight to Asmara, Adi Ugri, and other fortified places. Ras Alula and Ras Mangasha pleaded with Menilek for an order to set the cavalry upon the broken Italian mass as it bruised, bumped, and cartwheeled its way down from Adwa. Menilek refused, claiming a shortage of cavalry horses. The real reason, however, was his farsighted certainty that total annihilation of Baratieri and a sweep into Eritrea would force the Italian people to turn a bungled colonial war into a national crusade. With forty-three percent of the enemy dead, wounded, or missing, the Ethiopian empire had done well enough for one day.

For the white world, despite scattered predictions of Italian disaster, Adwa was an immense surprise, if not a bewildering shock. Each European Power had had its embarrassments, but an entire army had never been wiped out. "The suggestion has been made —absurd as it appears at present—that this is the first revolt of the Dark Continent against domineering Europe," the British authority George Fitz-Hardinge Berkeley mused in his book *The Campaign of Adowa and the Rise of Menelik* (1902). The formerly snide *Times* of London, which had amused its readers at the expense of the "barbarians of Abyssinia," made an about-face within hours after news of Adwa, deploring the cultural blinders that had caused the Italians so badly to miscalculate their formidable adversary.

The French newspaper *La Liberté* reflected the surprised conclusions of the Quai d'Orsay, editorializing that "all European countries will be obliged to make a place for this new brother who steps forth ready to play, in the Dark Continent, the role of Japan in the Far East." "We accept most willingly the propositions that your Majesty has made based on the independence of the empire," President Félix Faure found it appropriate to reply to Menilek after nearly two years of official silence. "Neighbors of Ethiopia through our possessions, we desire only the closest entente and the development of friendly relations and commerce." The Red Sea was soon to be filled with delegations from London, Paris, Rome, St. Petersburg, Austria-Hungary, and Greece, all headed for the Ethiopian highlands.

3

Adwa was a fateful paradox, for in saving themselves, the Ethiopians precipitated the European onslaught that would otherwise have been delayed for perhaps as long as two years. The sole possibility for much of East Africa to remain African depended on what arms, internal strength, and collaboration could be mustered in the short time remaining before France and Britain fought their way into the Nile basin. Adwa erased those hypothetical two years. France's final approval of Marchand's Congo-Nile mission followed soon thereafter.

For Menilek a period of grave danger began, less clear-cut than the recent Italian peril but potentially as fatal. Having been wise enough to avoid humiliating the Italians into continuing the war, he now had to use the other European Powers to Ethiopia's advantage, deceiving, manipulating, and cynically collaborating with them in order to save his empire.

His first diplomatic move was a message to the khalifa, five weeks after Adwa. *La Tribuna* reported the communiqué as saying, "I have beaten the Italians at Adwa, it is now your turn to conquer them at Kassala." If the Italian newspaper's translation was freewheeling, it nevertheless conveyed the gist of things. There had been a Mahdist attack on Sabderat, southeast of Kassala, just before Adwa, followed immediately by increased activity nearer Kassala. The khalifa had listened sympathetically to Menilek's messenger and signalled a willingness to hear more, but there was still no firm alliance in June when the emperor hurried another emissary to Omdurman. The khalifa's oldest son threw his support behind an Ethiopian compact, but it was only in September, after the Anglo-Egyptian army stormed into Dongola below the first bend in the Nile, that the pro-Ethiopian voices in Omdurman were given a fuller hearing.

Ten days after Dongola, the able Muhammad 'Uthman al-Hadj Khaled departed Omdurman by way of al-Qallabāt bearing Abdullahi's written proposals, as well as the indispensable oral message. This message must have proposed a period of trial detente and trade, for both began soon after Muhammad's return to Omdurman. But even though the khalifa's written demands omitted the usual call to conversion, they were still unacceptable. "As regards your desire for the conclusion of peace between us and you," Menilek read,

> be it known unto you that there is no incentive to any European to come to our Islamic territories for the profession of buying and selling, or on the pretext of travelling. There is only war between Us and them. If you are thus and you forbid all Europeans to enter your country, except in war, so that there is no connection between you and them, as it is with Us, on this condition peace may be concluded between Us and you.

"Menilek said that he had no intercourse with Europeans except for trade, which was necessary for the good of the Country," Muhammad 'Uthman reported. "To close that would be hard on both sides, but harder on the Ethiopians." It would take another eight months before the two African nations were ready for a treaty. By then, Menilek would be awash in treaties and informal understandings unleashed by Adwa.

Negotiations with Italy came to a head quickly. With eight hundred of its nearly naked, badly nourished officers and men building roads and repairing churches, some of them castrated and many others suffering from gangrenous wounds, the new government at Rome wanted only the quickest, least disgraceful terms possible. The Treaty of Addis Ababa was signed on October 26, 1896. Article II annulled the Treaty of Wichale. Article V put in a perpetual Ethiopian claim to Eritrea: "In the case where the Government of Italy should wish to abandon, by its own decision, a portion of territory in its possession, it will return it to Ethiopia." Under the fancy superintendence of Captain Ciccodiocola, a large, lavishly provisioned embassy was established by Italy in the Ethiopian capital.

The French were the first to test Menilek's alertness, with an embassy and two missions arriving in Addis Ababa within days of each other. A third mission, to be led by Captain Clochette, was even then assembling in the Ethiopian capital. After many delays and false starts, Paris was finally mobilizing for its Atlantic-Red Sea gambit. The abating of the ministerial round-robin helped. From the end of April 1896 until mid-June 1898, Prime Minister Jules Méline would occupy the Matignon Palace and André Lebon would direct colonial matters from the Pavillon de Flore.

Colonial Minister Lebon was a man of considerable culture and a republican elitist resolved to promote overseas expansion irrespective of public opinion. When policies had to be carried out vigorously, Lebon was the sort of minister able to bring more concentration and less conscience to his task than most of the anonymous, compromising politicians who participated in the usually meaningless exchanges of portfolios. It was Lebon's orders to Devil's Island that transformed Alfred Dreyfus's rough but sympathetic custodians into fierce tormentors.

Before Lebon became minister of colonies, the thrust from Ethiopia had been an idea without effective sponsorship or money. Prince Henri d'Orléans recalled that Parfait-Louis Monteil had been the first to broach the Congo-Nile pincer idea in May 1894, after an explorers' banquet in Paris. "Do you know what we should do? Two French columns, one of them starting from the Congo and the other from Abyssinia, would push toward the center of Africa. Would you lead the second?" Monteil asked excitedly. Delcassé, then master of colonial affairs, had felt obliged to be appalled by the prospect of the Pretender to the Throne serving the Republic officially.

Lebon, less the republican purist, seems not to have disapproved, so long as the Orléans prince was willing to finance the expedition himself. With the minister's covert blessings Henri d'Orléans set out for Ethiopia with a fellow prince and several counts under a plausible cover, disembarking at Djibouti in late February 1897. Meanwhile, ignoring the nervousness of his colleague Hanotaux, Lebon telegraphed precise instructions to Djibouti in mid-December about the two official missions, instructions intended to assure the arrival of supporting French and Ethiopian forces on the Nile well in advance of Marchand. Captain Clochette was to head for the Sobat River and the Nile as soon as possible. "He will be followed shortly by M. de Bonchamps, who leaves Paris at the end of January 1897. Without involving yourself in the actual direction of these missions," the cable continued, "you should extend them effective assistance." The man upon whose skill and energy the success of the missions depended was the thirty-six-year-old governor of French Somalia and minister to Ethiopia, Léonce Lagarde, a grandly self-possessed, intensely political, well-connected descendant of the signer of the 1848 friendship treaty between France and Ethiopia. Not only would Lagarde involve himself in the "actual direction of these missions," he would try to take complete control—especially as two powerful rivals, the Marquis Christian de Bonchamps and Charles Bonvalot, threatened to upstage the ambitious young diplomat.

Lagarde spent funds lavishly on camels, mules, drivers, and supplies. Leontiev, also at Djibouti and happy to be of service to the governor, paid for more pack animals to transport his own caravan, which was to follow Lagarde's. When Bonvalot and de Bonchamps arrived, they found the price of scarce animals and good drivers tremendously inflated, thanks to Lagarde and Leontiev. Lagarde was also profligate with promises. At Harar, where Ras Makonnen ordered a twenty-one-gun salute with captured Italian artillery, the minister offered thirty thousand Gras rifles and a quantity of Lebel machine guns. Before the year ended, nearly one hundred thousand rifles and two million rounds of ammunition came from France, but the government thought better of the machine guns.

In early March 1897, forty days after leaving Djibouti, Ambassador Lagarde arrived at Addis Ababa. Menilek was not happy to see him, and France's informal representative on the scene, ex-newspaperman Casimir Mondon-Vidailhet, had sent word that Lagarde might consider delaying his trip. Not only had Lagarde virtually invited himself, but the emperor had heard suspicious things about friendly dealings between Lagarde and General Baratieri. And even as Menilek disposed himself to lay on the appropriate ceremony, his intelligence service reported the movements of a second caravan of Frenchmen (carrying Bonvalot and de Bonchamps) only a few mountains behind the ambassador. Presently came news of a third—Prince Henri's on its way across the Danakil. Menilek wondered if the French were not going to be more of a problem than the Italians. Yet the apparently warm relationship that sprang up over the next few weeks between the emperor and France's minister was a masterpiece of lopsided deception. Lagarde's instructions, in any case, ordered him to give up a great deal in order to buy Menilek's cooperation. The mountain kingdom held one of the keys to open the Nile basin, not to mention the key to a brilliant coup for Lebon. Lagarde sought to deceive Menilek, but the Ethiopian ruler fully succeeded in beguiling the vain, inexperienced Frenchman.

Paris expected quick work from Lagarde. Ethiopians were needed on the Nile as soon as possible. Marchand was mistakenly believed to be within weeks of his destination. On March 14, Lebon telegraphed Djibouti, "Arrival on the Bahr al-Ghazāl appears imminent, if it has not already happened." Lagarde was told that it was indispensable for the Negus Negusti to "push his frontier line to the right bank of the Nile." The emperor was amused to learn that France wanted Ethiopia to reclaim and extend its ancient frontiers, from Lado in the south as far north as within two hundred miles of Omdurman and Khartoum. But Menilek was much more interested in acquiring rights in another direction—northeast toward Djibouti. The emperor pressed hard for as much of French Somalia as he could get. The Convention Relative to the Frontier of the French Coastal Zone, signed on March 2, gave him most of what he desired. France recognized the Solomonic kingdom's territorial integrity; in return, Menilek gave France most-favored-nation rights. Menilek also granted a railroad concession to French business interests, to be managed by his reliable Swiss technical advisor, Alfred Ilg, and to run from Djibouti to Addis Ababa. That same Saturday, Lagarde telegraphed Lebon details of another agreement—the White Nile Convention—intended to bind Ethiopia to active support of French moves in the Bahr al-Ghazāl. Because the White Nile Convention was secret, moreover, the emperor was willing to claim the southern Sudan and encourage the French, while waiting for a delegation from the khalifa in order to talk out the final terms of the treaty with Sudan.

Lagarde considered his mission a great success. Menilek even seemed to be genuinely fond of him. He was granted ready access to the imperial *gebi,* invited to participate in matters of state, encouraged to gossip over curried lamb and *t'ej* about politicians in Paris. Leontiev, who was so usefully influential in Russia, also seemed fond of Lagarde, and so Menilek seemed even more disposed to cultivate the Frenchman. Upon both men, the emperor

bestowed titles—duke of Entoto for Lagarde, count for Leontiev—
and was pleased to see the gravity the honor inspired in the egotisti-
cal ambassador. France's minister was now an Ethiopian peer, a
valued counsellor, and, so Lagarde believed, knowledgeable
enough of the ways and thoughts of Menilek to control him—just
the effect Menilek intended. With the pro-French engineer Ilg a
counsellor of state and charged with building the railroad, and two
other Frenchmen, Chefneux and Casimir Mondon-Vidailhet, also
promoted to positions of imperial privilege, the ambassador's self-
congratulatory dispatches depicting Ethiopia as a virtual French
satellite were convincing. Cautious Gabriel Hanotaux was still
doubtful, however. What he had been told by members of Czar
Nicholas's entourage the previous summer about Leontiev's chica-
nery left him deeply troubled. Experience and instinct warned the
foreign minister that the mountain kingdom held unpleasant surprises.

One of these surprises came just as Hanotaux and Lebon were
minuting Lagarde's dispatches. Only a few days after signing the
two French conventions, the emperor learned that the British were
coming. The cream of Her Majesty's junior officers vied for service
with Lieutenant Colonel Francis Wingate in Egypt. Wingate's intelligence service had carefully monitored developments between
Sudan and Ethiopia. The overbearing de facto ruler of Egypt, Evelyn Baring, now Earl of Cromer, pondering Wingate's information
with mounting concern at Cairo, decided to send his second-in-
command on a flying mission to Addis Ababa. Sir Rennell Rodd, the
smoothest of diplomats and a professional soldier, was told to offer
Menilek two options. The Negus Negusti could either become an
ally of Great Britain against France, or remain neutral. Her Majesty's government was "prepared to use its good offices to secure
some suitable territorial compensation for Abyssinia [Ethiopia]" if
the negus behaved himself. With the Italian ally trembling for the
security of Eritrea and frantic to abandon Kassala, London was truly
alarmed by the danger of France's Atlantic–Red Sea strategy.

Rodd chose his Ethiopian team with the flair of a theatrical im-
presario and the care of an Oxford don. Among them was Wingate's
accomplished subaltern, Captain Edward Gleichen, whose 1899
Handbook of the Sudan would remain the country's Baedeker until
recent years. Captain H. G. Swayne was a Somalia expert, as was
Captain T. Speedy of the Amharic language. Some were outstanding in size as well: several were over six feet tall.

The entire crew arrived at Zeila in British Somalia, just down the coast from Djibouti, on March 20. Despite "a touch of fever" that made him fear a flare-up of malaria, Rodd led his caravan of 115 straightaway into the desert for Harar. Passing a Russian Red Cross convoy of released Italian prisoners heading for the coast, the British learned of terrible Italian sufferings, especially at the hands of Ethiopian peasant women. An artillery officer described to Rodd how they had walked without boots more than five hundred miles, from Adwa through Addis, with scores of men stoned, beaten, and dropping to die. The officer himself had "sold his shirt for a chicken." But he praised Menilek's treatment and that of Ras Makonnen, "who had saved the lives of many Italians."

Leaving the 130-degree heat of the Danakil, Rodd's people were met at fifty-eight hundred feet by a "fantastic procession" of horn-blowing soldiers, clad in the regulation white *tobe* (a togalike garment) and commanded by one of Ras Makonnen's vassals, gorgeously arrayed in purple silk and crimson cloak, who escorted them to Harar. The Englishman was impressed by Makonnen's "alert and intelligent" face, and he found the governor's manner "quiet, cordial, and dignified." But Captain Speedy warned Rodd that accepting Makonnen's elaborate hospitality could easily bog the mission down in Harar. The British camped outside the picturesque white city. Then, cordially saluting two of Prince Henri d'Orléans's blue-blooded companions, who had preferred to fall back to hunt rather than dabble in politics in Addis Ababa, they reached the capital's outskirts, where, on April 25, they were greeted by a frock-coated delegation of Europeans headed by Counsellor of State Ilg. The formal reception by the emperor was set for the twenty-eighth.

Lagarde had left the scene two weeks earlier, not wishing to risk the dignity of France in competition with crimson uniforms and booted heel clicking. He was even more skittish about meeting the mission led by his own countrymen Bonvalot and de Bonchamps. The day before they were to arrive, Lagarde sent Captain Clochette a message from Djibouti, stressing the epic importance of the race to Fashoda and ordering him to leave Addis Ababa for the city of Goré. Captain Clochette, kicked in the side by a mule and suffered from a damaged liver, should have left instead for medical attention in Paris, but the officer was a pious patriot, and he dutifully obeyed. "He's gone that way, several days ago—toward the Nile," was all Casimir Mondon-Vidailhet would say to Bonvalot and de Bonchamps when they arrived. Prince Henri and his titled associates showed up to add to the confusion and the scarcely concealed amusement of Menilek. The Pretender had apparently begun to look upon Ethiopia as a business venture, especially after Leontiev told him about the riches of the south. Collaboration between the two missions vanished at the first moment of encounter. It was at just this moment that Rennell Rodd's delegation appeared.

Rodd's show was stunning, and all of Addis Ababa turned out for the official reception. Conducted to the *gebi* by the lord chief justice, Rodd, in a whirl of braid, sashes, and saber clanking, led his party of outsized Britons (some in bearskin helmets) and turbaned Sikhs through rows of warriors down the long aisle to the elevated throne where Menilek, in a purple cloak of silk displaying the Legion of Honor and the Russian Order of Saint Catherine, regally received them and inquired of Queen Victoria's health. The great Amhara nobles and the lords of the Coptic church formed ranks to the left of the throne, while Ilg, Prince Henri, Bonvalot and de Bonchamps, Chefneux, Mondon-Vidailhet, Leontiev and his cossacks, the Italians, the Austrians, and the Greeks, pomaded and starched, stood to the right. Rodd judged "the effect produced on the spectators" to have been "profound." Seeing how impressed Menilek and his nobles were, the French sulked, and Prince Henri wrote superciliously of Rodd's giants and their "less-than-successful" mission in *Le Temps* and the *New York Herald*.

In reality, Menilek was less impressed by the parade-ground spiffiness or the gift of an ornate, slightly dented silver plate (retrieved from a crevasse where a camel had fallen) than he was by the mission's no-nonsense proposals and the logic of British noninvolvement in Ethiopia. Whereas the French needed an Ethiopia fully engaged in and, ultimately, obedient to their African undertakings—and no doubt eventually reduced to protectorate status—the British were far more likely to live with an independent, neutral Ethiopia. France wanted Ethiopian armies streaming from the highlands into the Nile watershed; and if the khalifa proved to be a better Muslim than a diplomat, France obviously expected the Ethiopians to carve out and hand over a portion of the Bahr al-Ghazāl. Seemingly relaxed, inquisitive, and confiding, Menilek was in fact spinning out in his mind a politics for all comers and for all seasons.

The French and Russians, meanwhile, were reassured as to Menilek's admiration. The Russian Red Cross unit had established hospitals in Harar and Addis shortly after Adwa; the emperor and Ras

Makonnen genuinely respected its achievements. More Russians, a large diplomatic mission, were expected to reach Ethiopia toward the end of the year. French technical assistance had equipped and trained the army, established a postal system, and, under the direction of Mondon-Vidailhet, set up a newspaper. The capital for the railroad would come from them as well. Lagarde's and Leontiev's people were clearly as necessary as they might be dangerous to the kingdom's future, and the emperor unambiguously emphasized this point to one of the Italians: "If Europeans come into our house to bring us civilization, we thank them very much, but they must bring it without us losing our sovereignty." For the present, however, Menilek continued to flatter his allies, as he always did so expertly, in relaxed intimate smokers where talk was endlessly interesting and wide ranging. The cynical, well-travelled Prince Henri was captivated. According to some he reported Menilek was a genius "who must have come from heaven." For others, "he was just a barefoot nigger. But the admirers who seem to whip up flattery are nearer the truth than those who denigrate."

The British also had to guard against their host's charm. "His energy was astonishing," Rodd gasped. Menilek disdained pretense; protocol was never allowed to get in the way of essentials. He "wasted no time on phrases." Rodd formed "a high opinion both of his intelligence and of his character," but he was especially drawn by Menilek's "human side." The emperor, for example, was genuinely perplexed by his own occasional healing powers, the legendary thaumaturgy possessed by kings. "A man who was bitten by a snake would come to see him to be touched." He wondered of Rodd's medical officer how that man, "thus touched, frequently recovered." He was inclined to agree with the Englishman that the explanation must be the power of suggestion and great faith.

The negotiations, which went on over a two-week period, turned out to be the most demanding foreign service experience of Rodd's career. Menilek led the British to believe that Ethiopia was wholly contented with her Franco-Russian allies, that there was little Britain could offer to offset the relationship. When Rodd reminded the emperor during the first of their four meetings that the Hewett Treaty bound Ethiopia to refer all disputes with Egypt to Britain, Menilek replied that that treaty had been annulled when the Italians landed at Massawa. At their second meeting, Menilek dismissed Rodd's worries about Clochette's whereabouts and intentions ("only a sporting expedition") and shook the Englishman with the announcement that Ethiopia, in reclaiming her ancient boundaries, wanted half of British Somalia—after all, he exclaimed, "you are advancing right up to the gates of Harar!" The Somalis, moreover, had, since time immemorial, been but the "cattle keepers of the Ethiopians."

A third conference roughed out the treaty terms. Rodd decided to drop completely the question of Ethiopia's western frontiers (those frontiers the French had already secretly pushed to the Nile), proposing mutual acceptance of the status quo instead, "pending the final settlement." After much wrangling, Britain was also granted most-favored-nation rights and Ethiopia formally excused from recognizing the Anglo-Italian treaty of 1891, giving Italy certain claims in the Sudan. Trade between Zeila and Harar reopened and Menilek was granted the right to ship firearms. Article VI, the final article, promised that Menilek would prevent arms shipments to the khalifa. Article II agreed that Rodd and Menilek would accept whatever final demarcation line between Ethiopia and British Somalia would be subsequently decided at Harar. The final text (subject to the Somali border question) was signed on May 14, 1897. Menilek insisted on having its six articles reduced to simple declaratory sentences, all in the present tense, and a French translation made of the Amharic and English texts that was to be the final word in all disputes. Rennell Rodd then presented the emperor with a suitable decoration. Presents to Queen Victoria from Empress Taitu and Menilek were presented in turn.

As the ceremony closed, Rodd asked for a private audience. What was said has never been revealed, but the Englishman wrote suggestively twenty-five years later of having the "satisfaction of realizing that more had been accomplished by the mission than might appear from any concrete results recorded in a treaty." Certainly, Menilek was told of Lord Salisbury's promise of compensation for Ethiopian neutrality. And in all probability Menilek gave his word that, whatever the appearances, Ethiopia would distance itself from France. Menilek knew that he was buying the probable survival of the Kingdom of Solomon. Three weeks later, after the weary, exasperated Rodd threatened to decamp from Harar and scuttle the treaty, Ras Makonnen relented on his demands for half of British Somalia, settling for a hefty third.

The emperor had turned his full attention, meanwhile, to manipulating the troublesome French; it was Ethiopia's luck that they were remarkably willing to be deceived. Instead of displaying

the keen, accomplished negotiating skills for which they were notorious in Europe, they seized upon flimsy signs of Ethiopian fidelity
—such as Menilek's supposed handshake with all members of Lagarde's arriving delegation, as opposed to with only of some of the
British. They discounted disturbing symbolic portents, including
the most elaborate ceremony in Ethiopian memory to honor the
departing British. They uncritically reprinted Counsellor of State
Ilg's reassuring letter from the *Gazette de Zürich,* stating that
Rodd's delegation "had not had all the success that it should have
desired." Although Ilg worked closely with French interests, most
of his adult life had been spent in Ethiopia; his highest loyalty was
to the man who could make his fortune, Menilek. The French
disbelieved, discounted, and distorted so much because, above all,
they were incapable, even after Adwa, of crediting the warrior-
ruler, who was nonetheless hurrying his country into the modern
age, with the complicated intelligence and Bismarckian subtlety
necessary to make fools of them. They were soon to pay for their
blindness.

The dutiful, suffering Captain Clochette, whom Lagarde had
pushed out of Addis Ababa for Goré just before Bonvalot and de
Bonchamps's arrival, was the first victim. His reserve strength was
almost spent when he and his force of two hundred Ethiopians and
two French ex-NCOs reached Goré, after weeks of icy rains. From
Goré, with new instructions from Addis Ababa, Clochette was to
leave the highlands for the Baro River, following it into the Sudan
to its juncture with the Sobat River. Another week of travel would
then bring him to Fashoda. But Clochette's agony from his damaged liver was extreme, and he was increasingly unable to keep his
food down. The plans of Prince Henri's and Bonvalot's mission in
the capital had also begun to unravel. Before returning to Djibouti,
Lagarde had made it clear to Menilek that Henri d'Orléans and his
titled friends were neither official representatives of the French
Republic nor people in whom he had the slightest confidence. Sensing quickly that his gamble to play a role adding luster to the House
of Orléans was blocked, and spurned by Bonvalot and de Bonchamps because of previous professional clashes, Prince Henri
turned back for the coast two weeks after Rodd's departure.

Meanwhile, Bonvalot and de Bonchamps were stuck. There was
no sign of the equipment they expected from Djibouti—especially
the aluminum boat needed on the Baro and Sobat rivers (Lagarde
had left the boat and the other crates on the shore). Menilek, always

affable and accessible, insisted that the anxious Frenchmen enjoy the city's hospitality, which was a bearable diversion during the round of festivities occasioned by British presence. But with Lebon's orders in his pouch, Clochette presumably approaching Goré, Marchand somewhere in Central Africa depending on them, and his own career on the line, Bonvalot's nerves were fraying. What motivated his decision at this point is a mystery. Menilek granted his request to leave on May 17 for the Sudan, but twenty-four hours before the men and camels were ready Bonvalot told his companions that he was returning to France. "Start ahead of me and carry on to the Nile," he ordered. "I'm going to get us two boats —two gunboats—and I'll catch up with you." But the emperor had handed the mission a rough map of the route it must take, a round-about trail some 370 miles to Goré—three times longer than Clochette's route. With so much apparently amiss—Lagarde's hostility, vital equipment stranded, an inadequate budget, Menilek's indirect road map—Bonvalot may have concluded that the safest place for his career was Paris. Either that, or Bonvalot self-sacrificingly concluded that so long as he was in command, Lagarde would strangle the life out of the mission. On May 17 he walked out of the race to Fashoda, never to be heard from again.

De Bonchamps took charge of the mission, with Charles Michel-Côte now second-in-command. Menilek generously provided nine camels and an escort to the frontier. Leontiev, then Monsieur Ilg and his Swiss bride, gave de Bonchamps, Michel-Côte, the artist Maurice Potter, and mining engineer Léon Bartholin a lavish send-off. "All Addis Ababa in our honor," Michel-Côte gloated. After a few days on the mountain trails, the boring, pretentious Ethiopian capital must have seemed glorious. The rain began to fall like stalac-tites. "In another season, this six-hundred-kilometre trail would have been delightful," moaned Michel-Côte. They staggered on through forty-two days of torrent. Two of the camels died and several became useless. Their loads had to be transferred to the backs of Ethiopian escorts. Desertions began. And the Ethiopian guides refused to allow the mission to take shortcuts or make what little speedy headway it could, repeating over and again: "You must not take the same trail as the other white [Clochette], for you must reach Goré after him." Michel-Côte blamed Lagarde for the mission's misery. Menilek "had no wish to go against the wishes of our ambassador, even on so minor a matter," he wrote three years later. Three-quarters of a century would pass before a French scholar looked elsewhere for the blame. Lagarde wanted Clochette to have pride of place in the Fashoda race, but it was Menilek who enforced the conditions Lagarde desired. The Marquis de Bonchamps and Michel-Côte never knew that Lagarde's orders came from Menilek, or that the emperor, far more resolutely than the French ambassador, intended to delay the two missions from joining until both had been exhausted.

When de Bonchamps's men straggled into Goré on June 29, spirits as waterlogged as the sodden plateau stretching before them, they found Clochette shivering his last in a soaked tent. "The altitude and humidity are killing me! And you can see it—rain, mud, icy winds, that's my lot. I need sea air; I need warmth!" On their way to Goré, de Bonchamps's caravan had received a message from the governor of the province, Ras Tassama, suggesting that, "for friendship's sake," the marquis "await my return from Addis Ababa or, if I fail to return, a second letter from the Emperor." Three long weeks passed before Menilek's letter came permitting them to limp on to the Sudan, still without ammunition, photographic instruments, or the other equipment from Djibouti. Desertions reduced the French to eleven Ethiopians—"eleven men for six thousand kilos!" On July 27, de Bonchamps sent a courier to Addis Ababa bearing an angry cable for Paris about the Ethiopians "cowardly abandoning me." The local *fituari* (baron) speedily improved the Frenchmen's plight. Five of the supposed ringleaders responsible for desertions were dismissed, de Bonchamps was told he could reduce wages to five Maria Theresa dollars, and a mysterious contingent of new porters presented themselves, each bearing the ritual rock against the neck. On August 5, de Bonchamps folded tents and began the steep descent out of the highland rains into the warm land of the Baro. In ten days, Clochette was dead.

Twenty-six days later and but a gallop from the frontier, Michel-Côte, leading the advance party, was ordered to halt. "No Frenchmen are to go beyond this point!" an Ethiopian rider shouted, the order enforced by two thousand crack troops encamped at the frontier. The Frenchman galloped back to a place called Burei to confer with de Bonchamps and the others. Every other village along their route had been a test of diplomacy. Since Goré, especially, it seemed that every official, as well as every guide, had sworn to outdo the other in polite obduracy and maddening incomprehension of de Bonchamps's purpose. The French were certain that if Menilek knew how shabbily and stupidly these local potentates

were behaving, he would angrily put a stop to it. Michel-Côte and
Bartholin, mapless and virtually unescorted, raced almost three
hundred miles back to Addis Ababa. They reached the city in half
the best time—twenty-three instead of forty-seven days—despite
the rains. Menilek saw them on September 27, deplored the hap-
penings at the Sudanese border, but explained that he preferred to
await the arrival of Ambassador Lagarde, now minister plenipotentiary, from Djibouti before issuing new commands. When Lagarde
rode into the capital on October 3, Michel-Côte was nearly prostrate from anxiety. His friends were within three hundred miles of
the Nile basin; the scramble for Fashoda seemed all but decided in
favor of Marchand and France. Yet here he was, six hundred miles
later, at the starting point awaiting orders intended to clarify earlier
orders—while Kitchener's Anglo-Egyptian army was probably
marching from one victory to the next. The breakfast palaver on
Lagarde's first morning was explosive. Ilg, Mondon-Vidailhet, and
the painter Buffet agreed with the ambassador that Bonvalot was
the cause of the problems. "You were tainted with original sin,"
Lagarde magisterially proclaimed, referring to his departed rival,
"and you would never have got there. But now you have me!"
Mondon-Vidailhet soothingly explained that Menilek's orders were
"like a stone dropped into a pond—large waves near the stone, but
farther out, the water barely ripples."

Menilek's new orders, addressed to Ras Tassama, seemed to cover
every contingency, listing by name and title virtually every imperial
official de Bonchamps's caravan would encounter, as well as the
nature of the help to be provided. "In order that these gentlemen
can leave quickly, orders must be given that they are not to be
hindered if they need to buy mules and camels," they commanded.
Michel-Côte was given a copy of Tassama's orders for de Bonchamps, with Menilek's reassuring note that all was arranged "in
order to assist you with everything you need." Lagarde also had new
instructions for de Bonchamps: "The Minister of Colonies has decided that I shall take general direction of your mission." There were
to be no more telegrams, dispatches, and letters to Lebon. Everything, henceforth, was to flow through Léonce Lagarde—a traffic as
significant to the minister plenipotentiary as that on the Upper Nile.
Now that he had won the politics of the thrust from the Red Sea, he
was even generous enough to detach ten of the sixty-nine Senegalese and two camels with drivers from his escort.

But then Menilek, working at a distance through Lagarde, played the French a final, fatal trick. "The Emperor suggests taking the route along the left bank of the Sobat until its junction [with the Nile]," read Lagarde's new orders to de Bonchamps. The French were to build and garrison a fortress on the left bank of the Nile; Ethiopian forces, approaching from the right bank, would erect and occupy a second. "Whatever develops," ordered Lagarde, "there must be two solid forts." "This is crazy!" Michel-Côte thought to himself, but getting back to Burei to help de Bonchamps was what counted most. Leaving Addis Ababa on Tuesday morning, October 12, Michel-Côte remembered thinking, "We're going to have to count on luck alone." Months later, the impracticality of the new route would become apparent. Instead of heading through the marshy country in a fairly straight line for Fashoda, the trail kept the French seventy-five miles upriver from Marchand's destination, and drew them into the most debilitating wastes of the Sudan.

During all this—Michel-Côte's frantic, exhausting efforts, the writing of new orders for de Bonchamps—the Negus Negusti was quietly effecting a rapprochement with the khalifa. Soon after, Menilek would flatter the enormous vanity of "our superior, venerable, dearly beloved Khalifa al-Mahdi Abdullahi" in two letters accompanying a courier who carried the oral terms of the pact between the two powers. It was never a precise pact, and neither side ever fully agreed to (or fulfilled) the other's terms. Broadly, it called for the return of Ethiopian prisoners (many captured near Gondar ten years before) along with the ancient imperial crown taken from Yohannes's corpse. Trade was to continue. The Mahdiyya drew back from long-contested lands in the western regions known as the Bani Shangul, and Ethiopia vowed to prevent Europeans from invading Sudan through its territory. The great nobles —Makonnen, Mangasha, Tassama, and others—were told to send disingenuous protests of affection and brotherhood to Omdurman. It was certainly understandable that the khalifa needed reassuring, because three Ethiopian army corps were maneuvering on the Sudan border. Forces under Ras Makonnen had already made a lightning strike along the Blue Nile into the Bani Shangul. Makonnen's secret instructions were to occupy the entire region, if he heard the British had captured the city of Berber on the White Nile. Herbert Kitchener had not yet done so, and the Ethiopians dutifully withdrew. They had come to punish and not to stay, Menilek swore to Abdullahi, and "if any reports which he might hear [are] different from this statement, he must not believe them, but trust in their mutual friendship."

The huge Ethiopian maneuvers were easily misrepresented to the French. From the Pavillon de Flore a highly secret cable was flashed to the commissioner general of the French Congo. Marchand and Liotard were to be forwarded the following information in the shortest time possible, and told to increase their pace: Menilek had mobilized three large army corps. "Negus Negusti awaits with impatience news that Liotard has reached the White Nile, he reiterates orders to his three army corps chiefs so as to bring them into contact with Liotard or his emissaries, if the latter have been able to cross to the right bank." Paris was under the illusion that forty thousand Amhara and Oromo warriors were operating near Lake Rudolph and along the Blue Nile so that France could reach and secure the Bahr al-Ghazāl.

By the end of 1897, Menilek had used French arms and Russian artillery instructors to pulverize the Italians at Adwa; agreed by secret treaty to aid France militarily in its Congo thrust (in return for arms and technical assistance); signed a treaty with the British secretly committing himself to neutrality in Anglo-French rivalry (in exchange for assurances of Ethiopian independence); and negotiated an alliance with the khalifa against Britain, France, and Belgium. But then, Menilek had given Europe fair warning of his duplicity in his 1891 "Circular to the Kings in Europe." He did not intend, he had announced, "to listen quietly when governments from distant lands say that they will divide up Africa."

Not many years after de Bonchamps and Michel-Côte resumed their dogged course for the Nile, the British ambassador to Ethiopia concluded that he had "not yet seen that any of us have what I could really call influence, i.e., influence that would make Menilek do what he did not want to do." By then, the French had suffered a diplomatic Adwa.

CHAPTER SIX

Khalifa, Khedive, and Kitchener

1

Bilad al-Sudan, the "land of the blacks," begins in desert, at Wadi Halfa, and ends in rain forest thirteen hundred miles south at Nimule. It is larger than Europe, more than one-fourth the land mass of the United States. Before conquest and commerce opened its northern regions to Islam, commingling its Negro peoples with Egyptians, Turks, Arabs, and Circassians, the Sudan had truly been a land of very black inhabitants. Animists whose gods took the forms of crocodiles, fish, and cattle, the original Sudanese were iron-age herdsmen and fishermen when the explorers and then the regiments of Egypt's conquering state-builder, Muhammad Ali, began their ascent of the Nile in the 1840s. Where the White Nile, the Bahr al-Jebel, ends its great crook far south of Khartoum at Malakal, the true blacks—the Nilotes—more or less successfully resisted the rapacious slaving of the Arabs. Even today, the language, religion, and customs of the conqueror from the north have spread only the thinnest veneer over Shilluks, Dinkas, Nuers, Luo, and Bari. The Nilotes found Mahdism both strange and unwelcome.

The Sudan of the Mahdiyya, like Africa under Europe, remained a world of divided, hostile, uncomprehending peoples. "Africa," it is still said in Khartoum, "begins at Malakal." But even diverse and divided, the khalifa's Sudan was yet far from weak. Since the death of the Mahdi, Muhammad Ahmad, in the summer of 1885, the Mahdiyya had been transformed into the largest, most militant, and most organized political entity ruled by Africans. The neighboring empire of Ethiopia, now swarming with courteous European diplomats, had spent a thousand years contracting, disintegrating, and reassembling to reach its standing under Menilek II as the premier power on the continent. The Sudanese, on the other hand, had taken less than two decades to transform their cultural and political heritage and make their debut on the world stage through a bloody declaration of independence and an astonishingly workable new political order. But no water or mountains buffered the Sudan. Instead, the Nile, ancient artery for much of the right half of Africa, was a channel of destruction and death. The Mahdiyya, like French Louisiana energized by the Mississippi, was a success story inviting destruction from those whom capital and technology equipped with overwhelming advantages. As the saying goes, "When Allah created the Sudan, he laughed."

The Mahdiyya's assets and shortcomings depended on the strengths and weaknesses of its ruler; they were made possible, in large part, by the force of the leaders' personalities. Not long before he was stricken with typhus, Muhammad Ahmad had issued a proclamation ordaining Abdullahi as his successor—his principal khalifa: "He is of me, and I of him. Behave with all reverence to him, as you do to me; submit to him as you submit to me, and believe in him as you believe in me; rely on all he says, and never question any of his proceedings. All that he does is by order of the Prophet, or by my permission." When the khalifa emerged exhausted and exalted by his three-day vigil from the dead Mahdi's house, the will of the Prophet seemed as clear as the direction of Mecca. True, Abdullahi was expected to confer with the other two khalifas, Ahmad Wad Ali and Ahmad Sharif, in matters of great importance. As well, the young sons of the Mahdi were expected by the faithful to play a role. But those were expectations Abdullahi did not share.

Increasingly, the khalifa gave the Sudan structure and order at the expense of participation and vitality. Barely literate, he had never read the Shar'ia and other commentaries upon the Qur'an familiar to the Mahdi; instead, he made of them an ostentatious bonfire early in his ministry. Where the Mahdi had known enough of the world beyond the Sudan to be serenely positive that his people lost nothing by being sealed off from it, the khalifa knew nothing of the things the Mahdi ordained there was no need to know. Muhammad Ahmad was like a learned European of the Middle Ages; Abdullahi like a prodigy of the Dark Ages.

After becoming master of the Sudan, he remained for a few years accessible and engaging. Rudolf Slatin, Gordon's captured Austrian officer, recounted being entertained by Abdullahi's lighthearted memories of the early days when he and the mahdi straggled across the Sudan teaching and gathering many disciples but few alms. It had been a privilege to bear Allah's "troubles and afflictions," Abdullahi said once, smiling as he added, "teaching won't bring us food for our women and children."

Abdullahi was about thirty when the Austrian first saw him. He had "a light brown complexion, a sympathetic Arab face, on which the marks of smallpox were still traceable, an aquiline nose, a well shaped mouth . . . and a row of glistening white teeth." In those days of somewhat theatrical simplicity, the khalifa still wore the *jibba*—the cotton shirt reaching below the knee and patched with squares of varying colors. He was about five feet eight inches tall and well-built. If, as Slatin found, Abdullahi "generally spoke with a smile," what he said was often unpleasant. Those who displeased him were either tortured to death in ingenious ways or, if they were unlucky, locked away with little food and water in the dreaded Sayir (the prison). As he aged, the khalifa became more erratic and vicious. Slatin, hostile witness that he was, had little need to exaggerate Abdullahi's sadism, especially his "principal delight" in separating children from mothers by scattering them in distant provinces. "He firmly believes that he is capable of doing anything and everything," Slatin decided.

It was his shorter, broad-shouldered half brother, Ya'qub, who nurtured the khalifa's suspicions and sudden condemnations. Persecution "originated in Ya'qub's head, who, on feeling that somebody was not going in the way he liked, used to go to his brother at night through the secret door." Having married his daughter to the khalifa's oldest son, the highly literate Ya'qub was the second most powerful man in the Mahdiyya, chancellor and commander of the fierce Black Flag division. Prodded by Ya'qub, the khalifa's insecurities about the haughty, cosmopolitan merchants, or *jallaba*, verged on paranoia.

The destruction of Khartoum was an extravagant example of the khalifa's blend of madness and method. The sixty-five-year-old city was looked upon by the Mahdists as the symbol of alien domination, a citadel of Egyptian power upheld by arrogant Europeans and Americans. After their conquest of the city in 1895, the Mahdi had elected not to reside in Khartoum, establishing instead a new capital just a few miles below the fork of the White and Blue Niles at a place he named Umm Durr (Omdurman, "place of pearls"). Khartoum continued to thrive, nevertheless, with its Egyptianized Sudanese officials and enterprising *jallaba* behaving much as they had during Gordon's overlordship. Frequently, the Mahdi had journeyed to Friday services in its Grand Mosque. But the khalifa simmered resentfully, his bile against Khartoum's *ashraf* (those who claimed descent from the Mahdi) steadily rising. In August 1888, he struck. The population was ordered to vacate in three days. "On the fourth day," according to a British report, the destruction of the town commenced. "Houses were pulled down, and balconies was transported to Omdurman where it [*sic*] was used in the construction of the Khalifa's house and other buildings."

The Mahdist slaughter of Hicks's army at El Obeid and the martyrdom of Gordon at Khartoum had rankled Queen Victoria's subjects deeply, and the mere existence of this belligerent brown and black state was a destabilizing affront to Europe. For British imperialists, it was an article of faith that this desert theocracy would weaken and collapse of its own internal woes. Yet there was worrisome evidence of irregular, often chaotic but nonetheless persistent economic growth, tying the Mahdiyya to Ethiopia and, in the long run, to the Arabian peninsula. Promoting the market economy of slaves and grain, gum and cloth of the riverine tribes was of utmost importance to the Mahdi.

In the first years of Khalifa Abdullahi's rule, a relative decline from the prosperity of the Mahdi's days came about. "At first, the khalifa was behaving very well as regards the kingdom," the Amir Yusuf Mikha'il recalled. "All the farmers were regularly paid. A *mujihad* (regular soldier) was paid ten piastres, his family five piastres." But Abdullahi's ignorance of, and even innate hostility to, commerce soon began to tell. He belonged to the nomadic, cattle-herding Baqqara people, who deeply resented the wealth and pretensions of the city-bred *jallaba*—especially of the shrewd Ja'ali people. Soon the outlying enclosed markets—the *zaribas*—of the traders were being abandoned, the grain from the countryside badly distributed, and the town markets becoming bereft of salt, dates, spun goods, as well as luxuries. Good coin was being driven out by bad, and prices and taxes were steadily rising. The famine of 1888 greatly compounded the misery. Colonel Wingate's intelligence provided abundant confirmation of British expectations.

But suddenly there was a flow of bad news for the British. Apparently discomfited by a near coup d'etat in 1891, led by one of his most respected colleagues, the Khalifa Ahmad Sharif, Abdullahi changed his course. He agreed to the demands of the conspirators, most of them reflecting the concerns of traders and city dwellers. Among other things, taxes on trading boats and camels were abolished, tithes of goods passing through Berber and Omdurman were lifted, and goods stored in the treasury were distributed. Also, the khalifa promised to end the virtual house arrest of the Mahdi's sons, and swore that Khalifa Ahmad Sharif and his followers were not to be molested. Even though Abdullahi threw Ahmad Sharif in prison a few days later (the Prophet Muhammad in a dream had commanded it), the pledges concerning taxes and levies stood. Wingate's department reported in April 1892 that "the general feeling is one of greater security, and of hope that this period of tranquility may last."

Sir Evelyn Baring must have winced upon reading General Archibald Hunter's sunny report of August 14 from the vital Suakin district. "It is too soon to speculate yet," the general advised, speculatively,

> but with the gradual disappearance of religious fanaticism as the source of power, with the establishment of practically a military despotism, with the revival of trade, and with the counsels of merchants receiving daily more attention, to the neglect of the more restless and ambitious fighters, it is not now, as was once supposed, beyond the range of possibility that the day may come when the earthly ruler at Omdurman may listen to a proposal to come to terms, if the Egyptian Government entertain such an idea.

It was true that Britain had compelled Egypt to withdraw from the Sudan. It was also true that, except when faced by French designs in the region, the British even spoke of having abandoned the Sudan. Furthermore, Gladstone, who had once spoken of the Sudanese as "a people struggling to be free, and rightly struggling to be free," had recently delivered another speech about the "burdensome and embarrassing" misfortune of British occupation of Egypt. But Evelyn Baring had his pince-nez focused on the near future of a Salisbury cabinet. The invasion of the Sudan might or might not be inevitable—France would help decide that—but encouraging a prosperous, ordered, powerful Sudan was, for Baring, a flagrantly un-British activity. By the Anglo-Italian Treaty of May 1894, Britain gave the Italians a green light to harass the Mahdiyya in the southeast.

By then, Abdullahi's days of *jibba*-wearing simplicity—days of dwelling, as the Mahdi had, in a simple clay hut and moving among his people as humble if undisputed master—were long past. On the spot where the Mahdi's house had stood, a temple was built housing Muhammad Ahmad's remains, its gleaming, cone-shaped dome visible above Omdurman for twenty miles. For himself, Abdullahi constructed a commodious, two-level house and an enclosed courtyard facing a gigantic field. Behind the house at a suitable distance were erected the prison, the treasury (Beit al-Mal), and the arsenal (Beit al-Amana) with facilities for the construction and repair of Nile gunboats. Several other dwellings went up for the family of the Mahdi and for the khalifa's most trusted people. After two years of construction, a high brick wall enclosed the new center of power.

The khalifa's methods consolidated power in a land where the unity of Islam was as much a cultural reality as it was a political fiction. A smuggled report detailed what was happening. "There are many able men and larger hands among the Ja'aliyyin and other tribes in the Sudan . . . and it requires a great ability to keep these people down and make them nil before a man whom they so bitterly despise." The khalifa's first impulse, passionately encouraged by the bitter 'Uthman Diqna and scheming Ya'qub, had been of world conquest. Where the Mahdi's surprising admonitions to the rulers of Egypt, Ethiopia, and Europe had called for spiritual surrender to Islam for the sake of their souls, the khalifa and 'Uthman Diqna warned them of physical destruction. "The children of Egypt shall be your slaves and their womenfolk your concubines," 'Uthman Diqna once charged his followers after a battle. "From Egypt we will conquer Europe, if such is God's will, as did Sayyid Oman of Zanzibar so many years ago."

'Uthman and Ya'qub, both men of some learning, had glorious if inaccurate memories of Islam's rampage to the tips of Mediterranean Europe. What had been done before could be repeated. For Abdullahi, Europe was a much vaguer entity whose wealth and technology he would never be able to comprehend. Exhilarated by Sheikh al-Zaki Tumal's victory over the Ethiopians at al-Qallabāt, he had served notice to the queen of England of the Mahdiyya's expansionist plans. "If you believe in our religion, and confess that there is no God but God, and that Muhammad is His Prophet," he wrote Victoria on April 6, 1889, "we shall receive you with the greatest hospitality; but if you refuse to obey our summons, then do not doubt that your sins, and the sins of your people, will be on your head, and that you will fall into our hands." He had then sent an army into Upper Egypt, where General Grenfell's British regulars managed to halt them near Wadi Halfa after a five-hour battle.

Eventually, the khalifa came to realize that neither Khedive Abbas of Egypt nor Queen Victoria was likely to enter the Sayir. Gradually, he moved to rationalize the Mahdiyya; and if religious fanaticism never moderated into what Europeans called realpolitik, the impulse of the *jihād* became slowly mated to the imperatives of statecraft. By the early 1890s, despite the savage campaign against the Nilotics, much of the state's energy was channelled into a program of reorganization. Over the eight provinces and territories of Dongola and Berber in the north, of East Sudan, Equatoria, Bahr al-Ghazāl, and Kassala in the south, and of Kordofan and Darfur in the west, Abdullahi appointed closely watched governors. In a gesture of rare liberalism, the khalifa decreed in summer 1889 that even the smaller and weaker clans should have their own amirs. The clerk and chronicler, Yusuf Mikha'il, who rose to amir as a result, said the honor was due to fear of a British invasion after the battle near Wadi Halfa.

Reports continued to filter into Wingate's intelligence department of plots against the khalifa, of mass arrests and exiles to Fashoda, and of cruel deaths of prisoners. The Sayir remained crowded, and a scowl from Ya'qub or a nightmare for Abdullahi could have terrible consequences. Yet it was undeniable that order and prosperity were increasing. A supreme court of ten *qadis,* or justices, strove to uphold the Qur'an and the regulations of the Mahdiyya. The court began to function too well, for the incorruptible chief *qadi* forfeited his life in the Sayir for decreeing that property unlawfully accumulated should revert to the rightful owners, rather than to the khalifa and Ya'qub.

The Beit al-Mal contained specialized departments such as those of the chancery, personal treasury, sales, slaves, and granary, each headed by an amir chosen for his ability. Mahdist mechanics repaired and rebuilt seven Nile steamers—vessels of capital importance for transport and policing the Sudan. Rifles were stored here, where they were supposed to be carefully maintained, along with the sizable stock of captured artillery pieces.

The command structure for the military was also carefully worked out. *Mulazimin* were Arabs, who amounted to more than sixty percent of the seventy-thousand-man army. The rest was comprised of Negro soldiers or *jihādiyya,* equipped with smooth-bore

guns. An elite guard of fifty Ta'isha, a cattle-herding Sudanese people, protected the khalifa, and soon grew into a small army itself.

Even Father Paolo Rossignoli, a captive Italian priest, conceded
Abdullahi's skill in running the Mahdiyya. Rossignoli marvelled at
the khalifa's delving "into all important questions," despite the gain
in weight and infrequent public appearances "owing to the comparatively luxurious life he leads at present. . . . He shows his tact
by knowing how to treat the different tribes in the Sudan so as to
keep them under his hand." Reports handed to Sir Evelyn Baring
at the end of 1892 and in the following August supported the
priest's assessment: "Now that the authority of his own tribe, the
Baqqaras, is undisputed . . . he is doing his utmost to establish a more
lenient and popular system of government, and his efforts are not
altogether unsuccessful."

But neither tact nor terror could solve the currency problems.
The old Egyptian specie was disappearing, and much that continued to circulate was badly defaced. Maria Theresa dollars from
Ethiopia, various reals and piastres, all circulated with bewildering,
generally declining, values—many not accepted at all in parts of the
Mahdiyya. Henceforth, all coins "must pass in all dealings without
raising the prices," the *ansār* were warned. "If anybody makes
objections henceforth as to obliterated coins, even if it was [only]
a piastre—all his property will be confiscated and he will be punished." Minting his own currency was intended to stabilize inflating
prices. Instead, the seething *jallaba* cursed the khalifa under their
breath for his Maqbul dollar, at best containing by early 1894 some
six parts copper to one part silver. Like the currencies of some more
recent African states, the Mahdiyya's would soon become dangerously devalued.

Despite the brutality with which he had realized his accomplish-
ments, the khalifa might have succeeded in transforming his varied
and feuding peoples into a nation—but for threats to the Mahdiyya
from beyond its borders and for his reactions to those threats. In the
best of times, Abdullahi was subject to xenophobic spasms. But it
was significant of the changing khalifa that his governors and notables persuaded him to reopen the trade routes slammed shut during the last months of 1892. Though surrounded by voluptuous
concubines and becoming fleshier by the month, Abdullahi was just
as prone to moderation as to excess. The years after 1893, however,
saw a slowing and then a reversal of his benignity. As Italian and
Belgian forces arrived at the Mahdiyya's borders, he reverted to the

passions and policies that had temporarily been mastered as his power became entrenched. There was the shocking outburst in the Grand Mosque in September 1893, when he taunted the assembled Ja'aliyyin in rhyming Arabic, "If you die, you go to hell, and if you live, you work like donkeys." Then the great wealth of Sheikh al-Zaki Tamal (including Emperor Yohannes's crown and throne), proved too tempting for the increasingly decadent, devious Ya'qub. Al-Zaki Tamal, the destroyer of Yohannes and the Shilluks, died of thirst in the Sayir. "After my death, you will try to find men like me to take my place," he calmly warned Ya'qub, "and you will not find them."

During the next year, the situation in Omdurman became both more despotic and more anarchic. The few remaining positions of trust were now filled by Ta'isha and other Baqqara. Unpaid *jihād-iyya* rampaged the city, pillaging houses, accosting merchants, forcing traders to pay protection, and occasionally killing. By the end of 1895, the virtual worthlessness of the Maqbul dollar had turned a one-dollar piece of *jibba* cloth into a twenty-five-dollar luxury. By September, Wingate's sources reported that "trade had almost stopped in Omdurman." The following year, the khalifa ruefully imposed another embargo on trade with Suakin after learning that Mahdiyya currency was being heavily discounted by merchants there. New dollars with more silver content were minted, but they were too few to restore confidence. The portly khalifa was losing his grip. Completion of the high wall girdling his house and the major government buildings was now an obsession, and a press gang of three thousand slaves labored furiously on it.

What had happened in the Mahdiyya—beyond the lethal self-inflicted wounds—was invasion. Friction on the Ethiopian frontier had subsided, but the moves of the new emperor, Menilek, were watched from Omdurman with unflagging suspicion. In the west, there was a new threat from a rebellious Mahdist named Rabih ibn-Fadlallah, the adopted son of al-Zubayr Rahma Mansur, the conqueror of Darfur, whose slave empire had earned him the khedive's enmity and permanent house arrest in Cairo. Annoyed by Gordon, Rabih had finally vanished into the interior with less than a thousand followers. Probably secretly in touch with al-Zubayr (who never believed in the Mahdi's *baraka*), fending off the encroaching Belgians, and flirting with the advancing French, Rabih was a mysterious, magnetic sultan building an empire doomed to be overtaken by history. In 1893, however, having conquered the Dar Fertit region between Chad and the Bahr al-Ghazāl, Rabih's armies were pressing upon the outer flanges of the Mahdiyya. One of the khalifa's all-too-typical rages had caused several thousand veteran *ansār* to join Rabih in early 1892. If Anglo-Egyptian armies even invaded the Sudan, Abdullahi planned an emergency retreat westward—the very path Rabih's men were blocking. He worried about the western escape route, fretted about Queen Victoria and the khedive, and became almost apoplectic because of the 1893 Italian menace.

The khalifa's first hope had been that the Italians would swarm down upon the Ethiopians. Emperor Menilek's first suggestions of an alliance were, therefore, uninteresting. But the Italian armies were in the Horn of Africa to win an empire both in the mountains of Ethiopia and on the plains of the Sudan. Spreading from Massawa like an ink stain, they advanced in all directions. The khalifa's sermons in the Omdurman mosque turned increasingly shrill. Finally, in November 1893, Sheikh Ahmad Wad 'Ali, one of the boldest of the Ja'aliyyin, exceeded Abdullahi's orders and led his forces against Colonel Galliano's troops at Agordat. Galliano would die in 1896 at Adwa, calmly directing his overwhelmed *ascari*. At Agordat, some 120 miles due east of Kassala, the colonel's troops performed magnificently.

Prime Minister Crispi seized upon Agordat as an imperial moment to be memorialized by treaty. The Anglo-Italian Treaty of the following May (1894) gave the politician permission to grab Red Sea territory, provided it was kept in trust for Great Britain. Kassala, the hard-won prize of 'Uthman Diqna nine years before—the Mahdiyya's hoped-for springboard to Suakin, and Mecca—collapsed before General Baratieri's artillery and infantry attack in July. Abdullahi was staggered. He forgot about the "infidel British" for the moment, and the Grand Mosque reverberated to denunciations of the Italians. Rossignoli, who shortly escaped to Egypt, reported that Abdullahi saw himself "surrounded by antagonistic forces from all directions, by the Egyptian forces from the North, the Italians and Abyssinians from the East . . . and the Belgians from the South." Then there was Rabih in the west. The Mahdiyya of the mid-1890s was the African counterpart of Bismarck's Germany of the same period, imperilled by czarist Russia to the east, an unreliable Italy to the south, and a vengefully renewed France in the west. Unfortunately, the khalifa was no Bismarck.

Henry Morton Stanley, "Bula Matari"
(*Musée Royal de l'Afrique Centrale, Tervuren, Belgium*)

Léopold II, King of the
Belgians (*Musée Royal de
l'Afrique Centrale,
Tervuren, Belgium*)

Baron Dhanis (*Musée
Royal de l'Afrique Centrale,
Tervuren, Belgium*)

Stanleyville *(Musée Royal de l'Afrique Centrale, Tervuren, Belgium)*

The waterfront at Léopoldville in 1899 *(Musée Royal de l'Afrique Centrale, Tervuren, Belgium)*

Hamed bin Muhammad bin Juna al-Marjebi, "Tippu Tip" (*Bettmann Archive*)

Jean-Baptiste Marchand, "Paké-Bô" (*New York Public Library and the Section Outre-Mer, Archives Nationales, Paris*)

Louis Archinard *(Library of Congress)*

Joseph Germain by Castellani
(Library of Congress)

Albert-Ernest Baratier by
Castellani *(Library of Congress)*

Marchand and his men on the road to Djibouti: left to right, Largeau, Venail, Emily, Fouque (top), Landeroin (middle), Germain (bottom), Dat, Baratier, Mangin (top), Marchand (bottom), Dyé (*Archives Nationales, Paris*)

Emperor Yohannes IV and his son, Arya
Selassie *(Library of Congress)*

Ras Makonnen *(Library of Congress)*

The palace of Emperor Yohannes IV (*Library of Congress*)

Emperor Menilek II enthroned (*National Archives, Washington*)

Abbas II, Khedive of Egypt
(Bettmann Archive)

Herbert Kitchener, the Sirdar
*(National Portrait Gallery,
London)*

Ethiopian officers in dress uniform (*Library of Congress*)

Mwanga, Kabaka of Buganda, and Kabaraega, Omukamu of Bunyoro,
being led into exile *(Royal Commonwealth Society, London)*

Samori Turé captured *(Archives Roger-Viollet, Paris/Photo: Harlingue-Viollet)*

Mahmud Ahmad in captivity *(Royal Commonwealth Society, London)*

After Um Debreika: the body of the khalifa in the foreground
(Library of Congress)

Hauling the *Faidherbe* (*Archives Nationales, Paris*)

2

While the Mahdiyya was becoming more cohesive during the late 1880s, Egypt lost its independence in all but form. Rapid, sanguinary, and ignominious collapse of Egyptian power in the Sudan prolonged and then finally entrenched the British presence in Egypt. With the total annihilation in November 1883 of Hicks's army by the Mahdists, followed ten months later by the almost equally disastrous defeat of General Valentine Baker's forces, the British government ordered the Egyptian government to cut its losses and run. The puppet ruler, Khedive Tewfik, was privately distressed by London's will, and Sharif Pasha, his prime minister, preferred to resign rather than declare the Sudan legally abandoned. If one followed international law to the letter, the Sudan was not even Egypt's to abandon—not without formal approval of the Turkish sultan, from whom the Egyptian khedives derived their sovereignty.

There was no thought of these legal complications in London. It mattered little in the final turn of things whether Gladstone piously wished himself out of Egypt or whether Salisbury confided honestly that he "should be glad to be free of the companionship of the bondholders." The Egyptian debt of ninety-eight million dollars gradually assumed a policy-making inertia independent of prime ministers. As they had done twice before, with two steep upward revisions of the Egyptian international debt, the bankers made their considerable fears known to Her Majesty's servants. The reconquest of the desert beyond Wadi Halfa would exhaust the already strained Egyptian economy, said the financial community. Moreover, as the politicians well knew from their generals, Egyptian levies would have to be backed by crack British regiments to preclude more military calamities of the Hicks variety, a commitment that would consternate the British taxpayer. Much more palatable and profitable had been Sir Evelyn Baring's self-serving assurance in 1883 that, once the Sudan was written off, he could guarantee that "in twelve months there shall not be a British soldier in Egypt and that the country is put in such a position as to render it very improbable that any Egyptian question will be raised again for many years to come."

Egypt's fate was one of orderly exploitation. Adherence to khedival protocol and gentlemanly "advice" of British officialdom merely cloaked the country's increasing political impotence. Evelyn Baring's favorite aphorism—"We do not govern Egypt, we only govern the governors of Egypt"—was a perfect formulation of indirect rule. But then, Baring believed that he had "not yet come across a single man amongst the Pasha classes who appears to me really to understand the main elements of the local political problem with which the Egyptian government has to deal." Such a figure for Baring was a cultural impossibility. While Turks might evidence manliness and were even able occasionally to rule with sagacity, Baring's self-righteous essay, "The Government of Subject Races," slandered Egyptians as dolts and decadents. It followed that it would "never be possible to make a Western silk purse out of an Eastern sow's ear"; and hence, that Englishmen "need not always enquire too closely what these people themselves think."

Baring seldom did, and, to do him justice, the consequences of his indifference could have been worse. By 1891, the Egyptian budget had been balanced, reforms in the bureaucracy and army were well under way, and the pacification of Egypt was so complete that the khedive's subjects were obliged to defray the occupation costs of less than five thousand British regulars. That a quarter of the best farmland was mortgaged to the hilt; that the once rice-rich country was now exporting a mere 255,000 *kantars* (100 pounds to the *kantar*) of rice and importing 6,600,000; that the price of Egypt's most valuable export, cotton, dropped from 276 to 253 piastres a *kantar;* and that barely two percent of national expenditures was devoted to education were disparities occasioning scant protest beyond the eccentric circle of the Anglo-Catholic poet Wilfrid Blunt and the cultured nationalist leadership of the newspapers *al-Ahram* and *al-Muayyad.* Baring dismissed the Egyptian press as too insignificant even to bother censoring.

With its centenarian international debt securely funded, its trade imbalanced in favor of British manufactures, internal order restored, and imposing Cairo and Alexandria real estate available at bargain prices, Egypt became a winter resort for well-heeled Britons, French, Germans, and Austrians. Shepheard's, the sprawling hotel along the Cairo Nile, recreated the comfortable clutter and culinary blandness that upper-class English persons expected, but with just the desired modicum of costumed oriental obeisance. Shepheard's had unpleasant associations for the French community (one of Napoleon's marshals was believed to have committed suicide in its garden); nor did Gallic visitors especially care for the Turf

Club and the regal Gazira Sporting Club, where Baring played afternoon lawn tennis. But while the French could choose to suffer British smugness, not even the most aristocratic Egyptian was permitted to sup, bowl, or swat balls in such places. Embassies strove to excel in the sumptuousness of their banquets, the glitter of their cotillions, and above all in the panache of their ambassadors. Count Paul von Metternich, the German minister, was a credit to the preening kaiser and even more faithful heir to an illustrious name synonymous with accomplished intrigue. Baron H. Geidler von Egerigg of Austria became the terror of the Cairo golf course. The French and Russian ambassadors practiced cosmopolitan bonhomie and upheld the high standards of cuisine and conversation universally expected of French and Russian embassies.

Then there were the salons where Rennell Rodd, Baring's second-in-command, and Harry Boyle, Baring's learned "Oriental Secretary," could take the pulse of distinguished Egyptian and expatriate society. Princess Nazli Fazil, daughter of Khedive Ismail's half brother, defied every convention. "She was a clever woman," Rodd conceded, "and though she had good looks was curiously destitute of feminine vanity." She was certainly not destitute of patriotism, having backed the nationalist Colonel Urabi Pasha, and her palace was home to Egyptians and European (especially French) sympathizers for whom Sir Evelyn Baring's sublime paternalism was a source of unending shame and rage. The darkly handsome, enormously rich Wilfrid Blunt and his captivating wife (Byron's granddaughter) were regulars at Nazli's, more nationalist than the Egyptians and earning Blunt the affectionate title "the mad Englishman."

Ali Pasha Mubarak's salon was less grand and more businesslike, a salon befitting one of Muhammad Ali's *fellahin* who had trained as an engineer and risen from poverty to the rank of minister and respected educator. Although differing on who should run Egypt, the princess and the educator were agreed that Egypt must be run as an independent constitutional monarchy. A third circle, gathered around Riaz Pasha, saw the country's political problems as outward manifestations of religious apostasy. Let the people and their rulers return to Islam and the rule of the infidel British would be broken. The newspaper *al-Muayyad* was conceived and promoted by Riaz Pasha's associates.

In Alexandria and Cairo almost everybody was involved in schemes and plots, and almost everybody knew about them. Moreover, opposition to British rule was rarely an exclusive or even a primary passion among pashas and plutocrats. Ali Pasha Mubarak's twenty-volume study of Egyptian topography filled his days. Princess Nazli flitted to Istanbul and Paris. Sharif Pasha, who had resigned as prime minister rather than approve the abandonment of the Sudan, was too much the emeritus parliamentarian and gallicized sophisticate to conceive of politics as more than the reasonable civic obligation of persons born to privilege. So many delightful diversions took primacy over social and political realities: the Fencing Club; high tea at the Gazira Palace Hotel; the carousel of banquets during the "season" (November through February), occasionally made risky affairs by cholera. The story was well known (and not apocryphal) of the Cairo dinner party at which the guests' progress from one splendid course to the next was suddenly halted because the chef had expired from the dread contagion. After a decade on the job, and soon to be invested with the Earldom of Cromer, Sir Evelyn had, in this culture of political persiflage, every reason to be confident of the permanency of British rule in Egypt.

It was just at that moment, nevertheless, that the death of the pliant Khedive Tewfik and the accession to the throne of the eighteen-year-old Abbas Hilmi in 1892 appeared to jeopardize Consul General Baring's work. Abbas II had arrived, confident and cordial, from the Theresianum, Austria's military academy, and from intimate observation of the style of Habsburg rule. His manners, intelligence, and command of languages (except Arabic) instantly charmed the notoriously unresponsive Baring, who thought the young khedive "resembled a very gentlemanlike and healthy, muscled boy fresh from Eton or Harrow." Barely two years later, Lord Cromer would complain to London that Abbas played "with lunatics and is scarcely sane himself, according to his doctor." And long afterward, brooding in retirement on Abbas's behavior, Cromer would write a book about the khedive to explain why this perverse young man had matured into a resolute enemy of Great Britain.

What could one expect from a monarch who had consistently ignored Cromer's disinterested advice, surrounding himself instead with "those hybrid and nondescript Egyptians"? Abbas II had dared to try not simply to reign but to govern. He installed his old French tutor, from whom he had learned something of the politics of progress as well as the politics of British perfidy, as his European secretary. He adjourned his first cabinet meeting determined to replace the ministers who had responded to his every remark with, "as Your Highness pleases." He let Cromer know that he found the policy barring him from conferring with his own ministers without the presence of a British advisor intolerable. "I intend to work with men I can trust." "Of course," the astonished but still avuncular Cromer assured the khedive, "but it must happen gradually." Impatient, Abbas dismissed his British palace guard and replaced it with an elite Egyptian unit.

François Deloncle's colonial lobby encouraged the khedive to believe that France would offer Egypt strong material and diplomatic support for a policy of measured confrontation with Great Britain. But the mainsprings of khedival policy flowed less from French backing than from a combination of Abbas's assertive personality and the programs of formerly inconsequential habitués of salons, especially Ali Pasha Mubarak and his younger associate, the suave, romantic nationalist Mustapha Kamil. *Le Bosphore Égyptien* and *al-Ahram,* mouthpiece of Mustapha Kamil, defined "The Mission of a Prince" as becoming sole authority in his kingdom. Meanwhile, a new Gladstone ministry was again making conciliatory noises about the Egyptian occupation.

Abbas took his first decisive step in mid-January 1893, when a British police circular was sent to all provincial governors without the countersignature of the Egyptian minister of interior. Having already been sternly advised by Cromer not to replace his ailing, timorous prime minister with the able Coptic Christian Tigrane Pasha, Abbas exploded, firing not only the prime minister but the ministers of justice and finance.

Threatening resignation unless London fully backed him, Cromer delivered the British ultimatum three days later: "Her Majesty's Government expect to be consulted in such important matters as a change of ministers. No change appears at present either necessary or desirable." Abbas II yielded minutes before the expiration of the twenty-four-hour ultimatum. But Cromer still was not satisfied. More troops for the British garrison were required, he argued: "I do not feel the least confident that I can control the Khedive." Gladstone absolutely refused. Gladstone's private secretary disloyally lobbied the cabinet on the consul general's behalf; yet even he thought Cromer "had no doubt lost his head." Under pressure, however, Gladstone finally sent the troops. Nearly four years earlier, Cromer had told Salisbury, "The more I look at it, the more does the evacuation policy appear to me to be impossible under any conditions." His prophecy had fulfilled itself.

The khedive still did not know he was beaten. Egged on by his French secretary and some of his Egyptian advisors, he encouraged the advisory Legislative Commission to reject Cromer's 1894 budget. The consul general was steadily augmenting the excise taxes on Egyptian textile manufactures in order to make the more expensive Lancashire imports competitive; a similar policy suppressed the local tobacco industry. The budget also contained funds for the enlarged British occupation force. Publicly, Cromer justified bypassing the Legislative Commission because it was "not representative of the whole country." Privately, he communicated to Rosebery his worry that the Legislative Commission, "under the inspiration of an inexperienced, headstrong boy of no particular talent," had "publicly and officially declared that they want us to go." Whose country was Egypt, anyway, the Earl of Cromer must have wondered. "One of the peculiarities of the Anglo-Saxon race," he would write later, was an inability to "understand how anyone can question the excellence of their motives" as an occupying power.

Almost immediately, his lordship learned of another intolerable maneuver—a plot by the khedive to insult British officers serving with the Egyptian army. Herbert Kitchener, Sirdar or commander in chief of the Egyptian army, was proud of his work. Units pounded by the British during the Urabist revolt and demoralized by the Mahdi's "Dervishes" had been slowly rebuilt and honed to a fine edge. In January 1894, accompanied by his pro-British undersecretary of war, Abbas inspected the Wadi Halfa garrison. Although he praised the Egyptian officers, he informed Kitchener Pasha that he thought the British officers had done a poor job, that it was "disgraceful for Egypt to be served by such an army." The French ambassador reported to Paris that he was "quietly encouraging him in this way of thinking." Kitchener threatened the mass resignation of British officers (exactly what Abbas would have liked). The inevitable ultimatum from London arrived. Either his majesty would "give just satisfaction" for the "slights on British officers" or the Egyptian army would be removed from the control of the khedive. Was he "a monkey on a stick to dance to the British Consul General's tune"? Abbas protested to his tearful ministers. But again he surrendered, issuing an order of the day commending the army's British officers.

Abbas continued to struggle against his masters, but the war was won, although Rennell Rodd "sometimes wondered whether any better result would have been served by more cordial treatment of the young Khedive in this earlier stage." In 1895, the khedive accepted the support of Ali Pasha Mubarak and Mustapha Kamil. Khedival funds enriched the coffers of Kamil's Nationalist party and khedival advice resulted in anti-British articles by Kamil in such prominent French publications as *La Revue des Deux Mondes, Le Journal des Débats,* and *Le Figaro*—articles which, as one observer concluded, "roused much interest in Europe, [but] interest was all they roused." Abbas's minister of foreign affairs, Boutras Pasha, made a more substantial contribution to British embarrassment by secretly informing France's representative that Egypt welcomed Delcassé's scheme to rush an occupation force to the Bahr al-Ghazāl. The khedive's men watched Marchand's preparations with considerable excitement the following year, fully anticipating that before long a French force at Fashoda would compel the British to accept international mediation of the whole Egyptian question. Marchand's Congo-Nile mission offered a plausible prospect for unravelling the coils of British domination.

On March 16, 1896, Queen Victoria, who expected to be kept fully informed of her ministers' decisions, opened a telegram in cipher from Lord Salisbury, once again her prime minister. Twenty-four hours after the fact, she read that the cabinet in consultation with the military had "resolved on an advance up the Nile, having for its ultimate object the occupation and retention of Dongola." At about the same time Abbas II received an extraordinary visit at Abdin Palace from Lord Cromer, who had only just remembered that marching orders had been given to the Egyptian army without informing the khedive. Getting back the Sudan was certainly unobjectionable in principle, but nonobservance of even the formalities of Egyptian sovereignty humiliated Abbas II and convinced him that he would have as little influence in the Sudan as he did on Lord Cromer. In mid-September, the khedive was in Paris, bringing with him a draft scheme for Egyptian independence drawn up by nationalist intellectuals. The invasion of the Sudan had been decided so quickly that for three days Kitchener was uncertain whether he or the commander of the British garrison would be given supreme direction. Cromer himself had been surprised. His advice had been for a cautious advance by British regulars and Sudanese auxiliaries in order to divert Mahdist pressure on the Italians at Kassala. It was much too soon to throw the untested new Egyptian army at the khalifa, Cromer warned. "Approve decision," an uneasy Queen Victoria wired Salisbury from Balmoral Castle, "but in face of Lord Cromer's opinion I am a little anxious." As for the rest of Europe, there was only a terse Reuters announcement.

The de facto government of Egypt, the Caisse de la Dette, instantly voted (over the protests of the French and Russians) in favor of the five hundred thousand pounds the British requested to finance the operation. France and Russia sued successfully, compelling Egypt to return the money, but by then the first stage of the invasion was complete. The French, the Russians, and the sultan of Turkey (whose residual rights in the Sudan were obviously of no concern to the British) were left with their court decisions and their formal protests.

Official British justification for the bound to Dongola ranged from the provocation of an Ethiopian alliance with the Mahdiyya, to the need for a dramatic gesture to shore up Italian power in the eastern Sudan, to Salisbury's more touching explanation to Victoria that it was "for the sake of Egypt." But as Rennell Rodd, Cromer's trusted aide-de-camp, well knew, the prime minister cared almost as little about helping the Italians as he did about acquiring stretches of desert beyond Wadi Halfa. The reason for the invasion was France. French schemes for the Upper Nile had "been a subject of anxiety to me for some time," his lordship revealed. Annexation of Uganda and completion of the fantastically costly 1895 project of the railroad from Mombasa to Lake Victoria would eventually solve Britain's supply problems in East Africa and secure the Nile headwaters from the "encroachment" of other European powers. During the interim, however, Salisbury's nightmare was a French post at the other end of the Nile arrogantly flying the tricolor and sending out marine officers to negotiate treaties with the Nilotes and even, possibly, an accord with the khalifa's amirs. The paramount objective was to get to Fashoda before the French.

The French role gave the situation special force. Britain's diplomatic isolation at this moment was extreme. In a fit of Monroe Doctrine bravura, the president of the United States had virtually threatened war over supposed British interference in Venezuela. The international commission investigating the 1894 Turkish massacres of the Armenians made no secret of its views that Her Majesty's government was to blame for encouraging the Armenians in the first place. At the peace negotiations between China and Japan at Shimonoseki in March 1895, Europe and the United States had closed ranks to force the victorious Japanese to scale down their humiliating demands—all but Britain, which had reversed itself almost overnight and discovered in the Empire of the Rising Sun an oriental version of its maritime self. Annoyed by growing British coolness to the Triple Alliance, the kaiser had tried forcing London's hand with his notorious January 1896 telegram congratulating President Paulus Kruger on smashing Cecil Rhodes's scheme to overthrow Boer rule in the Transvaal. Not since Bonaparte had the prospect of wheeling and dealing at Britain's expense loomed so menacingly among the Powers.

3

By March 20, one of Kitchener's flying columns had already taken the outpost at Akasha, dashing from Wadi Halfa sixteen miles across the stretch of black, rocky hills known as the "Belly of Stones" to reach the district of Firka. "You must be quite prepared and on the watch," Muhammad Bushara wrote Hammuda Idris, the commander at Firka, "as I have received information that the God-forsaken Sirdar [commander in chief, i.e., Kitchener] says that he will occupy the district in seven weeks."

Muhammad Bushara had recently taken command of the Dongola region. Tall and black, he was the best of the khalifa's surviving generals, now that al-Zaki Tamal, Abu Anja, and Wad N'jumi were dead. The British abused Muhammad Bushara, calling him the "most cruel and black-hearted of all the Khalifa's evil horde." Yet they came to admire a commander whose personal courage and strategic intelligence would have greatly altered the course of the Sudan campaign had the amir possessed a fraction of the Anglo-Egyptian army's firepower. Muhammad Bushara, unlike the stealthy 'Uthman Diqna (now actively in the khalifa's service again), believed in attacking, in carrying the fight to the enemy, in keeping him off balance and concerned about his line of retreat.

On May 1, eleven days after Muhammad Bushara's alert to the Firka garrison, one of Hammuda Idris's scouting columns was sent flying by the Egyptian cavalry. Muhammad Bushara won the khalifa's permission to make the more aggressive 'Uthman 'Isa al-Azraq associate commander at Firka, but still the *ansār* held back. Meanwhile, enormously improved by the escaped Rudolf Slatin's detailed knowledge of the Mahdiyya, Wingate's intelligence bureau had been able to supply Anglo-Egyptian officers with accurate maps of the Firka defense. Suddenly, at 5:00 A.M. on June 7, after a flawlessly coordinated night march, Kitchener's desert column, approaching by way of the Nile River, converged nine thousand strong upon the Firka *zariba* (enclosure). Hammuda Idris and almost a thousand Dervishes were killed, while Egyptian forces counted twenty dead and ninety-one wounded. Muhammad Bushara prayed for Allah to strike down the Sirdar's host, "to have them brought to destruction by their own devices." Within days after the victory at Firka, 1,218 of Kitchener's officers and men were infected by cholera, and before the plague burned itself out, 919 were dead. Here, surely, was certain proof of the khalifa's *baraka*. 'Uthman Diqna and some of the others might call upon Abdullahi to order a general retreat in order to draw the infidel ever deeper into the vast Sudan and away from his supplies; for Muhammad Bushara this was the moment to advance. The khalifa agreed.

The Mahdist leader's thirteen thousand infantry and two thousand horsemen streamed out of Dongola in mid-September, heading down the Nile for the town of Hafir. Muhammad Bushara ordered his men to entrench themselves there. He positioned his artillery close to the bank in order to rake Kitchener's four aged armored gunboats. In order to attack Dongola, the Anglo-Egyptian army would have to cross from the right bank of the Nile at Kerma, directly across the river from Hafir. Muhammad Bushara intended to stop the Sirdar cold. On the morning of September 19, a young British journalist named Winston Churchill described the greeting of the army as it marched into Kerma:

> Behind the entrenchments and among the mud houses and enclosures strong bodies of the *jibba*-clad Arabs were arrayed. Still further back in the plain a large force of cavalry—conspicuous by the gleam of light reflected from their broad-bladed spears—wheeled and maneuvered. By the Nile all the tops of the palm trees were crowded with daring riflemen, whose positions were indicated by the smoke puffs of their rifles, or when some tiny black figure fell, like a shot rook, to the ground.

These were the Sudanese of old, the indomitable Hadendoa who had shattered a British square at Abu Klea, and who seemed not to die from their wounds. Churchill found it "thrilling." Three of Kitchener's boats futilely pounded the Mahdists for three hours (the fourth had failed to negotiate the Third Cataract). Machine-gun and rifle fire raced across the Nile, raking the Hafir *zariba*. Muhammad Bushara was wounded, but he continued to command. His hodge-podge artillery pieces, most of them captured during the Mahdi's time, had long since lost much of their firepower due to poor main-tenance and shortage of parts, and from belching scrap-metal am-munition. But the greatest defect was not in the guns themselves; at Hafir and for the rest of Kitchener's relentless advance, individu-alism and inadequate training of the khalifa's artillery batteries resulted in awful shooting. A Mahdist cannon almost never hit its mark. The breakthrough of the boats threw the amirs into confu-sion, especially after one of Wingate's Sudanese spies planted a report that the Anglo-Egyptian army had changed plans and now intended to march south before crossing to attack Dongola. Had the wounded commander's argument to hold Hafir not been overruled, the Sirdar would have been forced to take high casualties resulting from a direct assault on Muhammad Bushara's *zariba*.

Abandoning Hafir led to abandoning Dongola, for, as the various chiefs galloped toward the city, panic engulfed them. One of the three boats, the *Abu Klea*, had begun shelling the city just as Muhammad Bushara might have convinced his officers to stand and fight. Once again he was overruled and it was decided to evacuate the women and children farther upriver. On September 24, Kitch-ener pranced into an almost deserted Dongola on his white Ara-bian. It was the end of the campaign of 1896. Dongola was again Egyptian and British. The khalifa vanished for several days into his *kulwa*, or council, finally emerging still shaken to exhort the faithful from the Grand Mosque. "Deception and disobedience have in-creased amongst the *ansār*," he proclaimed. "What has happened is the result of deceit and disloyalty." There would be no more fighting beyond Omdurman. The armies of Dongola Province had been ordered back to the capital. Abdullahi had been warned by the Angel of the Lord that "the souls of the infidels would leave their bodies between Dongola and Omdurman." Herbert Kitch-ener was at that moment hurrying to London to present his own vision of the Sudan's future to Lord Salisbury.

CHAPTER SEVEN

From the Congo to the Nile

The notice in the "Colonial Affairs" section of *Le Temps* on June 25, 1896, was ostentatiously low key: "Captain Marchand, who is to take command of the military forces supporting us in the Upper Ubangi, leaves from Marseilles tomorrow. These forces are intended simply to occupy those posts in the Mbomu valley that were returned to us nineteen months ago by the Congo Free State." Attentive readers in the British Colonial Office knew better, and there was considerable satisfaction at having acted not one moment too soon. After its victory at Firka, Kitchener's army was only just beginning to recover from the cholera that Muhammad Bushara had begged Allah to visit upon the unbelievers. Exactly three months after the item in *Le Temps,* the fateful Mahdist miscalculations at Hafir would give the Sirdar an uncontested win at Dongola. But in late June neither Salisbury nor Cromer—and not even Kitchener himself—was certain of the campaign's outcome. Wingate's intelligence offered up reassuring reports of low morale and divided counsels, but no responsible voices in London or Cairo minimized the resiliency of the Sudanese, especially as the French obviously intended to befriend the khalifa. "Under no circumstances," *Le Temps* emphasized, "is this to be construed as an operation against the Dervishes." Here again was another slightly concealed signal to Omdurman that Paris hoped for an alliance.

In the backlash of recriminations after Fashoda, many of Marchand's ex-boosters would wonder at the preposterousness of the Congo-Nile strategy, the seemingly harebrained scheme of sending a dozen French officers slogging across Central Africa to snatch the Nile basin from the combined armies of Britain and Egypt—while at the same time winning the hearts and minds of the Mahdists. That was not the mood of the moment, though. Hanotaux had taken leave of the captain with the operatic exhortation to fire France's pistol on the Nile, and, in December, Jean Jaurès's socialists would join in ratifying Marchand's escalating budget without debate. Doubt was alien to Marchand's nature. Weighing the stupendous mandate of his mission against his negligible resources, Marchand found that the scales always balanced when he added the intangibles of character and discipline—and, of course, his own stupendous ego. When his second-in-command, Captain Baratier, wrote that "France alone possesses the colonial army with which such madness can be undertaken without risk," Baratier had in mind the incalculable asset of Marchand's kind of leadership.

Because Marchand appeared to have anticipated every contingency, those who dealt with or served under him inevitably came to believe that what had been anticipated was no longer problematical. Paké-Bô became France's version of Bula Matari. Mangin, who had been sent ahead to the French Sudan to recruit African troops, knew how carefully and insistently Marchand planned. One after another, before he sailed from Marseilles and immediately after he reached Loango in late July, the captain's letters of instruction meticulously guided Mangin's actions. Dialike, the former *tirailleur* corporal; Ba Issa, Marchand's garçon; Moussa, the cook who served with him at Tiéba, all had to be found, "whatever the cost." As for troops, none must have served in the cavalry—"they no longer have any value for us over there." Muslims, animists, Mangin could select all of them he wanted, "drunk or sober" —but no Christians and no brainy Africans. Good solid brutes, *"voilà l'idéal."*

Expected to locate favorite Africans and raise a battalion of veteran soldiers in less than a month, Mangin was yet admonished not to spend a single franc over budget. "In a word," Marchand wrote with his imperious humor, "you've got to work quickly, surmount all difficulties, overcome the impossible, and not spend a dime." Mangin overcame the impossible with dispatch and was ready with 154 *tirailleurs* and the physician Jules Emily at Dakar when the *Stamboul* collected them in early June. On the twentieth, the packed *Stamboul* dropped anchor at Libreville, Gabon, the administrative capital of the French Congo, where Mangin and the others were to complete final arrangements before leaving for Loango. From the coastal town of Loango the route of the Congo-Nile mission was supposed to take it around the roiling rapids to Brazzaville, then across Stanley Pool to Léopoldville, and from there up the Congo

River to its juncture, just above the equator, with the Ubangi; up the Ubangi to the administrative center at Bangui; from Bangui to Tambura on the Mbomu River at the end of the Congo River watershed. Fashoda lay another five hundred miles beyond.

Fanatic about details, Marchand was just as driven about imbuing his expedition with a philosophy. On this one point at least, he and Savorgnan de Brazza were in agreement: the African surface was not to be crossed in caravans stretching along miles of trails. Stanley's example—especially the botched and bloody rescue of Emin Pasha in December 1889, from which only a third of his original seven hundred had emerged—was not to be followed. Three hundred men would die on a mission across the heart of Africa; one hundred fifty just might make it. If Marchand was not the first European to grasp the reality that large caravans wasted everything in their path and drove otherwise friendly populations into wild flight or desperate warfare, he was one of the first to reach this conclusion from logic rather than necessity. He unhesitatingly sacrificed stores and numbers to speed and calculating humanitarianism. In his African memoirs, dedicated to Marchand, Baratier would dilate on the mission's principles. "To demand of [the natives] more than they can provide would condemn them to die of hunger, and consequently would provoke uprisings. Repression would cause time to be lost," he lectured. "Thus force becomes a source of weakness."

There was every reason to believe that Marchand, Baratier, Mangin, Lieutenant Largeau, and the others fully embraced this maxim. Yet, even before Largeau sailed from Marseilles ahead of the others, a powder trail of disastrous events had already detonated in the French Congo. Force, a great deal of it, was shortly to prove unavoidable. Throughout May into June, Basundis, a people in the up-country between Loango on the coast and Brazzaville on what was then Stanley Pool, had been in revolt. Certain notables—two in particular, Mabiala Nganga and Mayoke—had been preying upon commercial traffic with increasing frequency. At the village of Makabendilou, as convoys from the coast halted for breath, Chief Mayoke and his raiders routinely appeared from the brush. Just as suddenly and routinely, the priest Mabiala Nganga and his men came to the caravan's rescue. The traders were expected to pay generously for their deliverance.

As the French saw developments, Basundi chiefs were becoming an intolerable nuisance. When Mabiala removed the porcelain insulators from the telegraph poles in the belief that they caused the rains to cease, Albert Dolisie, Commissioner General de Brazza's second-in-command, punished the priest by seizing the arsenal of flintlock guns at Makabendilou and transferring it to the chief of Comba. Unchastened, Mabiala stole the Brazzaville mail, killing the postal courier in the attack. Dolisie promptly burned Makabendilou to the ground. On May 28, joined by many Bakongo to the south, Basundis rebelled and shut the three-hundred-mile trail between Loango and Brazzaville.

Just as the Belgians had little conception of the political and cultural forces that were shortly to unleash the Tetelas upon the Dhanis expedition, the French misunderstood Mabiala Nganga and seriously misjudged his influence among the hinterland peoples. Basundi and Bakongo believed him possessed of awesome spiritual powers. Three months after the uprising had been quelled, Sergeant Justin Deramond's garçon refused to enter the room in Brazzaville where Mabiala's fetishes were on display. Seventy-five years later, a French historian still found worshippers before Mabiala's grotto. Although experienced "Africans" like Mangin frequently took the trouble to know something of languages and peoples, marine officers had neither time nor inclination for amateur anthropology; and many civil administrators were too ignorant or besotted to make the effort.

Yet one of de Brazza's 1894 reports to the colonial ministry might have alerted the French to growing problems in their colony, of which the rebellion of Mabiala's Basundi was the inevitable symptom. The ten-year rampage of Europeans up and down the rivers of Central Africa cannot have left any doubt in even the most optimistic African mind of what was in store for the peoples. "Abandonment of Belgian territory has spread along the whole shore of the Congo . . . and on the Ubangi to the post at Bangui," the commissioner general informed the Pavillon de Flore. More than a thousand Africans had sought refuge on the French side of these rivers. With the Belgians systematically rounding up thousands of Congolese to transport equipment for the railroad, and thousands more to harvest rubber and timber, flight to French territory was hardly surprising. What these fugitives told their brothers and sisters on the left bank of the Congo about European brutality must have greatly nourished fears already deeply grounded. On the French side, the caravan revenues enjoyed by the peoples near Stanley Pool had been steadily eroded by the Loango, a coastal people favored by French authorities for portage. Finally, Basundi, Bakongo, Tetela, and other African peoples could hardly be blamed for failing to make the fine distinctions between Frenchmen and Belgians that colonial officials themselves, even after many years' residency, often could not draw between Africans. Once again Africa was responding to the challenge of European intrusion, with Mabiala Nganga acting the part in the French Congo that Malumba played in the Belgian Congo, Samori Turé in the Sudan and Ivory Coast, and Mutesa in Buganda.

In the south another Mabiala—Mabiala Nkinke (Mabiala "le Petit," the French called him, to distinguish him from his uncle, Mabiala "le Grand")—brought his people of Balimoeke into the fray. "Mabiala," he was fond of boasting, "doesn't budge for a white man." Mangin, who reached Libreville after Largeau, found the situation enraging. "Our caravans can't travel the Loango-Brazza-ville route as the result of a ridiculous incident." Even worse, de Brazza seemed more alarmed that Mangin's 154 *tirailleurs* might terrify the loyal Africans around Loango than he was concerned about suppressing the rebellion. Until countermanding instructions were telegraphed from Paris, the harried commissioner general "talked of keeping my company [of troops] here until July 20," the lieutenant fumed. Forty *tirailleurs* were finally sent from Libre-ville aboard a small steamboat to Boma-Matadi, from there they were to make their way to Brazzaville with orders to secure the expedition's arriving equipment.

Marchand reached Loango, supercharged and contentious, at the beginning of August. News from there had been discouraging. Lar-geau, complaining of Savorgnan de Brazza's conduct in late May, had written, just before leaving Libreville, that the aristocratic explorer-administrator found it "unbearable to think that anything whatsoever can be done without him." Largeau warned Marchand of the commissioner general's "dangerous spitefulness." Mangin was kinder to the "sleeping old lion" who wanted to play a major part in the "race that he himself began," but whom events were now overtaking. Captain Baratier had written Marchand of a barely averted public clash with the commissioner general just before leaving Libreville. De Brazza had made a "categorical declaration" that only five hundred of the expedition's cases could be carried. Coming down the coast from Libreville, Marchand fully expected major problems at Loango. What he found in the ragged, tin-roofed, enervatingly hot port surpassed his worst fears.

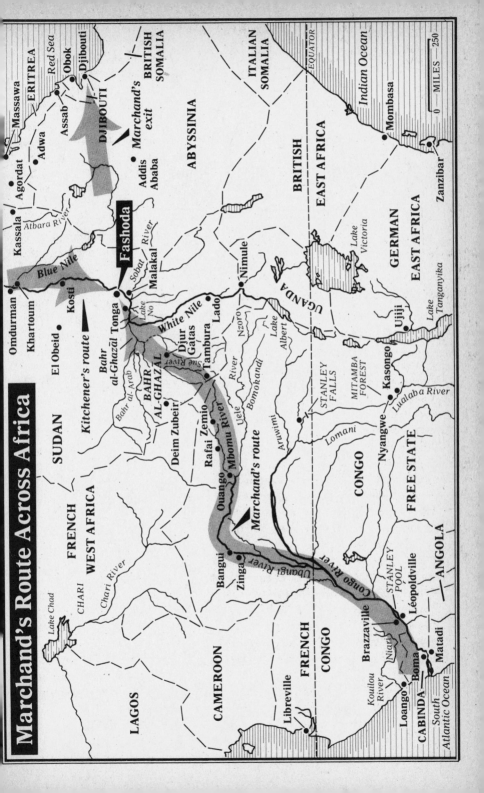

Marchand's Route Across Africa

For more than two years, heavy supplies for the up-country had been rusting and rotting in the beachside warehouses constructed by de Brazza. Equipment unloaded by the Monteil mission in 1894 bulged to the ceiling beside recently arrived cases and bundles for the Gentil mission in Chad. Another shed housed material of which Victor Liotard on the Upper Ubangi had long been in frantic need, and still another a mountain of boxes for the Brazzaville administration. There were twenty-five thousand loads in all—months of provisions for every Frenchman in Central Africa. From the outset, relations between the suave Roman nobleman and the marine officer from Thoissey had been soured by incompatible temperament. Furthermore, in the tight little world of colonial officers, de Brazza's swift, brilliant career was peevishly and bigotedly resented as that of a politically influential, self-advertising outsider. He was said to be an officer created by civilians, one who resisted the soldier's uncomplicated solutions to colonial problems. Just the opposite of Archinard, who used the politicians to widen the military's role in the colonies. For Marchand, then, the commissioner general was both personally and professionally suspect. But when he arrived at Loango and found most of the three thousand loads for his own expedition piled on the beach, Marchand exploded. "This is virtual treason," he told Captain Germain. "They're absolutely unaware of this state of affairs at the Ministry of Colonies."

Yet the commissioner general of the French Congo had repeatedly informed the Pavillon de Flore of Basundi harassment. Even without the hinterland troubles, he reminded Paris that his budget had never been large enough to pay the two thousand porters needed to transport the supplies that poured into Loango. When he had learned of the scale of the Congo-Nile equipment—3,049 cases weighing sixty-six pounds each—de Brazza had telegraphed a warning to the Ministry of Colonies. Someone at the Pavillon de Flore must have listened because in May, France's consul at Rotterdam negotiated a secret, careful, well-paid agreement with the Dutch firm Nieuwe Afrikansche Handelsvennvatschaf (NAHV) for transportation from Loango of Marchand's supplies. One Anton Greshoff, NAHV's agent in Cabinda (the bit of Portuguese coastal territory between the two Congos), was charged with overall arrangements and, specifically, with recruitment of porters along the southern route to Brazzaville. This southern route began at the mouth of the Congo River, moving from Boma-Matadi over the half-completed Belgian railroad to Comba, where supplies were unloaded for portage to Stanley Pool and Brazzaville.

Marchand had dispatched from Paris his usual precise instructions to the chief administrator at Brazzaville, Vittu de Kerraoul, peremptorily ordering him to hurry along Greshoff and his porters. Dashing from the *Taygète* to confer with de Brazza at Libreville on July 23, Marchand learned that NAHV preparations had bogged down. Lending his prestige and powers of suasion to the cause, the commissioner general immediately headed down the coast for Cabinda with Marchand. Discussions there were heated and only partially satisfactory. Despite the Rotterdam agreement, Greshoff refused to budge without additional money per load and a bonus because of Basundi and Bakongo hostilities. With the fate of the Congo-Nile expedition at risk, the two Frenchmen accepted NAHV's terms, and Greshoff promised swift collection of about half the three thousand loads from Loango for transport by river, rail, and trail through the Belgian Congo. Marchand, thoroughly disgusted, then chugged anxiously upcoast for Loango.

Six days before he reached Loango, Largeau and de Prat, with forty-two *tirailleurs* and eighty-five porters, had gamely headed across the sandy plain behind the port for Mbokou, the village at the entrance to the Mayombe forest. Beyond lay the long walk to Brazzaville. Mabiala Nganga's people allowed Largeau's caravan to pass without attacking, but they kept its desperately foraging porters from finding enough food. Loango Africans, whom Mangin sneeringly described as "coming into the world with loads on their heads," began choosing their heads over Largeau's loads as soon as they entered Mabiala's Mayombe. Sixty stayed with the caravan as far as Loudima. It straggled into Brazzaville with thirty-eight porters, the haughty Senegalese and Sudanese *tirailleurs* having been reduced not only to foraging but to balancing what remained of the sixty-six-pound boxes on their heads. No amount of money could persuade the Loango to march with another convoy.

Meanwhile, Baratier was straining to accomplish a far more ambitious breakthrough. Leaving Loango on July 2, the captain sailed for the mouth of the Kouilou, a winding, treacherous river about forty miles north of Loango. This river was known to be barely navigable, but Baratier was determined to haul some eight hundred loads past rapids until he reached a second, curving, narrow, hostile river, the Niari. Baratier was supplied with small steamers and funds to pay the hundreds of porters who would be needed for the final haul overland from Kimbedi to Brazzaville. If he managed somehow to pass the numerous rapids, he would never find porters, the experienced traders at Loango warned him. The Loango were the only Africans up to responsible portaging; and the peoples upcountry would never dare offend the leaders of the revolt. What Baratier proposed—a winding, three-hundred-mile gamble—was, they shrugged over their Pernod, impossible. Baratier nonetheless plunged onward, and for a time, Marchand lost all contact with him.

Paké-Bô saw that his mission was on the verge of ludicrous collapse. By early August, the Basundi had completely sealed the Mayombe-Niari trail, and, despite the fat wages offered by NAHV, Anton Greshoff still had no porters for the Comba-Brazzaville haul. A Belgian enterprise, the formidable Société Anonyme Belge pour le Commerce du Haut Congo, had more than a dozen branches on French territory and, by paying Loango porters more than its French competitors did, it controlled portage. Then came the equally distressing news that Belgian authorities were denying NAHV use of the railroad from Boma-Matadi to Comba. To make matters worse, the marquis and the captain were barely on civil terms, Marchand blaming the faltering mission on de Brazza's incompetence and threatening to return to Paris to wreck the explorer's career. It was becoming obvious to Marchand that it was not always easy to avoid the bloody tactics of a Stanley when Africans were determined to protect their lives and property. Something had to be done soon. By mid-August, the southern route was as sealed as the northern. On the other side of Africa, Kitchener's army was a month short of capturing Dongola. On the far side of the Belgian Congo, Dhanis's three-thousand-man force was about to strike for the Bahr al-Ghazāl. With three thousand cases on a beach standing between him and personal and national glory, Marchand found restraint temporarily intolerable. African resistance had to be rooted out, he told de Brazza.

Marchand's letters to powerful friends in Paris suggested that de Brazza's benign policies had caused the rebellion, and his increasing insolence toward the man whose enterprise and vision had given France equatorial Africa encouraged even the disrespect of French NCOs. Mangin, who spoke Arabic and could understand something of the languages of the region, was scandalized by the Pernod-sweating, whoring officials serving under de Brazza. Most could not even identify the names of the populations they were supposed to govern "or tell how far the next post was." Slurring de Brazza's administrative competency and even his Italian origins, Marchand later confided to Mangin that "for the first time in my life, I've vowed to destroy someone."

But first came the Africans. On Tuesday, August 18, the commissioner general yielded, signing a brief declaration of martial law drawn up by the expedition commander. De Brazza sailed for Libreville "that same evening," Marchand boasted, and "I've not heard a word from him since." The dedicated, fair-minded servant of the Republic had authorized not only a repression of Basundi and Bakongo, but an equally drastic campaign against himself. Four months later, Sergeant Deramond claimed that it was common knowledge that, immediately after the martial-law proclamation, de Brazza had authored a secret circular to his administrators ordering that "no coercion should be exerted with the goal of compelling things [from the natives] that violate their customs." Learning of this circular, Deramond wrote, Marchand was furious.

Meanwhile Baratier, as he was to do many times before reaching Fashoda, sent word from Brazzaville that he had pulled off the impossible. Moving the first Loango loads in August, over trails and then up the virtually unnavigable Kouilou River, Baratier and his men pulled their loaded whaleboats over the mean, shallow river's endless rocks. He had got the eight hundred cases up the Kouilou-Niari, and from Kimbedi overland to Stanley Pool. Without the powerful *tafia* drug he gave the porters, they would surely have failed. Drugged, exhausted, they had stumbled past Louvakou, Moutcheke, Bamboutate, and finally the large village of Koutissa, where, for the first time, people had not run away. Each night, the garçons picked Brazilian fleas—a parasite capable of destroying a toe or even a foot—from the Frenchmen's feet. Marchand wrote Baratier, "I would have been deeply pessimistic about our chances for arriving at Brazzaville within the desired timespan without your success on the Kouilou."

That success had nearly cost Charles Castellani his life. The strong-willed artist not only braved the noonday sun hatless, he also refused to take quinine. Prattling on about the fauna, the "natives," and the latest Parisian art vogues, Castellani seemed to relish the hardships of the Kouilou-Niari. The abscess on his foot (cut and drained by Baratier) barely slowed him. Suddenly he was stricken by malaria, falling unconscious within hours. Baratier was forced to leave him at one of the camps, instructing the bearers to carry him in a stretcher to Loudima. Day after day, the bearers lugged the unconscious Frenchman from village to village, unceremoniously dropping him in a heap off to the side while they palavered with friends and relatives on their leisurely way upcountry. Castellani not only survived his keepers but seemed positively recharged when Baratier found him at the village of Zilengoma, and immediately launched into a discourse on aesthetics. The extroverted Baratier listened, queried, then renewed the drive to Brazzaville, where new orders from Marchand awaited him.

Moving aggressively to implement conditions of martial law, the expedition commander left the coast for the village of Loudima about two-thirds the distance to Brazzaville. Largeau had strict orders to take charge of the sector between Comba and Brazzaville, but to avoid undue interference with NAHV's procedures. "You are there, in a word," Marchand explained severely, "to promote the undertakings of Monsieur Greshoff and Bakongo portage, without ever intervening in details of recruitment or transport." Other orders were rushed to Baratier and Sergeant de Prat. They were to reoccupy abandoned posts, set up a rapid mail service, and destroy the crops in rebel villages along the Loango-Brazzaville route. Baratier was ordered to spare the villages and the lives of the people; what the French army called *razzias* were intended to drive insurgent populations to the reoccupied French posts for food in exchange for surrender and portage service.

While Largeau and Baratier led *razzias* along the northern and southern trails, Marchand took command of the colony, to the formal outrage of Albert Dolisie, de Brazza's lieutenant governor. Rifles were distributed and a militia formed; civil administrators and traders were deputized as commanders. The mountain of crates was readied for rapid, gruelling transport to Brazzaville and farther up the Congo to Bangui. Truculent Basundi and Bakongo were flushed from the Mayombe and Niari and lined up for boxes to be balanced on their heads. The thousands of porters de Brazza had for many months only dreamt of in pessimistic dispatches to Paris suddenly materialized. But the cost was as high as de Brazza had feared. More than thirty villages were put to the torch by the Senegalese-Sudanese soldiers, who behaved in a manner appropriate to chastising "savages." The *tirailleurs* were such convincing Frenchmen that Sergeant Deramond's Bakongo garçon protested when ordered to do carpentering on the grounds that this was work for white men and Senegalese: "Senegalese, him not nigger like me." The paper commitment of NAHV was finally enforced. His troops far enough ahead of the French and anxious to win their support for a territorial grab on the Nile, Léopold himself had intervened directly, placing not only the unfinished railroad but the available steamboats on the Congo above Stanley Pool at the expedition's disposal. Greshoff and his agents no longer had an excuse for delay.

The first hundreds of some fourteen thousand loads began moving over the northern trails. In addition to his own three thousand cases, Marchand had agreed to oversee the transport of many of the supplies needed not only for the administration at Brazzaville, Bangui, and Zemio, but also those for the Chad mission and the Ouango post at the end of the Ubangi River. At the cost of several months, the captain's grand gesture transformed him from a junior officer on special mission into a heroic figure toasted well into the African night at French posts along the rivers. It was hoped that, if and when more men and supplies were sent from France to reinforce the Congo-Nile force, the bureaucrats whom Mangin derided would remember and return the favor, despite the Pernod and prostitutes.

Marchand was also fighting a decisive personal battle. At the end of September, undermined by fever, he staggered into Loudima, where, from the twenty-eighth through the thirtieth, he thought he had "had the curse." Dr. Emily, who had just pulled Baratier through an eight-day agony from copper-poisoned water, was rushed by express hammock from Brazzaville. Marchand was already on his feet when the physician and his bearers bounded into Loudima.

The rebel leaders Missitou and Mayoke, Mabiala Nganga's best officers, finally surrendered to Mangin and Sergeant de Prat after weeks of guerrilla skirmishing, but only after Mangin threatened to shoot thirty men, women, and children taken as hostages. De Prat shot Mayoke and Missitou at sunrise in front of one hundred Loango porters on October 17. Captain Baratier caught up with Mabiala Nkinke and liquidated the chief with a rifle shot.

Mabiala Nganga's end came three days after de Prat's firing squad had executed Missitou and Mayoke. In a series of firefights the religious leader had taught the *tirailleurs* to respect him, to the mounting annoyance of Marchand, who realized how fragile the line from Loango to Brazzaville remained while the Basundi guerrilla fighter was at liberty. He ordered Baratier to finish him. Two women revealed Mabiala's hideout, a cave with two entrances, and on October 20 Baratier and twenty soldiers attempted a surprise attack. Six *tirailleurs* were wounded by gunfire, Baratier himself just missing a bullet that killed a Senegalese. One of the two French administrators with Baratier ran back to the village of Kimbedi for reinforcements. On the way, he met Marchand and a detachment of troops on the trail for Brazzaville. A five-pound charge of explosives was placed against the far opening in the cave and set off after Marchand ordered a *tirailleur* to call for Mabiala's surrender several times. Grass was heaped up at the other entrance, set afire, and fanned into the cave. A few hours later, Marchand, Baratier, and several soldiers unsealed Mabiala's redoubt, entered, and found the priest and his men dead of smoke inhalation. Mabiala entered the pantheon of African resistance.

The final round in the Congo rebellion came on December 12, in a seven-hour battle between Mangin's *tirailleurs* and militia and a large force commanded by Tensi, the last significant insurgent leader. By the end of the month, Marchand announced the end of the revolt and the lifting of martial law. Within two years, however, Basundi and Bakongo would erupt again, closing their part of Africa to Europeans until a large French force broke them and handed their lands over to some forty corporations and cartels. Rubber and de facto slavery obliterated the kindly policies of Savorgnan de Brazza, recalled in 1897 and officially dismissed in 1898, ostensibly for exceeding his annual budget (which he had spent to assist Marchand), but in reality because the captain's allies ganged up on the courtly Roman nobleman.

Between late November and late January 1897, the French Congo experienced more action than had been seen in more than three years. Now deep in the Dinka country of Deim Zubeir, Liotard sent congratulations to Marchand for having accomplished what de Brazza "ought himself to have done long ago." By the northern route through the Mayombe and the Niari, eighty-five hundred cases of supplies reached Brazzaville. Of the twenty-five thousand cartons and cases Marchand and his officers had found stacked and deteriorating in Loango warehouses, fourteen thousand were slogged, week after week, over a thousand miles and five months from the Atlantic to remote Ouango. It was an operation involving "forty thousand porters or canoers, seventeen steamers, twenty-eight boats or barges, eight hundred dugout canoes—all that amounting to 1,060,000 workdays," Marchand's letter to a politician boasted. He was "curious to know what Stanley would think of it." Bula Matari was no doubt impressed, for the quashing of rebellion and movement of so much tonnage—superlative feats in themselves—were accomplished under conditions of awful, stoic suffering. "Nobody thought of resting," Emily recalled years afterward. "Wasn't it imperative to be first on the Nile, before the Belgian mission of Count Dangs [*sic*] and the Anglo-Egyptian army marching on Khartoum?" If hardship was occasionally relieved by succulent hippopotamus, a continent glass of evening wine, or the extraordinary appearance at Loudima in feathered hat and corseted gown of Princess Marie-Thérèse T'Chibemba, replete with trunk and French chaperone (the colonial ministry believed the European-educated "princess" to be the sultan of Dar Banda's kidnapped daughter), such moments were all too rare.

By the end of February the first phase of the race to Fashoda was about over. Still cooperating with the French, Léopold had ordered the new governor general of the Free State, Colonel Wahis, to give Marchand whatever assistance the captain reasonably required. All that was available for transport to the French at Brazzaville was one little boat and three undersized steamers belonging to the NAHV. Had the Belgians refused the loan of the 125-foot, steam-powered *Ville de Bruges,* Marchand could never have reached the Bahr al-Ghazāl before late 1899—if ever. With Colonel Wahis's best wishes, the powerful *Ville de Bruges* twice crossed from Léopoldville to Brazzaville, across Stanley Pool, to collect members and supplies for the eight-hundred-mile chug up the Congo and the Ubangi to Bangui.

The *Ville de Bruges* steamed from Brazzaville on a Wednesday morning, January 13, carrying half the French expedition toward Zinga, the last village the large craft could reach without scraping the Ubangi river bed. The steamer would return for Marchand and his crew; finally, from Zinga, the last lap to Bangui had to be covered in dugout canoes. Germain, Mangin, Emily, de Prat, and an ailing Lieutenant Simon were aboard, along with Sergeant Bernard and another NCO posted to Bangui. Castellani and Sergeant Venail followed in the NAHV steamer *Antoinette.* The artist Castellani's upriver account was as lushly detailed as the vegetation and as distorted as a colonial service map. This was the same route (in part) described by Joseph Conrad in stark, evil prose that fixed for much of this century Europe's vision of the Interior: "Going up that river was like travelling back to the earliest beginnings of the world, when vegetation rioted on the earth and the big trees were kings. An empty stream, a great silence, an impenetrable forest. The air was warm, thick, heavy, sluggish. There was no joy in the brilliance of the sunshine."

For Castellani, horror was tempered by voyeurism and frivolity of mind. The heat, hippopotami, hematuria, and the flea-infested sandbars where he and the others slept heaped together like cordwood were mere annoyances in the excitement of having his preconceptions confirmed. He could hardly wait to see these peoples' customs, superstitions, disunity, and lack of government. "It's the triumph of anarchy," he wrote, "it's the existence of a state of nature that I had to learn about first hand." These people "occupy the last degree on the human scale." Readers of *L'Illustration* were treated to startling, sensational, and even ghoulish sketches and essays, which the magazine's publishers fully expected, having paid handsomely in advance for permission to have Castellani accompany the mission.

Whether or not there were as many cannibals in the neighborhood as he alleged, Castellani and the others aboard the *Ville de Bruges* were arriving in the Interior when the delicate balance of food supply and integrity of traditional institutions came under steady assault from the warfare, slave raiding, and compulsory labor brought from outside. The eating of enemies was unquestionably spreading. At the picturesque village of Dundo not far downstream from Bangui, the French came upon a cannibal market. "You can't help shuddering when you see with your own eyes cadavers of babies disembowelled like sheep and hung from the branches of bushes," Castellani gasped.

Six months had been lost between Loango and Brazzaville, but now there was movement. Marchand's confidence, never far from the surface, was up again. "You can take it as certain," he dispatched via Paris to Lagarde on the other side of Africa, "that I'll be at Fashoda by January 1, 1898, at the latest—perhaps in November 1897—and you can undertake action with respect to the friends from the east." But however confident, Marchand never failed to calculate all the possibilities. Five weeks later, on February 14, he fired off a long priority dispatch to his old commander and patron, General Archinard. "We're rather behind the Belgians who ought to be at Bor about now," he estimated. Even more alarming, Marchand thought the British expedition from Uganda was probably on the right bank of the Nile somewhere between Dufile and Lado, within striking distance of Fashoda. He took it for granted that if Kitchener's Anglo-Egyptians seized Khartoum, they would be in the Bahr al-Ghazāl "a month afterward. It's in this neighborhood that the junction of the two [British] expeditions will take place." If that happened, he foresaw Belgium's being given the left bank of the Nile north to the Bahr al-Ghazāl and west to the Sué River. "Pretending that we'd be satisfied beyond our desires, one will grant the French the eastern border on the Sué and the northern border along the Boru River," he predicted, which would shut France out of the Bahr al-Ghazāl and confine it to Dar Fertit with Léopold's Force Publique across its path.

That was what might happen, but not if the French marines could save the situation by inserting the tricolor, like a block of wood in an alligator's mouth, at Fashoda. Victor Liotard, Marchand's nominal superior in the Congo and a kindred pathfinder, wrote from Zemio that it could be done, and offered advice on how to do it. "The British are at Dongola, you say? Then don't wait until all the supplies and men have reached the end of the line at Tambura," the commissioner of the Upper Ubangi urged. "In order to reach the Bahr al-Ghazāl before the rainy season, legs will have to be worked, but it's not impossible." The quickest way there, he wrote in a second dispatch in early February, was from Tambura northeast through the region of Djur Gatas. As an afterthought, Liotard suggested that, with a steamer at Djur Gatas, Marchand "would be able to dock it at Khartoum and, with the Mahdi's [khalifa's] permission, occupy Fashoda."

Impractical at first, the steamer idea was shortly to become a necessity; for the moment, however, Marchand was too busy organizing the departure from Brazzaville to catch the drift of Liotard's thinking. The *Ville de Bruges* was ready to make the second run to Zinga on March 10, 1897. Suffering badly from another attack of malaria, Marchand forced himself aboard along with Baratier, interpreter Landeroin, Sergeant Deramond, a Doctor Foutrein, and eleven hundred supply cases. With the Archinard dispatch and an alarming report of a frontier firefight between French and Belgian Africans on his mind, the slow, throbbing advance up the Congo to Bangui must have gnawed at Paké-Bô's innards. The firefight on the Ubangi had pitted infantry at Mobaye on the French side against Belgian forces at Banzyville on the river's south bank. The lengthy report from Ensign Alfred Dyé, a twenty-three-old naval officer just joining the Congo-Nile mission, mentioned misconduct by a French administrator, kidnapping by a Force Publique soldier of a woman from the French side, a "prolonged fusillade," but, somehow, no fatalities.

More troubling than advancing enemy columns or flare-ups along the route was nature itself. When the *Ville de Bruges* left the Congo for the Ubangi, the river was beginning to fall, more rapidly than in past years. With the boiler set at maximum pressure, the boat raced against the water level. It crashed on the rocks twenty miles from Zinga, damaging its hull, but not badly enough to prevent return to Brazzaville for repairs. Finally, Marchand reached Bangui in early April in command of a fleet of seventy-two dugouts. Baratier was sent ahead to the Mbomu River where Germain, Mangin, Largeau, and Simon were already exploring the various overland and river routes leading most directly to Fashoda. There were another 450 miles between Bangui and Ouango, the last post before the Mbomu rapids. Ouango, five months from Loango and the end of the Ubangi line for small boats, was a dot on the Mbomu less than a hundred miles above the point at which the river merged with the larger Ubangi. From Ouango, Marchand's route to Fashoda led northeast almost in a straight line through the flat country of Deim Zubeir, passing just above the Bahr al-Ghazāl's myriad lacelike system of canals. Beyond Deim Zubeir flowed the Bahr al-Arab, a modest waterway spilling into the less modest Bahr al-Ghazāl and the Bahr al-Jebel—the White Nile. At diamond-shaped Lake No, the Nile made its sharp left turn, and sixty-odd miles downstream on a spit of land surrounded by hot swamp stood the crumbling fort at Fashoda. It was mainly an overland route with the last 150 miles or more an easy paddle in the mission's special aluminum boats. Sticking to this course, Marchand could just keep his January 1898 arrival promise to Lagarde. A dispatch from the well-informed Liotard confirmed the captain's conviction that the British would not be able to besiege Omdurman before the end of the year. When news of the Tetela mutiny and massacre among Dhanis's forces in March reached him, Marchand was more confident than ever.

CHAPTER EIGHT

The Race to Fashoda

1

Marchand hardly noticed Castellani's departure for Paris. The past December, when the capering artist had tried to reach Bangui as a stowaway, Marchand's first furious reaction was to cashier Ensign Dyé, the boat's pilot, ordering him back to France, and to expel Castellani. "I'll not have some jokester whose only dream is adding ludicrous chapters to comic novels about his youthful pranks," he spluttered to Landeroin. The civilian only made matters worse when he reminded Paké-Bô of the 9,400 francs paid over by *L'Illustration* to the mission. Abject apology saved Castellani, and after his return to Paris and *L'Illustration*'s instant serialization of "Towards the French Nile with Marchand's Mission," Marchand wrote him, "My alleged severity, especially vis-à-vis you, was much more apparent than real."

The captain's severity could seem real enough. Marchand was the mission's engine. That the engine occasionally misfired and lurched was inevitable; the wonder was that it happened infrequently and only in short bursts. After many depressingly long days ("Nothing to read, not a single game except a checker board monopolized by Doctor Foutrein," wrote Sergeant Deramond in his journal), and nights spent huddled on sandbars trying vainly to escape swarming mosquitoes, civility and even friendships were bound to be badly strained. In Brazzaville, Paké-Bô had seemed ready to assault the cocky Lieutenant Largeau in the officers' mess after the lieutenant ridiculed the titles proudly rattled off by Marchand from his portable library ("Ugh! You haven't a single work by Taine"). Then, halfway to Bangui, had come Marchand's adolescent detonation over tangerines missing from the quartermaster supplies. Suspect-

175

ing theft, he imperiously informed the dysentery-racked Deramond and the other sergeants that he was disgusted with them, "turning on his heels" before they could explain that the fruit was rotten. When they reached Zinga, a raging Marchand had to be restrained by the local administrator from imprisoning Sango canoers whose two boats had capsized with cartridges and beads during the offloading of the stranded *Ville de Bruges.* Without saying so, Deramond found Marchand a combustible commodity.

Yet his admiration for the officer was to grow in the pressured days at Bangui and at Kuango, headquarters of the Ubangi civil administration. Deramond also found Administrator Henri Bobichon and his two deputies admirable. Bobichon and his men rapidly assembled the thousands of porters and hundreds of dugouts for the tonnage to be moved out of the Ubangi to the end of the line at Ouango. As more supplies trickled into Bangui and Kuango through the riverine arteries, Bobichon would send them along, giving priority attention, he promised Marchand, to equipment for the mission—especially the delayed battery of 42-mm guns. With the station at Mobaye his next stop on the Ubangi, Marchand set off in the direction already taken by the rest of his officers. But at Mobaye came the second biggest crisis of the expedition. The letter was dated April 8, 1897. It bore Liotard's signature and had come overland and downriver by runner from Deim Zubeir country.

Faidherbe and de Brazza had put France actively back into competition for empire, but it was Victor Liotard who more than any other single civilian saw to it that the peoples of Central Africa knew that they were subjects of France. The humiliating 1893 Belgian rebuff at Bangassou had been his sole miscalculation. Since then, neglected and unsupplied, Liotard had advanced up the Ubangi and the Mbomu season by season, occupying stations handed over by the Belgians and cutting new ones out of the vegetation. If elsewhere France ruled her possessions through bureaucracies bloated by resident Frenchmen, what was coming to be called French Equatorial Africa—Gabon, the Congo, Ubangi-Chari, and Chad—was, because of its handful of servants, an extreme exception. Leaving a couple of Senegalese or Sudanese sergeants at a river station here, a French officer and a few *tirailleurs* there, Commissioner Liotard governed the Upper Ubangi with less than two hundred troops and a few score administrators. Liotard had now advanced to the borders of the Bahr al-Ghazāl over a bridge of treaties with the principal potentates of the region.

As earlier discussed, when Liotard's long-delayed report had reached the Pavillon de Flore at the end of February 1896, four months before Marchand left France, the colonial ministry immediately grasped the potentially disastrous contradictions between Liotard's and Marchand's approaches. By slow and resourceful dealings among the Zande and Dinka of Deim Zubeir, the civilian administrator "assured France access to the Egyptian Sudan." By a lightning advance and audacious diplomacy among the Mahdists of the same region, the marine captain promised the same results. But Mahdists and Zande were mortal enemies, which explained the embrace of the tricolor among sultans along the Mbomu and beyond. Although Minister of Colonies Guieysse had once thought that it might be "possible to square the results obtained by Monsieur Liotard with the dispatch of the captain to the Upper Ubangi," he had finally thought it "necessary to subordinate the action of the latter to the views of the government commissioner." Two years of cautious advance were not to be risked. Léon Bourgeois had agreed. His successor Hanotaux was of the same opinion.

Liotard's previous hint of concern about the mission's route having been ignored, his April 8 letter to Marchand was a masterpiece of diplomacy. He had just learned from Germain, he wrote, that Marchand intended to advance from Ouango across Deim Zubeir, the most direct route to Fashoda. "For quite some time" he had been convinced that the line of entry into the Bahr al-Ghazāl "ought to pass through the inhabited regions along the Sué River." Deim Zubeir was not the route to take. The Mahdist devastation there and the vast, deserted stretches presented almost insurmountable hardships. No, clearly the Congo-Nile mission ought go up the Sué through the region known as Meschra'er Req, from there into the Ghazāl River and on to Fashoda. There would be Dinkas and Shilluks aplenty to supply food and carry supplies. More important, Marchand could place these peoples under the protection of the tricolor, as bargaining chips vis-à-vis the British. Conversely, it was likely that an advance by unknown armed Europeans across Deim Zubeir would alarm and mislead the Zande, and under no circumstances were the "Islamic and pagan populations" to be offended, Liotard admonished. These views, the commissioner added significantly, had been "submitted to the Minister of Colonies in a letter which I have allowed Captain Germain to copy."

Obliquely but firmly, Liotard meant to checkmate Marchand's plan to negotiate an alliance with the Mahdists. Nothing could have ruined work among the Zande, or the Dinka for that matter, more quickly. Saying nothing about cultivating Mahdists, Liotard's letters instead stressed their great numbers in Deim Zubeir as another compelling reason to avoid the region. To go the Meschra'er Req route Marchand would need a boat, a contingency to which Liotard had alluded in his earlier communiqué. This part of the Bahr al-Ghazāl was one colossal swamp, striated by more than a dozen narrow, winding waterways draining into the Nile. Paké-Bô cannot have been pleased by Liotard's recommendation, but it was tantamount to an order. Lebon, the current minister of colonies, respected the judgment of the experienced commissioner. Writing to Lebon later, the normally assertive captain was careful to stress that he "remained completely in agreement with Liotard in everything and for all things."

The boat was a problem. Yet the idea of sailing to Fashoda or even farther down the Nile with the flag flapping appealed to Marchand, imagining, as he must have, British surprise at a French steamboat brought from the heart of Africa and floated on the Nile. Then, too, Liotard had insisted in his first communiqués in January and February that the main thing was to take up an "effective and permanent position, not an exploration, expedition, or temporary mission" in the Bahr al-Ghazāl. A boat moored off Fashoda would certainly advertise the seriousness with which France took its rights under the Conference of Berlin ground rules. And why, as Liotard had disingenuously suggested, could he not steam straight to Omdurman before Kitchener besieged the capital of the Mahdiyya and favorably impress the khalifa? It was just the sort of dazzling, implausible gesture prized by Marchand. Baratier was amazed at how quickly his old companion convinced himself that a steamer, even if it delayed the mission's arrival, was indispensable. Once the diplomatic battle commenced, Marchand explained, it "would have a weight that the simple whale boats would not have."

There was one boat that seemed to meet the mission's needs admirably, the large, detachable, relatively new *Léon XIII,* owned by the Catholic diocese of the Upper Ubangi. But crusty Bishop Prosper-Philippe Agouard, fierce apostle of a church that regarded the republic served by Marchand as satanic, refused to discuss the matter, even after the modest tender of one hundred thousand francs. Whatever slim prospects there were for obtaining the *Léon XIII* had probably been dashed months earlier when Baratier, on

Marchand's orders, had turned back a Catholic caravan in order to keep the Brazzaville route open to essential civil and military supplies.

Marchand had already resolved, if necessary, to take another steamer—"to seize it, or rather steal it," said Baratier. The fifty-foot *Faidherbe*, now stranded in the shallows of the Mbomu below Mobaye, was a narrow, fast vessel belonging to the civil administration. Because of its width and the two-ton boiler occupying almost half the deck, the *Faidherbe*'s carrying capacity was limited. Disassembly of its unsegmented hull posed a daunting challenge. But these were mere details to Marchand. Since a formal request for the *Faidherbe* (the sole operating boat serving the Ubangi posts) would take time and probably be refused, the captain ordered Baratier and Dyé to commandeer it. Liotard's delegate, a Monsieur Rousset, was relieved to have the burden of decision preempted. Secretly, he agreed to rush a spare-parts order for the steamer out of the Ubangi budget. Germain was recalled from Deim Zubeir to solve the steamer's formidable engineering problems, along with a competent, complaining NCO from Bangui, Sergeant Souyri.

Now began the third phase of the Congo-Nile passage. It had taken the officers and men six months to open the way and move some seventeen thousand cases from Loango to Brazzaville, from mid-July to mid-January 1897. Three months more were needed to paddle up and out of the Congo River to the Ubangi. The third phase, the four-hundred-mile stretch beyond the Ouango rapids toward Tambura, had to be covered on foot. What had gone before —marauding Basundis, crocodiles and hippopotami, endless days in the water's stupefying glare, frayed nerves, dysentery and malaria —was but a rehearsal for the calvary of approaching Tambura. Baratier, accompanied by Deramond and three other officers, had left Mobaye with twenty-four dugouts and three hundred oarsmen on April 28 to map the course the rest of the mission would have to follow. Marchand advanced from Mobaye soon afterward, reaching Ouango, feverish and with a badly ripped toenail, a little before May 11. Pierre Simon, too ill to carry on and suffering his third hematuric attack at Bangassou, finally began the first lap of the long return to the coast and eventual death in late June.

Mangin and Landeroin had already headed for Rafai and Zemio in mid-May behind Baratier. Marchand would follow. Germain, Dyé, and Souyri, joined now by Lieutenant Eugène Gouly from the Kuango station, brought up the rear aboard the commandeered

Faidherbe in late May. Reaching the rapids above Ouango, they dismantled the steamer's hull, took apart the two-ton boiler, and with an army of Biasu, paid in beads and cloth, dragged and rolled the parts to navigable waters beyond, then sailed on to Zemio. When Mangin saw it puffing into Zemio in mid-June, he thought the *Faidherbe* a "highly risky" creation.

As the first rains of the May-October season fell, it was just possible that Marchand could push his men out of the rivers feeding the Congo and into those supplying the White Nile before they rapidly dried up at the end of the year. If the French failed to pass Tambura and reach the Sué River by October, it would mean having to camp for another seven months. The sultans were enthusiastically cooperative, and the other major people of the region, the cowed Karrari, had no choice but to serve resignedly as porters. Hundreds of porters and rowers were rounded up by Zande troops. Game was plentiful, and Mangin's group left its shallow boats to slaughter elephants below Rafai on May 23. The lieutenant found that "stewed elephant trunk is excellent" when wrapped in banana leaves and cooked for twelve hours. Months later, describing the sultans of Bangassou, Rafai, and Zemio, he dismissed them as "disgusting drunkards" who spoke "a few words of Arab patois," each one of them "begging gifts, especially rifles," and "adding to the shortcomings of black rulers all the vices of the Turks."

The ever-equable Baratier, on the other hand, found them firm, reasonable men, faithful to their bargains and deserving respect. Mangin notwithstanding, the Zande sultans knew how to impress. As long as the khalifa's armies menaced their borders, the Zande artfully welcomed in-transit European forces (Belgian and French). Marching through rows of armed uniformed troops, to bugled sounds of such martial clarity that he was "reminded, involuntarily," of a French parade ground, Justin Deramond wrote in his journal of the "astonishment at the honor paid us" at Bangassou, adding that, in returning the salute, "we did our best to render [it] as condescending as possible." Gorged on his hosts' honeyed chicken washed down with palm wine, the sergeant quickly recovered sufficient ethnocentrism to match Mangin's disdain for "these pure-blooded niggers (capable, certainly, of mental improvement) who take themselves for kings, for sultans without peer."

Beyond Zemio the going quickly became much harder. The hundred miles to Tambura, the last sultanate, took them away from the river and into the high grass. Since the end of May the rains had been torrential. Mangin, who had been ordered to forge ahead to catch Baratier, literally staggered into Tambura at the head of drenched, starving porters who had lost many of their cases. It was the same with Marchand's group, and for the first time Paké-Bô's magnificent confidence was taxed to the breaking point. "I almost believed for an instant that all was lost," he wrote in early July; "almost eight hundred loads abandoned in the grass by the [porters]; the grass blowing its worst in the rain." Liotard, whose advice, though not always welcome, had repeatedly saved the Congo-Nile force, once again served his countrymen. Awaiting them at Tambura's Fort Hossinger (a post less than two years old) was a year's supply of tinned food and enough equipment, Mangin wrote to a friendly general in Paris, "to stand up against a troupe of Mahdists." Although Mangin was displeased by the local sultan—"a greedy and sly brute who provokes not the slightest interest nor inspires the least confidence"—and although the ruler of Tambura had fought for both the Egyptians and the Mahdists, he and his people proved themselves, at least temporarily, an estimable ally for the French.

Mangin had no complaints about Fort Hossinger. They were "most comfortably housed in superb cabins, the likes of which we've not seen since Libreville," he told his sister. There was a first-rate garden with peas, potatoes, and cabbage, and chickens were for barter in the neighborhood. Better yet, he added, "the temperature rarely reaches 85 degrees in the shade." The post was restorative, and by the end of July Marchand's spirits were up again. "No matter what happens," his lengthy report to the minister of colonies vowed, "the flag will float over Meschra'er Req on January 1." Fashoda lay just beyond. But once more, confidence was tempered by anxiety. Although he wisely stressed that Liotard's advice and collaboration were splendid, and that his Fort Hossinger preparations were "all that I could hope for," Marchand told the Pavillon de Flore that it was his duty "to reiterate my requests concerning the immediate shipment of a second company of auxiliaries, of the 42-mm artillery battery belonging to Upper Ubangi and at this moment in Senegal, and of a detachable steamer for navigation of the Bahr al-Ghazāl and the Nile. The motorboat *Faidherbe* is only a simple flag bearer." Obviously uneasy about the reaction to his treatment of Basundi near Brazzaville, Marchand assured the minister, "Not one shot has yet been fired, except in the lower Congo in order to open the caravan route to Brazzaville." He was not planning to shoot his way to Fashoda or intimidate any of the peoples along his path. But, with thirty thousand Anglo-Egyptian troops fighting up the Nile, he obviously needed more than one hundred fifty *tirailleurs*. "What I'm asking is not superfluous in order to fix our flag temporarily at well-chosen points over which I am passing at this moment."

His requests were not being ignored. The mission's evolving needs were not always easy to know, however, because of the five months it now took for a message to reach Paris. Poised on the edge of the Congo watershed, Marchand was no longer uncertain about reaching Fashoda, but rather about what he needed to stay there. At the beginning of the next year, he would ask Liotard to hurry a telegraphic message to the coast for the Quai d'Orsay pleading for four hundred *tirailleurs* and twelve artillery pieces. Meanwhile, he counted on, as he explained to Mangin, the "plan of action organized in Paris before my departure in order to make a demarcation line of the 10th latitude north from one end of Africa to the other." Clochette striking for Fashoda from the east, naval officer Émile Gentil (with two other armed expeditions hurrying to reinforce him) occupying the Chari region leading to Lake Chad, and Bonvalot heading for the Sobat comprised the nub of that plan. But there was more. In addition to an Ethiopian army corps bearing down on the Lado Enclave, another mission coming from Timbuktu was to connect with Gentil in the Chari and Liotard in Deim Zubeir "in order to join with us."

Whether Marchand believed that all the elements of this complicated strategy were actually being coordinated so precisely is doubtful—a certain amount of pretense was essential to the mental health of the Congo-Nile mission. It would have taxed the senior staffs in the ministries of foreign affairs, colonies, and war to the fullest to execute such a plan; and it would have meant asking the notoriously stingy and fractious Chamber of Deputies for a great deal of money. To make matters worse the Quai d'Orsay, deeply averse to premature diplomatic confrontation with the British, wanted the Congo-Nile mission to succeed by underfunded stealth. Logistics of reinforcements could be managed once Marchand and his men were at the fort—depending also, of course, on what Kitchener and the khalifa had done to each other by then.

A little more than two months remained to move out of the Congo River system into the Nile. The rainfall was still heavy, but, once it slackened, the level in the Nile confluents would run down like water in an uncorked bathtub; and the *Faidherbe* was still more than three hundred miles downstream at Zemio. Until Baratier turned up at Fort Hossinger from exploring the upper reaches of the Mbomu on August 1, Marchand had expected to dismantle the steamer and begin lugging it overland from Zemio. But Baratier had paddled upstream to a point where a river unknown to the French—the Mboku—branched away to the northeast. Entering the Mboku he had discovered that, although it was crooked and badly clotted with vegetation, it was deep enough to take the *Faidherbe* as far as the unnavigable Méré, another uncharted watercourse about fifty miles from Tambura. This gave the steamer an additional 160 slow miles or more on the water. Once at the Méré, it would have to be hauled ashore, dismantled, dragged and rolled some one hundred miles to a place called Khojali, the nearest point on the Sué River.

Suffering his third hematuria at Hossinger, Justin Deramond was ordered back to France in mid-September. He left just as his journal pages were filling up with detailed accounts of friction between the officers and disciplinary problems among the men. On September 5, a Sunday night, several *tirailleurs* who had broken curfew stumbled back from Tambura, drunk, clutching stolen chickens, and belting out camp songs. A furious Marchand had not only been cursed by one of the Sudanese sergeants, but addressed with the familiar *tu*. Baratier's intervention probably prevented bloodshed. Sergeant Samba Rabi, winner of the Médaille Militaire, finally shrugged his shoulders, entering the stockade, he said, only because Baratier asked him—"If I didn't want to, he [Marchand] couldn't make me." The next morning, with the imprisoned sergeant still shouting curses at him, Marchand rounded on Mangin bitterly. "It's intolerable," he shouted, that the African troops Mangin had been assigned to recruit and train "don't want to hear of any authority but yours!" Feelings between the two officers worsened so much that Mangin took to wearing his revolver in camp. A few days later, Sergeant Samba Rabi apologized and was reinstated.

Arguments and indiscipline continued throughout that month and into the next. With Baratier taking an increasing hand in solving the engineering problems, the *Faidherbe* was hauled out of the Mboku and its hull taken apart piece by piece and assembled into forty-five-pound loads for portage. Together with the eight hundred-odd cases of mission supplies, the total number of loads needed more than two thousand carriers. In exchange for a heavy payment of cartridges, aging rifles, and handsomely wrought pistols, Mangin's "uninteresting brute," the sultan of Tambura, sent his Zande sol-diers to round up more than two thousand Madi and Duga people for the killing work demanded by the French. But before they carried, they had to clear. There was no road from the Méré to Khojali. One had to be built. The work on this road—fifteen feet wide and one hundred miles long—went on from September 12 to October 14, through the high grass and across the uneven terrain.

Food ran out. The sultan's supplies were gone. Marchand sent buyers far south for provisions. Grasshoppers had already stripped bare the vegetation to the west of Tambura, and one of the Suda-nese sergeants returned from Khojali to the north with the alarm-ing report that that region was under attack by the insatiable in-sects. The French learned of rumors among some of the people marked for labor that "the whites are shooting the porters instead of feeding them." "Under torrents of rain and without food," the road inched forward in mud and heat just a few miles in advance of the hundreds of *Faidherbe* parts, mission supplies, and the two one-ton sections of the steamer's boiler. Marchand's detailed ac-count of the herculean undertaking spoke of the stretch between the Méré and Rimbio when no more than "1300 yards followed thirteen hours of sustained efforts."

Because he demanded so much of himself, Paké-Bô rarely praised. Accomplishing the impossible was supposedly routine work for French marines. But now he gave way to unstinting admi-ration. "What bowls me over," he confessed, "is that the Basiri are still at it. These fellows are really terrific. I'm beginning to believe . . . that they don't eat while they're working." His Sudanese infan-trymen were also the stuff of myth, he found. Resourceful at every task, superb models for the local Africans, Sergeant Samba Rabi and his kind justified fully Baratier's later boast that only France pos-sessed such a colonial army. Ensign Dyé had been knocked out of the race at Zemio by dysentery and Germain was south of Tambura on one of the leader's impatiently ordered explorations. It was left to Baratier, Landeroin, Gouly, and the increasingly exasperated Sergeant Souyri to heave the two segments of boiler the hundred miles to Khojali.

Their first effort—nets made from local vegetation—failed. An-other try, with the boiler halves astride dugout canoes, collapsed under the tonnage. Baratier's third attempt worked. Yoking the huge boiler sections to the aluminum boats, he had lengths of wood cut from the few available trees, placing them under the boats so that the boilers could slide forward; the passed-over logs were then placed again in front of the advancing load. With nearly two hundred men pulling and pushing, the *Faidherbe*'s boiler eventually achieved a speed of about three miles a day, until, one hundred miles later, it reached the trench of water leading to Khojali on the Sué— the point on the river where the boiler could be reinstalled in the refloated steamer. The work of getting the boiler there became so gruelling that the sultan of Tambura had to be cajoled and paid from stocks intended for rulers deep in the Bahr al-Ghazāl before more laborers were found. The sultan cooperated, but complained to Liotard by courier that Marchand was stingy "in matters of arms, powder, percussion caps, cloth. Every week the gifts are less and less attractive and sufficient. I call your attention to this."

While the Zande ruler complained, the vegetation-clotted trench to the Sué was knifed through to make a channel for the boiler halves and boats. During one thirteen-hour day, the men chopped forward less than four hundred yards. "What astonishes me," Marchand marvelled six weeks later, "is that Baratier, Landeroin, and Gouly are still holding up. Their task is truly awful." Their task was not only truly awful; it failed in its purpose. The hard, steady, late October downpour which astounded Marchand—"never in my life even in the Sudan, have I seen so much water"—had stopped more than a month before the boiler arrived at Khojali. The Sué had nearly disappeared. To compound misfortune, the steamer's steel plates and rivets were late coming and partly defective. For Sergeant Souyri this was the last straw. He insisted on release to return to the Upper Ubangi. With no water at Khojali, Marchand decided the *Faidherbe* ought be dragged another 120 miles to the nearest point in the Sué with water enough to cradle the steamer. The French called the place "Poste des Rapides." There was little to do now but wait for the rains to begin in six months. Most of the mission would stay at Fort Hossinger until the spring. They had come almost three thousand miles since leaving Loango. Fashoda was five hundred miles away.

2

It was commonsense diplomacy for the British government never to justify publicly its invasion of the Sudan as an expensive maneuver to block the French on the Upper Nile. Official cognizance of the missions headed by Marchand, de Bonchamps, and Clochette would have risked conceding the French argument that the Nile basin was vacant territory available to the first serious occupier. Blocking the French was not the only reason Kitchener's army was now in winter quarters at Dongola, of course. The enormous popularity of Rudolf Slatin's year-old autobiography, *Fire and Sword* (translated by Wingate), was a masterpiece of propaganda, stirring vengeance for General Gordon's Khartoum martyrdom of 1885 and crusading righteousness against the black savagery of the Mahdiyya. British mothers and fathers choking with emotion on "Recessional," Kipling's just-published threnody glorifying the burden of empire, would still have been dismayed to learn that their sons were fighting and dying for an unknown place of no apparent value called Fashoda. Nor was there yet complete accord about Fashoda within the tight circle of ruling imperialists. Lord Cromer still saw no need to advance beyond Dongola, while Lord Salisbury had early and clearly perceived such a need, as had Colonial Secretary Chamberlain and Sirdar Kitchener. Officially, Fashoda remained a pinpoint on the map of British strategy, its incomparable importance unacknowledged and the pell-mell race to it undeclared (and thus the humiliation of losing refutable). That was the official line, even as Rennell Rodd's delegation hurried to Addis Ababa to checkmate Lagarde and Colonel Hector Macdonald's force dashed from Mombasa to the Nile basin to counter Marchand. But, occasionally, there were indiscreetly omniscient young journalists like Winston Churchill who felt no compunction about putting the geopolitics of the Sudan invasion in blunt perspective. "The movements of the French expeditions towards the Nile," he wrote of Kitchener's 1897 preparations, "counselled speed."

Eighteen ninety-seven was a year of speed—deliberate speed, greatly accelerating in the final quarter as the pitilessly methodical Sirdar's army steamrollered from Dongola. The compromise agreed upon (only after spirited discussions of Cromer's and Kitchener's opposing views) was Berber, the next large town on the Nile after Dongola and two hundred river miles from Omdurman. The forty-seven-year-old Sirdar was famous for his terseness. Some thought him capable of giving orders, but not of articulating the reasoning behind them. The clamped jaw (moustached to hide an old Mahdist bullet wound) and the steely, blue-eyed stare that would beckon millions of Englishmen to the trenches of the Great War was just then being discovered by awed war correspondents.

One of them, George W. Steevens of the *Daily Mail,* wrote that Kitchener's "precision is so inhumanly unerring, he is more like a machine than a man. You feel that he ought to be patented and shown with pride at the Paris International Exhibition." Laconic precision and perfect single-mindedness described Kitchener admirably, yet not completely. Behind the mask of Mars there were chasms of temperament, gulfs of self-doubt, and even rivulets of obsequiousness that could have had disastrous consequences for his career and the campaign. Lord Cromer unnerved him. But luck and the mask served him well. The Sirdar returned to Egypt in December 1896 with permission to advance to Berber. Cromer had fought him on a second year of warfare in the Mahdiyya and lost.

The battle over the railroad was harder. Once in Egypt, Kitchener immediately ordered his engineers to plan for the extension of the old Gordon Relief railroad beyond Wadi Halfa. In a more literal sense than Bismarck conceived the expression, Kitchener intended his superintendence of British imperialism to proceed by iron and blood. Armored steamers of the latest design were ordered from England. Squadrons of cavalry and a corps of camel troops were already assembled and being whipped into shape. But the Sirdar planned to meet the hosts of the khalifa not only with an armada of ironclads and waves of horses and camels, but at the head of parallel rails gleaming back to Wadi Halfa. It was to be Manchester versus Omdurman, the arsenal of the Industrial Revolution pitted against the implements of an African *jihād*. The engineers offered three possible routes: a line from the port of Suakin on the Red Sea to Berber; a line beginning at Korti, following the Nile to al-Metamma; and an improbable route plunging straight into the desert from Wadi Halfa to Abu Hamed, two hundred river miles from Omdurman. Kitchener unhesitatingly chose Wadi Halfa to Abu Hamed.

As it reaches Abu Hamed from its sources, the Nile begins a great five-hundred-mile loop until it more or less starts, at Wadi Halfa, to realign itself with the longitude for Abu Hamed. A diagonal line across the desert, connecting the ends of the loop and striking into the heart of the Mahdiyya, was irresistible to Kitchener. To Cromer it was preposterous, for the experts' unanimous verdict held that, "having due regard to the circumstances and remembering the conditions of war under which the work must be executed, it was impossible to construct such a line." But the Sirdar, bent on his unbroken steel lifeline to Manchester, won the dispute—simply by

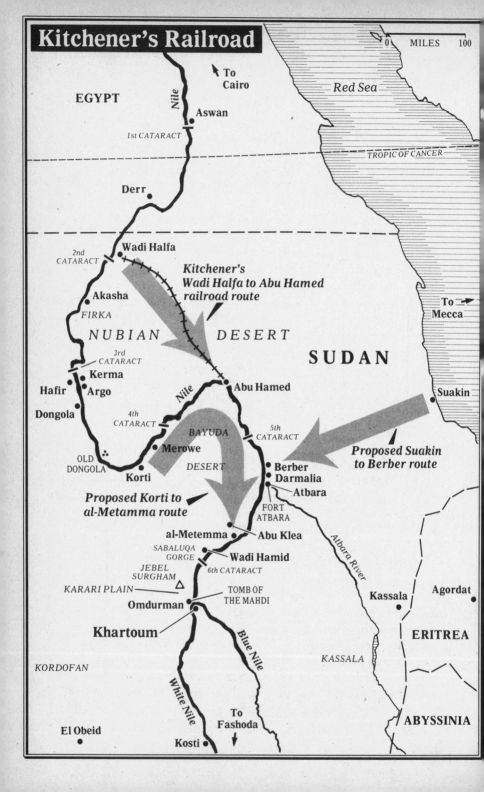

not debating. He then informed a flustered Cromer that the old three-foot, three-inch rail gauge was unsatisfactory for the extension beyond Wadi Halfa. Lord Cromer had become de facto viceroy of Her Majesty's second greatest possession because he was one of the realm's sharpest bankers. But the Sirdar's imperial vision was unencumbered by concerns for Egyptian bookkeeping. For him, the unacknowledged race to Fashoda galloped on to South Africa, where Cecil Rhodes's Cape-to-Cairo three-foot, six-inch gauge was anticipated soon to reach the Zambezi. Behind the Sirdar were other bankers and industrialists, and so Cromer also lost this round.

The Sirdar chose a brilliant young lieutenant of engineers, E. P. Girouard, French Canadian, unconventional, and charmingly disrespectful of rank, to work the impossible on schedule. Construction began in January 1897, paused almost four months while Girouard shopped for machinery and equipment in England, then resumed vigorously. By late July, Lieutenant Girouard's unstoppable work crew of one thousand *fellahin,* Mahdist prisoners, and Sudanese regulars had laid 130 miles of track. Abu Hamed was only a hundred miles ahead. But in the mosque at Omdurman, a shaken khalifa invoked the wrath of Allah, and what Churchill described as "cyclonic rains" wiped out fourteen miles of rail in an August flash. In any case, work on the line had to stop until the army captured Abu Hamed.

On the morning of August 9, Mahdists slain in battle at Abu Hamed floated on the Nile past a delighted Kitchener. It was Major General Archibald Hunter's sign that his surprise attack had succeeded. The general had lost two officers and twenty-four men; Mahdist losses had been heavy. The Anglo-Egyptian pace considerably quickened now. Abu Hamed, Berber, and al-Metamma were the three key points the khalifa had to hold if the invasion was to be stopped—or, if not stopped, halted long enough to raise doubts in London and Cairo about the cost of an advance to Omdurman. The loss of Abu Hamed made Zaki 'Uthman, the commander of Berber, so nervous that only word from Mahmud Ahmad, the khalifa's most aggressive general, arriving with a large reinforcement army, kept him at his post. Yet, with its large population and some ten thousand elite Mahdist troops, Berber was a formidable obstacle. Kitchener anticipated that it would be his most difficult test.

Before testing his men, though, the Sirdar tested his machines, the most deadly vessels yet launched on the Nile. The three old armored gunboats, with their twelve-pounder cannon and two Maxim-Nordenfelt machine guns, already outclassed the smaller and badly maintained steamers captured by the Mahdists during the mid-1880s. These were joined by three 1896-class stern-wheelers, 140 feet long, 24 feet wide, and steaming at twelve miles an hour. Three even more terrifying iron monsters were ready for crating in England. Seeing these devilish contraptions ready to bombard the city, and learning that Mahmud, after all, was not coming to his rescue, Zaki 'Uthman quietly withdrew, leaving a surprised Kitchener to send an occupation force into Berber without a battle on September 5. Girouard's railroad reached Abu Hamed on October 31.

Obedient to Cromer's view that, with the fall of Berber, the campaign should close, Cromer's director of finance began to reduce the invasion budget just as Kitchener thought that his easy victories should have convinced Cromer to support the final effort. The whole thing had to be finished off at Omdurman next year, he wrote the undersecretary for finance. "The strain on all of us is very great, and if we do not continue the advance the Dervishes will certainly assume the offensive." Worse yet, the undersecretary had "no idea what continual anxiety, worry, and strain I have through it all—I do not think I can stand much more, and feel sometimes so completely done up that I can hardly go on and wish I were dead." Four days later, on October 10, he cabled his resignation. The Sirdar's strain arose at least as much from military politics as from a Mahdist counteroffensive. Two days before his petulant telegram to Cromer, the old commander-in-chief of Egyptian forces, General Sir Francis Grenfell, had returned, this time to take charge of the British Army of Occupation in Egypt. To Herbert Kitchener this meant subordination of his Anglo-Egyptian command, if not his outright replacement. Only after an invitation to Cairo, reassurance of complete support, and Cromer's partial acquiescence to a reconsideration of policy did the "man of steel" agree to resume command. Even after returning to the front, he fretted, sending Grenfell a whiningly obsequious letter complaining of Cromer and professing his loyalty: "If you will place yourself in my position and tell me what you think I should do I will do my best to follow it."

The nerves left almost as suddenly as they had come. A month later, the Sirdar was on the offensive against Cromer. He paid a rapid visit to Massawa, where the Italian command, certain that the Ethiopians and the Mahdists were about to attack Kassala, had been in a state of high alarm since Adwa. Plans were completed for the transfer of the garrison on Christmas Day to the Sixteenth Egyptian Battalion, which would advance from Suakin. Kitchener's intention was to win permission to have Indian troops brought to Suakin to release the British-officered Egyptian and Sudanese infantry for combat. But the British government was not yet ready for a show-down, and Lord Cromer had powerful allies. Sensing the shifting current, the proconsul drafted a carefully reasoned memorandum, cabled to the prime minister in early November. In it Cromer made the strongest possible argument for halting at Berber. "Although I should of course much prefer that the French did not establish themselves on the Upper Nile, at the same time I do not share the somewhat extreme views—as they appear to me—which are often held as to the absolute necessity of preventing them from doing so," he began,

> What is it, after all, we want in Africa? I presume that we do not want to acquire on behalf of ourselves or the Egyptians large tracts of useless territory. . . . What we want, as it seems to me, is to trade with Central Africa. For the purpose of trade it would certainly be prefera-ble that no portion of the waterway of the Nile should be in the hands of an European Power. Let us, therefore, by all means do all that can be done by diplomacy, by negotiations with Menelik, who is the most important factor in the situation. . . . But whether it is desirable, merely in order to forestall the French on the Upper Nile, to send a large expedition to Khartoum with the possibility—for this also must not be forgotten—of being drawn by a combination of public pres-sures and military argument into further and more remote enter-prises appears to me to be very questionable.

But the Sudan invasion was becoming less susceptible of de-tached calculation with each bulletin from Kitchener's advancing headquarters. Then, as the year closed, the khalifa fatally played into the hands of Kitchener and Wingate.

Abdullahi had been plagued by disloyalty and self-doubt almost from the day the Anglo-Egyptian army crossed from Wadi Halfa into the Sudan. Suspecting the welling bitterness of the peoples along the river, Abdullahi was uncertain where to make a stand against the infidel. That had been the main reason for Zaki 'Uth-man's cowardly withdrawal from Berber, after the khalifa diverted the promised reinforcements to Omdurman. Abdullahi's best army and most aggressive amir, his cousin Mahmud Ahmad, commander of the Army of the West at Darfur, reached the capital in May, where it camped impatiently while Abdullahi reinterpreted his dreams, apostrophized the Mahdi, and exhorted the *ansār*. In one dream, which had come several times, the khalifa saw a carpet of bleached bones stretching across Omdurman's Karari Plain until it merged with the horizon—the remains of Kitchener's army. Yet he was not completely convinced by the dream, nor were those closest to him—Ya'qub, his half brother; 'Uthman Shaikh al-Din, his oldest son; Mahmud Ahmad of Darfur.

Mahmud had no experience with the killing power of a modern European arsenal, but he knew that, with sufficient numbers and a plan, the British and Egyptians could be made to bleed copiously for every mile advanced. Reinforce al-Metamma and attack Berber before it was solidly fortified by the enemy, he pleaded with his cousin. It made no sense to lose half the Mahdiyya's population while waiting for the enemy to arrive in force at Omdurman. Abdullahi should lead the army more than fifty thousand strong. But the ruler of the Mahdiyya had enemies everywhere, and as his *baraka* seemed to ebb from him he publicly abused those whose loyalty might have been greater. From Darfur to Equatoria the desert people were loyal. It was a different story among the Ja'aliyyin of the Nile, the people from whose ranks the Mahdi had come. The dismissal from positions of power of their amirs, the humiliation of the Mahdi's family, the punitive price controls and botched handling of currency had badly strained their trust in the khalifa.

Convinced that he could not rely on the people of al-Metamma, the khalifa ordered its proud sheikh to evacuate the populations and make way for Mahmud's occupation army. The sheikh was so much more fearful of sixteen thousand famished desert Arabs descending upon al-Metamma than of the well-provisioned, disciplined infidel that he sent a messenger to the Sirdar in late June offering to surrender the city, and pleading for a shipment of modern rifles to hold out until the Anglo-Egyptians arrived. The sheikh also sent the khalifa a letter renouncing obedience. Before the gunboats could deliver the rifles, Mahmud's army raced from Omdurman to throw itself against al-Metamma's walls in two blood-splattered waves. The attackers lost heavily, but they were able to carry out the khalifa's orders for the total massacre of the city's people. A year later, an appalled officer in the Grenadier Guards returned to his steamer from an inspection tour of the city, recording in his journal, "The place is thick with skulls and bones. . . . There must be several thousands of them lying about and the vultures still seem to find plenty of occupation."

When Kitchener returned from Massawa in November 1897, Wingate had alarming news. The khalifa's army was mobilizing. An Ethiopian delegation was arriving at Omdurman to put the final touches to an offensive alliance. There were strong indications of joint maneuvers down the Nile. Wingate was too politically astute not to color his intelligence findings. His December bomb exploded over the Salisbury cabinet just as it was grappling with Cromer's persuasive memorandum. It was true that nearly sixty thousand *ansār* were encamped on Karari Plain. It was true that Menilek's messengers were on their way to Omdurman with the Negus Negusti's extravagantly respectful greeting to "our superior, venerable, dear friend" the khalifa, and that, even though confidence in the Mahdiyya had been shaken by the loss of Dongola and Berber, the Ethiopians were willing to help the Sudanese—carefully, opportunistically, and up to a point. It was true that a large Ethiopian army under Ras Tassama was advancing toward the White Nile. But it was also true, as Wingate must have known, that the khalifa would not advance. The vision of bleached infidel bones on Karari Plain outside Omdurman held him fast to the city.

Then there was a new vision, this one of the archangel Gabriel appearing and promising extermination of his enemies if Abdullahi attacked on a certain day. But by now, the khalifa was not even capable of deciding among his jealous, spatting amirs whom to invest with command of the armies in the field. Mahmud he respected but liked increasingly less. 'Uthman Shaikh al-Din he liked but did not respect. Ya'qub the khalifa respected and liked, but not enough to deny his own son's passionate demand for the place of honor. Meanwhile, as Wingate also must have known, Ras Tassama's Ethiopians were not marching to join with the Mahdists, but were taking advantage of the khalifa's desperate need for peace between their two countries in order to occupy the contested Bani Shangul region. War councils were held late into the night, elaborate reviews of *jehādiyya* and *mulazimin* were mounted; on several occasions the great war drum boomed as the khalifa astride his mule seemed ready, amid deafening shouts of *"Ed din mansur!"* ("The faith is victorious!") to launch the *jihād*. Abruptly, on January 23, Abdullahi ordered the war flags lowered. He reentered Omdurman.

Wingate's intelligence bureau failed to report the Mahdist demobilization. It probably would have made no difference. By then, Cromer and others opposed to the race had changed their minds. There was a sudden hardness in the British government's dealings with France over the Nile basin. On December 10, the British ambassador, Sir Edmund Monson, had handed French Minister of Foreign Affairs Gabriel Hanotaux a blunt warning: "Her Majesty's Government must not be understood to admit that any other European Power than Great Britain has any claim to occupy any part of the Valley of the Nile. The views of the British Government upon this matter were plainly stated in Parliament by Sir Edward Grey some years ago." The shock among some British politicians caused by Grey's remarks at the time, and the ambiguous diplomatic signals sent to the French over the years, were gone. In late February, in strictest confidence, Monson relayed to Prime Minister Salisbury the unsettling prediction that, because of the polarization caused by the Dreyfus Affair, it was highly unlikely that France could "much longer escape an internal convulsion; a convulsion in which the army will take a prominent part, and which will equally be followed by a foreign war."

All the more justification, then, to have given the Sirdar the green light in December. It was now nonstop to Fashoda. Over the loudest protests heard in years from Istanbul, four thousand Indian troops marched down gangplanks into Suakin. Lieutenant Girouard extended the army's steel aorta beyond Abu Hamed to Bashtanab above the Fifth Cataract. Battalions from three crack British regiments were in place by the end of January, with a fourth on its way. A fifth, the Seaforth Highlanders, arrived a month later. South of Berber, six-foot-thick mud walls, gun emplacements, and infantry entrenchments presented a murderous face to the Mahdists.

Sixteen thousand of them were on the march. Mahmud Ahmad had not accepted the khalifa's decision to wait for the Anglo-Egyptians at Omdurman. Finally, after much argument and meditation at the Mahdi's tomb, Abdullahi gave Mahmud his blessings for an advance to retake Berber. Mahmud's force reached the outskirts of Berber in early March. Wad Bushara, "the Tiger of Hafir," whose fighting spirit matched Mahmud's, had joined the advance. Wad Bushara was a much wiser commander after two hard-fought engagements with the Sirdar's army. Mahdist warriors were capable of incredible physical endurance, so much so that British infantry had begun filing the tips of its Lee-Metford cartridges for greater stopping power. Riddled, even disembowelled, Mahdists were known to spring to life and kill after a battle was over. But howitzers and Maxims had taught Wad Bushara respect for strategy, respect he conveyed to the impetuous Mahmud. The caution of 'Uthman Diqna, the last of the early generals with whom the khalifa had won his empire, was even greater. Out of retirement in the Mahdiyya's hour of peril, preferring a strategy of measured retreat in order to draw the enemy almost to the Ethiopian border, the leader of the Hadendoa counselled a war of position rather than attack.

In any case, Mahmud had to concede that Berber was now too well defended for a frontal attack. He tried a wide, looping maneuver instead, hoping to circle behind the Anglo-Egyptian army and cut its line of communication. Kitchener promptly shifted his troops in a blocking movement. The Sudanese settled down at the juncture of the Nile and the Atbara River, building a sprawling, thorn-bush-encircled *zariba,* honeycombed with trenches. British officers had developed a grudging respect for the handsome Mahmud. Moreover, Wingate's usually accurate intelligence overestimated the amir's troop strength, another reason for British respect. Due to desertions, Mahmud had less than twelve thousand of his original sixteen thousand men—about two thousand less than Kitchener. Food was running low, the surrounding Ja'ali population was overtly hostile, and his desert troops had been corrupted by what seemed to them the fabulous booty and comely women gathered at al-Metamma. Friction between Mahmud and 'Uthman Diqna was intense. Meanwhile, the khalifa ordered a retreat up the Nile to the group of fortresses encircling the Sixth Cataract—the forts at Sabaluqa Gorge. If it withdrew from its *zariba* on the Atbara, Mahmud feared his army would fall apart. He brooded in his tent, unable to decide whether to advance or retreat.

Kitchener knew nothing of this, and he was both puzzled and unnerved by the amir's uncharacteristic behavior. For two weeks both armies stared at one another less than forty miles apart. The strain proved too great for the Sirdar. "The reconnaissance of Mahmud's position proves that we have in front of us a force of Dervishes of better fighting qualities and far greater numerical strength than we have ever met before," he telegraphed Cromer. What should he do? "You should not have asked me such a question," Cromer replied. Before the reply arrived, however, the attack was on; Kitchener had mastered his nerves and decided on a morning offensive on April 8.

Rockets and artillery fire opened up at precisely 6:15. The Cameron Highlanders led the perfect British columns straight into point-blank rifle fire, but the steady performance of the black troops, who moved ahead of the British, evoked unrestrained praise even from the racist correspondent Steevens. Pampered and paid, Kitchener's Sudanese and *fellahin* were the backbone of an advance that otherwise could never have succeeded. In the *zariba's* trenches, "*jibba*-clad figures sprang out of the ground, fired and charged, and were destroyed at every step," Winston Churchill recorded. Forty minutes of slaughter and the Battle of the Atbara was over. Wad Bushara and 'Uthman Diqna escaped, but Mahmud stood with his troops until the last, and was captured. He lost almost three thousand men.

Kitchener's tactics had been as unimaginative as the khalifa's: a whistle blew and the troops paraded into the enemy. They worked against the Mahdists' atrociously maintained, twenty-year-old Remingtons, low-grade gunpowder, and no artillery, but paid a high price for their victory. Over one hundred men, mostly brown and black, had been lost. When Chaplain Owen Spencer Watkins arrived at Dakla Fort the evening after the battle, he found the scene in the officers' mess reminiscent of a hospital. One colonel wore his arm in a sling. Another was "so bandaged that he was unrecognizable, for he had been wounded in the face." Queen Victoria's telegram, inquiring how her "brave wounded are progressing," cheered them immensely. Visiting the field hospital the following morning, Watkins saw heart-rending cases of heat prostration (the Sudan was "perpetual liquefaction," Steevens said), enteric fever, and "other young fellows lying, racked with pain, many of them maimed for life." He reflected upon the "terrible character of war" but he brought encouragement to those who would soon recover. "Turning their thoughts to higher and better things," the chaplain reminded them that "there would yet be another fight before the expedition was done."

The fighting was over for Mahmud, but his spirit flared up when he was paraded before Kitchener. Watkins and Steevens were impressed by the exchange. "Are you the man Mahmud?" the Sirdar asked. "Yes, I am Mahmud, and I am the same as you," snapped the proud commander. "Why did you come to make war here?" Kitchener continued—oddly, as he was standing five hundred miles into Mahmud's country. "I came," said the amir, "because I was told— the same as you." British officers went on vacation after Atbara.

Troops were marched off to Darmalia for soccer, cricket, and drill while awaiting the rise of the Nile in July. Meanwhile, Girouard's railroad snaked on to Berber, bringing the one hundred tons of food and supplies daily consumed. The three 1898-class, screw-driven armored steamers, behemoths bristling with four Maxim guns, two Nordenfelts, a howitzer, and a quick-firing twelve-pounder, arrived for assembly at Wadi Halfa. They were slower and clumsier than the older boats. Their Rube Goldberg superstructures, topped off by searchlights, gave them the incredible appearance of industrial townships set afloat on the Nile.

Now came the First Battalion of Grenadier Guards and Northumberland Fusiliers, and the Second Battalion of Lancashire Fusiliers and the Second Rifle Brigade—a full division commanded by the splenetic Lieutenant General Sir William Gatacre, whom the British troops affectionately called "Back-acher." There was more, for the War Office, now that the nation was fully committed, was unstinting of resources. The Thirty-second and Thirty-seventh Artillery Field Battalions with their forty-pounders and five-inch howitzers also clattered down Girouard's tracks to Berber. Finally, as full measure of national do-or-die, came the knightly Twenty-first Lancers, the posh unit in which correspondent Churchill's mother immediately arranged her son's lieutenancy, to the irritation of the Sirdar.

The khalifa obeyed his dream slavishly. He would meet the "Turk," as he called foreigners, on the plain of Karari. Sabaluqa Gorge, fifty miles north, was the logical point to make a stand. Had Mahmud eluded capture, he would almost certainly have insisted on occupying the seven thick-walled fortresses overlooking the rolling, cocoa-colored waters passing through the Sixth Cataract. Even the great gunboats would have found passage impossible until the guns of the Sabaluqa forts were silenced. And even then, the cautious Sirdar would almost certainly never have left his line of communications vulnerable by marching around the forts. The forts would have had to be stormed by infantry through the rubble created by artillery pounding, rubble in which the concealed enemy would exact a terrible toll. But the khalifa was afraid to move part of his forces. Abdullahi simply no longer trusted his soldiers, especially after the sack and massacre of al-Metamma. Instead, he made a halfhearted effort to mine the Sixth Cataract, ordering the boiler of a steamer packed with dynamite and submerged for detonation when the British flotilla passed over it. A pistol at the boiler's center, its trigger attached to a cord, was to ignite the charge. Somehow the charge exploded, atomizing the Mahdist crew in the boat above. Shaken by the mishap, the next crew surreptitiously punched a hole in the second boiler.

'Uthman Diqna urged that, like the Russians retreating before the Grande Armée, Abdullahi abandon the capital and draw the invaders south into the *sudd*. It would have been a strategy sorely perplexing to the cautious Sirdar and of much concern to the Foreign Office, always alert to Ethiopian complications. But the khalifa rejected the plan. Flexibility had never been natural to him. With his best generals now dead, mostly on his orders, and those who knew most about the larger world imprisoned, banished, or covertly rejoicing in his troubles, Abdullahi succumbed to the parochialism that was his true nature.

The last visit from the Ethiopians sadly showed how far gone was his political acumen. Menilek's delegation reached Omdurman either in late March or early April 1897, before news of the Atbara defeat had reached the capital. Wad Bushara, sent to Addis Ababa by the khalifa, returned with it bearing the customary written and oral messages from the Negus Negusti. The ban on wine was lifted, lamb for the Ethiopians was slaughtered by Ethiopian rather than Sudanese cooks, varieties of dates were ordered. Abdullahi intended to match the fabled hospitality of Menilek, to show the capital of the Mahdiyya as the center of a mighty, well-provisioned state. But there were moments when the thousand-year-old manners of the Ethiopians disconcerted the khalifa. When they entered the Grand Mosque with an elaborate salute, "by bowing their heads and putting their hands on their chests," he asked them bluntly, "Why do you bow your heads when saluting?" Four days later, actually receiving them under an embroidered tent taken from the captured baggage wagons of Yohannes IV, Abdullahi pulled out the stops to impress with a rocket-and-fireworks show. Only a partial account of Ethiopian-Sudanese negotiations has survived. Formal cession of the Bani Shangul region must have been discussed; assurances that the large armies operating beyond Ethiopia's customary borders were no threat to the Mahdiyya were definitely repeated. And one extraordinary matter, discussed in strict secrecy: as Wad Bushara left Addis Ababa, the Negus Negusti had told him to "take this flag," pointing to the furled tricolor held by Léonce Lagarde, "and give it to the khalifa and tell him that if the English advance against him he is to fly it at the head of his army."

Hanotaux would never have been a party to such a gambit, and even the more forceful Lebon would hardly have issued instructions on his own authority that put France in the position of defending the khalifa from more than twenty thousand British and Egyptian troops. What little exists about this bizarre episode suggests another instance of diplomatic intention mangled by calculated mistranslation. Sending the flag to Omdurman appears to have been Lagarde's impetuous idea. But what the Frenchman meant to convey by this—that the khalifa should recognize and welcome Europeans who marched under the tricolor (Liotard and Marchand)—was probably mischievously elaborated upon by Menilek in order to embroil these two troublesome powers: Britain and France. Ya'qub despised the proposal; it was a betrayal of the Mahdiyya's purity and purpose. Far better to trust in Allah and the dream, even if all was destroyed, than to hide behind the flag of the white devils. The uncertain khalifa called upon Yusuf Mikha'il for an opinion. Yusuf Mikha'il risked Ya'qub's wrath and urged his master to hoist the tricolor. Shaikh al-Din wanted to survive, even if it meant a pact with the French unbelievers, and also defied Ya'qub. Abdullahi decided to put the matter to the elders. They "have no good ideas," his son sighed. In the end, as the Anglo-Egyptians rolled forward, the French flag was stored in the khalifa's house.

As the sun rose on the last day of August 1898 over Jebel Surgham, the dark, cone-shaped mountain almost in the center of Karari Plain, the surviving power of the Mahdiyya surged out of Omdurman for review by the khalifa. Five thousand Deghein and Kenana soldiers formed the army's left wing, under the bright green flag of the steady Ali Wad Helu, an unexcelled cavalry officer. Under a huge, dark green battle standard intended to diminish Ali Wad Helu's, 'Uthman Shaikh al-Din led the main force of fourteen thousand spear-bearing *mulazimin* and thirteen thousand *jehādiyya,* or black riflemen. His troops were not the best—those had been given to Ya'qub, Wad Bushara, and 'Uthman Diqna—and this was Shaikh al-Din's first field command, but with his supply of rifles and weight of numbers he was expected to hold together the center. Behind the khalifa's son, the khalifa himself, under a black banner, commanded his bodyguard of two thousand with its nucleus of devoted Negro slaves. The army's right wing began with the Khalifa Sherif's brigade of two thousand Danaqla, identified by a broad red banner, and extended to 'Uthman Diqna's bannerless two thousand Hadendoa. In the rear, armed with spears and swords, were Ya'qub's fierce fourteen thousand Baqqara, a massive black flag in their midst. Stirred by the khalifa's exhortation and the moaning *ombeya*, or war horn, 52,000 *ansār* formed into a great crescent, awaiting the signal to sweep across the desert toward 25,800 methodically advancing British and Egyptians.

There was great exhilaration in the Mahdist high command, but also unease. Ali Wad Helu had broken his wrist when his mount slipped during a recent parade before the Mahdi's tomb. Then during the night, as special teams of *mulazimin* crisscrossed the city to flush out shirkers, some six thousand Mahdist soldiers slipped into the desert. Whether he had five thousand or a mere five at his side, Allah would grant him victory, Abdullahi proclaimed. Another vision had come, he said—of Muhammad the Prophet riding a horse before them into battle. But the next morning came another troublesome portent: a riderless steed, its head tamely lowered, cantered slowly toward the Mahdist position.

Suddenly, there was no more time to worry about portents. Scouts and the telegraph brought news that the enemy was a day's march from Omdurman. The crescent shot forward, like a scythe across the plain, and then placed itself about two miles from the foot of the range known as the Karari Hills. On Jebel Surgham, the British commander of Egyptian cavalry, Lieutenant Colonel R. G. Broadwood, saw the Mahdist advance and sent a courier with the warning to Kitchener. Reconnoitering from the Anglo-Egyptian encampment at al-Ageiga on the left bank of the Nile, the Twenty-first Lancers sped around from the Karari Hills with the same alert. The dimensions of the panorama were unlike anything yet experienced by the British, with few exceptions among them. "The great army of the Dervishes," Lieutenant Churchill wrote, "was dwarfed by the size of the landscape to mere dark smears and smudges on the brown of the plain." The Sirdar's six brigades, two British and four Egyptian, positioned and stiffened to meet them. The Mahdist storm moved more or less parallel with the Nile, raging on a course that, if unaltered, would miss the enemy entirely. Suddenly, it halted. The *ansār* spread their mats and squatted in the sand.

The khalifa and Kitchener passed the most anxious night of their lives. Thirteen years before, Abdullahi had taken up the Mahdi's sword, expanded his realm into Egypt and Ethiopia, inspired and bullied the peoples into accepting a central authority, imposed taxes, a bureaucracy, an army, and a postal system—and accomplished it all largely through his own intelligence and will. Yet, with so much achieved, the khalifa had an unshakable feeling that the forces arrayed against him were beyond surmounting. Although it was now too late for an offensive alliance, at least his understanding with Menilek allowed Abdullahi to concentrate his forces against the Anglo-Egyptians without much fear of an Ethiopian attack. He had numbers, and his men were ready to die. Yet, for the first time, the khalifa was truly unsure if courage and numbers were enough. Messengers arrived with the horrifying news that not only had nine gunboats silenced the new forts covering the approach to Omdurman, but British howitzers had shattered the sacred Tomb of the Mahdi. The battery's first shot had put a hole straight through the dome. Forty-pound shells packed with lyddite had crunched through the capital's mud walls like cookie cutters. Others had slammed into Omdurman's center like carpet-beaters, flattening and killing under an umbrella of dust. Hours later, the khalifa's troubled sleep was broken by cries from his men. The ancient night sky was scissored by blades of brilliant light. "What is this strange thing?" he asked 'Uthman Azrak. "Sire," the shaken khalifa was told, "they are looking at us."

Kitchener hoped that the searchlights would prevent a night attack. The *ansār* often fell upon enemies in the dark, as they had at Abu Klea and Tamai. If the khalifa sent his thousands slithering through the sands, noiselessly cutting the throats of sentries, and bunching together for a screaming charge against dozing Egyptian and British soldiers, there might be another Adwa. To counter that possibility, Wingate had sent Sudanese double agents into the Mahdist camp with stories of British plans for a night attack. In the stygian blackness just before daybreak, the Sirdar's nerves were at their keenest, for it had been at dawn that the Mahdi's faithful had stormed and breached the stout walls of Khartoum. Even if no attack came before dawn, the British commander was certain he would have to send his men across Karari Plain against an enemy entrenched before Omdurman. The high casualties of Atbara would probably be greatly exceeded.

By 3:30 A.M., the ruler of the Sudan had ranged his fifty-four thousand *ansār* across a five-mile front. A night attack had never seriously entered his head. Six thousand soldiers had padded out of Omdurman the night before to avoid fighting for him. Sending his army toward the hills in darkness would have been an incalculable risk. Nor was breaking camp and burrowing into the rubble of Omdurman (Kitchener's greatest fear) possible, for the archangel Gabriel had been quite precise about the victory taking place on the vast plain. Scouting Abdullahi's army from Jebel Surgham, Churchill gave the scene its appropriate majesty: "All the pride and might of the Dervish Empire was massed on this last great day of its existence." If 'Uthman Diqna, Wad Bushara, or 'Uthman Azraq still harbored doubts about a frontal attack on artillery and machine guns—even one certified by an archangel—they knew better than to give further voice to them now. Both the khalifa and their own culture were against maneuvering and retreating. If it was Allah's will that their *jihād* measure the shortest distance between life and death, then so be it.

A little after 5:30 A.M., to the complete surprise of Kitchener, who had just ordered the Anglo-Egyptian army to advance, the khalifa attacked. On Jebel Surgham, Churchill and his fellow lancers saw the Mahdists first. "The pace of their march was fast and steady, and it was evident that it would not be safe to wait long among the sandhills." At six sharp, the *ansār* could be seen by the British commanders. Chaplain Watkins was awed:

> We sighted the banner of one of their leaders, and soon as far as we could see were fluttering banners, and beneath them a seething mass of black humanity. The numbers seemed countless, their line of front extending for something like four miles across the plain and over the hill, looking solid and compact, a great contrast to our thin line, two deep, and making our 20,000 men, of which we had been so proud, look like a mere handful.

Seated on his prayer mat while his secretary brought reports, the khalifa heard the opening thunder of forty-pounders at 6:25, as twenty shells from the Thirty-second Field Battery scooped into the *ansār* mass. Next he heard the Krupps and Maxim-Nordenfelts of the Egyptian batteries, joined by the bark of the gunboats. The khalifa was only just beginning to realize that he had set his army on the wrong course. Perhaps it was misinformation cleverly planted by Wingate's spies or perhaps a misreading of the movements of Lieutenant Colonel Broadwood's cavalry, massed on the shanks of the Karari Hills, but the khalifa and his amirs believed that the bulk of the Anglo-Egyptian army had left its Nile beachhead and positioned itself near the hills. The Mahdists were on a course almost perpendicular to the British and Egyptian infantry squares in their semicircular *zariba* along the river when the field batteries brought a stinging correction to their attack. Ten thousand men under Shaikh al-Din's green banner and eight thousand led by 'Uthman Diqna swerved right, running and riding dead ahead for the enemy, their speed increasing in the hurricane of shrapnel and their war cries rising above the howitzers.

By 8:30, the battle appeared to be over. "It was a matter of machinery," Churchill noted. Although the outcome was never really in doubt, Kitchener made two major mistakes that could have made the Anglo-Egyptian victory a Pyrrhic win. Lieutenant Colonel Broadwood's Egyptian cavalry had found itself about to take the brunt of much of the rest of the Mahdist army, some twenty thousand soldiers under Ali Wad Helu and Shaikh al-Din. These were troops who had not swerved to attack the Nile beachhead, but continued on course for the Karari Hills. The Sirdar signalled Broadwood to head for the *zariba*, an order that would have brought the colonel's horsemen panting into the camps through the shaky Egyptians with more than twenty thousand Sudanese howling on their heels. Rather than risk pandemonium, Broadwood ignored the commander's instructions and began to retreat to the north, in the opposite direction from the *zariba*, intending to draw off Shaikh al-Din's formation.

It was an inspired tactical decision, but it left the slow Egyptian camel corps exposed and with barely enough time to fall back upon the camp. Only the last-minute appearance of the armored behemoth, *Melik*, saved the camel corps. Steaming downstream, every cannon and machine gun blazing away at close range, the gunboat ripped so many holes in the charging *ansār* that they were impeded by their own heaped dead. Relinquishing his prey, the inexperienced Shaikh al-Din regrouped his warriors and, instead of throwing them into the desperate fight at the *zariba*, galloped off into the hills after the Egyptian cavalry. Chaplain Watkins described the end of the frontal assault by 'Uthman Diqna's eight thousand:

With an utter fearlessness they rushed onto certain death, and as they rushed melted before the death-blast. But those left did not falter; soon but five remained, but they kept on their way; then three—still no check; and at last one only, but snatching the flag from his dead comrade's hand, alone he rushed onward, and tho bullets fell thick around him, it seemed as tho his life was charmed, and for another 150 yards he continued his mad rush; but at last he, too, fell dead, having reached nearer the English ranks than any other man in all that vast army.

"Our men were perfect," Steevens of the *Daily Mail* sportingly limned, "but the Dervishes were superb—beyond perfection." Churchill said, with terse honesty, "It seemed an unfair advantage to strike them thus cruelly when they could not reply."

Kitchener's second mistake was to assume he had won before the battle was over. A few minutes after 8:30, he ordered the Twenty-first Lancers to sweep Karari Plain of resistance pockets and cut off the retreating Mahdists. High-spirited knights who had twisted impatiently in their saddles while the Egyptian cavalry duelled the enemy, the lancers trotted out of the *zariba* toward Omdurman. A thin line of Mahdists lay across their path, and the cocky mass on hooves shifted into a gallop. Suddenly, what the lancers' colonel had mistaken for a few hundred stragglers turned out to be the decoys of more than two thousand of 'Uthman Diqna's riflemen, hidden in a *khor,* or dry stream bed. Regimental bugle blaring, sabers flashing, the Twenty-first Lancers made a mad, glorious cavalry charge. One hundred twenty seconds later, they had lost twenty-one officers and men out of four hundred, with another sixty-five seriously wounded. Steevens thought the charge splendid, showing that "the fighting devil has not, after all, been civilized out of Britons." Without intelligence from the lancers, Kitchener was unaware, when he finally gave the order to march on Omdurman at ten minutes to nine, that the khalifa and Ya'qub were behind Jebel Surgham with another twenty-one thousand fighters. Five of the Sirdar's six brigades raced each other for the honor of arriving first behind the lead British formation—the Second Brigade—before the gates of the city. Flushed with victory and now within an hour's march of the citadel of Mahdist power, the British troops, whose catechism for months had been "where a nigger can go, I can go," moved across the flat sands at a pace just short of a spring, leaving Colonel Hector Macdonald's Sudanese far in the rear.

Ya'qub's thousands sprang upon Macdonald. Risen from the ranks and worshipped by his troops, "Fighting Mac" found himself about to be supremely tested. Dismounting, pacing among his excitable Sudanese, the colonel steadied them for the impact of Ya'qub's fifteen thousand infantry, while a messenger raced after the Sirdar bearing an SOS. Macdonald's fire was deadly, but two thousand Martini-Henrys would never have been enough to stop the enemy; and Ya'qub, leading the charge on horseback, seemed immune to bullets. From his prayer blanket the khalifa shouted *"Abjakka!"* to his elite guard—"Attack!"—throwing his pampered but fearless Negro troops into what he knew was a last, desperate gamble. By then, and just as the distance between Ya'qub and Macdonald was less than a hundred yards, the two British and two Egyptian brigades had reeled about and come racing across the flanks of the Mahdists, gouging them with rifle fire, machine gunning, and shelling from armored boats. Horrified, the khalifa saw his brother disappear in the flash of a direct artillery hit. Kitchener had been slow to realize Macdonald's danger, but not too slow. With Ya'qub dead and the best of the *ansār* troops now a carpet of bodies stretching from Jebel Surgham almost to Macdonald's boots, the battle of Karari Plain was over. Abdullahi's dream of an army destroyed on this field had come to pass. Dazed, his flag seized by infidel British troops, the khalifa mounted his mule for Omdurman, where, after praying at the Mahdi's shattered tomb and gathering about him the last of the loyal, he escaped in disguise into the desert just as Kitchener entered the city.

CHAPTER NINE

The End of the Race

1

Where the White Nile makes a sharp right turn at Lake No, before straightening again at Fashoda and flowing 470 miles north to Khartoum, marks the center of the lands inhabited by the three dominant Nilotic peoples—Shilluk, Nuer, and Dinka. Isolated, inward-looking, they found themselves increasingly caught up in the three-cornered competition—Turco-Egyptian, Arab Sudanese, and European—for their seemingly limitless plane of weeds, water, and baked mud.

For the khedive's governors and soldiers, the winning of Shilluk notables and military conscription of their people had been crucial to the work of Egyptian expansion. Mahdist amirs had counted just as heavily upon Nuers in their drive to push the Sudan's frontiers into Central Africa, into what became Chad and the Congo Free State. The strategists in the colonial army of France had come to believe that by playing Nilotes against Mahdists, France could establish a protectorate in the Bahr al-Ghazāl from which its influence in the Sudan would be as irresistible as the flooding of the Nile itself. "I fear neither the Belgians nor the English," Marchand wrote Paris before reaching Fashoda; "we are living in the midst of at least seven to eight million Dinkas who, already friends, are becoming our allies. Now I'm going to work on the Shilluks."

The tall, sharp-featured Shilluks were the oldest of the indigenous African populations in the Bahr al-Ghazāl, with memory going back more than four centuries to the half-man, half-crocodile Nyikang, the divine king who had led them triumphantly to the west bank of the Nile. Omnipotent in principle, the Shilluk reth, or king, could in fact neither command his subjects to obey him nor stop them from fighting among themselves. His people looked to him for sacrifices to make the rains fall or bring victory in war, to maintain and purify the shrines to Nyikang, and to perform the ceremony of reconciliation between enemies. Above all, as the incarnation of his people's spirit, the reth must remain healthy; for if and when he could no longer do so, he was secretly slain by his courtiers. One dramatic account of an unfortunate reth's demise has him spending nights "in constant watchfulness, prowling fully armed, peering into the shadows. . . . Then, when at last his rival appeared, the fight would take place in grim silence . . . for it was said to be a point of honor for the reth not to call for help."

Whatever the precise powers of their king, the rule under which the Shilluks lived was more centralized and better organized than that of the Nuers and Dinkas. But then, with more than two hundred thousand of them crowded into a ten-mile-deep strip from Lake No northward beyond Fashoda for two hundred miles, a certain amount of cultural and political cohesion became necessary. They kept cattle, but not many; farmed and fished from the loamy, mile-long strips of hot marsh; and kept a thatched neatness to their clustered villages. They disdained the bow and arrow for the long metal-tipped spear. Like all Nilotes, they believed in their own cultural superiority. "The things of the Shilluks are good, and the things of the strangers are bad," was one of their favorite axioms. More than the others, however, their mythology of chosenness and of unbroken royal lineage made the yoke of the encroaching Turco-Egyptians unbearable as their homeland was reduced, between 1871 and 1874, to a province of Egypt.

Nuers and Dinkas watched from the sidelines at first. Unlike the Shilluks, these heronlike cattle herdsmen farther along the east bank of the Upper Nile had little political structure in their world, no royal traditions or overbearing aristocracies. Dinka priests who bore the sacred fishing spear were respected as intercessors between the powers of the divine world and Dinkaland, but they had no authority that could be seen as political. The cult of the sacred spear unified the clans through its powerful symbolism of phallic, natural, and spiritual renewal. Among the kindred Nuer, there was the leopard-skin chief, a nonhereditary religious potentate officiating over the deep spiritual needs of his people; but he also carried less political weight than the Shilluk reth.

Nuers and especially Dinkas were arrogant democrats, albeit ethnocentric ones. "Dinka" was the outsider's name for a people who knew themselves as Monyjang—"Men of Men"—denoting their standard for what is normal for the dignity of man and asserting superiority over " 'the others' or 'foreigners.' " "How can there be anything bad in the Dinka way?" they asked themselves. "If there were would it not have been abandoned a long time ago?" A towering sense of *dheeng*—"dignity"—infused the Dinka's every act; strangers were punctiliously respected so long as they deserved it —if not, they ceased to exist in his eyes. Successive waves of Arabs and Britons impressed the Nuers and the Dinkas, but overall these people of the Nile remained unintimidated by the outsiders' technology.

With the coming of the Turco-Egyptians and the Arabs of northern Sudan, the Dinkas had spoken in ever sadder tones of the spoilt world commencing in the 1870s. At first, they failed to see the common danger, and when the Shilluks rose in rebellion against the Egyptians in 1875, Dinkas and Nuers sat on their spears. Gordon's lieutenant, Romolo Gessi, was able to hold Bahr al-Ghazāl Province and, finally, to reestablish Khartoum's authority—so successfully that when the Mahdi's armies came crashing up the Nile in 1881, the pacified Shilluks now enrolled in the Egyptian army to fight them. But if Shilluks had learned to live with their Egyptian overlords, Dinkas and Nuers had not. Roused from indifferent neutrality by the Egyptians' high-handedness, they joined the Mahdists against Gessi's successor, Frank Lupton, believing the promise of the Mahdi that they would be delivered from the khedive's bureaucracy and taxes. With Dinka and Nuer spears in their ranks, Muhammad Ahmad's *jihād* swept Lupton's army aside.

But the Dinkas were to pay dearly for alliance with the Mahdists. Open season on slave-hunting and justified fear of forced Islamic conversion and circumcision turned them into guerrilla fighters by 1884. Their ferocity under the leader Chakchak infuriated the *ansār* as much as it had unnerved the unenthusiastic levies of the khedive. Dinka villages were flattened and burned, their cattle stolen, and women and young men yoked off to be sold. Retreating with what they could salvage of their beloved cattle into the swamps, the Dinka fought back furiously. The time spent hiding in the *sudd* from Mahdists reinforced the people's suspicions of the foreigner and nursed "that loathing and contempt for the stranger and all his ways."

After nearly ten years of the Mahdiyya's taxes and slave-raiding, the Shilluks rebelled again in 1891. Drought and famine, accompanied by a plague of grasshoppers, had ravaged much of the Sudan during 1889–90, sparing only the Fashoda region of the Shilluks. The Shilluks found themselves in a sellers' market for grain—until the khalifa ordered another invasion. The bloody Amir al-Zaki Tamal, who had routed the usually unbeatable Ethiopians, hurried to the scene with Nuer auxiliaries. A confused and brutal period ensued. Nuers fell upon the outnumbered Shilluks, and the reth was killed defending his capital at Fashoda in 1892. Kur Abd al-Fadil, a puppet reth, was placed on the throne. (He would still be in power when Marchand's expedition arrived six years later.) In December of that year, the Nuers suddenly realized that they might be the Mahdiyya's next victims. For about two years, Nuers slaughtered Mahdists, temporarily driving them out of their territory, while the badly mauled Shilluks also recovered sufficiently to set upon the Mahdists again. Enraged orders from the khalifa and reinforcements from Omdurman reversed the string of Nilotic victories. Both Shilluk and Nuer were beaten before the end of 1894, and a small garrison temporarily installed just downstream from Fashoda. Dinka resistance smouldered on. The result of all this rebellion and repression was that, instead of being able to mount a rolling Islamic barrage across the Nile watershed, the armies of the Mahdiyya were compelled to move more or less hopscotch into the deep Sudan, their lines of communication never secure enough for the bound into the Congo that might have made the khalifa master of much of King Léopold's new property.

As far as the Ethiopians were concerned, the Bahr al-Ghazāl region had limited value in itself. The climate of the place was deadly for highlanders, and their attitude toward the Nilotes was almost as contemptuous as it was incurious. If they had readily agreed with the French to extend the frontiers of the empire to the White Nile, they had done so to encourage French arms shipments and diplomatic support, on the one hand, and, on the other, to block European advances. The French were easily encouraged in the belief that the grateful Ethiopians would help win the Nile basin for the French and then docilely place themselves under French tutelage. For Menilek the goal was simply to pull Ethiopia through the certain crisis of Franco-British confrontation in the Sudan and the Horn of Africa. To do this, he had finally gotten an agreement with the khalifa which allowed the Sudanese to throw all their forces against the British. He had also signed a treaty with the British the consequences of which were supposed to guarantee Ethiopian independence if Ethiopia remained neutral vis-à-vis the Sudanese and the French. And finally, he pretended (in violation of his other pledges) to provide the manpower for Clochette and de Bonchamps to reach the Bahr al-Ghazāl.

Clochette had been dead more than three months when the reorganized forces led by de Bonchamps finally began their descent beyond Buré through the treacherous Baro gorge in early December 1897. Their trail was narrow—almost nonexistent in places—plunging rather than sloping to the Baro Plain, beyond which, some 240 miles due west, lay the village of Nasir at the head of the Sobat River. Four of the precious pack animals fell to their deaths—it was "a calvary for our beasts," Michel-Côte sighed. By the time they reached the country of the handsome king of Gambella the temperature registered just shy of one hundred degrees Fahrenheit in the shade. The Gambella king was well disposed, making a modest gift of provisions and placing his mark to a treaty making him a tributary of Menilek. But the Gambella lay in a valley of hideously misshapen trees devoid of leaves and encased in bark blackened by the annual slash-and-burn harvest. A place "vibrating with heat," Michel-Côte found it positively "lugubrious." Pressing on into Finkeo territory, then into Yambo territory, where the French again collected royal marks of assent to Ethiopian overlordship, the expedition entered the Baro Plain, turning south in order to place itself on the left bank of the Baro River in accordance with Lagarde's oddly inconvenient instructions.

It was now a few days before Christmas. Lion and hippo appeared; crocodile slithered; high grass and mud were everywhere. On the twenty-second, de Bonchamps, Bartholin, Michel-Côte, a certain Monsieur Faivre, Maurice Potter, and Veron and the thirty-five Ethiopians were down to two bags of rice. After seven hours, they came to a deserted village, then another, but near which they saw three men flee into the grass. Not far beyond, the French uncovered the African trio's two hundred pounds of dried fish, which saved them. The next day, de Bonchamps felled a magnificent elephant; not only were they unable to reach the beast because of the mud, but there was no wood for fire if they had. On Christmas Eve, they barely survived an attack of thirty elephants. The Ethiopians, wholly unused to the heat and low altitude, were prostrate, unable to walk more than ten minutes without taking half-hour rests. Two more camels dropped that day, despite Michel-Côte's bullwhip. The sickly, sweet, polluted water from the Baro undermined Europeans and Ethiopians alike.

On Christmas Day, they were reaching the end of their strength. The Ethiopian interpreter and the cook raved deliriously. They walked twelve miles in thirteen hours. The Yambo porters and guides finally refused to go on. Kill us, they challenged the French; for thirty-six hours their diet had consisted of only quinine. "The red sun crushed us under its heavy heat; we marched one step at a time until we could march no more," Michel-Côte wrote. Two days later, with two men dying and five more dangerously ill, and the Yambo porters vanishing into the brush, de Bonchamps halted in grass four yards high. It had taken five hours to cut through two miles. Three camels and several mules remained, and enough food for two more days. It would take at least seven to reach Fashoda. "The time of illusions is over," de Bonchamps announced. "A decision to go on means for all of us to die twenty or more kilometres beyond." Michel-Côte reflected bitterly on the expedition's unwisdom in obeying Lagarde's orders, which had added so many unnecessary miles to their ordeal. On December 31, the French turned back ninety miles from Fashoda.

When de Bonchamps's men straggled back to Goré in early February, they found an army under Ras Tassama slowly preparing for a sweep of the Sobat region. It was the smallest of the three armies Menilek had ordered to explore and, depending on events in the Sudan, occupy territory to which Ethiopia was now ready to lay claim. Tassama informed the French that they could return to the Bahr al-Ghazāl with him, an offer de Bonchamps immediately accepted. But with practically no money or provisions, the French decided that only de Bonchamps and Maurice Potter could go with Tassama. Michel-Côte and the others were to hurry back to Addis Ababa for money, reinforcements, and, above all, the crucial aluminum boats. Then, just as Michel-Côte was about to leave, de Bonchamps went out of his head with a violent malaria attack. By the end of February, Michel-Côte's formula of quinine, champagne, calomel, and *nux vomica* had saved the marquis, but he was clearly in no condition to return to the infernal Baro and Sobat regions. Instead, Faivre joined Potter when Tassama's four thousand armed troops and six thousand auxiliaries streamed out of Goré on March 10. De Bonchamps headed back to Djibouti.

Potter was a very different kind of artist from Castellani, even-

tempered, disciplined, and fully cognizant of the larger importance
of his assignment. When the Ethiopian army reached Nasir at the
head of the Sobat on March 30, Potter persuaded Ras Tassama that
the Marchand expedition had already arrived at Fashoda and must
be patrolling the stretch of the Nile in search of Clochette and de
Bonchamps. Establishing temporary headquarters at Nasir, the
Ethiopian commander agreed to send a flying squadron of eight
hundred men down the Sobat with Potter and a Russian colonel
named Artamanov. Tassama knew that even if they found Marchand, the flooding of the Sobat would soon make communication
with the Bahr al-Ghazāl impossible without a large number of boats
—boats that could not be built in the treeless swamp. Although
destined to fail, by supporting the Europeans' desperate Sobat gamble Tassama could satisfy his emperor's formal obligation to the
French. What had happened in December happened again. The
army wobbled through deserted villages. Food ran out. Game
crashed about more or less out of sight in the mud and high grass.
Crocodiles lay in wait for stragglers who fell asleep along the river-
bank. The heat wasted the Ethiopians. Disease racked the Europeans.

But this time, the French reached the White Nile. At precisely
8:00 A.M. on June 22, 1898, the Ethiopian commander, Fituari
Haile, ordered the flag of the empire raised at the place where the
Sobat poured into the Nile. The two Frenchmen and the Russian
insisted that they had to wait with at least a few of the fituari's
troops until a message was sent and received from Fashoda less than
sixty miles downriver. That was impossible, said the Ethiopian commander. "We're out of food. All my men are sick, and I've already
left too many of them along the road. Moreover, the river's rising.
If we don't leave immediately, we'll die in the swamp." Across the
Nile, 150 yards from where the anguished French stood, was a tiny
island. Potter was now barely able to stand, and Faivre was unable
to swim, but the honor of France demanded the posting of the
tricolor on what was to be French soil. At dawn on the twenty-fifth
as they prepared to break camp, a young Yambo agreed to paddle
the flag, attached to a pole inserted in an empty crate, to the other
side. Just as he splashed off, Colonel Artamanov pulled off his boots,
excitedly announcing, "It shall not be said that a nigger was the only
one who would raise the French flag!" The Russian snatched the
crate and swam to the island. Fifteen days later, when the Marchand expedition sighted Fashoda, the tricolor still floated over the
deserted plot.

2

Thirty-six years later, when Jules Emily published his rich account of the Congo-Nile mission, memories of the "capricious and stupid" Sué River still agitated him. In 1898, the river was at its most capriciously stupid. It would not begin to rise until mid-June, nearly a month late. "Total impossibility of using the Sué," Marchand fretted at the end of February; "there's nothing left in it but sand." But inactivity was not Paké-Bô's way. The long wait until the summer rains would have driven him mad and turned his fellow officers upon each other. The captious Mangin already believed that he could have led the entire expedition to Fashoda in December, ferrying it in the thirty-five canoes hollowed out by his *tirailleurs*, had Marchand not insisted on gearing logistics to the *Faidherbe*. Marchand had finally decided to send Mangin ahead in mid-September 1897 to found Fort Desaix, about two-thirds the way to Meschra'er Req and almost halfway to Wau, the old trading center downstream on the Sué.

Mangin not only created a model military encampment near Wau; he began to make it self-sustaining. A variety of vegetables and fruits was planted, three hundred chickens penned, a thousand sheep and a large number of cattle corralled. A wine cellar was dug for the Bordeaux and Burgundies bought more than three years earlier at the fashionable Fauchon in Paris's Place de la Madeleine. There was an abundance of wild duck and fresh fish. By the time Marchand reached Desaix at the end of December, his rival, seconded by Landeroin's green thumb, could furnish an officers' mess equal to the best in France. The hundred-odd men waited for the rains in fine style, their appetites slaked around Marchand's portable player piano. But Fort Desaix offered more than agreeable shelter. Establishing it had brought Mangin into the first close contact with the dreaded Dinkas, providing Marchand with a clearer picture of Nilotic vagaries. "After mistaking us for Turks," Mangin reported, "these ferocious Dinkas became tame rather readily." Arrogant, aloof, and utterly unwilling to accept the demeaning work of porters no matter what the reward, the local Dinkas were sufficiently impressed by the good manners and generous barter terms of the French to begin a brisk trade and to provide them with laborers drawn from subject Djur, Bongo, and Belande peoples.

This news of tame Dinkas relieved Marchand. As his expedition passed across the territory of the Zande sultans, he had brooded a good deal over the impression the sustained help from the sultans was likely to make upon the Dinkas. That had greatly concerned Liotard as well, prompting him to urge the Congo-Nile expedition to veer from its preferred route across Deim Zubeir and to choose Tambura instead. But Marchand had always believed that Zandes, Dinkas, and Mahdists, who despised each other as deeply as did French and Germans, could be manipulated to the advantage of France. Mangin's experience encouraged him. "Can't one make Dinkas understand," he lectured Captain Germain from Fort Hossinger, "that not being able to get to them except through Zande country, it's quite difficult not to accept the nominal patronage of the sultans? . . . We need the Zande route in order to make contact with the Dinkas, but it's with the Dinkas that we really want to make a solid alliance—if necessary against the Zande."

It was all very impractical, and certainly bound to raise understandable suspicions among the Nilotes. Using Zandes to reach Dinkas, then turning Dinkas on Zandes reeked of haughty opportunism, of divide-and-conquer at its most naked. By early February, though, Paké-Bô was boasting of the success of his policy, writing Mangin about a "palaver with neighborhood chiefs" at which he preached the message that "the French have come here to open all the trade routes; they're everybody's friends—Zandes, N'Dogos, Bongos, Golos, and Dinkas—but they especially protect the weak, and detest war. . . ." Arrival of an envoy from the Nuer, come to make certain Marchand's people were not Turks—"as rumors had it everywhere about"—seemed to bring the expedition's policies yet closer to success. But, in fact, it would soon become apparent that the Nilotes fully understood the essential weakness of the French position. All the while pretending to aid Marchand, they would later alert the Mahdists to the Frenchmen's vulnerability.

While Marchand plotted the future of the Nilotes, his fellow officers chafed at the inactivity forced on them by the fallen Sué. His concern for morale finally persuaded Marchand to agree to Baratier's scheme to find a way to the old Turco-Egyptian port of Meschra'er Req, and from there, if the old reports were true, to a clear water channel feeding directly into the Nile. With twenty-five *tirailleurs* and Landeroin, Baratier set out in several whaleboats from Fort Desaix on January 15. The Sué was still high enough to take them a few miles before it abruptly separated into two streams that dwindled into the high grass, inserting Baratier and his men into Africa's largest swamp. Heading north day after day in this hot, viscous world where the sounds of their own movement and those of the wildlife were muffled in the grass, and pushing boats forward barely four miles each day, provisions exhausted, and forced to eat fish and the occasional hippo raw because there was no wood, Baratier floundered for nearly a month. "Without guides, without food, without maps," Emily recalled, "and Dinkas vanishing at the approach of their boats, abandoned, sustained only by their own courage." Occasionally, a solitary Dinka would rise out of the reeds to gesture unmistakably that the desperately hungry travellers must not kill the sacred storks.

It was late February when Baratier's force began to break out of the swamp. It had missed the route to Meschra'er Req, overshooting the abandoned port by a hundred miles, chopping its way instead into a channel leading to Lake No, the huge pool at the end of the Bahr al-Ghazāl. Baratier's accomplishment was extraordinary. It proved that the Bahr al-Ghazāl could be crossed even in the dry season; it gave a firm sense of distance between Desaix and the Nile; and his discovery of a channel seemed to confirm the easy navigability of the waters between the Nile and Meschra'er Req. Heading back to Desaix, their sacks bulging with cured elephant and gazelle, Baratier and his men stumbled onto another near miracle. At the beginning of March, two Dinkas appeared, messengers from a lost Largeau, who had been sent to rescue Baratier. Slogging through the reeds on foot (they had found the boats too cumbersome) and in danger of dying from exhaustion and hunger as they went around in circles, Largeau and his men had heard one of Baratier's rifle shots. Two needles crossed in a haystack. Largeau's force crumpled into the whaleboats. Twenty days later, on March 26, they were all safely back at Fort Desaix. They had "the right to be satisfied," Baratier boasted. "Increasingly reassured and trusting, the peoples of the region are showing by their friendly behavior that nothing remains any longer of their initial fears, and that French domination is completely accepted and liked." Once again, the French distorted African reality. Nilotes had no intention of accepting French domination. All that Baratier's round trip had done was to convince the silently watching Africans that Frenchmen were not Turks.

Six weeks after Baratier and Landeroin had disappeared into the swamp, local Africans brought Marchand news of a large detachment of Europeans advancing into the Bahr al-Ghazāl from the southeast. Succumbing to his worst fears, Marchand decided that this must be the long-feared British expedition from Uganda. From what the Nuers said, it might even be a joint Anglo-Belgian force advancing on Meschra'er Req. The news could not have caught the French less prepared. Practically the entire force at Desaix had been allowed to disperse in late January. Sergeant Bernard was off exploring the left bank of the Sué. Captain Germain had been sent to the river's right bank and then due east into the region known as Djur Gatas. Marchand himself, accompanied by the hardy Emily, had left Desaix on January 20, following the general direction taken by Bernard. Finally, Lieutenant Simon's replacement, Lieutenant Fouques, was not expected until late March. Determined to block British access to the major roads, Marchand sent word to Eugène Gouly, the young commander from Tambura who was temporarily in charge of Fort Desaix, to lead a force to a place called M'Bia to the southeast. Gouly reached his destination on March 6, after a brutal forced march across parched country. A few days later, after drinking from an impure well, he was dead.

Marchand's alarm and Gouly's death were unnecessary. The dreaded British advance had never been launched. Captain J. A. L. Macdonald, who was to lead it, had been swamped by the mutiny of his African troops, the resistance campaign led by Kabaka Mwanga, disputes with the commissioner of Uganda over release of Indian reinforcement troops, and Macdonald's increasingly peculiar state of mental health. The real threat to the French would have come from the sizable Belgian force at Redjaf, nearly four hundred miles south on the White Nile. On February 18, 1897, one of Baron Dhanis's most brilliant tacticians, Louis-Napoléon Chaltin, had stormed the Mahdist center at Redjaf, eliminating a permanent Mahdist base in the Bahr al-Ghazāl. Chaltin had then awaited word from the advancing Dhanis, but within a month the commander of the Force Publique was in retreat from the Tetelas. By the time local Africans frightened Marchand with reports of advancing Europeans, Chaltin had left Redjaf well fortified to meet a Mahdist attack, but with a garrison too reduced in numbers to penetrate beyond the Lado Enclave. The French soon suspected the Africans of having intentionally panicked them in order to wear them down.

At the end of April, restlessness at Desaix was as thick as swamp water. Even if it came early, the rainy season was still at least three weeks away. For nearly two years, Marchand had managed to inspire and dominate his assertive fellow officers by setting a high example of intelligent discipline. The most difficult to control—Mangin—had been given a long leash, but Marchand made certain that whatever Mangin did directly benefitted the larger purpose of the mission. He had used the same tack with the less headstrong Baratier. But now, finally, Paké-Bô's volatile temperament burst its restraints. Ever since January, he had been sending candidly desperate appeals through Liotard to the colonial ministry. "Egyptians and Turks have left terrible memories here," a mid-February dispatch emphasized. There was no grand claim to Paris now of spontaneous African love of France. "Everything white here is feared, hated." "If possible," he pleaded the following month, "rush European and native personnel, ammunition for *Faidherbe* via Djibouti, Abyssinia."

On March 30, news came to Desaix that Lieutenant Fouques was still many weeks downriver. Marchand impatiently left Desaix that same day for a pointless trip to Gouly's grave at M'Bia, and then a ranging, month-long exploration of the south which covered 480 miles. He fully expected the rains to have begun before his return. He was back at Desaix on May 3, depressed and exhausted. There was no rain. Emily knew, despite "an obvious effort to chat with us at table," that Paké-Bô was "worn out." Over the next three weeks the doctor watched his patient's condition with increasing alarm as Marchand sank deeper into delirium. To make matters worse, when the long-delayed European newspapers arrived on the eighteenth, they carried accounts of the massacre of the Congo-Nile mission, a story probably originating in Brussels. The previous day, sick and depressed, Marchand had ordered Mangin to Meschra'er Req by land with Largeau, Sergeant Georges Dat, and fifty men. The objective was to make certain the channel running to the Nile from the old port was clear.

The rains refused to come. "This damned river doesn't flow any more," Marchand griped to Liotard. "Here we are stranded on the sand like flapping fish for want of sixteen inches of water and not a cloud in the sky. What a situation!" Finally, near the end of the month, as he and Emily recovered from malaria, the rains began, steady and heavy. But the malign Sué barely rose. "Despite the rains that have been falling in fairly large amounts the past few days," Germain's diary groaned, "the level of the Sué oscillates between 43 and 45 inches." Marchand knew the waiting had to end. Leaving Germain, Dyé, de Prat, Bernard, and some seventy *tirailleurs* and Yakoma auxiliaries to wait for Fouques and then, when the level was high enough, to sail from Desaix aboard the *Faidherbe* and the smaller boats, he led the vanguard away on June 4. At precisely 10:00 A.M., Marchand, Baratier, Emily, Landeroin, and about seventy men paddled down the Sué toward the vast swamp standing between them and the White Nile. "The sky is clear," Emily noted. "It rained part of last night," but the river "dropped more than six inches since yesterday." The Sué would hold back the force under Germain until July 19. For the vanguard, though, putting Fort Desaix behind it lifted spirits and completely restored the excitement of purpose.

The next day the wind was brisk, filling the sails Dyé had attached to the boats when they were under construction at the fort. That night it rained more heavily than ever, after a tornado had brushed the flotilla. The following day, under clouds and high winds, Marchand's dugout was smashed to pieces by a hippopotamus. Huge elephants watched curiously from the right bank of the Sué as the excited French blazed away at the half-submerged assailant. Overhead, ducks circled. On the morning of the eighth, Dinkas appeared along the right bank, erect and motionless, except for an occasional salute with the open palm of the right hand, "a mode of greeting not lacking a certain grandeur," Emily observed. Bumped by hippopotami and lashed by tornadoes, the convoy reached the edge of the swamp on June 11, having travelled about thirty miles in seven days. For the first time the spectral Dinkas intervened, signalling that the French were to advance no farther. These "egalitarian" people, whom Baratier now described as "essentially closed and inhospitable," apparently had not been won over by Mangin's and Baratier's earlier behavior after all. But Dinka egalitarianism appeared to work to the advantage of the French. Forced to wait in the shade of a tree, Marchand and his men watched the women argue and gesture their men into allowing the mission to continue.

The next morning, they glided Indian file into the swamp, with Marchand and Baratier leading in the aluminum whaleboat. A blizzard of mosquitoes engulfed them as the Sué vanished in the grass. Baratier was temporarily and painfully blinded in the right eye the next day. On the fourteenth, the water channel through the grass disappeared, not to be found until almost the end of the day. By the eighteenth, the ordeal was overwhelming. They were blocked by hippopotami. The air seemed liquid and so hot as almost to sear the lungs. The rains came down like a waterfall. The channel suddenly stopped before a wall of reeds. By day's end, they had advanced ninety yards. "How will we be able to continue?" Emily asked his diary.

In the late afternoon of June 25, after a last hippo attack which took the life of Private Badiara, Marchand brought his men out of the high grass into the Bahr al-Ghazāl, the waterway that would take them to Fashoda. They had spent thirteen days in the *sudd.* The following morning, Marchand divided his force, sending Landeroin, Sergeant Venail, and forty-three *tirailleurs* under Emily's command to an island in the Bahr al-Ghazāl called Ghyrdiga. They were to wait there for Marchand and Baratier to return from Meschra'er Req with Mangin and his men. Mangin's sojourn, meanwhile, had revealed that the channel from Meschra'er Req was too clotted to be used. Early on the morning of July 2, Sergeant Moktar-Kori on Ghyrdiga spotted the sails of Marchand's flotilla. Except for the group under Germain back at Desaix, the bulk of the Congo-Nile mission was finally assembled and ready for the last lap of its stupendous progress across Africa. They had come nearly four thousand miles. They set sail at 7:00 A.M. the next day: Baratier and Venail in the lead, Mangin and Dat in the aluminum boat, Marchand and Landeroin following, Emily behind them aboard the steel vessel, and finally Largeau—a distance of two hundred yards maintained between each. Strong winds whipped the twelve-foot-high reeds in the river, and, after so much hardship and danger, Emily found himself moved by the strange beauty of the undulating grass now that Fashoda was only days beyond. On July 5, they floated into Lake No, the pool joining the Bahr al-Ghazāl to the Nile. Leaving Meschra'er Req on June 27 with Marchand, Mangin had dashed off a letter to his sister telling her that they anticipated reaching Fashoda around July 10. "What'll we find there?" he speculated, "Englishmen, Dervishes or Ethiopians—or just the people of the country, those Shilluks with whom we get on so marvelously?" Baratier's diary asked the same questions. At ten the next morning, they entered the White Nile. "For the first time since Saint Louis and Bonaparte," Emily rejoiced, "the colors of France float on the river of the Pharaohs and the Ptolemys!"

They first saw Fashoda at about 5:00 P.M. on July 10, 1898, a Sunday. Earlier that day, stopping downstream at the village of Fashoda, the place where the ruler of the Shilluks resided in state, Marchand had given the reth a rifle. Kur Abd al-Fadil had proclaimed himself greatly pleased by the advent of the French, assur-

ing them that the long-deserted fortress lay some twenty miles
north, and briefly mentioning the recent presence of a force of
Ethiopians and Europeans in the neighborhood. Fashoda was a
landscape of rubble and desiccation populated by scorpions. The
old fort's walls were demolished almost to their foundations. But
the French were overjoyed. The morning after arriving, Marchand
had Mangin and his men busy clearing, stacking bricks, and measur-
ing an area within the walls for a new fort of thirty-five yards
square. The reth appeared late in the day in order to participate in
the official dedication ceremony the following morning. Less than
three weeks earlier, the force from the east—Ethiopians and their
French and Russian companions—had reached the junction of the
Nile at the Sobat, Kur Abd al-Fadil now related in much greater
detail. Shilluk messengers had hurried to make contact with them,
bearing an invitation for the strangers to come to Fashoda, he
continued, but nothing remained except two flags, one on the right
bank and the other on a small island.

The flagpole snapped just as Mangin gave the order to present
arms on the morning of the twelfth, an omen that Largeau said
would have caused the Romans to abandon the place. The second
try succeeded, and Marchand took possession of Fashoda in the
name of France. "The grand Nile has truly become a French river,"
Baratier exclaimed. Despite his pledge of friendship, however,
Marchand sensed that the reth was not overly impressed by eight
Frenchmen and ninety-eight *tirailleurs*. As soon as the celebrations
of the national holiday ended on the fourteenth, Marchand sent two
of the Yakomas in search of the Ethiopian relief force. He made
characteristically grand declarations to the reth about the might of
France and the justice and prosperity flowing from association with
Frenchmen. He bluffed about thousands of Ethiopian soldiers
awaiting his summons to Fashoda. The reth would be well advised,
Marchand counselled, to place himself under French protection.

But Kur Abd al-Fadil and his people remembered what the Mahdists had done to the Egyptians and their European agents. A tiny
band of foreigners was no protection from Omdurman's wrath—it
was even a potentially fatal provocation. The reth intended to govern with as little interference from outsiders as possible, even
though he himself was a creature of the Mahdists. In the final analy-
sis, he knew he must do nothing that would endanger his rule if the
Mahdists returned. Moreover, Kur Abd al-Fadil had an added cause

for unease when he learned that Tiok, the son of the reth murdered by the Mahdists, had come to the fort on the fifteenth in order to win French help in overthrowing him. Tiok was an impressive claimant who lived with his guerrillas in the *sudd*. Unlike the shifty Kur Abd al-Fadil, he needed the French even more than they needed him. Stalling, Marchand struck a posture of diplomatic neutrality until the various loyalties and risks were more calculable. But three weeks of diplomacy were a poor substitute for Ethiopian reinforcements and the promised *Faidherbe* with its supplies and men.

When Tiok hurried to the fort on August 25 to warn that two Mahdist steamers were an hour downriver, the French realized that the reth had communicated their presence to Omdurman, and that unless they gave a good account of themselves they would probably be attacked by Kur Abd al-Fadil's own troops. Precisely aimed firepower from the superb Lebels in the fort and a well-executed sortie led by Mangin shook the Mahdists. The armor of their steamers riddled by high-velocity bullets, the *ansār* disembarked out of range for an assault, only to be repulsed by Mangin's skirmishers. With only two men slightly wounded, but at the heavy cost of fourteen thousand cartridges (more than half the available supply), the French sent the Mahdists scampering back down the Nile. The Shilluks were greatly impressed, all the more so because the smokeless powder of the French made their victory seem magical. They still resisted Marchand's protectorate offer, however, Kur Abd al-Fadil probably having good reason to know that the Mahdist commander would be back.

The second battle of Fashoda (now rechristened Fort Saint-Louis) would have come four days later. Just as the *ansār* were about to advance on land, the *Faidherbe* was sighted. Marchand, who had charged out of his tent to shoot one of his Senegalese sergeants for allowing a surprise attack, realized just in time that his own men and supplies from Fort Desaix were causing the advancing puffs of smoke. "It's the *Faidherbe!* It's France!" Baratier shouted. "We're here now—all of us, gathered around our flag," a deeply moved Emily recorded. "We've paid for the right to stay here with our blood, and we shall stay here." "Give me your paper," a finally convinced Kur Abd al-Fadil said to Marchand. "I'm going to affix my seal." In return for Marchand's promise as "head of the Congo-Nile Mission" to "respect the usages, customs, manners, and religions of the country," the reth placed his realm under the protection of France. A copy in Arabic was also drafted. Marchand and his men thought they had won the race.

3

In a meeting almost as publicized and dramatic as that between Livingstone and Stanley, Marchand and Kitchener adroitly played out their roles for history on the morning of September 19. News of the victory at Omdurman had already come to Fashoda. The Sirdar's presence in the vicinity was announced the previous afternoon when two Sudanese NCOs paddled up bearing calculatedly supercilious greetings from the French-speaking Kitchener to "whatever sort of Europeans" he might find there. Kitchener well knew that these *"Européens quelconques"* belonged to the Congo-Nile mission. Lord Salisbury had carefully instructed Cromer to tell Kitchener to play the Fashoda meeting by ear, but not to recognize, even by implication, "a title to possession on behalf of France or Ethiopia to any portion of the Nile Valley." But Kitchener was also commanded to avoid "by all possible means any collision with the forces of the Emperor Menilek." Had the Amhara battalions sent to the Nile not turned back, the Sirdar would have had to implement contradictory instructions. But not only were Marchand and his men by themselves, their government was experiencing attacks of amnesia over Fashoda.

On June 28, the cabinet of Henri Brisson had replaced that of Jules Méline. The dynamic Delcassé succeeded the intellectual Hanotaux as foreign minister. But Delcassé, whose enthusiasm five years earlier for the Nile Valley strategy had made Marchand's walk across Africa possible, now conveniently forgot the captain's instructions. Had not Lebon sent orders many months ago "not to advance as far as Fashoda, but, preferably, to select an islet near the junction of the Sobat with the Nile"? he disingenuously asked. On September 8, while congratulating the British ambassador for Omdurman, Delcassé broached the possibility that Anglo-Egyptian forces might encounter a certain Captain Marchand. This gentleman has been "distinctly told," Ambassador Monson reported to Salisbury, "that he is nothing but an 'emissary of civilization.' " Yet, even as his memory lapsed, the foreign minister had approved a July 22 order for reinforcements. A Captain Julien was told to leave with a Lieutenant Archambault, Captain Delafosse, Lieutenant Galland, a medical officer, and four sergeants for Boma-Matadi. There were delays at Dakar (orders for equipment had not arrived). Julien's relief force only got under way for Matadi on September 19, the very day two Senegalese NCOs climbed aboard a British steamer with Marchand's greetings to Kitchener, and the further message that Marchand and Germain were rowing out to meet the Sirdar.

After perfectly correct formalities between the Sirdar and the captain, the two imperialists reached an impasse. Aware of the nervousness in Paris and of the unlikelihood of Ethiopian support for the tiny garrison, Kitchener had left Khartoum with an intimidating flotilla of five steamers; aboard were the Eleventh and Twelfth Sudanese Battalions, two companies of Highlanders, a battery of artillery, and four Maxim guns. In correct but heavily accented French, the Sirdar discoursed on the vulnerability of the Fashoda garrison, offered to facilitate an honorable withdrawal, and concluded by threatening to use force if the French opposed Anglo-Egyptian occupation of the fort and the hoisting of the Union Jack. Looking down from his full six feet at the compact officer, Kitchener must have sensed Marchand's total, almost suicidal dedication. Calmly, the Frenchman replied that his men were ready to die. Even with his overwhelming numerical advantage, the Sirdar was too cautious a man to risk the consequences of a shoot-out. War between France and England, with the rest of Europe soon drawn into it, was a distinct probability. The compromise that was struck was to leave Paké-Bô and his men where they were, to run up the Egyptian flag near the fort, and to post a detachment of Sudanese under the command of Major H. W. Jackson.

Before sailing farther south to the junction of the Sobat, Kitchener accepted the invitation to inspect the French handiwork. Landeroin's green thumb had turned a large plot behind the fort into a prolific garden bordered by flowers. There was no evidence whatsoever of illness or indiscipline, no symptoms of depression, no sandbar on which dilapidated shelters stood, and no lack of ammunition or food stores—none of the woes, in fact, that Kitchener and Wingate put into the official report to London. The Sirdar's commissary contained nothing to compare with the tinned delights and fine champagne from Fauchon. After Kitchener, Wingate, Major Lord Edward Cecil, son of the prime minister, and other officers drained the last of their champagne, they left their hosts a bundle of English and French newspapers. If the present was calculated to demoralize, it nearly succeeded, for it recorded the full details of the seismic Dreyfus Affair. The newspapers were dated August 20, Emily noted, "and the last to reach us by way of the Ubangi were from January!! But what wretchedness. . . . We read the details of the trial dividing France into two enemy camps." The mission was careful to hide its anguish from the British, but Emily had a sinking feeling about the future. Even the news brought by a British steamer on October 9 announcing Marchand's promotion to major was somewhat diminished by what the first direct message from Paris did not contain. Nothing about reinforcements, no injunction to stand fast while all France rallied around them, but simply the neutral order to avail themselves of British transportation to send an officer to Paris immediately.

When Baratier was ushered into the Quai d'Orsay on October 27, he found Delcassé at his amnesiac worst. For more than three years France's Nile policy had become progressively unrealistic. Britain had poured money and men into systematic reconquest of the Sudan. France had been content to sue for return of Egyptian funds disbursed to finance the invasion. The Quai d'Orsay and Pavillon de Flore solaced themselves with reports of hypothetical advances into the Bahr al-Ghazāl.

Hanotaux, meanwhile, had become an enthusiast. On June 21, his last day in office, he sent the French minister at Cairo a lengthy dispatch carefully rehearsing the origins, purpose, and current chances for success of Marchand's mission. There was the South African situation, the question of Portugal's African colonies, Anglo-Russian tensions, and Emperor Menilek's support of France. "From this ensemble of facts," Hanotaux reasoned, even "if the fall of Khartoum takes place at the end of this summer or during the fall," Britain would be compelled by the Powers to negotiate over Egypt. But new Foreign Minister Delcassé, the bold southerner, was now forced by events to adopt the caution that had once been second nature to Hanotaux. "The capture of Khartoum, Germany's rapprochement as much with Turkey as with England," Delcassé concluded in a note to the Pavillon de Flore, "have profoundly modified the situation which existed at the moment of the Marchand expedition's departure."

Did Baratier realize that France and Britain were on the brink of war? Why were they at Fashoda in the first place? Dismissed almost before he could reply, Baratier was ordered to return the next day. After a fifteen-minute wait, Marchand's spokesman met a more composed foreign minister. The meeting the previous day with Sir Edmund Monson, the British ambassador, had not been the debacle French intelligence had led Delcassé to expect. There was no ultimatum. But the ciphered telegram on its way from London would only confirm what Delcassé already knew—"no discussion with France before evacuation of Fashoda." The crisis had drained the foreign minister. Three days earlier, the minister of war, General Charles Chanoine, had destroyed the Brisson cabinet by unexpectedly resigning, leaving Delcassé a caretaker at the Quai d'Orsay. Paris was gripped by a two-week-old strike of railway and construction workers, with seventy thousand troops deployed by General Chanoine to keep order. The officer corps was thoroughly demoralized and, some believed, actually plotting a coup d'état because of the Dreyfus Affair, which was now entering its final agony. Much of the nationalist and anti-Semitic press howled for war rather than surrender at Fashoda. The American magazine *The Outlook* wrote of "a desperate plot which involves the turning to revolutionary account of the industrial troubles with which France is just now stirred." The naval minister's opinion was that France would suffer a second Trafalgar in the event of war, the construction program for the new fleet being underfunded and in disarray. The Russian ally, in whose economy some five billion gold francs were invested, had scanned the fine print in the Franco-Russian pact and sent regrets that its obligations did not extend to supporting France outside Europe. Listening to a fervent Baratier describe the ability of 150 men to defend themselves against an Anglo-Egyptian army of some 25,000, Delcassé morosely bowed to the inevitable. The captain was told to convey the thanks of a deeply stirred nation to Marchand, and to prepare the evacuation.

The end came fairly rapidly. The existence of a Franco-Ethiopian-Mahdiyya alliance had never been probable; the Ethiopians had no intention of serious collaboration with France. Not only did Delcassé understand this, but, despite the clamor of the press, French public opinion was decidedly lukewarm on going to war over Fashoda. Finally, it had dawned on the foreign minister and some members of the Comité de l'Afrique Française that, whatever the British said about negotiating the Nile Valley question, the logic of the situation meant war with France if France jeopardized reconquest of the Sudan. The Earl of Cromer's blunt language to the defeated Khedive Abbas shortly before Omdurman could have told the French what to expect: Her Majesty's government, said Salisbury speaking through Cromer, "expect that any advice which they may think fit to tender to the Egyptian Government, in respect to Sudan affairs, will be followed."

Marchand had not been able to wait for a decision. On October 24, he took passage on a British steamer for Cairo. He arrived on November 3, the day before Delcassé's preliminary telegram to the French minister at Cairo, Lefèvre-Pontalis, ordering the evacuation. Having left Fashoda in order to wire a comprehensive report from Cairo, Marchand found Delcassé's order to surrender—"even before you received my report"—incredible. He protested "with outraged honor" the lies Kitchener had spread about conditions at Fort Saint-Louis. He needed "only ten minutes with the men I now have in order to wipe out Jackson's battalion and the four artillery pieces, before going on to do the same thing on the Sobat." The Sudanese troops were only waiting for his signal to mutiny. Moreover, he had proof of British intentions to crush Ethiopia if France yielded on the Nile. With anger verging on insubordination, Marchand stated that duty as "a soldier and leader" commanded him to declare "formally that one does not lead a retreat of troops in conditions such as these; troops galvanized to the last bit of energy in order to reach a goal they believed was final." If the prime minister ordered the evacuation because of the "international political situation," he would obey. But Delcassé's instructions implied that the situation at Fashoda was untenable. Marchand was "ready for total obedience, however cruel,"

but I am also ready for total accomplishment of my duty to present the acts of the mission and the previous orders I have received, and I refuse formally to evacuate Fashoda so long as you do not give the chief of the French mission the sole order to evacuate that he can accept as the real reason. If you do not believe your duty is to proceed in this manner, it is useless to order me to evacuate. I believe I am a soldier for all tasks—but I refuse to fawn on anyone for whatever reason and no matter what the penalty.

Furious, Delcassé instructed Lefèvre-Pontalis on November 7 to tell Marchand to obey "in the higher interests of France." Lefèvre-Pontalis had already indicated that Marchand and Baratier were weakening, that they would obey if there were no hint of blame for conditions at Fashoda. That same day, less than a week after a new cabinet headed by Charles Dupuy was installed (with Delcassé still at the Quai d'Orsay), the colonial ministry sent formal, final evacuation orders to Cairo. "Motivated by the general interests of France," it announced, "the government has decided not to maintain itself at Fashoda." Marchand and Baratier were ordered to leave for Fashoda immediately. Six days later they started up the Nile, arriving, after stops in Dongola and Khartoum, on December 4. There was one consolation: the government had acceded to Marchand's insistence that he and his men be allowed to leave Africa by way of Ethiopia and Djibouti. Originally, Delcassé had accepted the anxious offer of the British to provide transportation through Egypt. That indignity for the Congo-Nile mission was to be spared. Only Sergeants de Prat and Bernard were sent out through Cairo on the eighth because Emily believed they were too ill to make the hard climb into the Ethiopian highlands. The Congo-Nile mission actually left the Fashoda vicinity on the morning of December 12, but its formal departure took place, with arms presented and "Marseillaise" played by Major Jackson's men, on the morning of the eleventh, a Sunday. The French raised their hats to the British and Sudanese as the *Faidherbe* chugged past with five whaleboats in tow. "And so, we moved on," Emily wrote, "moved on sad but proud, eyes wet but heads high, knowing that we had done nothing to deserve the humiliation inflicted upon us by circumstance." "We are fleeing," Baratier said simply. Later, Marchand made the enigmatic remark that one day the Sphinx would laugh.

Emily was certainly right: the humiliation was imposed. Thirty months after leaving the west coast of Africa, the mission had crossed the middle of the continent with the loss of three Europeans and one Senegalese or Sudanese soldier, hauling boats and enough supplies to revitalize France's African empire. It was a stunning achievement, doomed by the realities of African travel and politics, the incompetence and lack of resolve at Paris, and the resolution and military superiority of Britain. When they finally reached Addis Ababa on March 9, 1899, the *Faidherbe* having been abandoned in the Baro two months earlier, there was news of a promotion for Emily and elevation of Mangin and Germain to officers in the Légion d'Honneur, with Landeroin, Largeau, de Prat, and Dat presented with the rank of chevalier. The Russians Vlasov and Leontiev, the Swiss advisor Ilg, the Italian minister Captain Ciccodicola, and much of the European community opened a vast number of bottles of champagne in their honor. Lagarde held a promotions ceremony at the legation. While they were at Lagarde's, the British minister Captain Harrington left his card at the home of the resident French minister, Monsieur Mondon-But, a gracious gesture under the circumstances. On April 1, Menilek returned to the capital. Two days later, he received Marchand, his officers, and the *tirailleurs*, who executed snappy steps to Paké-Bô's commands for the impressed Negus Negusti. Ten days later, the Congo-Nile mission headed for Djibouti.

The European war was postponed. Had it come during the winter of 1898, as many in France's military, aristocratic, and ultranationalist circles wished, the end of European imperialism in Africa might have been advanced by half a generation. In the unsettled conditions of world war, with their financial and manpower resources greatly stretched, Britain, France, Belgium, Germany, and Italy would have been denied those years of uninterrupted military repression and administrative consolidation that, by 1914, had brought the Scramble for Africa to its European conclusion. War between France and Britain in the winter of 1898 might well have reprieved the khalifa his fate. That other genius of the *jihād*, Samori Turé, had finally been run to ground and sent into exile by the French only a few days before Baratier reached Paris to report to Delcassé, but Abdullahi was still free with more than five thousand troops in the southern Sudan, near Jebel Gedir. His men had little food, and the khalifa's last surviving written message was a pitiful plea to a local sheikh to return rifles taken from *ansār* ambushed while looking for grain stores in a small village: "Oh! Sheikh of Lokbu, bring me my guns and the animals you have taken. My three hundred are dead. It is finished. Their blood remains in the ground, and I shall trouble Lokbu no more." Four months later, on November 24, 1899, at a place called Um Debreika, Colonel Wingate attacked Abdullahi with 3,700 cavalry. The khalifa died fighting on his prayer blanket. In 1915, his grave was plowed over because of the large numbers of Sudanese who came to it to sustain faith in the liberation of their country from the British. Hours after entering Omdurman, Kitchener had thrown the Mahdi's bones into the Nile, keeping the skull as a souvenir until shocked British public opinion condemned the new governor general's lack of taste.

Yet, even without war, and even with the elimination of the khalifa, Menilek's strategy of survival through manipulation of

France and Britain had succeeded. And in the long term, Menilek had won his struggle. The Fashoda incident led to the final partition of sub-Saharan Africa—it was the penultimate African partition before the Powers ceded Morocco as a French sphere of influence —but it also led to the end of the Europe established at the Congress of Vienna, the wrecking of the so-called Pax Britannica, and the demise of European world hegemony. Delcassé had hoped until the last that France might emerge from the Fashoda incident with a colony on the Upper Nile. Why, for instance, could Ambassador Monson's government not accept a French sphere bordered on the north by the Bahr al-Ghazāl and Bahr al-Arab, and on the east by the left bank of the White Nile as far south as the fifth parallel? With most of the British press abusing the French as "irregular marauders" and the "scum of the desert," Salisbury would not. On March 21, then, while Marchand and his men were still on the road from Goré to Addis Ababa, the new French ambassador, Paul Cambon, joined with Salisbury in signing the innocuously characterized Addition to Article IV of the 1898 Niger Convention. By its terms, the Nile Valley became British; the sixteen-year-old dispute over Egyptian occupation was definitively closed. Though not part of the written accord, it was understood that France, in compensation, could have (if she could take it) that remainder of North Africa west of the Nile Valley as yet unoccupied by another European power.

The humiliation was large, the loss of objectives utter. But for these very reasons, those who now argued that France and Britain must reinvent their diplomatic relations were to carry the day. There were prominent hotheads who clamored for rapprochement with Germany, but the august newspaper *Le Matin* spoke the final truth with its pronouncement that the honor of France could never be compromised by a colonial enterprise. Prodded by Eugène Étienne and other chastened members of the Comité, Delcassé embarked on a course that was to draw Britain, five years later, into an unprecedented continental understanding: the Entente Cordiale, which would allow France to face what she had never ceased to regard as her real nemesis, the German Reich. Egypt and the Sudan became British; Morocco was set aside for France. Fashoda was erased from the map and renamed Kodok. Léopold, whose Force Publique had flooded into Equatoria and begun to penetrate the Bahr al-Ghazāl itself after Fashoda, was finally pushed out by the British in 1906.

The players in the tragedy of 1914 found their scripts revised by

Fashoda. Delcassé and his supporters, having lost the Nile gambit, decided to cultivate Britain as an ally, since no one had ever seriously doubted that the real enemy was Germany. In the fateful summer of 1899 Delcassé sailed to Saint Petersburg to close the loophole in the Franco-Russian Alliance, so that future crises involving France outside Europe would find the Russians bound to support it. With Britain on the side of France, and Russia now as tightly committed to France as France was to Russia's Balkan objectives, the era of loose-fitting compacts and fence-sitting was largely over. Two large armed, rivalrous, and increasingly hostile blocs grew up —the Allied Powers versus the Central Powers. It could only be a matter of time before a first or second Moroccan crisis, some Balkan war, or the murder of a Habsburg ignited the tinder. Three of the Congo-Nile mission's officers would fight as generals in that war— Marchand, Baratier, and (acquiring a reputation as sanguinary as Kitchener's) Mangin. Largeau, who returned to Africa to become the "Conqueror of Chad," died at the head of his brigade at Verdun in March 1916. Second Lieutenant Georges Dat disappeared in action on August 25, 1914.

The peoples who had been stirred and shaped by Mutesa, Samori, and the Mabialas, Ahmadu, Malumba, and Sefu, Urabi, the khalifa, and Menilek continued to work for their independence, even as they collaborated with and learned from their technologically advanced conquerors. Outright resistance became much less common, though it never entirely disappeared. German troubles in South-West Africa with the Herero and Nama peoples and in Tanganyika with the Maji-Maji would explode into bloody, two-year military campaigns shortly after the beginning of the twentieth century. The Congo Free State continued to seethe with Yaka rebellion until 1906, as did the Zambezi Valley with Tonga, Shona, and Ndebele warfare against the Portuguese and British. Ten years after the Congo-Nile mission broke camp at Fashoda, a Tonga priest summoned the peoples of Nyasaland to take command of their destiny: "The time has come for us to fight the white people, we will start now and fight through the rainy season. The black people [will] rise and drive all the white people out of the country." From Stanley's advent on the Lualaba to Marchand's encampment at Fashoda, it had taken the Europeans less than twenty-five years to overwhelm Africa, twenty-five years in which the tragic and bloody cry of the Tonga priest became nothing so much as the cry for survival of a slowly reemerging, free Africa.

APPENDIX

Chronology

1840 Seyyid Sa'id, sultan of Oman, moves his official residence from Muscat to Zanzibar.

1855 Egyptian government establishes antislavery patrol station at Fashoda.

1862 FEBRUARY: The first Europeans, John Hanning Speke and James Augustus Grant, reach the court of Mutesa II, kabaka of Buganda.

1869 NOVEMBER: Opening of Suez Canal.

1875 NOVEMBER: Egyptian army defeated by Ethiopians at Gundat.

1876 FEBRUARY: Second Egyptian defeat at Gura.
      SEPTEMBER: Léopold II convenes International Geographical Conference, leading to formation of the Association Internationale Africaine (AIA).
      DECEMBER: Henry Morton Stanley begins descent of Lualaba and Congo rivers.

1877 AUGUST: Stanley arrives at Boma, forty miles from the Atlantic coast of Africa.

1878 JULY: Emin Pasha becomes governor of Equatoria Province.

1879 AUGUST: Stanley ("Bula Matari") enters service of Léopold II in the Congo Free State.

1881 SEPTEMBER: Colonel Urabi Pasha leads military coup d'état in Egypt.
      NOVEMBER: Muhammad Ahmad proclaims himself Mahdi.

1882 JUNE: Savorgnan de Brazza returns to France with Makoko treaties.
      JULY: British troops occupy Alexandria.

1883   JANUARY: Mahdists capture El Obeid.

DECEMBER: Stanley hoists flag of Congo Free State at Stanley Falls on the equator in the eastern Congo. British Parliament votes to evacuate Sudan.

1884–85 NOVEMBER to FEBRUARY: Berlin Conference meets. Recognition of Congo Free State.

1885   JANUARY: Khartoum falls to Mahdists. General Charles Gordon slain.

JUNE: Death of Mahdi. Succeeded by Khalifa Abdullahi.

1886   FEBRUARY: Italians take possession of Massawa in coastal sphere claimed by Ethiopia.

1887   APRIL: France-Congo Free State Protocol defining respective boundaries in Central Africa.

DECEMBER: Emin Pasha Relief Expedition organized. Expedition disbanded in DECEMBER 1889.

1888   SEPTEMBER: William Mackinnon's Imperial British East Africa Company (IBEA) granted royal charter for exploitation of Uganda.

1889   MARCH: Ethiopian ruler, Yohannes IV, dies fighting Mahdists at al-Qallabāt.

MAY: Italo-Ethiopian Treaty of Wichale signed.

1891   DECEMBER: Assassination of Msiri, ruler of Katanga, by Force Publique officer.

1892   OCTOBER: Swahili War begins in Belgian Congo.

1894   MAY: Anglo-Congo Free State Treaty, enraging France and causing Major P.-L. Monteil to be sent to West Africa.

AUGUST 15: Annulment of Monteil's orders.

1895   JULY: Earl of Salisbury becomes British prime minister.

SEPTEMBER 11: Marchand presents Congo-Nile proposal.

NOVEMBER 6: Baron Dhanis leaves Antwerp for Congo Free State to lead large expeditionary force to the Nile watershed.

NOVEMBER to MAY 1896: Léon Bourgeois ministry in power in France. Gabriel Hanotaux is minister of foreign affairs, Pierre Guiyesse presides at colonies.

NOVEMBER 30: Official approval of Congo-Nile scheme.

1896   MARCH 1: Italian military debacle at Adwa, Ethiopia.

MARCH 12: Anglo-Egyptian army, commanded by Sirdar Herbert Kitchener, invades Sudan, objective Dongola.

MAY to SEPTEMBER: Basundi revolt in French Congo.

JUNE 25: Captain Marchand sails from Marseilles for French Congo.

SEPTEMBER 24: Dongola occupied.

1897 JANUARY 13: Marchand sends first detachment from Brazzaville for Ubangi aboard Belgian steamboat *Ville de Bruges.*

FEBRUARY: Khalifa agrees to discuss mutual defense with Menilek.

MARCH: Ambassador Léonce Lagarde, followed by the Bonvalot-de Bonchamps mission and Henri, Prince d'Orléans, arrives at Emperor Menilek's capital, Addis Ababa. Two Franco-Ethiopian conventions signed, MARCH 20.

MARCH 18: Baron Dhanis's expedition destroyed by Tetela mutiny.

APRIL: British mission, comanded by Rennell Rodd, arrives at Addis Ababa. Anglo-Ethiopian Treaty signed, MAY 14.

APRIL through NOVEMBER: Congo-Nile mission passes through territories of the Mbomu sultans.

JUNE 25: Russian colonel plants French flag on island in Nile at junction with the Sobat River.

AUGUST 7: Kitchener's forces capture Abu Hamed, crucial to desert railroad route.

NOVEMBER to JUNE 1898: Marchand waits for Sué River to rise.

DECEMBER: Marchand joins his men at Fort Desaix.

1898 JUNE 28 to OCTOBER 25: Henri Brisson ministry presides over resolution of Fashoda incident. Théophile Delcassé presides as interim minister of foreign affairs.

JULY 10: Congo-Nile mission reaches Fashoda.

SEPTEMBER 1: Kitchener defeats khalifa near Omdurman.

SEPTEMBER 19: Marchand and Kitchener meet at Fashoda.

SEPTEMBER 29: French Court of Cassation begins review of 1894 treason conviction of Captain Alfred Dreyfus. Samori Turé captured by French forces in the Ivory Coast.

NOVEMBER 4: France formally yields to Britain over Fashoda.

DECEMBER 12: Marchand and men leave Fashoda.

1899 MARCH 21: Prime Minister Salisbury and Ambassador Cambon sign addendum to Article IV of the Niger Convention of 1898, ratifying Fashoda agreement.

NOVEMBER 24: Khalifa dies fighting at Um Debreika.

1904 Entente Cordiale—Anglo-French understanding.

Acknowledgments

This book might not have been written but for several freewheeling lunchtime conversations in the spring of 1981. On a hilltop near Palo Alto, two think-tank colleagues, William Goetzmann of the University of Texas at Austin and Charles Kindleberger of Harvard, rekindled a dwindling enthusiasm for the project. Uncrating Fashoda notes going back some seven years, I felt again the excitement of the Roman proconsul's dictum *"Semper novi quid ex Africa."*

Seeing that I would not be dissuaded, Harold Marcus of Michigan State University, leading Africanist and gruff, good friend of many years, volunteered conceptual and methodological cautions that saved time and avoided many errors. George Neville Sanderson of Royal Holloway College, University of London, and Robert O. Collins of the University of California, Santa Barbara, two great names in Horn of Africa studies, offered advice about how to say new things about old matters and, in Sanderson's four-page letter, about what should be said that was new. Bob Collins also did me the favor, one afternoon at the University of Khartoum, of forcing me to think harder than I ever had before about what it was I really wanted to say.

In a café near the Sorbonne in the summer of 1982, Marc Michel of the Université de Clermont-Ferrand ticked off pieces of the Congo-Nile mission that had, for one reason or another, escaped his own detailed monograph. More than that, his telephone call to Mademoiselle Élisabeth Rabut of the Section Outre-Mer of the Archives Nationales resulted in my being vouchsafed one of those finds of which historians dream—in this case, the diary of Sergeant Jules Deramond. Equally forthcoming was Louis Mangin, who, though working up a family history at the time, graciously returned his father's papers to the Archives Nationales for my examination during the 1982 Christmas holidays. Although I failed to meet Henri Brunschwig of the École des Hautes Études, his letter to me

235

(a virtual annotated bibliography of recent Fashoda scholarship) was invaluable.

From the moment I first entertained the Fashoda monograph fourteen years ago, my research in the repositories of France—the Archives du Ministère des Relations Extérieures, the Archives Nationales and its Section Outre-Mer, the Bibliothèque Nationale, and the Bibliothèque de l'Institut—were assisted with gratifying efficiency and friendliness. My quest among sources in the United Kingdom was equally recompensed, and with the same graciousness on the part of the staffs of the old British Museum Reading Room and the Public Record Office. Demands upon Belgian repositories were lighter than upon either French or British, but the Musée Royal de l'Afrique Centrale at Tervuren always responded with alacrity.

In Africa, where, as in Europe, historical research is sometimes suspected of being handmaiden to current political activism, private briefings and letters of introduction brought access to crucial documents in Ethiopia and the Sudan. But getting to Africa would have been far more problematical without the special 1982 research and travel budget appropriated by Chancellor Richard Atkins of the University of California, San Diego, during my first year in the history department. I cannot imagine, once in Africa, that without the coaching of Tesfaye Demeke in Washington and James McCann in Addis Ababa, my approach to the staff of the Institute of Ethiopian Studies (IES) could have been so successful. My gratitude to the staff of IES—especially to Taedessa Tamarat, its director, who closed the facility for the better part of a day in order to translate Tigrinya and Amharic documents—is large and lasting.

Similarly, the counsel of my erstwhile colleague at the University of the District of Columbia, Muhammad al-Bashir, enabled me to make optimal use of virtually every hour spent on the campus of the University of Khartoum and in the Central Records Office (CRO). Muhammad Abu Selim, director of CRO, and his staff were striving heroically to accommodate scholarship in physical circumstances that cried out for improvement by the Sudan government. Muhammad al-Bashir (unrelated to my Washington colleague) was equally forthcoming at his far better endowed Institute of African-Asian Studies, University of Khartoum. Whatever success I have had in seeing the Horn of Africa through nineteenth-century African eyes, I owe to talks with Oman al-Nagar and Muhammad Gadal of Khartoum's history department. Sociologist Steve Howard, convert to a heterodox Islamic sect and another Michigan State graduate student, made the country far more comprehensible to me. Without him, a memorable (and forbidden) bus ride to the site of the battle of Omdurman would have been impossible. A final African debt is owed Didier Morin, hastily departing professor of Kushitic languages, who delayed packing his bags in order to give me a tour of the Djibouti that Léonce Lagarde would have recognized.

The first draft patently demanded guidance from specialists in African anthropology. George Bond of Teachers College, Columbia University, and William Shack of the University of California, Berkeley, alerted me to the vastness of my anthropological innocence, mercifully providing a basic reading list. Fellow historians Hollis Lynch of Columbia and Kennell Jackson of Stanford, ever generous with their clear-headed advice, instructively suggested how to write. Africanists who read much or most of the penultimate draft, and to whom I am as grateful for what works in it as I am absolving of what does not, were Joseph Harris and Richard Sigwalt of Howard University, Edward Reynolds of the University of California, San Diego, and Wendell Holbrook of Rutgers (Newark).

At the National Humanities Center, where half of the first draft was done during the 1983–84 academic year, there were several fellow fellows whose interest in this topic extended beyond obligatory lunchtime colloquy. In this regard, I especially remember Robert Hill of UCLA, Martin Meisel of Columbia, Linda Kauffman of the University of North Carolina at Chapel Hill, Jack Hexter of the University of Washington, and Franklin Ford of Harvard. Above all, there was Nell Painter of Chapel Hill, who indulged both the evolving author and the evolving manuscript with generous criticism for nearly a year. At Rutgers, there was time to polish the final draft, thanks to Provost Kenneth Wheeler's generosity, as well as to the often provocative responses of the undergraduate students upon whom portions of it were tried out in my course on imperialism.

Mark Polizzotti is the sort of editor, patient and perfecting, that one would wish for all authors, but neither his skills nor my energy could have produced a final draft in the time allotted without the extraordinary word-processing speed and competence of Catherine Core of the Howard University Foundation, James Partee and Diane Carter of the Joint Center for Political Studies, and Florentina Whaley and Maggie Blades of the National Humanities Center. Also greatly appreciated was an allocation from Howard University's history department to help defray the costs of typing and photographs.

Among the many friendships that make research and writing a complex pleasure, none has meant more through the years than Richard and Carolyn Thornell's, Jean-Claude Boffard's, and Marie-Laure Meilhaud's. To the memory of my friendship with Harold and Sarah Blank I now pay a tragically belated acknowledgment. Lastly, I must thank Ruth for being Ruth.

Notes

PREFACE

xii. THE DEVELOPED WORLD: T. O. Ranger, ed., *Emerging Themes in African History* (London: Heinemann Educational Books, 1968), p. xv.

INTRODUCTION

3. "CLIMATE KILLS THEM": Quoted in Ruth Slade, *King Leopold's Congo: Aspects of the Development of Race Relations in the Congo Independent State* (London: Oxford University Press, 1962), p. 30.

4. ONE HUNDRED MILES: On Fashoda origins and ecology, Edward Gleichen, *Handbook of the Sudan* (London: HM Stationery Office, 1899) and *The Anglo-Egyptian Sudan: A Compendium Prepared by Officers of the Sudan Government* (London: HMSO, 1905); Robert O. Collins, *The Southern Sudan, 1883–1898: A Struggle for Control* (New Haven: Yale University Press, 1962) and *Land Beyond the Rivers: The Southern Sudan, 1898–1918* (New Haven: Yale University Press, 1971), esp. pp. 18–38; and Sir William Garstin, "Fifty Years of Nile Exploration, and Some of Its Results," *Geographical Journal*, vol. 33 (1909), pp. 117–52.

4. "DENSITY OF POPULATION SO GREAT": Georg Schweinfurth, *The Heart of Africa, Three Years' Travels and Adventures in the Unexplored Regions of Central Africa from 1868 to 1871.* 2 vols. (London: Gregg International Publishers, 1969; orig. pub. 1873), vol. 1 pp. 79, 87–88.

4. "LOCAL GREEK TRADERS": Wilhelm Johann Junker, *Travels in Africa: 1875–1878; 1879–1883; 1882–1886.* 3 vols. (London: Chapman and Hall, 1890), vol. 1, p. 212.

4. MOMBASA ON THE COAST: Richard Hill, *Egypt in the Sudan* (London: Oxford University Press, 1959), esp. p. 14; Frederick Cooper, *Plantation Slavery on the East Coast of Africa* (New Haven: Yale University Press, esp. pp. 115–23; al-Zubayr Basha, *Black Ivory or the Story of El Zubeir Pasha, Slave and Sultan,* trans. H. C. Jackson (New York: Negro Universities Press, 1970; orig. pub. 1913); Henri Deherain, *Le Soudan Perdu et Reconquis,* vol. 7 of Gabriel Hanotaux, *Histoire de la Nation Egyptienne* (Paris: Plon, 1940). Philip Curtin et al., *African History* (Boston: Little, Brown, 1978), chs. 11, 13.

5. BEEN SWEPT AWAY: Peter Malcolm Holt, *The Mahdist State in the Sudan, 1881–1898: A Study of Its Origins, Development and Overthrow* (Oxford: Clarendon Press, 1958), p. 132. Alan B. Theobald, *The Mahdiya: A History of the Anglo-Egyptian Sudan, 1881–1899* (London: Longmans, Green, 1951), pp. 186–87.

6. "SO VIEWED BY ENGLAND": Deloncle quoted, in William L. Langer, *The Diplomacy of Imperialism, 1890–1902* (New York: Knopf, 1960, 2d ed.), p. 263. Grey quoted, in T. W. Riker, "A Survey of British Policy in the Fashoda Crisis," *Political Science Quarterly*, vol. 44 (1929), p. 58.

7. "PLEDGES . . . GIVEN TO EUROPE": Gladstone quoted, in Charles W. Hallberg, *The Suez Canal: Its History and Diplomatic Importance* (New York: Columbia University Press, 1931), p. 272. On British inconsistency on Egypt, Cedric James Lowe, *The Reluctant Imperialists: British Foreign Policy, 1878–1902* (London: Routledge and Kegan Paul, 1967), pp. 50–55; John Marlowe, *Cromer in Egypt* (London: Elek Books, 1970), pp. 120–21.

8. "FROM WEST TO EAST": James Rennell Rodd, *Social and Diplomatic Memories* (Second Series) *1894–1901, Egypt and Abyssinia* (London: Edward Arnold & Co., 1923), p. vi.

10. "BEST FOR THEIR OWN INTERESTS": Earl of Cromer (Evelyn Baring), "The Government of Subject Races (pub. 1919)," in Afaf Lutfi al-Sayyid, *Egypt and Cromer: A Study in Anglo-Egyptian Relations* (New York: Praeger, 1969), pp. 62, 68; Marlowe, *Cromer in Egypt*, pp. 120–21.

11. ON AFRICAN LEGS: On European imperialist dogma, Winfried Baumgart, *Imperialism: The Idea and Reality of British and French Colonial Expansion, 1880–1914* (New York: Oxford University Press, 1982); Henri Brunschwig, *Mythes et Réalités de l'Impérialisme Colonial Français, 1871–1914* (Paris: A. Colin, 1960), pp. 109–10; Jean Ganiage, *L'Expansion Coloniale de la France sous la Troisième République (1871–1914)* (Paris: Payot, 1968), pp. 42–59; Prosser Gifford and William Roger Louis, eds., *Britain and Germany in Africa: Imperial Rivalry and Colonial Rule* (New Haven: Yale University Press, 1967), esp. R. L. Hess, "Germany and the Anglo-Italian Entente"; Ronald Robinson and J. Gallagher, *Africa and the Victorians: The Official Mind of Imperialism* (London: Macmillan, 1961); John Mackenzie, ed., *Imperialism and Popular Culture* (Manchester: Manchester University Press, 1986); Bernard Porter, *The Lion's Share: A Short History of British Imperialism, 1850–1983* (London: Longman, 1984), pp. 25–26; C. M. Andrew, P. Grupp, and A. S. Kanya-Forstner, "Le Mouvement Colonial Français et ses Principales Personnalités, 1890–1914," *Revue Française d'Histoire d'Outre-Mer*, vol. 62 (1975), pp. 640–73; M. D. Biddiss, "Racial Ideas and the Politics of Prejudice, 1850–1914," *Historical Journal*, vol. 15 (1972), pp. 570–82.

13. "THOSE FROM THE DEAD": Buhaya quoted, in Henry M. Stanley, *Through the Dark Continent, or the Sources of the Nile Around the Great Lakes of Equatorial Africa and Down the Livingstone River to the Atlantic Ocean.* 2 vols. (New York: Harper & Bros., 1878), vol. 2, p. 152. On some African attitudes toward Europeans, Joseph C. Miller, ed., *The African Past Speaks: Essays on Oral Traditions and History* (London: William

Dawson & Sons, 1980), pp. 62–66; and Slade, *Leopold's Congo,* p. 56; also, William Fagg, *Tribes and Forms in African Art* (New York: Tudor, 1965), pp. 51, 81; and Douglas Fraser, ed., *African Art as Philosophy* (New York: Interbook, 1974), p. 110. Similar Arab reactions to whiteness, Bernard Lewis, *Race and Color in Islam* (New York: Harper & Row, 1971), pp. 33–34.

13. "BEDIMO!": Slade, *Leopold's Congo,* p. 56.

13. "WORLD WAS SPOILT": Quoted in Francis Mading Deng, *The Dinka of the Sudan* (New York: Holt, Rinehart and Winston, 1972), p. 7. On Nilotic Sudan, Francis Mading Deng, *Africans of Two Worlds: The Dinka in Afro-Arab Sudan* (New Haven: Yale University Press, 1978), esp. p. 116; and Khalid Ahmed Mustafa Hagar, "Dynamics of Socioeconomic Transformation Among the Nilotes of Southern Sudan." Ph.D. dissertation, University of Connecticut, 1980, esp. ch. 4.

13. "LIVING CREATURES": Quoted in Jon M. Bridgman, *The Revolt of the Hereros* (Berkeley: University of California Press, 1981), p. 17.

14. LIVINGSTONE DID IN JULY 1871: Tim Jeal, *Livingstone* (New York: G. P. Putnam's Sons, 1973), p. 333. Robert I. Rotberg, ed., *Africa and Its Explorers; Motives, Methods, and Impact* (Cambridge: Harvard University Press, 1970), esp. pp. 9, 48, 226, and *Joseph Thomson and the Exploration of Africa* (New York: Oxford University Press, 1971), p. 76; Catherine Coquery-Vidrovitch, *Brazza et la Prise de Possession du Congo, La Mission de l'Ouest Africain* (Paris: Mouton, 1969). Richard West, *Brazza of the Congo: European Exploration and Exploitation in French Equatorial Africa* (London: Jonathan Cape, 1972), p. 110; also Christopher Hibbert, *Africa Explored: Europeans in the Dark Continent, 1769–1889* (New York: Penguin Books, 1983), chs. 11, 12, 13.

14. TO POSTURE: Rotberg, *Africa and Its Explorers,* p. 9.

14. "IMMENSE AMOUNT OF TROUBLE": Stanley quoted, in Slade, *Leopold's Congo,* p. 23. John Hanning Speke's account of his Royal Geographical Society trip to Uganda is a masterpiece of racial presumptuousness. He and his companion James Augustus Grant were the first Europeans to penetrate the kingdoms of that country. Speke it was who first postulated the racial red herring of the Hamites, reasoning that the white dead of Baganda legend were evidence of primeval immigration of Caucasian "Hamites." These Hamites explained for Speke the sharp features and copper skin prominent among Uganda's aristocracies, as well as the complex political structures of the Uganda monarchies. See also Miller, *African Past Speaks,* pp. 62–63; and Edith R. Sanders, "The Hamitic Hypothesis: Its Origins and Functions in Time Perspective," *Journal of African History,* vol. 10 (1969), pp. 521–32.

14. "CONTINUE MY WANDERINGS": Thomson quoted, in Alan Moorehead, *The White Nile* (Middlesex: Penguin Books, 1963).

15. ABEOKUTA, TIMBUKTU: Moorehead, *White Nile,* pp. 104–06. Russell John Linnemann, "The British Literary Image of Africa in the Nineteenth and

Twentieth Centuries: A Study of the Images of Africa in British Fiction, 1845–1968." 3 vols. Ph.D. dissertation, University of Michigan, 1972.

CHAPTER ONE: THE SPOILT WORLD

16. A DECADE LATER: Rotberg, *Africa and Its Explorers,* pp. 117–21. Hibbert, *Africa Explored,* pp. 191–269.

17. "NO TIME TO GIVE . . . [AFRICANS]": Stanley, *Dark Continent,* vol. 1, p. 148. Stanley on Africa and Africans, *ibid.,* vol. 1, p. 71. On Stanley's character, Richard Hall, *Stanley: An Adventurer Explored* (Boston: Houghton Mifflin Co., 1975); Roger Jones, *The Rescue of Emin Pasha: The Story of Henry Morton Stanley and the Emin Pasha Relief Expedition, 1887–1889* (New York: St. Martin's Press, 1972), esp. pp. 17–26; Byron Farwell, *The Man Who Presumed: A Biography of Henry M. Stanley* (New York: Henry Holt and Co., 1975); Moorehead, *White Nile,* ch. 7.

17. "PEARL OF AFRICA": Stanley, *Dark Continent,* vol. 1, pp. 185, 222–23; and quoted, in Margery Perham, *Lugard and the Years of Adventure, 1858–1898* (London: Collins, 1957), p. 172.

17. "EXTORTING TO EXCESS": Stanley, *Dark Continent,* vol. 1, p. 185. On Uganda, M. S. M. Semakula Kiwanuka, *A History of Buganda: From the Foundation of the Kingdom to 1960* (New York: Africana Publishing Corp., 1972), pp. 150–60; Lucy Mair, *Primitive Government: A Study of Traditional Political Systems in Eastern Africa* (Bloomington: Indiana University Press, 1962); David Apter, *The Political Kingdoms in Uganda: A Study in Bureaucratic Nationalism* (Princeton: Princeton University Press, 1961), esp. p. 67; Crawford Young, "Buganda," in Rene Lemarchand, ed., *African Kingships in Perspective: Political Change and Modernization in Monarchical Settings* (London: Frank Cass, 1977); John Waller Gregory, *The Foundation of British East Africa* (New York: Negro Universities Press, 1979; orig. pub. 1901).

17. "MANNERISMS OF A EUROPEAN'S": Stanley, *Dark Continent,* vol. 1, p. 195.

18. "AROUND LAKE VICTORIA!": *ibid.,* p. 223.

18. BATTING HIS EYELASHES: Heinrich Brode, *Tippoo Tib: The Story of His Career in Central Africa* (Chicago: Afro-American Press, 1969; orig. pub. 1907), p. 14. Also, Leda Farrant, *Tippu Tip and the East African Slave Trade* (New York: St. Martin's Press, 1975). On Swahili origins and influence, Cooper, *Plantation Slavery;* Christine Nicholls, *The Swahili Coast: Politics, Diplomacy and Trade on the East African Littoral, 1798–1856* (London: Allen & Unwin, 1971); Roland Oliver and G. N. Sandersons, eds., *The Cambridge History of Africa: from 1870 to 1905.* 8 vols. (Cambridge: Cambridge University Press, 1985), vol. 6; esp. pp. 70–77; Basil Davidson, *The African Slave Trade* (Boston: Little, Brown, 1980; rev. ed.).

18. FORBIDDING . . . TO THE EUROPEANS: Brode, *Tippoo Tib,* p. 113.

18. MEMORABLE SALUTATION IN 1871: Hibbert, *Africa Explored,* pp. 289–90.

18. "IDEAS AND MANNERS": Verney Lovett Cameron, *Across Africa* (New York: Harper & Bros., 1977), p. 270.

19. COAST TO COAST: Rotberg, *Africa and Its Explorers,* p. 264.

19. WORLD'S MIGHTY RIVERS: Stanley, *Dark Continent,* vol. 2, p. 91. Sidney Langford Hinde, *Fall of the Congo Arabs* (London: Methuen & Co., 1897), esp. pp. 180–81. Rotberg, *Africa and Its Explorers,* pp. 265–66.

19. MITAMBA FOREST: Brode, *Tippoo Tib,* p. 118.

19. HEROIC POINTLESSNESS: Stanley, *Dark Continent,* vol. 2, p. 152.

20. IGNORED OBSTACLE: On African portaging, Hinde, *Fall of the Congo Arabs,* pp. 34–35; Perham, *Lugard,* p. 194; Daniel R. Headrick, *The Tools of Empire: Technology and European Imperialism in the Nineteenth Century* (New York: Oxford University Press, 1981), ch. 14.

20. "TO NO PURPOSE": Tippu Tip quoted, in Stanley, *Dark Continent,* vol. 2, p. 76.

20. TWENTY-SIX HUNDRED DOLLARS: Negotiations between Stanley and Tippu Tip, Brode, *Tippoo Tib,* pp. 109, 118–27; and Stanley, *Dark Continent,* vol. 2, pp. 139–40.

20. "GO BACK, *WASAMBYE!*": Wagenia leader quoted, in Stanley, *Dark Continent,* vol. 2, p. 152. On African opposition to traffic down the Lualaba, Peter Forbath, *The River Congo: The Discovery, Exploration and Exploitation of the World's Most Dramatic River* (New York: Harper & Row, 1977). "They all think that my buying a canoe means carrying war to the left bank [Livingston]"; and "No good had ever resulted from the advent of strangers who had gone before him [Cameron]," in Forbath, *River Congo,* pp. 222–89.

21. "SING OUT A SIMILAR NOTE!": Stanley, *Dark Continent,* vol. 2, p. 119.

21. TOOK THEIR LEAVE: Stanley quote, *Dark Continent,* vol. 2, p. 179. On Swahili, Brode, *Tippoo Tib,* p. 127. Forbath, *River Congo,* pp. 301–04.

21. TERRITORIAL JEALOUSY: On linguistic connections and resistance, Joseph H. Greenberg, *The Languages of Africa* (Bloomington: Indiana University Press, 1970, 3d ed.); Forbath, *River Congo;* Oliver and Sanderson, *Cambridge History of Africa,* vol. 6, ch. 6; A. Adu Boahen, ed., *General History of Africa: Africa Under Colonial Domination, 1880–1935.* 8 vols. (London: Heinemann, 1985), vol. 7, chs. 3–9.

21. RED-HOT FROM VOLLEYS: Stanley, *Dark Continent,* vol. 2, p. 217.

22. MARROW AND BLOOD: Stanley, *Dark Continent,* vol. 2, p. 273. Description of battles, *ibid.,* pp. 270–73. Hall, *Stanley,* p. 77.

22. "BEARING THIS NAME": Ethnographer quoted, in Crawford Young, *Politics in the Congo: Decolonization and Independence* (Princeton: Princeton University Press, 1965), p. 242.

23. "ABORIGINES AND STRANGERS": Stanley, *Dark Continent,* vol. 2, p. 302.

23. THE HEART OF AFRICA: Stanley, *Dark Continent,* vol. 2, p. 357. On Stanley's costly determination to reach Boma by boat, Hall, *Stanley,* p. 84. Congo's navigability, Forbath, *River Congo,* pp. 5–10.

23. "YEAR AFTER YEAR": Gambetta quoted, in Hall, *Stanley,* p. 243.

24. ZANZIBAR ALONE: *The African Slave Trade from the Fifteenth to the Nineteenth Century: Reports and Papers of Experts organized by UNESCO at Porte-au-Prince, Haiti, 31 January to 4 February 1978* (UNESCO 1979).

24. KISWAHILI: Basil Davidson, *The Growth of African Civilisation: East and Central Africa to the Late Nineteenth Century* (London: Longmans, Green, 1967).

24. GOODWILL USUALLY FOLLOWED: On Swahili penetration, Brode, *Tippoo Tib,* esp. pp. 141–49; Cooper, *Plantation Slavery,* esp. pp. 28–35; Iain R. Smith, *The Emin Pasha Relief Expedition, 1886–1890* (Oxford: Clarendon Press, 1972), p. 99.

25. EQUATORIA PROVINCE: Hagar, "Dynamics," pp. 100–05.

25. REST OF THE SUDAN: *Ibid.,* pp. 106–28. Jacques Berque, *Egypt, Imperialism and Revolution* (New York: Praeger, 1972). Deherain, *Le Soudan Perdu.* Hill, *Egypt in the Sudan.* Holt, *Mahdist State.*

25. AFRICAN REAL ESTATE: Jules Cocheris, *De l'Egypte et du Soudan: Situation Internationale (Juridique et Politique)* (Paris: Plon, 1903). Lowe, *Reluctant Imperialists,* p. 50. William L. Langer, *European Alliances and Alignments, 1871–1890* (New York: Knopf, 1962), p. 251. Robinson and Gallagher, *Africa and the Victorians,* pp. 96–108. G. N. Sanderson, *England, Europe and the Upper Nile, 1882–1899* (Edinburgh: Edinburgh University Press, 1965). Baumgart, *Imperialism,* p. 3. J. D. Hargreaves, "Entente Manquée; Anglo-French Relations, 1895–1896," *Cambridge Historical Journal,* vol. 11 (1953–55), p. 65.

26. HALF THAT SUM: Hallberg, *Suez Canal,* pp. 231–36, 291; and David Landes, *Bankers and Pashas: International Finance and Economic Imperialism* (Cambridge: Harvard University Press, 1979; orig. pub. 1958), ch. 5; John Marlowe, *Spoiling the Egyptians* (London: Andre Deutsch, 1974), pp. 77–79. W. S. Blunt, *Secret History of the English Occupation,* (New York: Howard Fertig, 1967; orig. pub. 1922), pp. 15–16; Lord Kinross (John Patrick Balfour), *Between Two Seas: The Creation of the Suez Canal* (New York: William Morrow & Co., 1969), p. 231; Pierre Crabites, *Ismail the Maligned Khedive* (London: Routledge and Sons, 1933), pp. 42–49.

26. "TELEGRAPHED ACCORDINGLY": Disraeli quoted, in Hallberg, *Suez Canal,* p. 242.

27. MORE THAN A DECADE: Crabites, *Ismail,* pp. 120–22; Haggai Erlich, *Ethiopia and Eritrea during the Scramble for Africa: A Political Biography*

of Ras Alalu, 1875–1897 (East Lansing, Michigan: African Studies Center, 1982), pp. 10–11; Richard Pankhurst, "Fire-Arms in Ethiopian History (1800–1935)," *Ethiopian Observer*, vol. 6 (N.D.), p. 148.

27. DEPOSE THE KHEDIVE: On European presence, Berque, *Egypt, Imperialism and Revolution*, p. 192; al-Sayyid, *Egypt and Cromer*, p. 4; Landes, *Bankers and Pashas*, ch. 3; Hallberg, *Suez Canal*, p. 255; Blunt, *Secret History*, p. 49; G. N. Sanderson, "Egypt: The End of Ismail's Reign," in Oliver and Sanderson, *Cambridge History*, vol. 6, pp. 597–99.

27. TENETS OF ALLAH: Holt, *Mahdist State*, esp. pp. 38–44; Theobald, *Mahdiya*, esp. pp. 28–29.

27. WHOLLY UNEXPECTED: Holt, *Mahdist State*, p. 22.

27. GOVERNOR OF THE BAHR AL-GHAZĀL: On politics and slavery, Holt, *Mahdist State*, pp. 28–32; *African Slave Trade*, p. 166; al-Zubayr, *Black Ivory*, pp. 84–85; Hagar, "Dynamics," pp. 102–06.

28. ABOUT TWELVE THOUSAND: Hagar, "Dynamics," p. 105; Holt, *Mahdist State*, p. 28; Cooper, *Plantation Slavery*, p. 115; Nicholls, *Swahili Coast*, p. 204.

28. METED OUT TO MALEFACTORS: Holt, *Mahdist State*, pp. 30–31.

28. IN HIS DIARY: Gordon quoted, in Francis Reginald Wingate, *Mahdism and the Egyptian Sudan, being an account of the Rise and Progress of Mahdism, and the Subsequent Events in the Sudan to the Present Time* (London: Frank Cass, 1968; orig. pub. 1891), p. 11.

28. KHEDIVE'S LAST YEARS: Blunt, *Secret History*, p. 99.

29. REBELS MADE COMMON CAUSE: On Urabi's slogan, al-Sayyid, *Egypt and Cromer*, pp. 13, 15–20. John Marlowe, *Arab Nationalism and British Imperialism: A Study in Power Politics* (New York: Praeger, 1961), ch. 1.

29. TOTAL INSOLVENCY: Hallberg, *Suez Canal*, p. 258.

29. TO SAIL WITH THEM: al-Sayyid, *Egypt and Cromer*, p. 21. Langer, *European Alliances and Alignments*, pp. 266–67. Sanderson, "Egypt: The End of Ismail's Reign," p. 603.

30. "NOT GOING TO DO": Gladstone quoted, in Hallberg, *Suez Canal*, p. 272.

30. "PUT INTO PRISON": *Times* correspondent quoted, in Theobald, *Mahdiya*, pp. 25–26.

30. "REST OF THE MUSLIMS": On becoming the Mahdi, Holt, *Mahdist State*, pp. 47–48. Mahdi's proclamation, *ibid.*, p. 34.

30. JANUARY 1883: Wingate, *Mahdism*, pp. 444–48. Richard A. Bergmann, *The Mahdi of Allah: The Story of the Dervish Mohammed Ahmed* (New York: Macmillan, 1932), pp. 200–01.

31. THEY WERE SKEWERED: John Colborne, *With Hicks Pasha in the Sudan, Being an Account of the Senaar Campaign in 1883* (London: Smith, Elder and Co., 1884); Theobald, *Mahdiya,* pp. 51–54; Byron Farwell, *Prisoners of the Mahdi,* (New York: Tower Publications, 1967; abridged edition), pp. 33–44.

31. VINYA NYAZA: "Tippu-Tib had watched [Stanley] depart into the un-known where nobody dared to venture. When the news came at last that Stanley had survived, the spell guarding the peoples of the plateau was broken." Hall, *Stanley,* p. 264. Slade, *Leopold's Congo,* p. 91.

31. EXTRACTING IVORY AND RUBBER: Slade, *Leopold's Congo,* p. 91.

32. "FOR HOURS TOGETHER": On Leteta, Hinde, *Fall of the Congo Arabs,* p. 88; Demetrius Boulger, *The Congo State and the Growth of Civilisation in Central Africa* (London: W. Thacker & Co., 1898), p. 176; Young, *Politics in the Congo,* p. 186; Jean Stengers, "King Leopold's Congo," in Oliver and Sanderson, *Cambridge History,* vol. 6, p. 332.

32. CENOTAPHS OF PROGRESS: Henry M. Stanley, *The Congo and the Found-ing of Its Free State.* 2 vols. (New York: Harper & Bros., 1885), vol. 2, pp. 79–80, 139–41. On Stanley's shock upon returning to Congo, Hall, *Stan-ley,* pp. 263–64.

32. LAKE VICTORIA: On African cannibalism, André Singer and Brian V. Street, eds., *Zande Themes, Essays Presented to Sir Edward Evans-Pritch-ard* (Totowa, N.J.: Rowman and Littlefield, 1972), p. 58. On famine and trypanosomiasis, Geoffrey Mark and William K. Beatty, *Epidemics* (New York: Scribners, 1976), pp. 182–83: the authors believe Stanley intro-duced tsetse fly to the Interior during the late 1880s; John T. McKelvey, Jr., *Man Against Tsetse: Struggle for Africa* (Ithaca: Cornell University Press, 1973), p. 34; John Lonsdale, "Frontiers of Change," in Oliver and Sanderson, *Cambridge History,* vol. 6, p. 691.

CHAPTER TWO: THE SPOILERS

34. "ENTERPRISING THAN OURSELVES": Léopold quoted, in Demetrius Boulger, *The Reign of Leopold II: King of the Belgians and Founder of the Congo Free State, 1865–1909.* 2 vols. (London: Ardenne Publishers, 1925), vol. 1, p. 126.

34. CENTERED ON THE NILE: A. J. Wauters, *Souvenirs de Fachoda et de l'Expé-dition Dhanis* (Bruxelles: M. Weissenbruch, 1910), pp. 9–10. Neal Ascher-son, *The King Incorporated: Leopold II in the Age of Trusts* (Garden City, N.Y.: Doubleday, 1964), pp. 39–40. Robert O. Collins, *King Leopold, England and the Upper Nile* (New Haven: Yale University Press, 1968), p. 14.

34. "REFLECTIONS FROM ATTACK": Minister quoted, in Ascherson, *King In-corporated,* p. 61.

35. HEART OF THE CONTINENT: Ascherson, *King Incorporated,* pp. 89–90.

35. TO EXCITE THEM: Léopold's letter quoted, in Roger Antsey, *Britain and the Congo in the Nineteenth Century* (Clarendon: Oxford University Press, 1962), p. 59.

35. "CURRENT IS WITH US": Léopold's address quoted, in Ascherson, *King Incorporated,* p. 94; Boulger, *Reign of Leopold,* vol. 1, p. 129. Brunschwig, *Mythes et Réalités,* p. 35.

36. SUMMER OF 1879: Stanley, *Congo,* vol. 1, pp. 21–24. Forbath, *River Congo,* p. 333.

36. "TWO DIFFERENT THINGS": Léopold quoted, in Ascherson, *King Incorporated,* p. 117.

36. EASTERN CONGO: Forbath, *River Congo,* p. 343. Young, *Politics in the Congo,* p. 243. Boulger, *Reign of Leopold,* vol. 1, pp. 135–36. Hall, *Stanley,* pp. 263–65.

36. STUPENDOUS SURFACE: Hall, *Stanley,* p. 257.

37. "TO STRIVE FOR": Stanley quoted, *ibid,* p. 248, see also p. 266.

37. 1879 TO 1890: Boulger, *Reign of Leopold,* vol. 1, p. 215. Wauters, *Souvenirs de Fachoda,* pp. 8–9. Slade, *Leopold's Congo,* p. 181. Stengers, "King Leopold's Congo," pp. 337–44.

37. "TO BE A PHARAOH!": Léopold, quoted in Deherain, *Le Soudan Perdu,* p. 419.

37. BELGIUM'S GRANDEUR: Forbath, *River Congo,* p. 329. Stengers, "Leopold's Congo," pp. 319–20. Jean Stengers, "Leopold II Takes the Initiative," in Robert O. Collins, ed., *The Partition of Africa: Illusion or Necessity* (New York: John Wiley & Sons, 1969), p. 23–25.

38. RAMPANT PROTECTIONISM: Baumgart, *Imperialism,* pp. 127–32. Brunschwig, *Mythes et Réalités,* pp. 31–34. Ganiage, *L'Expansion Coloniale de la France,* esp. pp. 42–165. Stephen H. Roberts, *The History of French Colonial Policy,* 1870–1925 (London: Frank Cass, 1963, orig. pub. 1929), esp. pp. 15–20.

38. MODEST INHERITANCES: Mackenzie, *Imperialism and Popular Culture,* ch. 6; Linnemann, "British Literary Image of Africa"; G. N. Sanderson, "The Partition and the Ideology of Imperialism," in Oliver and Sanderson, *Cambridge History,* vol. 6, pp. 335–37. J. Vansina, "Occupation and Administration of the State," in Oliver and Sanderson, *Cambridge History,* vol. 6, pp. 335–337.

38. "EVEN IN RAILROADS": Léopold's book quoted, in Brunschwig, *Mythes et Réalités,* p. 32 (author's trans.).

38. CONGO VENTURE: Ascherson, *King Incorporated,* p. 11.

39. LÉOPOLD'S PRESENCE INSUFFERABLE: *Ibid.,* p. 12.

39. BANK OF THE CONGO RIVER: West, *Brazza*, pp. 110–23. Roberts, *French Colonial Policy*, pp. 338–41. On de Brazza, Catherine Coquery-Vidrovitch, *Brazza et la Prise* and *Le Congo au Temps des Grandes Compagnies Concessionnaires, 1898–1930* (Paris: Mouton, 1972).

39. "HOSPITABLE PEOPLE": De Brazza quoted, in Eric Halladay, "Stanley," in Rotberg, *Africa and Its Explorers*, p. 226.

39. AND HIS FRIENDS: West, *Brazza*, p. 123. Baumgart, *Imperialism*, p. 19.

40. DEGREES OF LATITUDE: Sanderson, *England, Europe and Upper Nile*, p. 123.

40. "CIVILIZATION, AND COMMERCE": Livingstone's motto. On Mackinnon, Léopold, and Africa; Antsey, *Britain and the Congo;* John S. Galbraith, *Mackinnon and East Africa, 1878–1895: A Study in the "New Imperialism"* (Cambridge: Cambridge University Press, 1972); Jones, *Rescue of Emin Pasha*.

41. GORDON AT KHARTOUM: Emin's message, Jones, *Rescue of Emin Pasha*, p. 69.

41. FATHER . . . NEVER KNOWN: On Emin's past and character, George Schweitzer, *Emin Pasha: His Life and Works, Compiled from His Journals, Letters, Scientific Notes and from Official Documents* (New York: Negro Universities Press, 1969; orig. pub. 1898); Jones, *Rescue of Emin Pasha*, p. 40; Moorehead, *White Nile*, pp. 301–03; Sanderson, *England, Europe and Upper Nile*, ch. 2; and despite invented dialogue and inaccuracies, but because of deft personality portrayal and knowledge of Schweitzer family lore, Alan Caillou, *South from Khartoum: The Story of Emin Pasha* (New York: Hawthorne Books, 1974).

41. "A TURKISH NAME": Emin's letter to sister quoted, in Jones, *Rescue of Emin Pasha*, p. 41.

42. EGYPT IN 1871: *Ibid.*, pp. 7–11. R. O. Collins, "Samuel Baker," in Rotberg, *Africa and Its Explorers*, pp. 141–54. A. E. Atmore, "Eastern Africa: The Trading Sphere of the Swahili Arabs," in Oliver and Sanderson, *Cambridge History*, vol. 6, pp. 70–77.

42. ANTICIPATED FOR 1883: Smith, *Emin Pasha Relief Expedition*, p. 19; Galbraith, *Mackinnon*, p. 5.

42. "WELL ARMED": Lupton's letter quoted, in Jones, *Rescue of Emin Pasha*, p. 66.

43. AN EVACUATION EXPEDITION: *Ibid.*, p. 72; Langer, *Diplomacy*, p. 113.

43. SIDELINED FROM LEADERSHIP: Jones, *Rescue of Emin Pasha*, p. 71.

43. FOR A TROPHY: On mixed goals of rescuers, Smith, *Emin Pasha Relief Expedition*, pp. 68–80; Jones, *Rescue of Emin Pasha*, p. 209; Galbraith, *Mackinnon*, p. 118; Wauters, *Souvenirs de Fachoda*, pp. 10–11; Stanhope

White, *Lost Empires on the Nile: H. M. Stanley, Emin Pasha and the Imperialists* (New York: Roy Publishers, 1969), pp. 200–10, 245.

43. BELGIAN KING: Smith, *Emin Pasha Relief Expedition,* p. 51.

44. PROJECTED IBEA: Jones, *Rescue of Emin Pasha,* p. 215; Smith, *Emin Pasha Relief Expedition,* p. 80; White, *Lost Empires,* pp. 200–10.

44. BROAD CONSEQUENCES: Galbraith, *Mackinnon,* p. 116. Langer agreed: *Diplomacy,* p. 113. To Roger Jones, however, the motives of Mackinnon, Léopold, and Stanley were transparent: *Rescue of Emin Pasha,* pp. 83–84. G. N. Sanderson, "The Scramble for the Interior," in Oliver and Sanderson, *Cambridge History,* vol. 6, pp. 142–43.

44. INTO THE BUSH: Slade, *Leopold's Congo,* pp. 90–93.

44. THE GERMANS: White, *Lost Empires,* p. 203.

45. FROM THE CAPE TO CAIRO: Galbraith, *Mackinnon,* pp. 179–80. Langer, *Diplomacy,* p. 119.

45. MAJESTY'S GOVERNMENT: Sanderson, *England, Europe and Upper Nile,* p. 93.

45. INTERNATIONAL LEGITIMACY: Langer, *Diplomacy,* p. 119. Sanderson, *England, Europe and Upper Nile,* p. 93.

45. LATE 1880s: Boulger, *Reign of Leopold,* vol. 2, p. 194.

46. NINE-TENTHS OF THE LAW: On Belgian and French forces in the Congo, R. P. Lotar, *La Grande Chronique du Bomu* (Bruxelles: Van Campenhout, 1940), pp. 41–54; Marc Michel, *La Mission Marchand,* 1895–1899 (Paris: Mouton, 1972), pp. 17–18; Wauters, *Souvenirs de Fachoda,* pp. 11–12.

46. "LIKE A PESTILENCE": Wauters, *Souvenirs de Fachoda,* p. 11.

46. KILLING VAN KERCKHOVEN: Boulger, *Reign of Leopold,* vol. 1, p. 200.

46. SWAHILI KNIFE: Death of Emin, Perham, *Lugard,* p. 279. "Epilogue," in Jones, *Rescue of Emin Pasha,* pp. 379–95. Milz's progress, Boulger, *Reign of Leopold,* vol. 1, pp. 201–02.

47. POST AT GANDA: Boulger, *Reign of Leopold,* vol. 1, pp. 201–02. Wauters, *Souvenirs de Fachoda,* pp. 12–13, R. P. Lotar, *La Grande Chronique de l'Uele* (Bruxelles: Institut Royal Belge, 1944), p. 140. A. Thuriaux-Hennebert, *Les Zandes dans l'Histoire du Bahr el Ghazal et de l'Equatoria* (Bruxelles: Editions de l'Institut de Sociologie et de l'Université Libre, 1964), p. 216.

47. JOIN THE MAHDISTS: Wauters, *Souvenirs de Fachoda,* p. 13. Sanderson, *Europe, England and Upper Nile,* p. 95.

47. THEIR FINAL RUN: Lotar, *Bomu*, p. 3.

48. BATHTUB SPIGOT: Parfait-Louis Monteil, *Souvenirs Vécus, Quelques Feuillets de l'Histoire Coloniale, Les Rivalités Internationales* (Paris: Sociétés d'Editions Géographiques maritimes et coloniales, 1924), p. 67. Langer, *Diplomacy*, p. 127. Michel, *Mission Marchand*, p. 21. Credit for the original conception of the Congo-Nile scheme goes to de Brazza: Michel, *Mission Marchand*, p. 16.

48. THE ENDGAME: "Hanotaux became a much stronger colonialist once he was out of office. But as long as there was a chance of accomplishing peaceably by diplomatic means rather than by military expedition, a settlement of the Upper Nile question, Hanotaux refused to sanction the planned Nile penetration. During 1894 and 1895, he sparred almost continually with his colleagues at the Colonial Office," in Alf Andrew Heggoy, *The African Politics of Gabriel Hanotaux, 1894–1898* (Athens, GA: University of Georgia Press, 1972), pp. 32, 62. Michel, *Mission Marchand*, pp. 22–24. Roger Glenn Brown, *Fashoda Reconsidered: The Impact of Domestic Politics on French Policy in Africa, 1893–1898* (Baltimore: Johns Hopkins University Press, 1969), pp. 40, 77.

49. EVEN AT FASHODA: Lotar, *Bomu*, p. 42.

49. OUTSTANDING PROCONSULS: Liotard quoted, *ibid.*, p. 40.

49. APPRECIATED BY DE BRAZZA: Liotard profile in (otherwise unreliable) Michel Morphy, *Le Commandant Marchand et Ses Compagnons d'Armes à Travers l'Afrique, Historie Complète et Anecdotique de la Mission.* 2 vols. (Paris: H. Geffroy, 1899–1900), vol. 1, pp. 207–10; Lotar, *Bomu*, p. 39.

50. BRIEF, CONTENTIOUS SOJOURN: Liotard-Belgian exchange, in Lotar, *Bomu*, pp. 54–55; also, Thuriaux-Hennebert, *Les Zandes*, p. 232.

50. "I WILL OBEY": Monteil, *Souvenirs*, p. 67. On Monteil's expedition, Jean Stengers, "Aux Origines de Fachoda, L'Expédition Monteil," Parts 1, 2. *Revue Belge de Philologie et d'Histoire*, vol. 36 (1958), p. 439.

50. WATERSHED MUST BE DONE: Delcassé to Chamber, Michel, *Mission Marchand*, p. 19.

51. "FORCE THAN MINE": Alis quoted, in Stengers, "Origines de Fachoda," *Revue Belge de Philologie et d'Histoire*, vol. 38 (1960), p. 384.

51. LOBBYING POLITICIANS: Alis's influence and letters, *ibid.*, pp. 384–91; Baumgart, *Imperialism*, pp. 78–79; Brunschwig, *Mythes et Réalités*, ch. 8; Brown, *Fashoda Reconsidered*, pp. 25, 33; Collins, *King Leopold*, pp. 36–37; John D. H. Hargreaves, *West Africa Partitioned.* Vol II. *The Elephants and the Grass* (Madison, WI.: University of Wisconsin Press, 1985), p. 27; Sanderson, *England, Europe and Upper Nile*, p. 152.

51. *"VOUS ÊTES INSATIABLE":* Officer quoted, in Camille Vergniol, "Les Origines de la Mission Marchand," *La Revue de France*, (August 1, 15; Septem-

ber 1, 1936), August 15 edition: pp. 630–45. Monteil's motives are still *insaisissables*; for analyses of them (to which this author does not fully subscribe), Sanderson, *England, Europe and Upper Nile,* pp. 151–52.

52. ALONG THE NILE: Lugard, in Stengers, "Origines de Fachoda," vol. 38, pp. 1043–44.

53. "REST OF THE WORLD": Léopold telegram, *ibid.,* p. 1055.

53. "ZERO RAMIFICATIONS": Hanotaux quoted, *ibid.,* vol. 38, p. 1041.

53. ICILY DECLINED: Young, "Buganda," p. 204.

53. FRAGILE TRUCE: Apter, *Political Kingdoms,* pp. 72–77; Kiwanuka, *History of Buganda,* p. 225; Perham, *Lugard,* pp. 228–36.

54. DIVIDED BUGANDANS: Kiwanuka, *History of Buganda,* p. 228; Perham, *Lugard,* p. 400.

54. FOREIGN OFFICE: Lugard quotes (Mwanga), in Perham, *Lugard,* p. 232; and "waste places," in Galbraith, *Mackinnon,* p. 8.

54. TROUBLINGLY ODD: Langer, *Diplomacy,* p. 122.

54. OVERLORDS OF THE KINGDOM: Perham, *Lugard,* pp. 236, 461. Apter, *Political Kingdoms,* pp. 74–75.

54. TALLEYRAND: Heggoy, *Hanotaux,* pp. 6–7.

55. LOSING HIS THRONE: Stengers, "Origines de Fachoda," vol. 38, p. 1064.

55. "BAHR AL-GHAZĀL": *La Réforme* quoted, *ibid.,* p. 1057.

55. "THE LAST CENTURY": Dufferin quoted, *ibid.,* p. 1045.

55. AT THE TIME: *Ibid.,* p. 1047.

55. THE ORDERS READ: *Ibid.,* p. 1042; Michel, *Mission Marchand,* p. 22.

56. FOURTH PARALLEL: Michel, *Mission Marchand,* p. 22; Langer, *Diplomacy,* pp. 139–40.

56. "LOST . . . SIGNIFICANCE": Dispatch quote, in Stengers, "Origines de Fachoda," vol. 38, p. 1053.

56. CANCEL MONTEIL'S ORDERS: Michel, *Mission Marchand,* pp. 23–24.

57. "UNFRIENDLY ACT": Grey, in Riker, "Fashoda Crisis," p. 58. On Hanotaux's optimism, Michel, *Mission Marchand,* p. 24; Langer, *Diplomacy,* pp. 266–68.

57. COMPETE WITH THE BELGIANS: Langer, *Diplomacy,* pp. 130–31.

58. CONGO-NILE EXPEDITION: Brown, *Fashoda Reconsidered,* p. 33.

58. ON THE RIVIERA: Victoria quoted, in George Earle Buckle, ed., *The Letters of Queen Victoria: A Selection from Her Majesty's Correspondence and Journal Between the years 1886 and 1901.* 3 vols. (London: John Murray, 1932, 3d series), vol. 3, p. 243.

58. CHALET AT OSTENDE: Wauters, *Souvenirs de Fachoda,* pp. 18–19; Ascherson, *King Incorporated,* p. 192.

58. BELGIUM, AND ETHIOPIA: Léopold's pincer—*"une triplice africaine"* Wauters, *Souvenirs de Fachoda,* pp. 20–21, 26.

59. "ABREAST OF AFRICAN AFFAIRS": Léopold's quote, Langer, *Diplomacy,* pp. 269–70.

59. VICTORIA CONFIDED: Victoria quoted, *ibid.,* p. 270. Salisbury wrote Victoria's secretary, Léopold's "confidences are so extraordinary that I hesitate to put them into a despatch": Buckle, *Letters of Queen Victoria,* vol. 3, p. 24.

59. *LA BELGIQUE COLONIALE:* Anonymous article quoted, in Wauters, *Souvenirs de Fachoda,* pp. 36–37.

CHAPTER THREE: THE BEGINNINGS OF RESISTANCE

61. ONLY FOR PYGMIES: E. Evans-Pritchard, *The Azande, History and Political Institutions* (Oxford: Oxford University Press, 1971), pp. 234–40.

61. "IDEAL OF THE WARRIOR": *Ibid.,* p. 260.

61. LANGUAGES AND CULTURES: P. M. Larken, "An Account of the Zande," *Sudan Notes and Records,* vol. 9 (1962), pp. 1–56; C. G. Seligman and Brenda Z. Seligman, *Pagan Tribes of the Nilotic Sudan* (London: George Routledge & Sons, Ltd., 1932)—two culturally biased but still useful early sources for the Zande. Classic Evans-Pritchard sources are *Azande; The Zande State* (London: Huxley Memorial Lecture, 1963); and, invaluable, "A History of the Kingdom of Gbudwe (Azande of the Sudan)," *Zaire* (May-July-October 1956). Singer and Street, *Zande Themes*; Curtin et al., *African History,* pp. 272–73.

61. PROBABLY WERE NOT: Evans-Pritchard, *Azande,* p. 71. Seligman and Seligman, *Pagan Tribes,* p. 497. Schweinfurth, *Heart of Africa,* vol. 2, p. 3.

61. AVUNGARA RULE: Evans-Pritchard, *Azande,* pp. 24–25, 158. Evans-Pritchard, *Zande State,* p. 135; Armand Hutereau, *Histoire des Peuplades de l'Uele et de l'Ubangi* (Bruxelles: Goemaere, date unknown, p. 144. Seligman and Seligman, *Pagan Tribes,* pp. 495–502; Larken, "Zande," pp. 22–24.

61. "THEY WERE TERRIBLE": Zande nobleman quoted, in Evans-Pritchard, *Azande,* p. 372. On Gbudwe's reign, Evans-Pritchard, *Azande,* p. 112;

Evans-Pritchard, "Kingdom of Gbudwe," May 5, pp. 451–91, esp. pp. 457–58; Singer and Street, *Zande Themes,* pp. 7, 55.

62. BEGUN, BY ABOUT 1870: Evans-Pritchard, *Azande,* pp. 112, 323–40.

62. KING GBUDWE: Evans-Pritchard, *Azande,* p. 112.

62. UBANGI RIVER BASIN: Lotar, *L'Uele,* pp. 14–16.

62. "HEART OF AFRICA": de Ryhove quoted, in Lotar, *Bomu,* p. 32.

63. CIRCUMSPECTION AND DELICACY: Hutereau, *Histoire des Peuplades,* p. 185. Lotar, *Bomu,* p. 32.

63. FORT THE FOLLOWING YEAR: Slade, *Leopold's Congo,* p. 176.

63. LAKE TANGANYIKA: Marcia Wright, "East Africa, 1870–1905," in Oliver and Sanderson, *Cambridge History,* vol. 6, pp. 539–91, esp. pp. 562–63. Farrant, *Tippu Tip,* p. 92.

63. "GARENGANZE . . . NO OTHER": Msiri quoted, in Slade, *Leopold's Congo,* p. 132. A. E. Atmore, "Africa on the Eve of Partition," in Oliver and Sanderson, *Cambridge History,* vol. 6, p. 75.

64. BODYGUARD COULD REACT: Slade, *Leopold's Congo,* pp. 133–34.

64. "KNOW NOTHING OF THIS": Barghash quoted, in Brode, *Tippoo Tib,* p. 181. Tippu Tip wrote, "In accordance with the Sultan's plenary powers at the time, he promulgated a decree, mainly directed against the Belgians, that no one would enlist carriers until Hamed bin Mohammed was sufficiently supplied," *Ibid.,* p. 159.

64. WITHDRAWAL IN THE EASTERN SUDAN: Yves Person, "Samori and Resistance to the French," in Robert Rotberg and Ali Mazrui, eds., *Protest and Power in Black Africa* (New York: Oxford University Press, 1970), pp. 80–112; and J. I. Kanya-Forstner, "French Military Imperialism in the Sudan," *ibid.,* pp. 93–94.

65. TO THE ATLANTIC COAST: Slade, *Leopold's Congo,* pp. 91, 93, 109, 176.

65. COMMERCIALLY FINISHED: Hinde, *Fall of the Congo Arabs,* pp. 2–3. "The Arabs, moreover, realized that, in the event of a European success, the greater part of the ivory and rubber trade would be taken out of the hands of the Mohammedans, and would, instead of going to the east coast, go down the Congo to the Atlantic": *Ibid.,* p. 22. Farrant, *Tippu Tip,* pp. 140–43.

65. DOMAINS IN THE MANYEMA: Brode, *Tippoo Tib,* p. 216. Cooper, *Plantation Slavery,* p. 115.

65. THIRTY POUNDS A MONTH: Olivia Manning, *The Remarkable Expedition: The Story of Stanley's Rescue of Emin Pasha from Equatorial Africa* (New York: Atheneum, 1985), p. 52. Slade, *Leopold's Congo,* p. 95.

65. ENSUING PANDEMONIUM: Jones, *Rescue of Emin Pasha,* ch. 7. Manning, *Remarkable Expedition,* p. 67.

66. CONGO FREE STATE: Hinde, *Fall of the Congo Arabs,* p. 23.

66. IGNITE . . . WEST COAST: On some intriguing might-have-beens in the Scramble: on unrest in French West Africa, Michel, *Mission Marchand,* pp. 83–119; on general insurrections, M'Baye Gueye and A. Adu Boahen, "African Initiatives and Resistance in West Africa, 1880–1914," and A. Isaacman and J. Vansina, "African Initiatives and Resistance in Central Africa, 1880–1914," in Boahen, *General History of Africa.*

66. EXIT FROM EGYPT: Langer, *Diplomacy,* p. 124.

66. OVERTHROW . . . CABINETS ENSUED: Thomas Francis Power, Jr., *Jules Ferry and the Renaissance of French Imperialism* (New York: King's Crown Press, 1944). Jacques Chastenet, *Histoire de la Troisième République,* vol. 2, *La République des Républicains,* 1879–1893. 7 vols. (Paris: Librairie Hachette, 1954), pp. 162–65.

66. ALL THE WAY TO OMAN: Kiwanuka, *History of Buganda,* p. 218. Perham, *Lugard,* p. 217.

66. TENS OF THOUSANDS: For details of Swahili leadership and warfare, Farrant, *Tippu Tip,* pp. 140–43; Hinde, *Fall of the Congo Arabs,* p. 19; Slade, *Leopold's Congo,* pp. 107–19. Wright, "East Africa," pp. 562–63.

67. TETELA RIFLEMEN: Oscar Michaux, *Au Congo: Carnets de Campagne, Episodes et Impressions de 1889 à 1897* (Bruxelles: Librairie Falk Fils, 1907), p. 168; Hinde, *Fall of the Congo Arabs,* pp. 19, 139; Slade, *Leopold's Congo,* p. 109.

67. DOWN THE LUALABA: Hinde, *Fall of the Congo Arabs,* pp. 96–97; Stengers, "Leopold's Congo," p. 331.

67. "CANNIBAL TENDENCIES . . . FIRST TIME": Quotes, in Hinde, *Fall of the Congo Arabs,* p. 63. Belgian historian quoted, in Boulger, *Reign of Leopold,* vol. 1, p. 236.

67. EASTERN CONGO: "An estimate of 70,000 dead on the Swahili-Arab side is probably exaggerated, while figures for Congo State losses are not available. At all events, tens of thousands died during this campaign." Stengers, "Leopold's Congo," p. 331.

68. A HUNDRED CANOES: Michaux, *Au Congo,* pp. 220–22.

68. "FORTIFIED CAMP": Hinde, *Fall of the Congo Arabs,* p. 180.

68. "MOSQUITO CURTAINS": *Ibid.,* p. 184.

68. FATALLY WOUNDED: Brode, *Tippoo Tib,* p. 247; Hinde, *Fall of the Congo Arabs,* p. 231.

68. FLED TO TANGANYIKA: Slade, *Leopold's Congo,* p. 113.

68. BY FIRING SQUAD: Hinde, *Fall of the Congo Arabs*, p. 208.

68. "LOST A SINGLE LOAD": *Ibid.*, p. 211.

69. "EXAMPLE . . . FOLLOWED BY MANY OTHERS": *Ibid.*, p. 217.

69. "I WILL FIGHT THE WHITES": Mangbetu chief quoted, in Boulger, *Reign of Leopold*, vol. 2, p. 197.

69. *"KPEKPE LI ABORO"*: Gbudwe quoted, in Evans-Pritchard, "Kingdom of Gbudwe, Part I" (May 1956), p. 457.

70. ONCE-INVINCIBLE ZULUS: Curtin et al., *African History*, pp. 281–84, 410–11.

70. UNYAMWEZI AS EQUALS: Brode, *Tippoo Tib*, p. 149. Oliver and Sanderson, *Cambridge History*, vol. 6, pp. 73, 562–63. Robert W. July, *A History of the African People* (New York: Scribners, 1980, 3d ed.), chs. 11, 14, 15, 17.

70. "THIS BLOODY LAND": Michaux, *Au Congo*, p. 284.

70. BILI RESISTANCE: Hutereau, *Histoire des Peuplades*, p. 186. H. F. Fox Bourne, *Civilisation in Congoland: A Story of International Wrong-Doing* (London: P. S. King and Son, 1903), pp. 228–30.

70. SIXTY-MAN FORCE: Bourne, *Civilisation*, p. 228.

71. LUPTON . . . BAHR AL-GHAZĀL: Hutereau, *Histoire des Peuplades*, p. 113. Boulger, *Reign of Leopold*, vol. 1, p. 196.

71. FINALLY OVERWHELMED: Sanderson, *England, Europe and the Upper Nile*, p. 96.

71. "ASSAIL THEM ON THEIR ROUTE": Quoted in Evans-Pritchard, "Kingdom of Gbudwe," pp. 844–45.

71. "ALL HAD HEARD OF IT": *Ibid.*, p. 845.

72. AGAINST BRITISH RULE: T. O. Ranger, "Connexions Between 'Primary Resistance' Movements and Modern Mass Nationalism in East and Central Africa," *Journal of African History*, vol. 9 (1968), p. 442; D. Chanaiwa, "African Initiatives and Resistance in Southern Africa," in Boahen, *General History of Africa*, vol. 7, pp. 194–220.

72. "OBLITERATION . . . [OF THE WESTERN CONGO]": Boulger, *Reign of Leopold*, vol. 1, p. 235.

CHAPTER FOUR: SOLDIERS AND STATESMEN

73. PLAYGROUND DREAMS: On Marchand's early years (with caution), Michel Morphy, *Le Commandant Marchand*, vol. 1, pp. 46–51; (again with cau-

tion), Charles Castellani, *Marchand l'Africain* (Paris: Flammarion, 1900); Julien Maigret, *Marchand l'Africain* (Tours: Maison Mame, 1937); Michel, *Mission Marchand.*

73. DAYS SHY OF TWENTY: Maigret, *Marchand,* p. 15; Castellani, *Marchand l'Africain,* p. 63.

74. IMPROVE WHAT WAS THERE: On recruitment and ethos of the French colonial army, *Paul-Marie de la Gorce, The French Army: A Military-Political History* (New York: George Braziller, 1963), pp. 87–89; and William Serman, *Les Officiers Français dans la Nation, 1848–1914* (Paris: Aubier Montaigne, 1982), pp. 9–10.

74. " 'GOODBYE OLD FELLOW' ": Gerald Herbert Portal, *The British Mission to Uganda in 1893* (Westport, Conn.: Negro Universities Press, 1970), p. 34.

74. MID-MARCH 1887: Maigret, *Marchand,* p. 15.

75. THE STRONGEST TERMS: Edouard Réquin, *Archinard et le Soudan* (Paris: Editions Berger-Levrault, 1946), p. 36.

76. "SILLY, BUT INEVITABLE": Marchand quoted, in Jacques Delebecque, *Vie du Général Marchand* (Paris: Librairie Hachette, 1936), p. 31.

76. ORDER OF THE DAY: Hargreaves, *The Elephants and the Grass,* p. 36. Yves-J. Saint-Martin, *L'Empire Toucouleur, 1848–1897* (Paris: Le Livre Africain, 1970), pp. 142–46.

76. "I SAY WHAT I THINK": Marchand quoted, in Réquin, *Archinard,* p. 67.

77. AHMADU'S CAPITAL: Delebecque, *Général Marchand,* p. 36.

77. TO PAY THEIR WAY: *Ibid.,* p. 23.

77. FARAWAY PLACE: Paul Moreau-Vauthier, *Un Chef: Le Général Mangin, 1866–1925* (Paris: Les Publications Coloniales, 1936), p. 3.

77. TUKULORS . . . DURING 1890–91: A. S. Kanya-Forstner, "Mali-Tukulor," in Michael Crowder, ed., *West African Resistance: The Military Response to Colonial Occupation* (New York: Africana Publications, 1971), esp. pp. 69–71. Ganiage, *L'Expansion Coloniale de la France,* pp. 174–75.

78. PART OF HIS EMPIRE: Yves Person, *Samori: Une Révolution Dyula,* 3 vols. (Dakar: Mémoires de l'Institut Fondamental d'Afrique Noire, 1968, 1970, 1975), vol. 3, p. 1489. A. S. Kanya-Forstner, "Mali-Tukulor," in Crowder, *West African Resistance,* p. 74, believes Ahmadu belatedly allied with Samori in 1890. July, *History of African People,* p. 254.

78. CHAMBER OF DEPUTIES IN 1879: Baumgart, *Imperialism,* pp. 28–29; Saint-Martin, *L'Empire Toucouleur,* pp. 119–20; Réquin, *Archinard,* p. 4.

78. PLACE OF SULTANS AND CHIEFS: Kanya-Forstner, "Mali-Tukulor," pp. 71–74. Saint-Martin, *L'Empire Toucouleur*, p. 160. Hargreaves, *The Elephants and the Grass*, pp. 34–42.

78. *"MON CHER PAPA":* Mangin quoted, in Moreau-Vauthier, *Un Chef,* pp. 10–11; Maigret, *Marchand,* p. 17.

78. FINE EXAMPLE: Moreau-Vauthier, *Un Chef,* p. 9.

78. ALLAH'S CHOSEN ONE: July, *History of African People,* pp. 251–54. Saint-Martin, *L'Empire Toucouleur,* p. 159.

79. "THOSE WHO FREQUENT MARKETS": Person, *Samori,* vol. 1, p. 97; and for socioeconomic background to Samori Turé and his empire, *ibid.,* pp. 236–58.

79. FURTHER PROVOCATIONS DISCONTINUED: Person, "Samori and Resistance to the French," in Rotberg and Mazrui, *Protest and Power in Black Africa,* pp. 93–94.

79. EUROPEAN TACTICS: *Ibid.,* pp. 100–103. Person, *Samori,* vol. 2, esp. pp. 891–1013. July, *History of African People,* p. 254.

79. CONTENTED WITH ITS BORDERS: Person, *Samori,* vol. 2, p. 632. Ganiage, *L'Expansion Coloniale de la France,* p. 176.

79. ARMS PIPELINE: Person, *Samori,* vol. 2, p. 632.

79. TIMBUKTU . . . WERE RENOWNED: Roberts, *French Colonial Policy,* p. 306.

80. DE BRAZZA'S . . . FRENCH CONGO BY 1892: Réquin, *Archinard,* pp. 146–50; Coquery-Vidrovitch, *Le Congo,* pp. 48, 72.

80. MARCHAND'S PROMOTION TO CAPTAIN IN 1892: Delebecque, *Général Marchand,* p. 49; Gorce, *French Army,* p. 87.

80. "KNIGHTLY FINENESS": Colonel quoted, in Morphy, *Le Commandant Marchand,* vol. 1, p. 234.

80. "REVOLUTION IS NEVER PEACEFUL": Albert Ernest Baratier, *Au Congo: Souvenirs de la Mission Marchand, de Loango à Brazzaville* (Paris: Arthème Fayard, 1914?), p. 64.

81. MODEL FOR THE FUTURE: On the Tunisian model and this debate, Roberts, *French Colonial Policy,* pp. 129, 64–75; Brunschwig, *Mythes et Réalités,* pp. 25–26; July, *History of African People,* p. 499–502.

81. AT ANOTHER CROSSROADS: Roberts, *French Colonial Policy,* pp. 392–95.

81. REVOLUTION WAS WELL UNDER WAY: Gabriel Hanotaux, *Le Général Mangin* (Paris: Plon, 1925), pp. 16, 48.

82. TUKULOR POTENTATES: Saint-Martin, *L'Empire Toucouleur,* p. 160.

82. STRONGHOLDS ON THE NIGER, CRUMBLED: *Ibid.*, p. 162.

82. HAD BEEN KILLED: *Ibid.*

82. CIVILIAN ADMINISTRATORS: *Ibid.* Person, *Samori*, vol. 3, p. 1486. Michel, *Mission Marchand*, p. 28.

82. BONUA IN NOVEMBER 1894: Castellani, *Marchand l'Africain*, p. 102.

83. FOR YEARS AFTERWARD: *Ibid.*, p. 107.

83. "FIRE A METAL CARTRIDGE": Charles Mangin, *Regards sur la France d'Afrique* (Paris: Plon, 1924), p. 196. Person, "Guinee-Samori," in Crowder, *West African Resistance*, p. 123; Person, "Western Africa, 1870–1886," in Oliver and Sanderson, *Cambridge History*, vol. 6, pp. 240–41.

83. MAKE REGIMENTAL HISTORY: Castellani, *Marchand l'Africain*, p. 102.

83. "THE AFRICAN": Patricia Wright, *Conflict on the Nile: The Fashoda Incident of 1898* (London: Heinemann, 1972), p. 126.

83. "COURAGE ENVELOPED THEM": Hanotaux, *Mangin*, p. 1.

83. PRINCE AUGUSTE D'ARENBERG: Brown, *Fashoda Reconsidered*, pp. 45–46.

83. ON ACTIVE DUTY: Michel, *Mission Marchand*, p. 28.

84. " 'ATLANTIC TO THE RED SEA' ": Deloncle quoted, in Charles Michel, *Mission de Bonchamps: Vers Fachoda à la Rencontre de la Mission Marchand* (Paris: Plon, 1900), p. 5.

84. MUTUALLY ACCEPTABLE AGREEMENT: Wright, *Conflict on the Nile*, p. 59; Camille Vergniol, "Fachoda," *La Revue de France*, September 1, 1936, pp. 117–18; Hargreaves, "Entente Manquée," p. 83.

84. LIOTARD . . . NILE WATERSHED: Liotard quoted, in Robert de Caix, *Fachoda, La France et L'Angleterre* (Paris: J. André, 1899), p. 148.

85. RIBS IN A KITE: Jean Marchand, "Projet du Mission Etabli par le Capitaine Marchand," September 11, 1895, Document No. 1, Title 1, Africa III, pp. 31–34, Section Outre Mer (SOM).

85. "EGYPTIAN SUDAN . . . RESOLVED": Jean Marchand, "Note Analytique Complémentaire à Annexes au Projet de Mission Congo-Nil Dressé par le Capitaine Marchand," November 10, 1895, Document No. 2, Africa III, SOM.

85. 150,000 FOR 1898: Marchand, "Projet du Mission," Title 3, Africa III.

85. 128,180 FRANCS: *Ibid.*

86. MONSIEUR ANTOINE CONGA: Marchand to Roume, January 26, 1896, Document No. 4, Africa III, SOM. Maigret, *Marchand,* p. 50.

86. A "LEFT WING" CABINET: Vergniol, "Mission Marchand," p. 114.

86. WAY OF UGANDA: Marchand, "Note Analytique Complémentaire." Marc Michel, *Mission Marchand,* pp. 40–42.

86. "UNDERSTANDING WITH THE DERVISHES": Marchand, "Note Analytique Complémentaire."

87. "HASTENING THIS SETTLEMENT": Berthelot to Affaires Etrangères (AE), November 30, 1895, Document No. 3, Africa III, SOM.

87. "MONOTONOUS AND DISHEARTENING": Marchand to Mangin, February 6, 1896, Papiers Charles Mangin, AP 149 3, Archives Nationales (AN).

87. ENTIRE UPPER UBANGI: Marc Michel, *Mission Marchand,* p. 42.

88. "RECOMMENDED BY M. LIOTARD": Roume, "Note," January 1896, Document No. 6, Africa III, SOM.

88. "AT ANY SECOND": Marchand to Roume, Dir. des Affaires Politiques du Ministre des Colonies sur les Conditions de la Mission, January 26, 1896, Document No. 5, Africa III, SOM.

88. "IN THIS CASE": *Ibid.*

89. "ALREADY AT . . . REDJAF": *Ibid.*

89. RECALLING LIOTARD: Archinard to Roume, "Note pour la 2eme Direction, Chef," October 31, 1895, Document No. 4, Africa III, SOM.

89. SERVED UNDER ARCHINARD: Brown, *Fashoda Reconsidered,* pp. 50–51.

89. LIOTARD'S AUTHORITY: "Le Ministre à M. Marchand, Capitaine d'Infanterie de Marine," February 24, 1896, Document No. 9, Africa III, SOM.

90. "MASTER OF MY WILL": Marchand to Mangin, February 6, 1896, Papiers Charles Mangin, AP 149 3, AN.

90. "ABLE TO STUDY": *Ibid.*

90. "DEPOPULATION AND DISMEMBERMENT": Largeau to Marchand, December 22, 1895, Fonds Baratier, 99 AP 1, No. 1 (Largeau—1895–1897), AN.

90. "SOMETHING OF A RENAISSANCE": Castellani, *Marchand l'Africain,* pp. 3–4.

90. REOCCUPYING PART OF THE SUDAN: Langer, *Diplomacy,* p. 537; Buckle, *Letters of Queen Victoria,* vol. 3, pp. 37–38.

91. GUIEYSSE'S INSTRUCTIONS: Minister of Foreign Affairs, Léon Bourgeois, April 7, 1896, Document No. 12, Africa III, SOM.

91. MARCHAND WROTE MANGIN: Marchand to Mangin, April 24, 1896, Papiers Charles Mangin, AP 149 3, AN.

91. DAKAR AND LOANGO: Marc Michel, *Mission Marchand*, p. 82.

91. "FIRE HER PISTOL": Hanotaux quoted, in Langer, *Diplomacy*, p. 538.

92. WAS INCALCULABLE: Wauters, *Souvenirs de Fachoda*, p. 9; Stengers, "Leopold's Congo," pp. 340–41.

92. "LABOR TAX": Young, *Politics in the Congo*, pp. 26–27.

93. MOST OF THE MANYEMA: Wauters, *Souvenirs de Fachoda*, p. 8.

93. EVEN MORE FEASIBLE: Stengers, "Leopold's Congo," p. 323.

93. DUMMY FINANCIAL ORGANIZATIONS: Wauters, *Souvenirs de Fachoda*, p. 9; Ascherson, *King Incorporated*, pp. 190–94.

93. SUPPLY OF CAPTURED ARMS: Young, *Politics in the Congo*, p. 282.

94. LAND GRABS IN HISTORY: Brunschwig, *Mythes et Réalités*, pp. 33–34.

94. TO SHARE THE TERRITORY: Wauters, *Souvenirs de Fachoda*, p. 28; Deherain, *Le Soudan Perdu*, pp. 423–44.

95. UNNERVED EVEN STANLEY: Bourne, *Civilisation*, pp. 239–40; Deherain, *Le Soudan Perdu*, p. 424.

95. "MAKING FASTER PROGRESS": Boulger, *Reign of Leopold*, vol. 2, p. 35.

95. MOMENT OF REVENGE: *Ibid.*, vol. 2, p. 37; Bourne, *Civilisation*, p. 230.

96. "ON CANE CHAIRS": Boulger, *Reign of Leopold*, vol. 2, p. 37.

96. "LIBERTY AND REVENGE": Malumba quoted, in Bourne, *Civilisation*, p. 230.

96. "DISASTER WAS TOTAL": *Mouvement Géographique* quoted, in Wauters, *Souvenirs de Fachoda*, p. 40.

97. ENOUGH FOR RECONQUEST: Boulger, *Reign of Leopold*, vol. 2, p. 60.

97. SANGUINARY MATCH: *Ibid.*, pp. 38–40.

98. "END TO THE SCANDAL": German officer quoted, in Bourne, *Civilisation*, p. 238. Stengers, "Leopold's Congo," p. 333.

98. UPPER UBANGI: Marc Michel, *Mission Marchand*, p. 152.

CHAPTER FIVE: PAWNS OF PAWNS—ETHIOPIA AND THE MAHDIYYA

99. PORT OF MASSAWA: Harold Marcus, *The Life and Times of Menelik II: Ethiopia, 1844–1913* (Oxford: Oxford University Press, 1975), p. 82; Richard Pankhurst, *Economic History of Ethiopia, 1800–1935* (Addis Ababa: Haile Sellassie I University Press, 1968), p. 18; Erlich, *Ethiopia and Eritrea*, pp. 58–63.

100. GOODS THROUGH . . . MASSAWA: Marcus, *Menelik II*, p. 81. E. Hertslet, *The Map of Africa by Treaty*, 2 vols. (London: Frank Cass, 1967), vol. 2, Document No. 98.

100. SHOA, AND WOLLO: George Fitz-Hardinge Berkeley, *The Campaign of Adowa and the Rise of Menelik* (London: Archibald Constable and Co., 1902), pp. 6–7.

100. THEIRS FOR THE TAKING: Guebre Sellassie, *Chronique du Règne de Ménélik II, Roi des Rois d'Ethiopie* (Paris: Librarie Orientale et Américaine, 1930), p. 252; Zewde Gabre-Sellassie, *Yohannes IV of Ethiopia: A Political Biography* (Oxford: Clarendon Press, 1975), pp. 147–50; Pankhurst, *Economic History of Ethiopia*, p. 18.

100. "MASSAWA THIS DAY": Admiral quoted, in Hertslet, *Map of Africa*, Vol. 2, Document No. 114.

100. YOHANNES MOANED: Yohannes quoted, in Erlich, *Ethiopia and Eritrea*, p. 58.

100. "SHALL BE VICTORIOUS": Yohannes quoted, in Marcus, *Menelik II*, p. 85.

101. AMERICAN OFFICERS: Assisted by archivists of the Institute of Ethiopian Studies, the author examined the highly illuminating correspondence between Menilek and Ismail for this period contained in the Sven Rubenson, Collection, 70. E 3. Most revealing is Menilek to Ismail, 1st Mescaran 1868 (September 11, 1875), a letter both protesting Egyptian incursions and reaffirming Menilek's offer of a firm alliance, while it also implicitly encourages Ismail against Yohannes. Sven Rubenson, *The Survival of Ethiopian Independence* (New York: African Publishing Co., 1976), p. 324.

101. "POSSESSION OF THIS KINGDOM": Ismail's letter quoted, in Pankhurst, "Fire-Arms in Ethiopian History (1800–1935)," *Ethiopian Observer*, vol. 6, p. 150.

101. APPEARANCE AT YOHANNES'S CAMP: Erlich, *Ethiopia and Eritrea*, p. 20; Marcus, *Menelik II*, p. 55.

101. AFTER HIS ELDEST SON: Patrick J. Rollins, "Russia's Ethiopian Adventure, 1888–1905." Ph.D. dissertation, Syracuse University, 1967, p. 129.

101-02. ANNEX SHOAN TERRITORY: Hertslet, *Map of Africa*, vol. 2, Document No. 117; Marcus, *Menelik II*, p. 96.

102. POLITICS OF ETHIOPIA: Marcus, *Menelik II*, p. 31; Alan Moorehead, *The Blue Nile* (New York: Harper & Row, 1962).

102. "COME TO AN AGREEMENT": Yohannes to Queen Victoria, in Erlich, *Ethiopia and Eritrea*, p. 113.

103. EQUIVALENT TO CAPTAIN: *Ibid.*, p. 9.

103. "DEMAND . . . YOU WITHDRAW THE TROOPS": Alula quoted, in Erlich, *Ethiopia and Eritrea*, p. 94.

103. ROMAN CIVILIZATION: Donald O. Limoli, "Francesco Crispi's Quest for Empire—and Victories—in Ethiopia," in Collins, *The Partition of Africa: Illusion or Necessity*, p. 132.

103. "WATCHING THE TIGREANS' FLIGHT": Erlich, *Ethiopia and Eritrea*, p. 120.

103. TACTICS OF ETHIOPIAN ARMIES: Marcus, *Menelik II*, p. 86.

104. "AND FOUGHT WITH HIM": Yohannes quoted, in Erlich, *Ethiopia and Eritrea*, p. 106.

104. "GOVERNOR OF ROME": Alula quoted, in Marcus, *Menelik II*, p. 98; Portal, *British Mission to Uganda*, p. 6.

104. TIME FOR THE EMPIRE: Erlich, *Ethiopia and Eritrea*, p. 106; Pankhurst, *Economic History of Ethiopia*, p. 18.

104. KEPT TO THE COAST: Erlich, *Ethiopia and Eritrea*, p. 113.

104. ENDLESSLY ADVANCING *JIHĀD:* Theobald, *Mahdiya*, p. 150.

105. "COME OUT AND MEET US": Hadol's letter to Alula quoted, in Erlich, *Ethiopia and Eritrea*, pp. 64–65. Henry Cecil Jackson, *Osman Digna* (London: Methuen, 1926), p. 150.

105. DESIRE FOR REVENGE: Holt, *Mahdist State*, p. 78; Theobald, *Mahdiya*, p. 96; Jackson, *Osman Digna*, pp. 22–23.

105. ABU KLEA: Farwell, *Prisoners of the Mahdi*, p. 55; Mackenzie, *Imperialism and Popular Culture*, p. 57.

105. SUSPICIOUS KHALIFA: Theobald, *Mahdiya*, p. 95.

105. "RETURN TO SUAKIN . . .": Khalifa's letter to Digna quoted, in Erlich, *Ethiopia and Eritrea*, p. 65.

106. AL-QALLABĀT'S SEIZURE: Richard A. Caulk, "Yohannes and the Mahdists: Mere Pawns in European Diplomacy or Unsuspecting Collaborators with Colonialism," *Historical Journal* [Addis Ababa], vol. 2 (1968), p. 24.

106. NEGUSTI EMBRACED ISLAM: Theobald, *Mahdiya*, p. 154.

106. LITURGICAL SCRIPT OF ETHIOPIA: Caulk, "Yohannes and the Mahdists," p. 24.

106. "THEY HAVE PROFANED": Erlich, *Ethiopia and Eritrea*, p. 119.

106. IMPORTED BY THE ITALIANS: Richard Pankhurst, "The Great Ethiopian Famine of 1888–1892; A New Assessment," Institute of Ethiopian Studies Mimeograph (1964), p. 7.

107. LETHARGICALLY FOR THE FRONT: Gabre-Sellassie, *Yohannes IV*, p. 247.

107. GROOMED FOR THE THRONE: Rollins, "Russia's Ethiopian Adventure," p. 129.

107. LACKLUSTER RESPONSE: Sanderson, *England, Europe and the Upper Nile*, p. 69.

107. "THEY WILL NOT SPARE YOU": Yohannes quoted, in G. N. Sanderson, "Contributions from African Sources to the History of European Competition in the Upper Nile Valley," *Journal of African History*, vol. 3 (1962), p. 70.

107. AL-ZAKI TAMAL . . . TOOK HIS PLACE: Theobald, *Mahdiya*, p. 155.

108. SAID OF MENILEK: Wylde quoted, in Erlich, *Ethiopia and Eritrea*, p. 187.

108. RULE THE EMPIRE: Roland Oliver and Michael Crowder, *The Cambridge Encyclopedia of Africa* (Cambridge: Cambridge University Press, 1981), p. 111.

108. "TROUBLE IN THE FUTURE": Augustus Wylde, *Modern Abyssinia* (London: Methuen & Co., 1901), p. 11.

108. EXPLOSIVE ENERGY: *Ibid.* "Oily" voice quote, in Herbert Vivian, *Abyssinia: Through the Lion-Land to the Court of the Lion of Judah* (London: C. Arthur Pearson, 1901), p. 203. Erlich, *Ethiopia and Eritrea*, p. 187.

109. "FOR ANOTHER IN SHOA": Alula quoted, in Erlich, *Ethiopia and Eritrea*, p. 164.

109. FIVE-THOUSAND-MAN ARMY CORPS: Marcus, *Menelik II*, p. 95.

109. THE *ASCARI:* Berkeley, *Campaign of Adowa*, pp. 48–49.

109. ITALIAN PROTECTORATE: *Ibid.*, pp. 23–32.

109. SERVING AS COLLATERAL: *Ibid.*, p. 21.

110. "ITALY AS A POWER": Baring quoted, in Sanderson, *England, Europe and the Upper Nile*, p. 75.

110. "THOUSAND TONS OF LEAD": Clerk quoted, in Marcus, *Menelik II*, p. 117.

110. FORFEITURE OF PROPERTY: *Ibid.*, p. 117.

110. "POWERS OR GOVERNMENTS": Wichale Treaty quoted, in Ernest Work, *Ethiopia: A Pawn in European Diplomacy* (New Concord, Ohio: published by author, 1935), pp. 79, 120. Fascinating cultural-linguistic discussion of Wichale in Donald N. Levine, *Wax and Gold: Tradition and Innovation in Ethiopian Culture* (Chicago: University of Chicago Press, 1965), p. 6. Marcus, *Menelik II*, pp. 114–15.

111. LEARN THEIR ALPHABET: Thomas Leiper Kane, "Amharic Fictional Literature." Ph.D. dissertation, University of California, Los Angeles, 1971, pp. 4–5.

111. SPELLED OUT THE ESSENTIAL: Levine, *Wax and Gold*, pp. 5–9.

111. WRITING MATTERED: Siegfried Pausewang, "The History of Land Tenure and Social Personality in Ethiopian History." Paper presented to Conference on Current Research Trends in Ethiopian History [Addis Ababa], March 14, 1970, pp. 2–4, 6.

111. "POSTMAN" EXPLANATION: Rollins, "Russia's Ethiopian Adventure," pp. 138–39.

111. "THIS SHALL NEVER BE": Taitu quoted, in Work, *Ethiopia*, p. 118.

111. ANNULMENT OF THE ARTICLE: *Ibid.*, pp. 122–23; Marcus *Menelik II*, p. 145.

111. "ADVISE ME TO DO SO": Menilek's letter to Umberto quoted, in Berkeley, *Campaign of Adowa*, p. 33.

111. "DIVIDE UP AFRICA": One version of Menilek's circular quoted, *ibid.*, pp. 35–36; another version, Sven Rubenson, "Adwa 1896: The Resounding Protest," in Rotberg and Mazrui, *Protest and Power*, p. 129.

112. SENT TO UMBERTO: Berkeley, *Campaign of Adowa*, p. 55. Marcus, *Menelik II*, p. 145.

112. HEARTILY APPROVED: Berkeley, *Campaign of Adowa*, p. 37.

112. "COULD RESTORE ORDER": Alula quoted, in Erlich, *Ethiopia and Eritrea*, p. 188.

112. LIRE IN AUGUST: Marcus, *Menelik II*, p. 162.

112. BARATIERI AGAINST MANGASHA: Wylde, *Modern Abyssinia*, p. 52. "Special Issue on the Battle of Adowa," *Ethiopian Observer*, vol. 1 (December 1957).

112. EXPELLED FROM ETHIOPIA: Marcus, *Menelik II*, p. 161.

112–13. MANGASHA'S MEAT GRINDER: *Ibid.*, p. 164.

113. VENGEFUL FRENZY: Wylde, *Modern Abyssinia,* pp. 52–53.

113. 38,063 SOLDIERS DISEMBARKED: Berkeley, *Campaign of Adowa,* p. 196.

113. MANGASHA AND HIS VASSALS: *Stampa* editorial, in Paul Combes, *L'Abyssinie en 1896, Le Pays—Les Habitants, La Lutte Italo-Abyssine* (Paris: J. André, 1896), p. 109.

113. "TRAMPLED UNDER OUR FEET": Menilek's letter to Umberto quoted, in Berkeley, *Campaign of Adowa,* p. 217.

114. "CROSS THE BORDERS OF ISLAM": Khalifa's letter to Menilek, Safar 1313 (October 1895), Menelik-Khalifa Folder, *Institute of Ethiopian Studies* (IES).

114. "ONE ANOTHER IN JERUSALEM": Yohannes's letter to Czar Alexander quoted, in Rollins, "Russia's Ethiopian Adventure," p. 25.

114. ANGLO-ITALIAN CONVENTION: Marcus, *Menelik II,* p. 160. Prince A. Lobanov-Rostovsky, *Russia and Asia* (New York: Macmillan, 1933), p. 212; Rollins, "Russia's Ethiopian Adventure," pp. 153, 155.

114. "BROTHERLY ASSISTANCE": Czar's letter to Menilek, in Rollins, "Russia's Ethiopian Adventure," p. 153. Lobanov-Rostovsky, *Russia and Asia,* p. 212.

114. INTENDED TO INVEST HEAVILY: Marcus, *Menelik II,* p. 152.

115. HONEY CALLED T'EJ: Rollins, "Russia's Ethiopian Adventure," p. 241.

115. GOOD ARTILLERY OFFICER: *Ibid.,* p. 188. Dedjaz Comte N. de Leontieff, *Provinces Equatorials d'Abyssinie* (Paris: publisher unknown, 1900).

115. WAR COUNCIL: Rollins, "Russia's Ethiopian Adventure," p. 199.

115. TRIPLE ALLIANCE: *Ibid.* pp. 201, 209.

116. SEVERAL MACHINE GUNS: *Ibid.,* p. 206.

116. ITALIAN ARSENAL: Wylde, *Modern Abyssinia,* p. 53.

116. MACHINE GUN PRACTICE: Pankhurst, *Economic History of Ethiopia,* p. 58.

116. SUBJECT TO ITALIAN APPROVAL: Berkeley, *Campaign of Adowa,* p. 229.

116. HIS RIVAL BARATIERI: *Ibid.,* p. 255.

116. "THE PRESTIGE OF THE MONARCHY": Crispi's telegram, *ibid.,* p. 256.

117. ARRIVING AT MASSAWA: *Ibid.* p. 196.

117. ARGUED FOR AN ATTACK: *Ibid.* pp. 164, 258–59.

117. "DISHONORABLE RETREAT": Dabormida quoted, in "Special Issue," *Ethiopian Observer*, p. 350.

117. "ENEMY'S CAMP": Baratieri quoted, in Berkeley, *Campaign of Adowa*, p. 259.

117. MENILEK'S ARMY: "Special Issue," *Ethiopian Observer*, p. 350.

117. UNDER FORTY THOUSAND: Berkeley, *Campaign of Adowa*, p. 124.

118. "THE ANGER OF GOD": Italian officer quoted, in "Special Issue," *Ethiopian Observer*, p. 351.

118. ON THE MOVE: "Special Issue," *Ethiopian Observer*, p. 353. Wylde, *Modern Abyssinia*, p. 204.

118. TO DECEIVE MENILEK: Erlich, *Ethiopia and Eritrea*, p. 193.

118. ARRIVING AT ABOUT 8:30: Albertone message quoted, in Berkeley, *Campaign of Adowa*, pp. 286 and 282–344. "Special Edition," *Ethiopian Observer*, pp. 353–57.

118. SECOND OF MARCH: Berkeley, *Campaign of Adowa*, p. 259. Marcus, *Menelik II*, p. 172.

119. "PRAY FOR US": Menilek's proclamation quoted, in Berkeley, *Campaign of Adowa*, pp. 126–27.

119. "FOR THE FAITH!" Marcus, *Menelik II*, p. 172.

119. ON THEIR FLANKS: "Special Issue," *Ethiopian Observer*, p. 352; Achille Bizzoni, "The Battle of Adowa, 1896, a Contemporary Italian View," *Ethiopian Observer*, vol. 14 (1971), pp. 15–39; Roberto Battaglia, *La Prima Guerra d'Africa* (Torino: Giulio Einaudi editore, 1958), p. 772; Berkeley, *Campaign of Adowa*, pp. 280–81.

119. SIX HUNDRED CAVALRY . . . NEARBY: "Special Issue," *Ethiopian Observer*, p. 352. Berkeley, *Campaign of Adowa*, p. 281.

119. THEIR OWN ERITREANS: Berkeley, *Campaign of Adowa*, p. 286.

120. *"EBALGUME! EBALGUME!"*: War cry, *ibid.*, p. 344. Disappearance of Dabormida, *ibid.*, p. 339.

120. "GOLDEN STARS": Berkeley, *Campaign of Adowa*, p. 339, footnote 1.

120. NATIONAL CRUSADE: Sellassie, *Chronique*, p. 2. Marcus, *Menelik II*, p. 176; Wylde, *Modern Abyssinia*, p. 211.

120. FOR ONE DAY: "Special Edition," *Ethiopian Observer*, p. 351. Berkeley, *Campaign of Adowa*, p. 348.

120. *THE RISE OF MENELIK*: *Ibid.*, p. viii.

121. "THE FAR EAST": *La Liberté* quoted, in "Special Edition," *Ethiopian Observer,* p. 366.

121. "FRIENDLY RELATIONS AND COMMERCE": Faure's letter to Menilek, in André Lebon, "La Mission Marchand et le Cabinet Méline," *Revue des Deux Mondes* (March 15, 1900), p. 287.

121. CONVEYED THE GIST OF THINGS: *La Tribuna,* quoted in "Special Edition," *Ethiopian Observer,* p. 366. Holt, *Mahdist State,* p. 209.

121. ACTIVITY NEARER KASSALA: "There is little doubt that owing to the news of Abyssinian success against the Italians, and possible communication received from Menelik, that the Khalifa resolved to enter into an active campaign against the Kassala district": British intelligence report, No. 44, (February/March 1896), Sudan Intelligence Reports (SIR) (University of Khartoum Library). Marcus, *Menelik II,* p. 178.

122. ANOTHER EMISSARY TO OMDURMAN: Holt, *Mahdist State,* p. 209.

122. "BETWEEN US AND YOU": Khalifa to Menilek, Rabih II 1314 (September-October 1896), Menelik-Khalifa Folder, IES.; Holt, *Mahdist State,* p. 209.

122. "BUT HARDER ON THE ETHIOPIANS": Muhammad 'Uthman quote, in "Statement of Mohammed Osman El Haj Khaled, Jaali; Khalifa Abdulla's emissary to Menelik," Folder—1/34/16, Central Record Office (CRO).

122. "RETURN IT TO ETHIOPIA": in Hertslet, *Map of Africa,* vol. 2, Document No. 124.

123. IN THE ETHIOPIAN CAPITAL: Vivian, *Abyssinia,* pp. 183–84.

123. IRRESPECTIVE OF PUBLIC OPINION: David Levering Lewis, *Prisoners of Honor: the Dreyfus Affair* (New York: William Morrow, 1973), p. 125.

123. "WOULD YOU LEAD THE SECOND?": Monteil quoted, in Prince Henri d'Orléans, *Une Visite à l'Empéreur Ménélik, Notes et Impressions de Route* (Paris: Dentu, 1898), p. 1.

124. "EFFECTIVE ASSISTANCE": Lebon dispatch quoted, in Jules Emily, "Les Missions du Haut-Nil en 1897–1898," *Revue de l'Histoire des Colonies Françaises,* No. 3 (1931), p. 266.

124. BETWEEN FRANCE AND ETHIOPIA: Charles Michel, *Mission de Bonchamps,* p. 18. Marc Michel, *Mission Marchand,* p. 140.

124. TO FOLLOW LAGARDE'S: Czeslaw Jesman, *The Russians in Ethiopia: An Essay in Futility* (London: Chatto and Windus, 1958), pp. 116–18.

124. THE MACHINE GUNS: Charles Michel, *Mission de Bonchamps,* p. 18. Marc Michel, *Mission Marchand,* p. 143.

124. DELAYING HIS TRIP: Charles Michel, *Mission de Bonchamps,* p. 18. Jacques Vanderlinden, "Casimir Mondon-Vidailhet: A Propos d'un Manuscrit de C. Mondon-Vidailhet," Typescript. 983.3 VAN, IES.

124. ACROSS THE DANAKIL: Charles Michel, *Mission de Bonchamps,* p. 90.

125. "THE RIGHT BANK OF THE NILE": Lebon's telegraph, Marc Michel, *Mission Marchand,* p. 142.

125. WHAT HE DESIRED: Holt, *Mahdist State,* p. 208. Marcus, *Menelik II,* p. 180.

125. FRENCH MOVES . . . BAHR AL-GHAZĀL: Sanderson, *England, Europe and Upper Nile,* p. 294. Marcus, *Menelik II,* p. 180. Marc Michel, *Mission Marchand,* p. 142.

126. FRENCH SATELLITE WERE CONVINCING: Alfred Ilg, "Ethiopie," *Journal des Débats, Politiques et Littéraires,* October 9, 1897, p. 2. Charles Michel, *Mission de Bonchamps,* p. 102.

126. ATLANTIC–RED SEA GAMBIT: Harold Marcus, "The Rodd Mission of 1897," *Journal of Ethiopian Studies,* vol. 3 (July 1965), pp. 25–35.

127. "LIVES OF MANY ITALIANS": Italian officer quoted, in Rodd, *Memories,* p. 128.

127. FORMAL RECEPTION: D'Orléans, *Visite à l'Empéreur Ménélik,* p. 160. Rodd, *Memories,* p. 132.

127. TO BONVALOT . . . WHEN THEY ARRIVED: Mondon-Vidailhet quote, in Charles Michel, *Mission de Bonchamps,* p. 96.

128. AMUSEMENT OF MENILEK: Rodd, *Memories,* p. 153.

128. THE RICHES OF THE SOUTH: Langer, *Diplomacy,* p. 542.

128. QUEEN VICTORIA'S HEALTH: Rodd, *Memories,* p. 150. D'Orléans, *Visite à l'Empéreur Ménélik,* p. 160.

128. "THE EFFECT . . . PROFOUND": Rodd, *Memories,* p. 149.

128. *LE TEMPS* AND *NEW YORK HERALD*: Casimir Mondon-Vidailhet, "En Ethiopie," *Le Temps,* June 16, 1897, p. 1.

128. NONINVOLVEMENT IN ETHIOPIA: Rodd, *Memories,* pp. 167–74.

129. RESPECTED ITS ACHIEVEMENTS: M. V. Right, "Russian Red Cross Expedition to Ethiopia," *Russia and Africa* (Moscow: 'Nauka Publishing House, 1966).

129. END OF THE YEAR: Rollins, "Russia's Ethiopian Adventure," p. 269.

129. RAILROAD . . . AS WELL: Richard Greenfield, *Ethiopia: New Political History* (New York: Praeger, 1965), p. 125.

129. "LOSING OUR SOVEREIGNTY": Menilek quoted, in Pankhurst, *Economic History of Ethiopia,* p. 24.

129. "HUMAN SIDE": Rodd, *Memories*, p. 162.

129. SUGGESTION AND GREAT FAITH: Menilek quote, *ibid.*, p. 157.

130. "CATTLE KEEPERS OF THE ETHIOPIANS": Menilek quote, in Marcus, "Rodd Mission," p. 31.

130. ARMS SHIPMENTS TO THE KHALIFA: Marcus, "Rodd Mission," p. 32.

130. "RECORDED IN A TREATY": Rodd, *Memories*, p. 174.

130. DISTANCE ITSELF FROM FRANCE: Sanderson, *England, Europe and the Upper Nile*, p. 259. Marcus, *Menelik II*, p. 185.

131. ONLY SOME OF THE BRITISH: D'Orléans, *Visite à l'Empéreur Ménélik*, p. 162.

131. UNABLE TO KEEP HIS FOOD DOWN: Charles Michel, *Mission de Bonchamps*, p. 146.

132. "I'LL CATCH UP WITH YOU": Bonvalot quoted, *ibid*, p. 108.

132. LONGER THAN CLOCHETTE'S ROUTE: *Ibid.*, p. 115.

132. TO THE FRONTIER: *Ibid.*, p. 252.

132. "IN OUR HONOR": *Ibid.*, p. 111.

132. "REACH GORÉ AFTER HIM": *Ibid.*, p. 119.

132. THREE YEARS LATER: *Ibid.*, p. 115.

133. ELSEWHERE FOR THE BLAME: Marc Michel, *Mission Marchand*, p. 143. Sanderson, "Contributions from African Sources": "The received account that the Negus had committed himself more or less completely to the support of the French policy on the Upper Nile evidently requires drastic revision," p. 89. Yet Ganiage, *L'Expansion Coloniale de la France*, p. 215, writes: "Despite the good will of Menelik, this expedition failed, at least in part, due to inadequate preparation."

133. HAD BEEN EXHAUSTED: The Marquis de Bonchamps, after the great Nile stretch was over, decided that "the Ethiopians didn't help the mission; they did everything possible in order to prevent its departure for the Nile." De Bonchamps quote, in Sanderson, "Contributions from African Sources," p. 87.

133. "I NEED WARMTH!": Clochette quote, in Charles Michel, *Mission de Bonchamps*, p. 146.

133. "SECOND LETTER FROM THE EMPEROR": *Ibid.*, p. 139.

133. "SIX THOUSAND KILOS!": *Ibid.*, p. 165.

133. ROCK AGAINST THE NECK: *Ibid.*, pp. 170–71.

134. ISSUING NEW COMMANDS: Emily, "Missions du Haut-Nil," p. 268; Charles Michel, *Mission de Bonchamps,* p. 236.

134. "NOW YOU HAVE ME": Lagarde quoted, in Charles Michel, *Mission de Bonchamps,* p. 245.

134. "WATER BARELY RIPPLES": Mondon-Vidailhet quote, *ibid.*, p. 237.

134. "MULES AND CAMELS": Menilek text, *ibid.*, pp. 250–51.

134. ON THE UPPER NILE: *Ibid.*, pp. 252–53. Marc Michel, *Mission Marchand,* p. 145.

135. OCCUPY A SECOND: Charles Michel, *Missions de Bonchamps,* p. 254.

135. "ON LUCK ALONE": *Ibid.*, p. 252.

135. INVADING SUDAN THROUGH ITS TERRITORY: Khalifa to Menilek, Safar 1313 (October 1895), Menelik-Khalifa Folder, IES. Salih Mohammad Nur, "A Critical Edition of the Memoirs of Yusuf Mikha'il," Ph.D. dissertation, School of Oriental and African Studies, University of London, 1962. Holt, *Mahdist State,* p. 209. Marcus, *Menelik II,* p. 179. Sanderson, *England, Europe and Upper Nile,* pp. 174, 297.

135. DISINGENUOUS PROTESTS . . . TO OMDURMAN: Mangasha to Khalifa, 6 Safar 1314 (October 1896), Khalifa Correspondence, IES. Sanderson, *England, Europe and Upper Nile,* p. 297.

136. "THEIR MUTUAL FRIENDSHIP": Menilek quote, from "Statement of Mohammed Osman El Haj Khaled," p. 147.

136. "CROSS TO THE RIGHT BANK": "Ministre des Colonies à Commissaire Général, Libreville, 30 December 1897, III Periode—2 août 1897—10 juillet 1898," Fonds Baratier AN/99 AP 1 a 8/.

136. "DIVIDE UP AFRICA": Menilek quote, in Rubenson, "Adwa 1896," p. 129.

136. "DO WHAT HE DID NOT WANT TO DO": British ambassador quoted, in Pankhurst, *Economic History of Ethiopia,* p. 4.

CHAPTER SIX: KHALIFA, KHEDIVE, AND KITCHENER

137. VERY BLACK INHABITANTS: Richard Gray, *A History of the Southern Sudan, 1839–1889* (London: Oxford University Press, 1961).

137. "BEGINS AT MALAKAL": On region's history and ethnography, Hagar, "Dynamics"; Francis Mading Deng, *Tradition and Modernization: A Challenge for Law Among the Dinka of the Sudan* (New Haven: Yale University Press, 1971), and *Dinka of the Sudan;* Evans-Pritchard, *Azande;* P. Stefan Santandrea, *A Tribal History of the Western Bahr el Ghazal* (Bologna: Editrice Nigrizia, 1964).

138. "BY MY PERMISSION": Mahdi quote, in Nur, "Memoirs of Yusuf Mikha'il," pp. 166–67. Rudolf C. Slatin Pasha, *Fire and Sword in the Sudan: A Personal Narrative of Fighting and Serving the Dervishes, 1879–1895* (New York: Negro Universities Press, 1969; orig. pub. 1896), p. 369.

138. BONFIRE EARLY IN HIS MINISTRY: Slatin, *Fire and Sword*, p. 374.

138. OF THE DARK AGES: *Ibid.*, p. 547.

139. "FOOD FOR OUR WOMEN AND CHILDREN": Khalifa quote, *ibid.*, pp. 139–40.

139. "GLISTENING WHITE TEETH": *Ibid.*, p. 285.

139. WAS OFTEN UNPLEASANT: *Ibid.*

139. SCATTERING THEM IN DISTANT PROVINCES: *Ibid.*, p. 517.

139. "CAPABLE OF . . . EVERYTHING": *Ibid.*, p. 516.

139. FIERCE BLACK FLAG DIVISION: Winston Churchill, *The River War: An Account of the Reconquest of the Sudan* (London: Eyre and Spottiswoode, 1933; orig. pub. 1899), p. 262.

140. *ASHRAF* . . . STEADILY RISING: *Ibid.*

140. KHALIFA'S HOUSE AND OTHER BUILDINGS: E. G. S.-Hall, C.M.G., Governor of Khartoum Province, "Handbook of Khartoum Province," 2/2/10, Cairo Intelligence (CAIRINT), CRO, p. x.

140. "HIS FAMILY FIVE PIASTRES": Nur, "Memoirs of Yusuf Mikha'il," p. 169.

141. NOT TO BE MOLESTED: Gordon Brooke-Shepherd, *Between Two Flags: The Life of Baron Sir Rudolf Slatin Pasha* (London: Weidenfeld and Nicolson, 1972), p. 92. British intelligence reports, No. 1 (2 May), with "Covering Note" from Sirdar Kitchener; No. 2 (May); No. 4 (July); and No. 41 (August/September 1895), SIR (University of Khartoum Library).

141. "TRANQUILITY MAY LAST": British intelligence report, No. 5 (August 1892), p. 5: SIR (University of Khartoum Library).

141. "ENTERTAIN SUCH AN IDEA": Archibald Hunter, Lewa, Commanding Suakin District to DMI, 14 August 1892, p. 7, SIR (University of Khartoum Library).

141. "BURDENSOME" . . . OCCUPATION OF EGYPT: Gladstone quote, in al-Sayyid, *Egypt and Cromer*, p. 102. Langer, *Diplomacy*, p. 101.

142. "SO BITTERLY DESPISE": Father Rossignoli, "Report on the Sudan," 1894, 1/40/240, CAIRINT-CRO.

142. WARNED THEM OF PHYSICAL DESTRUCTION: Deherain, *Le Soudan Perdu*, p. 354.

142. "ZANZIBAR SO MANY YEARS AGO": 'Uthman Digna quote, in Jackson, *Osman Digna*, p. 191.

143. "FALL INTO OUR HANDS": Khalifa's Queen Victoria letter, in Wingate, *Mahdism*, p. 448.

143. A FIVE-HOUR BATTLE: Deherain, *Le Soudan Perdu*, pp. 411–12.

143. AFTER THE BATTLE NEAR WADI HALFA: Nur, "Memoirs of Yusuf Mikha'il," p. 10.

143. CRUEL DEATHS OF PRISONERS: British intelligence reports, No. 41 (August/September); No. 42 (November/December 1895), SIR (University of Khartoum Library).

143. RIGHTFUL OWNERS RATHER THAN . . . KHALIFA: British intelligence report, No. 41 (August/September 1895), SIR (University of Khartoum Library). Vera Maria Plasilova, *Le Soudan dans le Différend Anglo-Egyptien* (Paris: Editions A. Pedone, no date), p. 34.

143. POLICING THE SUDAN: Dervish Steamers information, in 9/9/97, 1/50/292, CAIRINT-CRO.

144. "TO KEEP THEM UNDER HIS HAND": Rossignoli, "Report on the Sudan."

144. "EFFORTS ARE NOT ALTOGETHER UNSUCCESSFUL": British intelligence report, No. 9 (December 1892), p. 7, SIR (University of Khartoum Library).

144. IN PARTS OF THE MAHDIYYA: British intelligence report, No. 1 (May 2, 1892), SIR (University of Khartoum Library).

144. TO ONE PART SILVER: *Ibid.*

144. TO MODERATION AS TO EXCESS: *Ibid.;* and No. 17 (August 1893), SIR (University of Khartoum Library).

145. "YOU WORK LIKE DONKEYS": Khalifa quote, in British intelligence report, No. 18 (September 1893), SIR (University of Khartoum Library), p. 3.

145. "YOU WILL NOT FIND THEM": Zaki Tamal quote, in Slatin, *Fire and Sword*, p. 501. British intelligence report, No. 23 (February 1894), p. 3; Nur, "Memoirs of Yusuf Mikha'il," p. 219.

145. *JIHĀDIYYA* . . . OCCASIONALLY KILLING: British intelligence report, No. 41 (August/September 1895), SIR (University of Khartoum Library).

145. "TRADE HAD ALMOST STOPPED IN OMDURMAN:" *Ibid.*

145. CURRENCY . . . DISCOUNTED BY MERCHANTS THERE: Babikr Bedri, *The Memoirs of Babikr Bedri*, Yousef Badri and George Scott, trans.; introduction by P. M. Holt (London: Oxford University Press, 1969), p. 202.

145. LOSING HIS GRIP: British intelligence report, No. 17 (August 1893), SIR (University of Khartoum Library). Theobald, *Mahdiya*, p. 196.

145. A THOUSAND FOLLOWERS: July, *History of African People*, pp. 251–56.

145–46. EMPIRE . . . OVERTAKEN BY HISTORY: Gray, *A History of Southern Sudan*, pp. 121–23. Thuriaux-Hennebert, *Les Zande*, p. 55. *The African Slave Trade*, p. 166.

146. JOIN RABIH . . . 1892: British intelligence report, No. 2 (May 1892), SIR (University of Khartoum Library).

146. TROOPS PERFORMED MAGNIFICENTLY: Theobald, *Mahdiya*, p. 170.

146. ARTILLERY AND INFANTRY ATTACK: Slatin, *Fire and Sword*, p. 506.

146. "THE BELGIANS FROM THE SOUTH": Rossignoli, "Report on the Sudan."

147. DERIVED THEIR SOVEREIGNTY: Mekki Abbas, *The Sudan Question: The Dispute over the Anglo-Egyptian Condominium, 1884–1951* (London: Faber and Faber, 1952), p. 45.

147. INDEPENDENT OF PRIME MINISTERS: al-Sayyid, *Egypt and Cromer*, pp. 2–4.

147. CONSIDERABLE FEARS . . . HER MAJESTY'S SERVANTS: Berque, *Egypt, Imperialism*, pp. 171–72. Al-Sayyid, *Egypt and Cromer*, p. 5.

147. "FOR MANY YEARS TO COME": Cromer quote, in al-Sayyid, *Egypt and Cromer*, p. 56.

148. "EGYPTIAN GOVERNMENT HAS TO DEAL": Cromer quote, *ibid.*, p. 59.

148. "WHAT THESE PEOPLE THEMSELVES THINK": Cromer quote, *ibid.*, p. 62.

148. FIVE THOUSAND BRITISH REGULARS: Berque, *Egypt, Imperialism*, p. 192.

148. EVEN TO BOTHER CENSORING: *Ibid.*, pp. 179–87. Al-Sayyid, *Egypt and Cromer*, p. 159.

148. *AL-MUAYYAD:* Berque, *Egypt, Imperialism*, pp. 181–87.

148. BRITONS, FRENCH, GERMANS, AUSTRIANS: *Ibid.*, p. 192.

149. SWAT BALLS IN SUCH PLACES: *Ibid.*, p. 194.

149. FRENCH AND RUSSIAN EMBASSIES: Rodd, *Memories*, p. 68.

149. "DESTITUTE OF FEMININE VANITY": Nazli quote, *ibid.*, p. 63.

149. "THE MAD ENGLISHMAN": *Ibid.*, p. 70.

150. THE DREAD CONTAGION: Berque, *Egypt, Imperialism*, p. 125. Rodd, *Memoirs*, p. 110.

150. "FRESH FROM . . . HARROW": Baring quote, in al-Sayyid, *Egypt and Cromer*, p. 99.

150. "SCARCELY SANE . . . HIS DOCTOR": *Ibid.*, p. 128.

150. "NONDESCRIPT EGYPTIANS": Earl of Cromer (Evelyn Baring), *Abbas II* (London: Macmillan, 1915), p. 9.

151. BRITISH ADVISOR INTOLERABLE: al-Sayyid, *Egypt and Cromer*, p. 100.

151. "IT MUST HAPPEN GRADUALLY": Cromer quote, in Berque, *Egypt, Imperialism*, pp. 164–65.

151. MUSTAPHA KAMIL: al-Sayyid, *Egypt and Cromer*, pp. 155–56.

151. FIRST DECISIVE STEP . . . 1893: *Bosphore Egyptien, ibid.*, p. 100. *Ibid.*, p. 101.

151. "NECESSARY OR DESIRABLE": Rosebery message, *ibid.*, p. 108.

151. "CONTROL THE KHEDIVE": Cromer to Rosebery, *ibid.*, p. 115.

151. "IMPOSSIBLE UNDER ANY CONDITIONS": Baring to Salisbury, June 15, 1889, in Lowe, *Reluctant Imperialists*, p. 68.

152. LOCAL TOBACCO INDUSTRY: al-Sayyid, *Egypt and Cromer*, p. 138.

152. "DECLARED THAT THEY WANT US TO GO": Cromer quote, *ibid.*, p. 120.

152. "EXCELLENCE OF THEIR MOTIVES": Cromer, *Modern Egypt*, p. 222.

152. "DISGRACEFUL . . . ARMY": Abbas quote, in al-Sayyid, *Egypt and Cromer*, p. 122. Marlowe, *Cromer in Egypt*, p. 174.

152. "THIS WAY OF THINKING": French ambassador quote, in Berque, *Egypt, Imperialism*, p. 165.

152. CONTROL OF THE KHEDIVE: Rosebery ultimatum, in al-Sayyid, *Egypt and Cromer*, p. 123.

152. HIS TEARFUL MINISTERS: Abbas quote, *ibid.*, p. 124.

153. "THIS EARLIER STAGE": Rodd, *Memories*, p. 5.

153. "INTEREST . . . ROUSED": al-Sayyid, *Egypt and Cromer*, p. 158.

153. FORCE TO THE BAHR AL-GHAZĀL: Hargreaves, "Entente Manquée," pp. 75-76. Al-Sayyid, *Egypt and Cromer*, p. 133.

153. "RETENTION OF DONGOLA": Salisbury to Victoria, March 16, 1896, in Buckle, *Letters of Queen Victoria*, vol. 3, p. 33.

153. WITHOUT INFORMING THE KHEDIVE: Rodd, *Memories*, p. 86.

153. NATIONALIST INTELLECTUALS: "The Khedive in France," September 28, 1896, *Times* (London).

153. GIVEN SUPREME DIRECTION: Sir George Arthur, *Life of Lord Kitchener*. 3 vols., (London: Macmillan, 1920), vol. 1, pp. 219–20.

153. PRESSURE ON THE ITALIANS AT KASSALA: Rodd, *Memories*, pp. 84–85.

154. VICTORIA . . . "A LITTLE ANXIOUS": Victoria to Salisbury, March 16, 1896, in Buckle, *Letters of Queen Victoria*, vol. 3, p. 34.

154. TERSE REUTERS ANNOUNCEMENT: Rodd, *Memories*, p. 85.

154. THE INVASION WAS COMPLETE: Theobald, *Mahdiya*, p. 196. Deherain, *Le Soudan Perdu*, pp. 174–84.

154. "FOR THE SAKE OF EGYPT": Buckle, *Letters of Queen Victoria*, vol. 3, p. 38.

154. "ENCROACHMENT" OF OTHER EUROPEAN POWERS: Salisbury to Bigge, September 2, 1896, *ibid.*, p. 73. "The French advance towards the Nile was in his [Salisbury's] eyes a more serious matter, so far as one could diagnose his thoughts": Rodd, *Memories*, p. 187.

154. ACCORD WITH THE KHALIFA'S AMIRS: Salisbury to Lyons, July 20, 1887, in Lowe, *Reluctant Imperialists*, p. 59.

155. LOOMED SO MENACINGLY AMONG THE POWERS: Langer, *Diplomacy*, chs. 5, 6, 7.

155. "IN SEVEN WEEKS": Muhammad Bushara letter, in A. Hilliard Atteridge, *Towards Khartoum: The Story of the Soudan War of 1896* (London: A. D. Innes, 1897), p. 243.

155. ABU ANJA, AND WAD N'JUMI WERE DEAD: Theobald, *Mahdiya*, p. 228.

155. "OF ALL THE KHALIFA'S HORDE": Owneñ Spencer Watkins, *With Kitchener's Army, Being a Chaplain's Experience of the Nile Expedition, 1898* (London: S. W. Partridge, 1899), p. 52.

155. ANGLO-EGYPTIAN ARMY'S FIREPOWER: George W. Steevens, *With Kitchener to Khartoum* (New York: Dodd, Mead, 1898), p. 153.

155. FLYING BY THE EGYPTIAN CAVALRY: Theobald, *Mahdiya*, p. 200.

156. THE FIRKA DEFENSE: *Ibid.*, pp. 201–02.

156. "DESTRUCTION BY THEIR OWN DEVICES": Muhammad Bushara, in Atteridge, *Towards Khartoum*, p. 243.

156. 919 WERE DEAD: Theobald, *Mahdiya*, p. 203.

156. THE MOMENT TO ADVANCE: Philip Ziegler, *Omdurman* (New York: Knopf, 1974), p. 31.

156. "FELL . . . TO THE GROUND": Churchill, *River War,* p. 153.

157. CROSSING TO ATTACK DONGOLA: *Ibid.,* pp. 154–55. Theobald, *Mahdiya,* pp. 205–06.

157. TO STAND AND FIGHT: Churchill, *River War,* pp. 159–60.

157. "BODIES BETWEEN DONGOLA AND OMDURMAN": Khalifa's dream, British intelligence report, No. 50 (August 28–December 31, 1896), SIR (University of Khartoum Library).

CHAPTER SEVEN: FROM THE CONGO TO THE NILE

158. HEARTS AND MINDS OF THE MAHDISTS: Marchand, "Note Analytique Complémentaire."

159. ESCALATING BUDGET WITHOUT DEBATE: Marc Michel, *Mission Marchand,* p. 122.

159. MARCHAND'S KIND OF LEADERSHIP: Baratier, *Au Congo: Souvenirs de la Mission Marchand,* p. 9.

159. *"VOILÀ L'IDÉAL":* Marchand to Mangin, February 6, 1896, Papiers Charles Mangin, AP 149 3, AN.

159. "NOT SPEND A DIME": Marchand to Mangin, March 4, 1896, Papiers Charles Mangin, AP 149 3, AN.

159. LEAVING FOR LOANGO: Baratier, *Au Congo: Souvenirs de la Mission Marchand,* pp. 18–21.

160. STANLEY'S EXAMPLE . . . NOT TO BE FOLLOWED: "Lorsqu'on passe comme Stanley, on emmene une armée qui ravage tout, et laisse derrière elle des cadavres fait par le balles ou par la famine qu'on a provoquée": Baratier, *Au Congo: Souvenirs de la Mission Marchand,* p. 9. Tony Gould, *In Limbo: The Story of Stanley's Rear Column* (London: Hamish Hamilton, 1979).

160. ONE HUNDRED FIFTY JUST MIGHT MAKE IT: Baratier, *Au Congo: Souvenirs de la Mission Marchand,* p. 10.

160. "A SOURCE OF WEAKNESS": *Ibid.,* p. 9.

160. HAD BEEN IN REVOLT: Bernier, chef du Bureau des Douanes, Manyanga, to Monsieur le Commissaire du Gouvt. en mission spéciale, December 28, 1896, Fonds Baratier, 99 AP 1, AN. Baratier, *Au Congo: Souvenirs de la Mission Marchand,* p. 51. Marc Michel, *Mission Marchand,* p. 113.

160. PAY GENEROUSLY FOR THEIR DELIVERANCE: Baratier, *Au Congo: Souvenirs de la Mission Marchand,* p. 51.

161. BETWEEN LOANGO AND BRAZZAVILLE: Mangin to Marie, Libreville, July 6, 1896, Papiers Charles Mangin, AP 149 3, AN. Marc Michel, *Mission Marchand,* p. 113.

161. BEFORE MABIALA'S GROTTO: Marc Michel, *Mission Marchand,* p. 113. Baratier, *Au Congo: Souvenirs de la Mission Marchand,* pp. 50–51. Justin Deramond, "Journal de Route de Deramond," 575 MI, AN, p. 391.

161. FRENCH SIDE OF THESE RIVERS: "Rapport Périodique sur la Situation au delà de la Colonie du 20 novembre au 20 décembre 1894," No. 46, Série Gabon I, 46 à 48, SOM.

162. "BUDGE FOR A WHITE MAN": Mabiala quote, in Marc Michel, *Mission Marchand,* p. 114.

162. "A RIDICULOUS INCIDENT": Mangin to Marie, July 6, 1896, Papiers Charles Mangin, AP 149 3, AN.

162. THE LIEUTENANT FUMED: *Ibid.*

162. "DANGEROUS SPITEFULNESS": "Je croirais manquer à mes devoirs si je ne vous disais mon impression sur M. de Brazza: nous nous trouvons en présence d'un homme qui a crée la colonie et auquel il est insupportable de penser qu'on puisse faire quoi que c'était en dehors de lui": Largeau to Marchand, Libreville, May 20, 1896, Fonds Baratier, 99 AP 1, AN.

162. EVENTS WERE NOW OVERTAKING: Mangin to Marie, July 6, 1896, Papiers Charles Mangin, AP 149 3, AN.

162. CASES COULD BE CARRIED: Baratier to Marchand, June 2, 1896, Fonds Baratier, 99 AP 1, AN. Baratier, *Au Congo: Souvenirs de la Mission Marchand,* p. 13.

164. SELF-ADVERTISING OUTSIDER: West, *Brazza,* p. 84. Coquery-Vidrovitch, *Brazza et la Prise,* p. 12. Marc Michel, *Mission Marchand,* p. 83.

164. "AT THE MINISTRY OF COLONIES": Marchand quote (credible), in Morphy, *Le Commandant Marchand,* vol. 1, p. 325.

164. NAHV . . . SUPPLIES: Delebecque, *Général Marchand,* p. 98. Marc Michel, *Mission Marchand,* pp. 99–101.

165. GRESHOFF AND HIS PORTERS: Marchand to Kerraoul, Vittu de, May 1896– January 1897, Fonds Baratier, 99 AP 1, AN.

165. RAIL, AND TRAIL . . . CONGO: Baratier, *Au Congo: Souvenirs de la Mission Marchand,* p. 95.

165. MABIALA'S MAYOMBE: *Ibid.,* p. 14.

165. BOXES ON THEIR HEADS: *Ibid.,* p. 92.

166. THE LEADERS OF THE REVOLT: Marc Michel, *Mission Marchand,* p. 41.

166. CONTROLLED PORTAGE: *Ibid.*, p. 95.

166. EXPLORER'S CAREER: West, *Brazza*, pp. 154–58.

167. "HOW FAR THE NEXT POST WAS": Mangin to Marie, July 6, 1896, Papiers Charles Mangin, AP 149 3, AN.

167. "I'VE VOWED TO DESTROY SOMEONE": Marchand to Mangin, Comba, October 24, 1896, Papiers Charles Mangin, AP 149 3, AN. Marc Michel, *Mission Marchand*, p. 102.

167. "A WORD FROM HIM SINCE": Marchand quote, in Marc Michel, *Mission Marchand*, p. 102. Brazza to Minister of Colonies, August 21, 1896, Document No. 23, Africa III, SOM.

167. MARCHAND WAS FURIOUS: Deramond, "Journal de Route," p. 190. West, *Brazza*, p. 154.

167. "SUCCESS ON THE KOUILOU": Marchand to Baratier, August 24, 1896, Fonds Baratier, 99 AP 1, AN.

168. DISCOURSE ON AESTHETICS: Baratier, *Au Congo: Souvenirs de la Mission Marchand*, pp. 46–48.

168. "RECRUITMENT OR TRANSPORT": Marchand to Largeau, May 1896–January 1897, Fonds Baratier, 99 AP 1, AN.

168. SURRENDER AND PORTAGE SERVICE: Marchand to Baratier, August 24, 1896, Fonds Baratier, 99 AP 1, AN.

168. DE BRAZZA'S LIEUTENANT GOVERNOR: "Les diverses instructions qui vous ont été remises ne contiennent aucune délégation de pouvoirs administratifs, vous avez néanmoins procédé à des achats et à des positions de marches au nom du service local du Congo Français": Commissaire Général du Gouvt. to Monsieur le Capitaine Marchand, March 30, 1897, Document No. 3bis, Africa III, SOM.

168. CHASTISING "SAVAGES": Wauters, *Souvenirs de Fachoda*, pp. 27–28.

168–69. "NOT NIGGER LIKE ME": Deramond, "Journal de Route," p. 391.

169. "HAD THE CURSE": Castellani, *Marchand l'Africain*, p. 22.

169. BOUNDED INTO LOUDIMA: Baratier, *Au Congo: Souvenirs de la Mission Marchand*, p. 75.

169. CHILDREN TAKEN AS HOSTAGES: Castellani, *Marchand l'Africain*, p. 150.

169. PORTERS ON OCTOBER 17: *Ibid.*, p. 150.

169. WITH A RIFLE SHOT: Baratier, *Au Congo: Souvenirs de la Mission Marchand*, p. 68.

170. KILLED A SENEGALESE: *Ibid.,* p. 84.

170. DEAD OF SMOKE INHALATION: *Ibid.,* p. 84.

170. SIGNIFICANT INSURGENT LEADER: Marc Michel, *Mission Marchand,* pp. 118–19.

170. FORTY CORPORATIONS AND CARTELS: Roberts, *French Colonial Policy,* pp. 350–55. Coquery-Vidrovitch, *Le Congo au Temps des Grandes Compagnies Concessionnaires,* p. 25. Coquery-Vidrovitch, "French Congo and Gabon," in Oliver and Sanderson, *Cambridge History,* vol. 6, pp. 305–15.

170. "HAVE DONE LONG AGO": Liotard to Marchand, May 8, 1897, Fonds Baratier, 99 AP 1, AN.

171. "WHAT STANLEY WOULD THINK OF IT": Marchand to Monsieur Le Herisse, député d'Ille-et-Vilaine, December 13, 1897, cited by the none-too-reliable Morphy, *Le Commandant Marchand,* vol. 1, pp. 152–53.

171. "FIRST ON THE NILE . . . MARCHING ON KHARTOUM?": Jules Emily, *Fachoda, Mission Marchand, 1896–1899* (Paris: Hachette, 1935), p. 12.

171. SUCH MOMENTS WERE ALL TOO RARE: Baratier, *Au Congo: Souvenirs de la Mission Marchand,* pp. 87–88. Deramond, "Journal de Route," p. 355.

171. STEAMER ANTOINETTE: Marc Michel, *Mission Marchand,* p. 152. Castellani, *Marchand l'Africain,* pp. 211–12. Travel of Sergeant Venail, Papiers Charles Mangin, AP 149 3, AN.

172. "BRILLIANCE OF THE SUNSHINE": Joseph Conrad, *Heart of Darkness* (New York: Norton, 1963; orig. pub. 1902), p. 34.

172. LACK OF GOVERNMENT: Castellani, *Marchand l'Africain,* pp. 188–89. For Mangin's more composed reactions, see Mangin, "Lettres de la Mission Marchand," *La Revue des Deux Mondes,* September 15, 1931, pp. 241–83, esp. Mangin to sister, February 15, 1897, p. 253.

172. "FRIENDS FROM THE EAST": Marchand quote, in Marc Michel, *Mission Marchand,* p. 149.

173. ACROSS ITS PATH: "Extrait d'une lettre écrit au Général Archinard par le capitaine Marchand à la date du 14 février 1897," Document No. 32d, Africa III, SOM.

173. "IT'S NOT IMPOSSIBLE": Liotard to Marchand, Semio, January 17, 1897, Fonds Baratier, 99 AP 1, AN.

173. "MAHDI'S [KHALIFA'S] PERMISSION, OCCUPY FASHODA": *Ibid.*

174. SEVENTY-TWO DUGOUTS: Marc Michel, *Mission Marchand,* p. 158.

174. OMDURMAN BEFORE THE END OF THE YEAR: Liotard to Marchand, May 8, 1897, Fonds Baratier, 99 AP 1, AN.

CHAPTER EIGHT: THE RACE TO FASHODA

175. "ABOUT HIS YOUTHFUL PRANKS": Marchand to Landeroin, Kimbedi, December 15, 1896; Marchand, December 13, 1896, Fonds Baratier, 99 AP 1, AN.

175. "MUCH MORE APPARENT THAN REAL": Marchand to Castellani quote, in Castellani, *Marchand l'Africain*, p. 32.

175. BADLY STRAINED: Deramond, "Journal de Route," pp. 366–67, 440–41, 445, 470.

175. "A SINGLE WORK BY TAINE": Largeau quote, *ibid.*, p. 367.

176. HIS SOLE MISCALCULATION: Lotar, *Bomu*, pp. 54–55.

176. AN EXTREME EXCEPTION: "In 1900 the total strength of the white community . . . was merely 800, of whom most were stationed at Brazzaville (248), Pointe Noire and Libreville": Coquery-Vidrovitch, "French Congo and Gabon," p. 304.

177. "VIEWS OF THE GOVERNMENT COMMISSIONER": Ministry of Colonies to Ministry of Foreign Affairs, February 24, 1896, Document No. 10, Africa III, SOM.

177. A MASTERPIECE OF DIPLOMACY: Liotard to Marchand, February 5; April 8, 1897, Deuxième Période—Fonds Baratier, 99 AP 1, AN.

177. CHIPS VIS-À-VIS THE BRITISH: Liotard to Marchand, April 8; February 5, 1897, Deuxième Période—Fonds Baratier, 99 AP 1, AN.

178. COMPELLING REASON TO AVOID REGION: Liotard to Marchand, April 8; February 5, 1897, Deuxième Période—Fonds Baratier. Castellani, *Marchand l'Africain*, p. 226. Gabriel Hanotaux, *Histoire des Colonies Françaises et de l'Expansion de la France dans le Monde*, 6 vols. (Paris: Plon, 1931), vol. 4, pp. 522–23.

178. "LIOTARD . . . FOR ALL THINGS": Marchand to Ministry of Colonies, Fort Hossinger, July 28, 1897, Deuxième Période—Fonds Baratier, 99 AP 1, AN.

178. "PERMANENT POSITION" . . . IN THE BAHR AL-GHAZĀL: Liotard to Marchand, January 17; February 5, 1897, Deuxième Période—Fonds Baratier, 99 AP 1, AN.

178. "WHALE BOATS WOULD NOT HAVE": Marchand quote, in Albert Ernest Baratier, *Vers le Nil: Souvenirs de la Mission Marchand, Brazzaville à Forte Desaix* (Paris: Arthème Fayard, 1914?), p. 22.

178. MODEST TENDER OF ONE HUNDRED THOUSAND FRANCS: "Germain est encore à Zemio où il vient d'arriver avec le bateau qu'il a du couper en tranche, puisque l'évêque Agouard n'a pas voulu vendre le sien": Mangin to Marie, July 11, 1897, Papiers Charles Mangin, AP 149 3, AN. Coquery-Vidrovitch, "French Congo and Gabon," pp. 304–05.

179. CIVIL AND MILITARY SUPPLIES: Marc Michel, *Mission Marchand*, p. 158. Baratier, *Au Congo: Souvenirs de la Mission Marchand*, p. 94.

179. "STEAL IT," SAID BARATIER: Baratier, *Vers le Nil*, p. 21.

179. THE UBANGI BUDGET: *Ibid.*, p. 22.

179. SERGEANT SOUYRI: Wright, *Conflict on the Nile*, pp. 144–45.

179. RIPPED TOENAIL . . . MAY 11: Marchand to Mangin, Ouango, May 11, 1897, Papiers Charles Mangin, AP 149 3, AN.

179. SIMON . . . LATE JUNE: Mangin to Mme. Menard, May 23, 1897, Papiers Charles Mangin, AP 149 3, AN.

180. "HIGHLY RISKY" CREATION: Mangin to Marie, Zemio, June 21, 1897, Papiers Charles Mangin, AP 149 3, AN.

180. COOKED FOR TWELVE HOURS: Mangin to Louise Menard, Rafai, May 24, 1897, Papiers Charles Mangin, AP 149 3, AN.

180. "VICES OF THE TURKS": Mangin to Général des Garets, Fachoda, November 6, 1898, Papiers Charles Mangin, AP 149 3, AN.

180. DESERVING RESPECT: Baratier, *Vers le Nil*, p. 43.

180. "AS CONDESCENDING AS POSSIBLE": Deramond, "Journal de Route," p. 571.

180. "SULTANS WITHOUT PEER": *Ibid.*, pp. 585–86.

180–81. RAINS HAD BEEN TORRENTIAL: *Ibid.*, p. 605.

181. "GRASS BLOWING . . . IN THE RAIN": Marchand quote, in Castellani, *Marchand l'Africain*, p. 227.

181. "A TROUPE OF MAHDISTS": Mangin to Général des Garets, November 6, 1898, Papiers Charles Mangin, AP 149 3, AN.

181. ALLY FOR THE FRENCH: *Ibid.*

181. "85 DEGREES IN THE SHADE": Mangin to his sister, *ibid.*

181. "MESCHRA'ER REQ ON JANUARY 1": Marchand to Minister of Colonies, Fort Hossinger, July 28, 1897, Fonds Baratier, 99 AP 1, AN.

181. "A SIMPLE FLAG BEARER": *Ibid.*

182. "PASSING AT THIS MOMENT": *Ibid.*

182. TWELVE ARTILLERY PIECES: Report from Marchand to Liotard, February 17, 1898, Document No. 65, Africa III, SOM.

182. "IN ORDER TO JOIN WITH US": Marchand to Mangin, Fort Hossinger, September 26, 1897, Papiers Charles Mangin, AP 149 3, AN.

183. "HE COULDN'T MAKE ME": Sergeant Samba Rabi quote, in Deramond, "Journal de Route," p. 867.

183. MANGIN . . . REVOLVER IN CAMP: Marchand's reproach of Mangin, *ibid.*, p. 869. Marc Michel, *Mission Marchand,* p. 70. Emily, *Fachoda, Mission Marchand,* p. 133.

184. THE INSATIABLE INSECTS: Marchand to Mangin, Fort Hossinger, October 18, 1897, Papiers Charles Mangin, AP 149 3, AN.

184. SECTIONS OF THE STEAMER'S BOILER: *Ibid.*

184. "THIRTEEN HOURS OF SUSTAINED EFFORTS": *Ibid.*

184. IMPATIENTLY ORDERED EXPLORATIONS: *Ibid.*

185. "I CALL YOUR ATTENTION TO THIS": Sultan of Tambura to Liotard, in Liotard letter to Marchand, Zemio, November 10, 1897, Fonds Baratier, 99 AP 1, AN.

185. "THEIR TASK IS TRULY AWFUL": Marchand to Mangin, Fort Hossinger, October 18, 1897, Papiers Charles Mangin, AP 149 3, AN.

185. BOILERS ARRIVED AT KHOJALI: *Ibid.*

186. UNKNOWN PLACE . . . CALLED FASHODA: Cf. John M. Mackenzie, *Propaganda and Empire: The Manipulation of British Public Opinion, 1880–1960* (Manchester: Manchester University Press, 1984), chs. 1–2.

186. MOMBASA . . . TO COUNTER MARCHAND: Churchill, *River War,* pp. 312–13. Ronald Robinson, John Gallagher, Alice Denny, *Africa and the Victorians: The Official Mind of Imperialism* (London: Macmillan, 1961), pp. 358–62.

186. "COUNSELLED SPEED": Churchill, *River War,* p. 168.

186. ARTICULATING THE REASONING BEHIND THEM: Arthur, *Lord Kitchener,* vol. 1, p. xiii.

187. "PARIS INTERNATIONAL EXHIBITION": Steevens, *Kitchener to Khartoum,* p. 46.

187. CHOSE WADI HALFA TO ABU HAMED: Arthur, *Lord Kitchener,* p. 210.

187. "IMPOSSIBLE TO CONSTRUCT SUCH A LINE": Churchill, *River War,* p. 169.

189. CROMER ALSO LOST THIS ROUND: "Cecil Rhodes's scheme for the Cape to Cairo railway was then taking shape, and Kitchener was determined to do his share from the northern end": Arthur, *Lord Kitchener,* p. 219.

189. RESUMED VIGOROUSLY: Churchill, *River War,* p. 172.

189. MILES OF RAIL IN AN AUGUST FLASH: *Ibid.,* p. 166.

189. MAHDIST LOSSES HAD BEEN HEAVY: Deherain, *Le Soudan Perdu,* p. 465. Ziegler, *Omdurman,* p. 31.

189. KEPT HIM AT HIS POST: Theobald, *Mahdiya,* pp. 215–16.

190. CRATING IN ENGLAND: Churchill, *River War,* pp. 3–4.

190. "WISH I WERE DEAD": Kitchener to Sir Clinton Dawkins, Abu Hamed, October 6, 1897, in Arthur, *Lord Kitchener,* p. 221–22.

190. RESUME COMMAND: Theobald, *Mahdiya,* p. 217.

190. "MY BEST TO FOLLOW IT": Arthur, *Lord Kitchener,* p. 219.

191. ADVANCE FROM SUAKIN: *Ibid.,* pp. 223–25.

191. "APPEARS . . . TO BE VERY QUESTIONABLE": Baring to Salisbury, November 5, 1897, Cabinet No. 37/45/46. Lowe, *Reluctant Imperialists,* vol. 2, p. 115.

191. A STAND AGAINST THE INFIDEL: Churchill, *River War,* p. 186.

192. YA'QUB . . . MAHMUD AHMAD OF DARFUR: *Ibid.,* p. 186.

192. TOTAL MASSACRE OF THE CITY'S PEOPLE: *Ibid.,* p. 189.

193. "VULTURES . . . PLENTY OF OCCUPATION": Grenadier officer quote, in Ziegler, *Omdurman,* p. 56.

193. JOINT MANEUVERS DOWN THE NILE: Sanderson, "Contributions from African Sources," p. 72. Theobald, *Mahdiya,* p. 224.

193. RAS TASSAMA . . . TOWARD THE WHITE NILE: Sanderson, "Contributions from African Sources," p. 85.

193. CONTESTED BANI SHANGUL REGION: G. N. Sanderson, "The Foreign Policy of the Negus Menelik, 1896–1898," *Journal of African History,* vol. 5 (1964), pp. 96–97.

193. "THE FAITH IS VICTORIOUS!": Khalifa exhortation, in Churchill, *River War,* p. 186.

193. HE REENTERED OMDURMAN: Theobald, *Mahdiya,* p. 218.

194. "GREY SOME YEARS AGO": Monson to Hanotaux declaration, in Langer, *Diplomacy,* pp. 550–51.

194. "FOLLOWED BY A FOREIGN WAR": Monson to Salisbury, FO France 3393 (No. 109), February 26, 1898 in G. P. Gooch and Harold Temperly, eds., *British Documents on the Origins of the War, 1894–1914.* 2 vols. (London: H. M. Stationery Office, 1927), vol. 1, p. 146.

194. DOWN GANGPLANKS INTO SUAKIN: Theobald, *Mahdiya,* p. 199.

194. BASHTANAB ABOVE THE FIFTH CATARACT: Watkins, *With Kitchener's Army,* p. 30.

194. HIGHLANDERS ... A MONTH LATER: *Ibid.,* pp. 37–38. Ziegler, *Omdurman,* pp. 31–32.

195. KILL AFTER A BATTLE WAS OVER: Bennett, *The Downfall of the Dervishes* (London: Methuen, 1899), p. 183.

195. POSITION RATHER THAN ATTACK: Churchill, *River War,* p. 218. Jackson, *Osman Digna,* p. 150.

195. TWO THOUSAND LESS THAN KITCHENER: Sanderson, "Contributions from African Sources," p. 75.

195. MAHMUD AND 'UTHMAN DIQNA WAS INTENSE: Jackson, *Osman Digna,* pp. 150–51.

195. CROMER REPLIED: Kitchener-Cromer exchange quoted, in Arthur, *Lord Kitchener,* pp. 224, 229.

196. AT PRECISELY 6:15: Theobald, *Mahdiya,* p. 221.

196. "DESTROYED AT EVERY STEP," CHURCHILL RECORDED: Churchill, *River War,* p. 239.

196. THE ATBARA WAS OVER: Steevens, *Kitchener to Khartoum,* p. 150.

196. THREE THOUSAND MEN: Theobald, *Mahdiya,* p. 221. Deherain, *Le Soudan Perdu,* p. 469.

196. CHEERED THEM IMMENSELY: Watkins, *With Kitchener's Army,* pp. 37–38.

196. "PERPETUAL LIQUEFACTION": *Ibid.,* p. 200.

196. "BEFORE THE EXPEDITION WAS DONE": *Ibid.,* p. 42.

196. "TOLD—THE SAME AS YOU": Kitchener-Mahmud exchange, in Steevens, *Kitchener to Khartoum,* p. 153.

197. SUPPLIES DAILY CONSUMED: Watkins, *With Kitchener's Army,* p. 79.

197. AFLOAT ON THE NILE: Ziegler, *Omdurman*, p. 37.

198. PUNCHED A HOLE IN THE SECOND BOILER: Churchill, *River War*, p. 253.

198. "BOW YOUR HEADS WHEN SALUTING:" Khalifa query, in Nur, "Memoirs of Yusuf Mikha'il," p. 229. Holt, *Mahdist State*, p. 209.

198. "AT THE HEAD OF HIS ARMY": Statement of Mohammed El Haj Khaled, Jaali, Khalifa Abdullah's emissary to Menelik, 1/34/16 Folder CRO, p. 150.

199. FLAG WAS STORED IN THE KHALIFA'S HOUSE: *Ibid.* Nur, "Memoirs of Yusuf Mikha'il," pp. 229–37. Sanderson, *England, Europe and Upper Nile*, pp. 299–300.

199. OR BLACK RIFLEMEN: Churchill, *River War*, p. 260.

200. SLIPPED INTO THE DESERT: *Ibid.* Ziegler, *Omdurman*, p. 70.

200. TOWARD THE MAHDIST POSITION: Ziegler, *Omdurman*, p. 88.

200. "THE BROWN OF THE PLAIN": Churchill, *River War*, p. 264.

201. "THEY ARE LOOKING AT US": 'Uthman Azrak quote, *ibid.*, p. 270.

201. FOR A NIGHT ATTACK: Jackson, *Osman Digna*, pp. 154–55.

202. "LAST GREAT DAY OF ITS EXISTENCE": Churchill, *River War*, p. 271.

202. "LONG AMONG THE SANDHILLS": *Ibid.*, p. 271.

202. "A MERE HANDFUL": Watkins, *With Kitchener's Army*, p. 164.

203. "IT WAS A MATTER OF MACHINERY": Churchill, *River War*, p. 273.

204. "IN ALL THAT VAST ARMY": Watkins, *With Kitchener's Army*, pp. 168–69.

204. "THEY COULD NOT REPLY": Churchill, *River War*, p. 273. Steevens, *Kitchener to Khartoum*, p. 282.

204. "CIVILIZED OUT OF BRITONS": Steevens, *Kitchener to Khartoum*, p. 274.

204. "NIGGER CAN GO, I CAN GO": British troops quote, *ibid.*, p. 18.

204. TO BE SUPREMELY TESTED: Watkins, *With Kitchener's Army*, p. 48.

205. "ABJAKKA": Khalifa shout, in Bedri, *Memoirs*, p. 236.

CHAPTER NINE: THE END OF THE RACE

206. SHILLUK, NUER, AND DINKA: Edward Gleichen, *Handbook of the Sudan (July 1899)* (London: H. M. Stationery Office, 1899), p. 9.

206. THE CONGO FREE STATE: Diedrich Westermann, *The Shilluk People: Their Language and Folklore* (Westport, Conn.: Negro Universities Press, 1970; orig. pub. 1912), p. lix.

206. "TO WORK ON THE SHILLUKS": Marchand quote, source unidentified (probably authentic), in Morphy, *Le Commandant Marchand*, vol. 1, p. 154.

207. CEREMONY OF RECONCILIATION BETWEEN ENEMIES: E. Evans-Pritchard, *The Divine Kingship of the Nilotic Sudan* (London: Cambridge University Press, 1948), pp. 16–19. Mair, *Primitive Government*, pp. 61–62.

207. "TO CALL FOR HELP": Seligman and Seligman, *Pagan Tribes*, p. 91.

207. POLITICAL COHESION BECAME NECESSARY: Mair, *Primitive Government*, p. 24. Schweinfurth, *Heart of Africa*, p. 87.

207. "THINGS OF THE STRANGERS ARE BAD": Shilluk quote, in Westermann, *Shilluk People*, p. xxviii. Schweinfurth, *Heart of Africa*, pp. 90–91.

207. WEIGHT THAN THE SHILLUK RETH: Godfrey Lienhardt, *Divinity and Experience: The Religion of the Dinka* (Oxford: Clarendon Press, 1961). Hagar, "Dynamics," p. 66. Deng, *Dinka of the Sudan*, p. 111.

208. " 'OTHERS' OR 'FOREIGNERS' ": Dinka quote, in Deng, *Dinka of the Sudan*, p. 3.

208. "ABANDONED A LONG TIME AGO": *Ibid.*, pp. 13–14.

208. CEASED TO EXIST IN HIS EYES: *Ibid.*, p. 6.

208. SAT ON THEIR SPEARS: Westermann, *Shilluk People*, pp. liii–liv.

208. EGYPTIAN ARMY TO FIGHT THEM: *Ibid.* Hagar, "Dynamics," p. 105.

208. SWEPT LUPTON'S ARMY ASIDE: Collins, *The Southern Sudan*, p. 41–42.

208. LEVIES OF THE KHEDIVE: Santandrea, *Tribal History of the Western Bahr el Ghazal*, p. 64.

208. YOKED OFF TO BE SOLD: Hagar, "Dynamics," p. 128.

208. "THE STRANGER AND ALL HIS WAYS": Deng, *Africans of Two Worlds*, p. 131.

209. EXPEDITION ARRIVED SIX YEARS LATER: Albert Ernest Baratier, *Au Congo: Souvenirs de la Mission Marchand*, p. 68.

209. JUST DOWNSTREAM FROM FASHODA: Westermann, *Shilluk People*, p. lix.

210. "CALVARY FOR OUR BEASTS": Charles Michel, *Mission de Bonchamps*, p. 269.

210. TRIBUTARY OF MENILEK: *Ibid.*, p. 268.

210. POSITIVELY "LUGUBRIOUS": *Ibid.*, p. 278.

210. DRIED FISH, WHICH SAVED THEM: *Ibid.*, p. 328.

211. "WE COULD MARCH NO MORE": *Ibid.*, p. 339.

211. NINETY MILES FROM FASHODA: *Ibid.*, p. 364.

212. "WE'LL DIE IN THE SWAMP": *Ibid.*, p. 454.

212. "RAISE THE FRENCH FLAG": *Ibid.*, p. 455.

213. SUÉ RIVER STILL AGITATED HIM: Jules Emily, "Suite de l'Histoire des Colonies Françaises," *Revue de L'Histoire des Colonies Françaises*, No. 3 (1931), p. 335.

213. "NOTHING LEFT IN IT BUT SAND": Marchand observation, February 28, 1898, Papiers Charles Mangin, AP 149 3, AN.

213. LOGISTICS TO THE *FAIDHERBE:* Mangin to Général des Garets, November 6, 1898, Papiers Charles Mangin, AP 149 3, AN.

213. "DINKAS BECAME TAME RATHER READILY": *Ibid.*

214. "IF NECESSARY AGAINST THE ZANDE": Marchand to Germain, Fort Hossinger, December 10, 1897, Papiers Charles Mangin, AP 149 3, AN.

214. EXPEDITION'S POLICIES YET CLOSER TO SUCCESS: Marchand to Mangin, Limbo, February 4, 1898; Marchand to Mangin, Kaiango, February 9, 1898, Papiers Charles Mangin, AP 149 3, AN.

215. "SUSTAINED ONLY BY THEIR OWN COURAGE": Emily, *Fachoda, Mission Marchand*, p. 29.

215. SAFELY BACK AT FORT DESAIX: *Ibid.*, pp. 29–30. Delebecque, *General Marchand*, p. 113.

215. "COMPLETELY ACCEPTED AND LIKED": Baratier, *Souvenirs de la Mission Marchand*, p. 16.

216. ANGLO-BELGIAN FORCE . . . MESCHRA'ER REQ: Document No. 56, Report from Marchand to Liotard, February 17, 1898, series 31–34, Africa III, SOM.

216. HE WAS DEAD: Morphy, *Le Commandant Marchand*, p. 157. Marc Michel, *Mission Marchand*, p. 181.

216. STATE OF MENTAL HEALTH: Robinson, Gallagher, Denny, *Africa and the Victorians*, p. 363.

216. RETREAT FROM THE TETELAS: Wauters, *Souvenirs de Fachoda*, p. 40. Hutereau, *Histoire des Peuplades*, pp. 185–86. Deherain, *Le Soudan Perdu*, p. 424.

216. TO WEAR THEM DOWN: Marc Michel, *Mission Marchand*, p. 181.

217. "AMMUNITION FOR *FAIDHERBE* VIA DJIBOUTI . . .": Document No. 57, Marchand telegram to Colonial Ministry, March 1, 1898, Africa III, SOM.

217. PAKÉ-BÔ WAS "WORN OUT": Emily, *Fachoda, Mission Marchand*, p. 35.

217. ORIGINATING IN BRUSSELS: *Ibid.*, p. 37.

217. OLD PORT WAS CLEAR: Mangin to Louise, Fashoda, July 11, 1898, Papiers Charles Mangin, AP 149 3, AN.

217. "WHAT A SITUATION!": Marchand quote, source unidentified, in Darrell Bates, *The Fashoda Incident of 1898: Encounter on the Nile* (London: Oxford University Press, 1984), p. 94.

217. "BETWEEN 43 AND 45 INCHES": "Journal de Route de Germain," Fort Desaix, June 29–August 4, 1898, Fonds Baratier, 99 AP 1–8, AN.

218. "SIX INCHES SINCE YESTERDAY": Emily, *Fachoda, Mission Marchand*, p. 42.

218. "MODE OF GREETING . . . GRANDEUR": Emily quotes, *Ibid.*, p. 46.

218. BARATIER'S EARLIER BEHAVIOR . . .: Baratier, *Souvenirs de la Mission Marchand*, pp. 30–31.

218. ALLOWING THE MISSION TO CONTINUE: *Ibid.*, p. 30.

219. "ABLE TO CONTINUE?": *Ibid.*, p. 57.

219. THIRTEEN DAYS IN THE *SUDD:* Baratier, *Souvenirs de la Mission Marchand*, p. 53.

219. MANGIN AND HIS MEN: *Ibid.* p. 54. Emily, *Fachoda, Mission Marchand*, p. 70.

219. NEARLY FOUR THOUSAND MILES: Emily, *Fachoda, Mission Marchand*, p. 73.

219. FASHODA ONLY DAYS BEYOND: *Ibid.*, p. 75.

219. "SHILLUKS . . . SO MARVELOUSLY?": Mangin to Louise, Meschra'er Req, June 27, 1898, Papiers Charles Mangin, AP 149 3, AN.

219. BARATIER'S DIARY . . . SAME QUESTIONS: Baratier, *Souvenirs de la Mission Marchand*, pp. 58–59.

219. "THE PHARAOHS AND THE PTOLEMIES!": Emily, *Fachoda, Mission Marchand*, p. 82.

219. JULY 10, 1898, A SUNDAY: *Ibid.*, p. 92.

220. ETHIOPIANS AND EUROPEANS IN THE NEIGHBORHOOD: *Ibid.*, p. 94. Baratier, *Souvenirs de la Mission Marchand*, p. 64.

220. ON A SMALL ISLAND: Emily, *Fachoda, Mission Marchand*, p. 94. Baratier, *Souvenirs de la Mission Marchand*, p. 68.

220. ABANDON THE PLACE: Emily, *Fachoda, Mission Marchand*, p. 96.

220. "FRENCH RIVER": Baratier, *Souvenirs de la Mission Marchand*, p. 73.

220. NINETY-EIGHT *TIRAILLEURS:* Marc Michel, *Mission Marchand*, p. 203.

221. RISKS WERE MORE CALCULABLE: Baratier, *Souvenirs de la Mission Marchand*, p. 82.

221. KUR ABD AL-FADIL'S OWN TROOPS: *Ibid.*

221. "IT'S FRANCE!" BARATIER SHOUTED: *Ibid.*, p. 122.

221. "WE SHALL STAY HERE": Emily, *Fachoda, Mission Marchand*, p. 137.

221. "AFFIX MY SEAL": Kur Abd al-Fadil quote, in Baratier, *Souvenirs de la Mission Marchand*, p. 125.

222. ARABIC COPY . . . DRAFTED: Traité de Protectorat entre Marchand, capitaine de l'Infanterie de Marine, détaché aux Colonies, chef de la Mission Congo-Nil . . . et Kour Abd-el-Fadil, Sultan des Chillouks, Dossier 34, Document No. 39, Annexe No. 6, Africa III, SOM.

222. "WHATEVER SORT OF EUROPEANS": Kitchener to "Chef de l'expédition européenne à Fachoda," September 18, 1898, Document No. 40, Africa III, SOM.

222. "ANY PORTION OF THE NILE VALLEY": Salisbury to Cromer, No. 185. FO Turkey (Egypt) 5050 (No. 109), August 2, 1898, in Gooch and Temperly, *British Documents* vol. 1, p. 160.

222. "COLLISION . . . WITH . . . EMPEROR MENILEK": *Ibid.*, p. 160.

222. "JUNCTION OF THE SOBAT WITH THE NILE": Delcassé, Ministre des Affaires Etrangères à Ministre des Colonies, September 7, 1898, Document No. 72, Africa III, SOM.

222. "EMISSARY OF CIVILIZATION": Monson to Salisbury, No. 188. FO France 3396 (No. 441), September 8, 1898, in Gooch and Temperly, *British Documents*, vol. 1, pp. 163–64.

223. ROWING OUT TO MEET THE SIRDAR: Rapport du Capitaine Julien de la Relève de la Mission Marchand, January 6, 1899, Document No. 38, Africa III, SOM.

223. ARTILLERY, AND FOUR MAXIM GUNS: Churchill, *River War*, p. 318.

224. "FRANCE INTO TWO ENEMY CAMPS": Emily, *Fachoda, Mission Marchand*, p. 163.

224. OFFICER TO PARIS IMMEDIATELY: *Ibid.*, pp. 171–72.

224. TO NEGOTIATE OVER EGYPT: Hanotaux to the French Minister at Cairo, June 21, 1898, I Fachoda (France-Angleterre), Papiers Delcassé, Archives des Affaires Etrangères (AAE).

224. "MARCHAND EXPEDITION'S DEPARTURE": Delcassé to Ministry of Colonies, in Christopher Andrew, *Theophile Delcassé and the Making of the Entente Cordiale: A Reappraisal of French Foreign Policy, 1895–1905* (New York: St. Martin's Press, 1968), p. 92.

225. THERE WAS NO ULTIMATUM: *Ibid.*, pp. 98–99.

225. "BEFORE EVACUATION OF FASHODA": Baron Courcel to Delcassé, October 29, 1898, Carton 7 D (France-Angleterre), Papiers Delcassé, AAE.

225. "FRANCE IS JUST NOW STIRRED": *The Outlook* quote, in Lewis, *Prisoners of Honor*, p. 252.

225. SUPPORTING FRANCE OUTSIDE EUROPE: Langer, *Diplomacy*, pp. 562–63. Andrew, *Delcassé*, pp. 121–22.

225. TO PREPARE THE EVACUATION: Baratier, *Souvenirs de la Mission Marchand*, p. 211.

225. LUKEWARM . . . GOING TO WAR: Robinson, Gallagher, Denny, *Africa and the Victorians*, p. 375.

226. "ADVICE TO EGYPTIAN GOVERNMENT . . . WILL BE FOLLOWED": Salisbury to Cromer, No. 185. FO Turkey (Egypt) 5050 (No. 109), August 2, 1898, in Gooch and Temperly, *British Documents*, vol. 1, pp. 159–60.

226. "A GOAL THEY BELIEVED WAS FINAL": Marchand to Delcassé, telegram, Cairo, November 4, 1898, Papiers Delcassé, AAE.

226. "NO MATTER WHAT THE PENALTY": Marchand to Delcassé, Cairo, November 5, 1898, Papiers Delcassé, AAE.

226. "THE HIGHER INTERESTS OF FRANCE": Delcassé to Lefèvre-Pontalis, telegram, November 7, 1898, Papiers Delcassé, AAE.

226. BLAME FOR CONDITIONS AT FASHODA: Marchand to Delcassé, Cairo, telegram, November 1, 1898, Papiers Delcassé, AAE.

227. "NOT TO MAINTAIN ITSELF AT FASHODA": Guillain to Lefèvre-Pontalis for Marchand, November 7, 1898, Papiers Delcassé, AAE.

227. HARD CLIMB INTO THE ETHIOPIAN HIGHLANDS: Emily, *Fachoda, Mission Marchand*, p. 202.

227. RAISED THEIR HATS . . . WITH WHALEBOATS IN TOW: *Ibid.,* p. 205.

227. "INFLICTED . . . BY CIRCUMSTANCE": *Ibid.,* p. 205.

227. "WE ARE FLEEING": Baratier, *Souvenirs de la Mission Marchand,* p. 225.

227. SPHINX WOULD LAUGH: Riker, "Fashoda Crisis," p. 77.

227. PRESENTED WITH THE RANK OF CHEVALIER: Emily, *Fachoda, Mission Marchand,* pp. 235–36.

228. HEADED FOR DJIBOUTI: *Ibid.,* pp. 241–42.

228. "I SHALL TROUBLE LOKBU NO MORE": Abdullahi quote, in Intelligence Diary, (Bikhit Ahmed, secret agent), Fashoda, September 1899, Intel 5/4/47 CAIRINT-CRO.

228. KHALIFA DIED . . . ON HIS PRAYER BLANKET: Deherain, *Le Soudan Perdu,* pp. 476–77.

229. SOUTH AS THE FIFTH PARALLEL: Delcassé to de Courcel, telegram, October 4, 1898, I Fashoda, (France-Angleterre) Papiers Delcassé, AAE.

229. SALISBURY WOULD NOT: Riker, "Fashoda Crisis," p. 69.

229. HONOR . . . COMPROMISED BY A COLONIAL ENTERPRISE: *Ibid.,* p. 75.

229. THE GERMAN REICH: Andrew, *Delcassé,* pp. 30, 103–04.

229. PUSHED OUT BY THE BRITISH IN 1906: Langer, *Diplomacy,* p. 572.

230. DAT DISAPPEARED IN . . . 1914: Marc Michel, *Mission Marchand,* p. 74.

230. BEGINNING OF THE TWENTIETH CENTURY: Alison Redmayne, "Mkwawa and the Hehe Wars," *Journal of African History,* vol. 9 (1968), pp. 631–41.

230. AGAINST THE PORTUGUESE AND BRITISH: A. Isaacman and J. Vansina, "African Initiatives and Resistance in Central Africa, 1880–1914," in Boahen, *General History of Africa,* vol. 7, pp. 176–85.

230. "THE WHITE PEOPLE OUT OF THE COUNTRY": Tonga priest quote, *ibid.,* p. 189.

Index

Abarambo people, 61
Abbas II, Khedive of Egypt, 11, 12, 43, 47, 143, 150-53, 225-26
 defiance of British rule, 151-53
Abdullahi, Khalifa of the Sudan, 4-5, 8, 9, 11, 12, 138-44, 158, 173, 209, 228, 230
 Anglo-Egyptian invasion and, 155, 156, 157, 182, 189-205 *passim*
 dreams and, 192, 193, 197, 200
 escape after battle of Karari Plain, 205, 228
 death of, 228
 described, 139, 145, 146
 Ethiopia and, 104, 105, 106, 107, 113-14, 121-22, 135-36, 193, 198, 209
 viciousness of, 139-40, 143, 144-45
 see also Sudan, as Mahdiyya
Abu Anja, 106, 107, 155
Abu Hamed:
 battle at, 189
 railroad to, 9, 187-89, 190
Abu Klea, 105, 156, 201
Abu Klea (boat), 157
Achte, Father, 96
Addis Ababa, 108, 127, 128, 131, 134, 227
 railway from, to Djibouti, 114, 125, 126
Addis Ababa, Treaty of, 122
Adigrat, 112
Adi Ugri, 120
Adwa, 99, 100
 battle at, 6, 8, 116-21, 131, 136, 146, 191, 201
"African Cross," 85
Agibu, 78
Agordat, 146
Ahmad Sharif, Khalifa of the Sudan, 138, 140, 141
Ahmadu, Sultan, 76-78, 81, 82, 230
Ahmad Wad Ali, Khalifa of the Sudan, 138, 146
Akasha, 155
al-Ageiga, 200
al-Ahram, 148, 151
Albertone, General, 116, 117, 118, 119, 120
Alexander II, Czar of Russia, 114
Alexander III, Czar of Russia, 114
Alexandra, Empress of Russia, 115
Algeria, 80-81
Al-Hadj Khaled, Muhammad 'Uthman, 122

Al-Hajj Umar, 78
Ali Pasha Mubarak, 149, 150, 151, 153
Alis, Harry (Hippolyte Percher), 51, 52, 58
Ali Wad Helu, 199, 200, 203
al-Metamma, 187, 189, 192, 195
 massacre at, 192-93, 197
 sheikh of, 192
al-Muayyad, 148, 149
al-Qallabāt, 105-106, 107, 142
Alula Wādi Qubi, Ras, 100, 101, 102-103, 104, 105, 107, 109, 112, 118, 119, 120
al-Zaki Tamal, Amir, 107, 142, 145, 155, 209
al-Zubayr Rahma Mansur, 145
Amba Alagi, 112-13
Ambomu people, 61
Amharic language, 110, 111, 126
Anglo-Belgian India Rubber Company (ABIR), 93
Anglo-Congo Treaty, 52-55
Anglo-Egyptian army, 134, 152
 invasion of Sudan, 6, 9, 153-54, 155-57, 158, 166, 171, 172, 181, 182, 185-205, 224, 228
 battle at Karari Plain, 9, 199-205
Anglo-Italian Convention, 112, 114
Anglo-Italian treaties, 57, 130, 141, 146
Angola, 19
animists, 4, 137
Ankole, 54
Antonelli, Pietro, 107-108, 109, 110, 111
Arabs, 4-5, 14, 18, 19, 23-32, 62, 72
 three sources of, 24, 31
Archambault, Lieutenant, 223
Archinard, Louis, 75-82, 84, 89, 164, 172, 173
 Samori Turé and, 77, 78-79, 82
 Tukulors and, 75-78
Arimondi, General, 116, 117, 118, 120
Armenians, 154
Arnodala, *see* Malumba
Artamanov, Colonel, 212
Arusi, 101
Atbara River, 195
 battle at, 195-96, 198, 201
Aruwimi River, 21, 22, 43, 44, 45, 63-64, 65, 93, 95
Ashanti (Asante) people, 23, 25
Asmara, 109, 117, 120
Association Internationale Africaine (AIA), 36

293

ABOUT THE AUTHOR

David Levering Lewis was born in Little Rock, Arkansas, in 1936. He received a bachelor's degree from Fisk University, a master's degree in American history from Columbia University, and a doctorate in modern French history from the London School of Economics and Political Science. He has been awarded fellowships by the Woodrow Wilson International Center, the Center for Advanced Study in the Behavioral Sciences, the National Humanities Center, and the John Simon Guggenheim Memorial Foundation. He is Martin Luther King, Jr., Professor of History at Rutgers University (New Brunswick). His previous books are *King: A Biography; Prisoners of Honor,* a study of the Dreyfus Affair; *District of Columbia: A Bicentennial History;* and *When Harlem Was in Vogue,* a social history of the Harlem Renaissance. He is the father of three children.